MCSE
TestPrep

Windows NT
Server 4

MCSE TestPrep: Windows NT Server 4

By Hillary Contino, Emmett Dulaney, Howard Hilliker, Ron Milione, Joseph Phillips, Christoph Wille, David Yarashus

Published by:
New Riders Publishing
201 West 103rd Street
Indianapolis, IN 46290 USA

Copyright © 1997 by New Riders Publishing

Printed in the United States of America 1 2 3 4 5 6 7 8 9 0

Library of Congress Cataloging-in-Publication Data

CIP data available upon request

Warning and Disclaimer

This book is designed to provide information about the **Windows NT Server 4 Microsoft Certified Professional Exam**. Every effort has been made to make this book as complete and as accurate as possible, but no warranty or fitness is implied.

The information is provided on an "as is" basis. The authors and New Riders Publishing shall have neither liability nor responsibility to any person or entity with respect to any loss or damages arising from the information contained in this book or from the use of the disks or programs that may accompany it.

Publisher	*David Dwyer*
Executive Editor	*Mary Foote*
Marketing Manager	*Sarah Kearns*

Acquisitions Editor
Danielle Bird

Development Editor
Kezia Endsley

Project Editor
Brad Herriman

Copy Editor
Molly Warnes

Technical Editors
Brian Komar, Bob Reinsch

Coordinator of Editorial Services
Suzanne Snyder

Software Acquisitions and Development
Dustin Sullivan

Assistant Marketing Manager
Gretchen Schlesinger

Team Coordinator
Amy Lewis

Manufacturing Coordinator
Brook Farling

Book Designer
Glenn Larsen

Cover Designer
Dan Armstrong

Cover Production
Casey Price

Director of Production
Larry Klein

Production Team Supervisor
Laurie Casey

Graphics Image Specialists
Steve Adams, Debi Bolhuis, Kevin Cliburn, Sadie Crawford, Wil Cruz, Tammy Graham, Oliver Jackson

Production Analysts
Dan Harris, Erich J. Richter

Production Team
Kim Cofer, Linda Knose, Kristy Nash, Elizabeth SanMiguel

Indexer
Kevin Fulcher

About the Authors

Emmett Dulaney is an MCSE and MCPS, as well as CNE, CNA, and LAN Server Engineer. A trainer for a national training company, Emmett is also a consultant for D S Technical Solutions in Anderson, IN. He can be reached at `edulaney@iquest.net`.

Howard F. Hilliker built his first computer in the late 70s. His major source of influence came from his father, whose career in Electrical Engineering, communications, and Defense work challenged his engineering mind. He has been involved in the microcomputer industry since its infancy. He holds over 70 certifications with major vendors including Microsoft, IBM, Hewlett-Packard, Epson, Zenith, NEC, and Okidata. Howard has been involved as a Microsoft Certified Professional since the program's infancy (LAN Manager 2.0). He has nearly a decade of network and hardware field experience and holds key networking credentials, including Compaq ASE and Hewlett-Packard Network Professional. Howard has done technical editing and illustration work on several occasions in the past. He has taught classes on Microsoft Windows and Microsoft Networking products. His experience includes advanced topics such as SNA Server and SQL. Howard also enjoys the benefits associated with being an experienced Pascal, C++, and Foxpro developer. He has been involved with several key Microsoft BETA programs. Howard also holds an amateur radio license and is an active member of the Network Professional Association. He lives with his charming wife and two beautiful young daughters.

Ronnie P. Milione, an MCSE, MCT, MCNE, CNE, CNA, and ASE, is Chief of Technology Services for ISG, Inc., for New York and for New Jersey, and is both Manager and Head Trainer for ISG's Microsoft Training Center. Ronnie earned his BS and MS in Electrical Engineering from City College of New York. He has a wide range of skills and is a member of the IEEE, CNEPA, SARA, and both the Microsoft and Novell Developer's Networks. Ronnie has written articles for *PC Week* and *Computer World* magazines.

Joseph Phillips, an independent Microsoft Certified Trainer, has been teaching computers for the past five years. He attended the writing program at Columbia College, Chicago where he later taught computer education. Currently, he resides in Indianapolis, IN.

Christoph Wille, an MCSE and MCSD, has an extensive background working with OLE, MFC, Microsoft SQL Server, Microsoft operating systems, and Access. He is currently developing web sites with integrated e-commerce as well as working as a consultant for companies that want to connect their private networks to the Internet and who need someone to design their Internet presence.

David Yarashus is a Senior Consultant for Chesapeake Computer Consultants, Inc. in Annapolis, MD. He specializes in network infrastructure management, troubleshooting, and design for large, multiprotocol networks. Mr. Yarashus has contributed to many books and articles on networking-related topics, and is a member of Novell's Master CNE Advisory Council. His major industry certifications include: Cisco Certified Internetwork Expert (CCIE), Microsoft Certified Systems Engineer (MCSE), Master CNE, and Certified Network Expert (CNX).

Trademark Acknowledgments

All terms mentioned in this book that are known to be trademarks or service marks have been appropriately capitalized. New Riders Publishing cannot attest to the accuracy of this information. Use of a term in this book should not be regarded as affecting the validity of any trademark or service mark.

Contents at a Glance

Table of Contents

Introduction

The *MCSE TestPrep* series serves as a study aid for people preparing for Microsoft Certification exams. The series is intended to help reinforce and clarify information with which the student is already familiar by providing sample questions and tests, as well as summary information relevant to each of the exam objectives. This series is not intended to be the only source for student preparation, but rather a review of information with a set of practice tests—used to increase the student's familiarity with the exam questions and thus increase the student's likelihood of success when taking the exam.

Who Should Read This Book

MCSE TestPrep: Windows NT Server 4 is specifically intended to help students prepare for Microsoft's Windows NT Server Exam (#70-67). This is one of the core tests in the MCSE program for the Windows NT 4 track.

How This Book Helps You

In addition to presenting a summary of information relevant to each of the exam objectives, this book provides a wealth of review questions similar to those you will encounter in the actual exam. This book is designed to help you make the most of your study time by presenting concise summaries of information that you need to understand to succeed on the exam. The review questions at the end of each objective help reinforce what you have learned. The final exam at the conclusion of each chapter helps you determine if you have mastered the facts. In addition, the book contains two full-length practice exams.

How to Use This Book

You should use this book to make sure that you are ready to take the exam after you are some-what familiar with the exam concepts. At that point, take the practice tests at the back of the book and see how well you really know your subject.

After you are doing well on the practice tests, you are ready to schedule your exam. Use this book for a final quick review just before taking the test to make sure that all the important concepts are set in your mind. See Appendix B for more information about taking the test.

What the Windows NT Server Exam (#70-67) Covers

The Windows NT Server Exam focuses on determining your skill in six major categories of implementing and supporting Windows NT Server. These categories (along with the chapters in this book that cover them) follow:

- Planning (Chapter 1)
- Installation and Configuration (Chapter 2)
- Managing Resources (Chapter 3)
- Connectivity (Chapter 4)
- Monitoring and Optimization (Chapter 5)
- Troubleshooting (Chapter 6)

The Implementing and Supporting Microsoft Windows NT Server 4.0 certification exam uses these categories to measure your ability to implement, administer, and troubleshoot information systems that incorporate Windows NT Server version 4.0 in a *simple computing environment*. A simple computing environment is typically a homogeneous LAN. It might include one or more servers, a single domain, and a single location; and it might have file-sharing and print-sharing capabilities. More complex Windows NT Server networking issues are tested in other exams. Before taking this exam, you should be proficient in the following skills.

Objectives for Planning

The Planning section of the exam is designed to make sure that you understand the implications of the various installation options so that you can choose the best way to meet any particular set of requirements. The test objectives for this section follow:

- Plan the disk drive configuration for various requirements. Requirements include choosing a file system and choosing a fault-tolerance method.
- Choose a protocol for various situations. Protocols include TCP/IP, NWLink IPX/SPX Compatible Transport, and NetBEUI.

Objectives for Installation and Configuration

The Installation and Configuration section of the exam tests your understanding of how to install Windows NT Server to meet the requirements of different server roles. You must understand server hardware, network protocols, installation from different types of media, basic domain issues, server services, printing, and client support. The test objectives for this section follow:

- Install Windows NT Server on Intel-based platforms.
- Install Windows NT Server to perform various server roles. Server roles include primary domain controller (PDC), backup domain controller (BDC), and member server.

- Install Windows NT Server by using various methods. Installation methods include:

  - Using CD-ROM

  - Installing over-the-network

  - Using Network Client Administrator

  - Performing express versus custom

- Configure protocols and protocol bindings. Protocols include TCP/IP, NWLink IPX/SPX Compatible Transport, and NetBEUI.

- Configure network adapters. Considerations include changing IRQ, IO base, and memory addresses as well as configuring multiple adapters.

- Configure Windows NT Server core services. Services include Directory Replicator and License Manager.

- Configure peripherals and devices. Peripherals and devices include:

  - Communication devices

  - SCSI devices

  - Tape device drivers

  - UPS devices and UPS service

  - Mouse drivers, display drivers, and keyboard drivers

- Configure hard disks to meet various requirements. Requirements include:

  - Allocating disk space capacity

  - Providing redundancy

  - Improving performance

  - Providing security

  - Formatting

- Configure printers. Tasks include adding and configuring a printer, implementing a printer pool, and setting print priorities.

- Configure a Windows NT Server computer for various types of client computers. Client computer types include Windows NT Workstation, Windows 95, and MS-DOS–based computers.

Objectives for Managing Resources

The Managing Resources section of the Windows NT Server exam covers the most common day-to-day tasks of a typical network administrator. It focuses on managing users, groups, and disk resources effectively. The test objectives for this section follow:

- Manage user and group accounts. Considerations include:

  - Managing Windows NT groups

  - Managing Windows NT user rights

- Managing Windows NT groups

- Administering account policies

- Auditing changes to the user account database

- Create and manage policies and profiles for various situations. Policies and profiles include local user profiles, roaming user profiles, and system policies.

- Administer remote servers from various types of client computers. Client computer types include Windows 95 and Windows NT Workstation.

- Manage disk resources. Tasks include:

  - Copying and moving files between file systems

  - Creating and sharing resources

  - Implementing permissions and security

  - Establishing file auditing

Objectives for Connectivity

The Connectivity section of the Windows NT Server test has two main sections: interoperation with and migration from NetWare servers is the first one, whereas the Remote Access Service (RAS) is the other. The test objectives for this section follow:

- Configure Windows NT Server for interoperability with NetWare servers by using various tools. Tools include Gateway Service for NetWare and Migration Tool for NetWare.

- Install and configure Remote Access Service (RAS). Configuration options include:

  - Configuring RAS communications

  - Configuring RAS protocols

  - Configuring RAS security

  - Configuring dial-up networking clients

Objectives for Monitoring and Optimization

The Monitoring and Optimization section of the Windows NT Server exam tests your understanding of system limitations as well as using Performance Monitor to identify them. The more you understand performance management on computer systems, the better you are likely to do on this section. The test objectives for this section follow:

- Monitor performance of various functions by using Performance Monitor. Functions include processors, memory, disks, and networks.

- Identify performance bottlenecks.

Objectives for Troubleshooting

Microsoft tests your Troubleshooting skills to determine if you know how to solve typical problems. Getting experience solving problems on a typical network is the best way to prepare for this section of the exam. The test objectives for this section require you to choose the appropriate course of action to take to resolve these errors:

- Installation failures

- Boot failures

- Configuration errors

- Printer problems

- RAS problems

- Connectivity problems

- Resource access problems and permission problems

- Fault-tolerance failures. Fault-tolerance methods include:

  - Tape backup

  - Mirroring

  - Stripe set with parity

  - Disk duplexing

Hardware and Software Recommended for Preparation

MCSE TestPrep: Windows NT Server 4 is meant to help you review concepts with which you already have training and experience. In order to make the most of the review, you need to have as much background and experience as possible. The best way to do this is to combine studying with working on real networks using the products on which you will be tested. This section gives you a description of the minimum computer requirements you need to build a good practice environment.

The minimum computer requirement to study everything on which you are tested is one or more workstations running Windows 95, Windows NT Workstation, and two or more servers running Windows NT Server—all connected by a network.

Windows 95 and Windows NT Workstations require:

- Computer on the Microsoft Hardware Compatibility List

- 486DX 33 Mhz (Pentium recommended)

- 16 MB of RAM (32 MB recommended)

- 200 MB (or larger) hard disk

- 3.5 inch 1.44 MB floppy drive

- VGA (or Super VGA) video adapter

- VGA (or Super VGA) monitor

- Mouse or equivalent pointing device

- Two-speed (or faster) CD-ROM drive
- Network Interface Card (NIC)
- Presence on an existing network, or use of a hub to create a test network
- Microsoft Windows 95

Windows NT Server requires:

- Two computers on the Microsoft Hardware Compatibility List
- 486DX2 66 Mhz (or better)
- 32 MB of RAM (64 recommended)
- 340 MB (or larger) hard disk
- 3.5 inch 1.44 MB floppy drive
- VGA (or Super VGA) video adapter
- VGA (or Super VGA) monitor
- Mouse or equivalent pointing device
- Two-speed (or faster) CD-ROM drive
- Network Interface Card (NIC)
- Presence on an existing network, or use of a hub to create a test network
- Microsoft Windows NT Server

How to Contact New Riders Publishing

The staff of New Riders Publishing is committed to bringing you the very best in computer reference material. Each New Riders book is the result of months of work by authors and staff who research and refine the information contained within its covers.

As part of this commitment to you, New Riders invites your input. Please let us know if you enjoy this book, if you have trouble with the information and examples presented, or if you have a suggestion for the next edition.

If you have a question or comment about any New Riders book, there are several ways to contact New Riders Publishing. We will respond to as many readers as we can. Your name, address, or phone number will never become part of a mailing list or be used for any purpose other than to help us continue to bring you the best books possible.

You can write us at the following address:

> New Riders Publishing
> Attn: Publisher
> 201 W. 103rd Street
> Indianapolis, IN 46290

If you prefer, you can fax New Riders Publishing at:

> 317-817-7448

You can also send electronic mail to New Riders at the following Internet address:

> mfoote@newriders.mcp.com

New Riders Publishing is an imprint of Macmillan Computer Publishing. To obtain a catalog or information, or to purchase any Macmillan Computer Publishing book, call 800-428-5331 or visit our Web site at http://www.mcp.com.

Thank you for selecting *MCSE TestPrep: Windows NT Server 4!*

CHAPTER 1

Planning

This chapter helps you prepare for the "Planning" section of Microsoft's Exam 70-67, "Implementing and Supporting Microsoft Windows NT Server 4.0." Microsoft provides the following objectives for the "Planning" section:

- Plan the disk drive configuration for various requirements. Requirements include choosing a file system and choosing a fault-tolerance method.

- Choose a protocol for various situations. Protocols include TCP/IP, NWLink IPX/SPX Compatible Transport, NetBEUI.

1.1   Windows NT Among Microsoft Operating Systems

Microsoft has three operating system products now competing in the marketplace:

- Windows 95
- Windows NT Workstation
- Windows NT Server

A.   Windows 95

Windows 95 provides a 32-bit platform and is designed to operate with a variety of peripherals. The minimum hardware requirements for Windows 95 are:

- 386DX/20 processor or better
- 4 MB RAM (8 MB is recommended)
- 40 MB of free disk space

Like Windows NT, Windows 95 supports preemptive multitasking, but unlike Windows NT, doesn't support multiple processors. Windows 95 supports plug and play, not to mention a vast number of hardware devices and device drivers (more than Windows NT).

Windows 95 supports 16-bit and 32-bit Windows and MS-DOS applications, including applications that access the hardware directly. Windows 95 runs only on Intel platforms.

Windows 95 uses the File Allocation Table file system, which is less secure than the NTFS file system that Windows NT supports. Windows NT also supports FAT, but NT does not support the FAT32 file system that is supported by recent versions of Windows 95 (OEM Release 2).

You can network a Windows 95 computer in a workgroup, and you can use a Windows 95 computer as a client in a domain-based Windows NT network. However, Windows 95 alone cannot provide a network with centralized authentication and security.

B.   Windows NT Workstation

The original Windows NT operating system has evolved into a pair of operating system products—Windows NT Workstation and Windows NT Server. These two products are virtually the same except that they include some different tools and are configured for different roles. NT Server is designed to operate as a network server and domain controller. NT Workstation, like Windows 95, is designed to serve as a network client and desktop operating system.

Windows NT Workstation can serve as a stand-alone operating system, act as a client in a domain-based NT network, or participate in a workgroup. The most striking difference between Windows NT Workstation and Windows 95 is security. Windows NT Workstation is an extremely secure operating system, and for almost every facet of Windows NT administration and configuration, there are security implications. Windows NT provides security for files, directories, printers, and nearly everything else; in fact, a user must be authenticated to even use Windows NT at all.

Windows NT Workstation's minimum hardware requirements are as follows:

- 486DX/33 or better processor
- 12 MB of RAM (16 MB recommended)
- 120 MB of free disk space

Windows NT is designed to provide system stability; each application can run in its own memory address space. Windows NT supports preemptive multiprocessing and as well as true multiprocessing (more than one processor).

Although Windows NT doesn't support the vast array of devices Windows 95 supports, it supports more processor platforms. Because Windows NT is written mostly in C, it can be compiled separately for different processors. In addition to the Intel platform, versions of Windows NT are available for DEC Alpha and others.

Microsoft designed Windows NT for backward-compatibility with MS-DOS 5.0, Windows 3.1x, OS/2 1.x, and lateral-compatibility with POSIX-based applications.

C.   Windows NT Server

Windows NT Advanced Server had some clear advantages over NT Workstation 3.1. Unlike Windows NT Workstation 3.1, it supports Macintosh clients, for example, and provides its users with RAID fault tolerance.

With version 4, NT Server and NT Workstation continue to differentiate themselves as they adapt to their respective markets.

1. Features

The following features are available on Windows NT Server but not on Windows NT Workstation:

- Services for Macintosh
- RAID fault tolerance
- Domain logon validation
- Directory replication
- Windows NT Directory Services (NTDS)
- Multiprotocol routing and advanced network services, such as DNS, DHCP, and WINS

2. Capacity

The following facets of Windows NT differ in capacity on Workstation and Server:

- **Concurrent Client Sessions:** Windows NT Server supports an unlimited number of inbound sessions; Windows NT Workstation supports no more than 10 active sessions at once.
- **Remote Access Sessions:** Windows NT Server accommodates an unlimited number of Remote Access connections (although Microsoft only supports up to 256); Windows NT Workstation supports only a single Remote Access connection.
- **Multiprocessors:** Although both Windows NT Workstation and Server can support up to 32 processors in an OEM (Original Equipment Manufacturer) configuration, Windows NT Workstation can support only two processors out-of-the-box, whereas Windows NT Server can support four.
- **Internet Service:** Both NT Workstation and NT Server come with Internet-type server applications, but the NT Server application (Internet Application Server) is more powerful and better suited to the open Internet than is the NT Workstation application (Peer Web Services), which is designed primarily for in-house intranets. (Personal Web server software packages are available for Windows 95 systems.)
- **BackOffice Support:** Both NT Workstation and NT Server provide support for the Microsoft BackOffice family of software products (SQL Server, Systems Management Server, SNA Server, Exchange Server), but NT Server provides a higher level of support for BackOffice products.

3. Performance

Some of the performance differences between Windows NT Workstation and Server are as follows:

- *Windows NT Workstation preloads a Virtual DOS Machine (VDM), the 32-bit MS-DOS emulator that supports legacy applications.*

  Because older applications are more likely to run on a workstation than a server, the preloading of the VDM speeds up the load time of the first DOS or Win16 application at the expense of the RAM used by the VDM, which most likely would need to be loaded anyway.

- *Caching is handled differently on workstations and servers, enabling better network throughput on Windows NT Server and better local disk access time on Windows NT Workstation.*

- *Windows NT Server includes a configurable server service that enables you to tune the server as an application server or as a file/print server.*

  Windows NT Workstation does not provide this feature, because it is limited to 10 inbound sessions.

- *The server files system driver used in both Windows NT Workstation and Server (SRV.SYS) is more subject to paging under Windows NT Workstation than under Windows NT Server.*

  When Windows NT Workstation runs out of physical RAM, it pages the server code out to disk, which means its network sharing performance takes a hit, but local application performance gets a boost. Windows NT Server does not page out much of the server code.

4. Minimum Hardware Requirements

The minimum requirements for NT Server and NT Workstation are roughly the same, but NT Server needs a little more RAM and a little more disk space, namely:

- 486DX/33 processor
- 16 MB of RAM
- 130 MB of disk space

1.1   Practice Problems

1. Which of the following machine configurations meets the minimum hardware
   requirements for Windows NT Server?
   Select all that apply:

   A. Pentium 133, 12 MB RAM, 1 GB
      hard disk space free

   B. 486 DX2/66, 16 MB RAM, 120
      MB hard disk space free

   C. Pentium 200, 32 MB RAM, 200
      MB hard disk space free

   D. 486 DX33, 16 MB RAM, 150 MB
      hard disk space free

2. Your department bought six new DEC
   Alpha workstations. Which of the
   following operating systems can be
   installed? Select all that apply:

   A. Windows 3.11a

   B. Windows 95 for Alpha

   C. Windows NT Server

   D. Windows NT Workstation

3. Which of the following services are not
   available on Windows NT Workstation?
   Select all that apply:

   A. DNS

   B. Directory Replication

   C. DHCP

   D. WINS

4. Which of the following statements is
   true? Select the best answer:

   A. Both Windows NT Workstation
      and NT Server support multiple
      processors.

   B. Both Windows NT Workstation
      and NT Server support unlimited
      number of inbound sessions.

   C. Both Windows NT Workstation
      and NT Server support RAID fault
      tolerance.

   D. Both Windows NT Workstation
      and NT Server support four
      processors out of the box.

5. Your boss asks you to enable Mac users
   from the graphics department to share files
   with PC users. Which operating systems
   support file shares for both Macintosh and
   PC users? Select all that apply:

   A. Windows 95

   B. Windows NT Server

   C. Windows NT Workstation

   D. You have to buy MS MacShare for
      Windows NT Server

6. Dan manages a workgroup for chemistry
   research in the company MEGACORP.
   There are currently 14 computers in this
   workgroup, with a mix of Windows 95,
   Windows for Workgroups 3.11, and
   Windows NT Workstation installed on
   these. There is a share on his NT Workstation computer that needs to be
   accessed by every user, but not all users
   can connect. What is the most likely
   cause? Select the best answer:

   A. He needs to buy additional client
      licenses because NT Workstation
      comes only with ten licenses in the
      box.

   B. If he intends to share resources
      effectively, he really should upgrade
      to NT Server.

   C. He has used up all possible inbound
      sessions; NT Workstation supports
      only a maximum of ten.

   D. He needs to restart his computer.

7. Which of the following operating systems
   support fault-tolerant RAID? Select all
   that apply:

   A. Windows NT Workstation

   B. Windows NT Server

   C. Windows 95

   D. Windows 3.11a

1.1 Answers and Explanations: Practice Problems

1. **C, D** The minimum hardware requirements for NT Server are a 486DX/33 processor, 16 MB of RAM, and 130 MB of disk space.

2. **C, D** Only Windows NT is available as a Windows operating system for Alpha.

3. **A, B, C, D** All of these services are available only on NT Server.

4. **A** Both NT Server and Workstation support multiple processors.

5. **B** NT Server offers Services for Macintosh, which enable file shares for Mac and PC users.

6. **C** NT Workstation is limited to a maximum of 10 inbound connections.

7. **B** Only NT Server supports fault-tolerant RAID levels 1 and 5.

1.1 Key Words

BackOffice Support

DHCP (Dynamic Host Configuration Protocol)

DNS (Domain Name Service)

FAT (File Allocation Table)

FAT32

Hardware requirements

Multiprocessor

NTFS

Operating system

Platform independent

RAID

Remote Access

Services for Macintosh

Windows 95

Windows NT Server

Windows NT Workstation

WINS (Windows Internet Naming Service)

1.2   Workgroups and Domains

Every networked Windows NT-based computer can participate in one of two environments:

- Workgroup
- Domain

The difference between a workgroup and a domain boils down to the question of where the user accounts are stored. Users must—and it should be stressed that this logon process is completely mandatory—log on to Windows NT to use a Windows NT-based computer.

When a user successfully logs on to Windows NT, an access token is generated that contains the user's security identifier and group identifiers, as well as the user rights granted through the User Rights policy in User Manager or User Manager for Domains.

The access token identifies the user and all processes spawned by the user. No action can take place on a Windows NT system without somebody's access token attached to it.

A.   Workgroups

A *workgroup* is a collection of computers grouped together for a common purpose, however, each computer in the workgroup has to manage its own user accounts. The security information necessary to verify the user's credentials and generate the access token resides on the local machine. Thus, every Windows NT computer in a workgroup must contain accounts for each person who might need to access the workstation. This involves a great deal of administration in workgroups that consist of more than a few members.

A workgroup is, however, simpler than a domain and easier to install. A workgroup does not require an NT Server machine acting as a domain controller, and the decentralized administration of a workgroup can be an advantage in small networks because it does not depend on the health of a few key server and controller machines.

Unless a Windows NT Server computer is configured as a stand-alone server, it cannot participate in a workgroup. Windows NT Workstation computers, Windows 95 computers, and older networkable Microsoft systems, such as Windows for Workgroups, can participate in workgroups.

B.   Domains

In a domain environment, all nodes must authenticate logon requests with a domain controller that contains the central accounts database for the entire domain. A password needs to be changed only one time to be usable on any member computer of the domain. Likewise, a user needs only a single account to access resources anywhere in the domain. Only Windows NT Server machines can serve as domain controllers in a Windows NT network.

1.2   Practice Problems

1. Which statements are true about domains? Select all that apply:

   A. Centralized user management

   B. Decentralized user management

   C. Works best for small groups of users

   D. Works best for large groups of users

2. Which statements are true about
   workgroups? Select all that apply:

   A. Centralized user management

   B. Decentralized user management

   C. Works best for small groups of users

   D. Works best for large groups of users

3. To create a domain, which type of
   operating system should you choose?
   Select the best answer:

   A. Windows NT Workstation

   B. Windows NT Workstation with
      Domain Extensions

   C. Windows NT Server

   D. Windows NT Server with Domain
      Extensions

4. Select all operating systems that enable a
   user to log on to a domain:

   A. Windows 3.11 for Workgroups

   B. Windows 95

   C. Windows NT Workstation

   D. Windows NT Server

5. The chemistry lab is running a
   workgroup with a mix of Windows 95
   and Windows NT Workstations. Three of
   the Windows NT Workstation computers
   have file and printer shares that are
   accessed from all workgroup users. Dan,
   who administers this workgroup, complains that every time a user joins, he has

to change the account database on all
three NT Workstation computers to
enable the new user to access all resources.
What can Dan do? Select the best answer:

   A. This is easy to solve: Set up user
      account replication between the
      three computers so that you have to
      maintain only one computer, and
      all changes are propagated to the
      other two.

   B. Dan has to migrate the workgroup
      to a domain, because only domains
      allow central user management.

   C. Dan has to download service pack
      3, which solves this problem.

   D. One of the NT Workstation
      computers must be promoted to
      master browser for this workgroup.

1.2   Answers and Explana-
tions: Practice Problems

1. **A, D**   A domain is used for centralized
   user management for large environments.

2. **B, C**   Workgroups are best for decentralized management of small networks.

3. **C**   For a domain, a PDC is needed and
   only NT Server can be installed as a
   PDC.

4. **A, B, C, D**   All these operating systems
   support domain logon.

5. **B**   Centralized user-management is
   possible only with an NT domain.

1.2   Key Words

Centralized user management

Decentralized user management

Domain   Workgroup

1.3 Plan the Disk Drive Configuration

Microsoft lists the following objective for the Windows NT Server exam:

Plan the disk drive configuration for various requirements. Requirements include choosing a file system and choosing a fault-tolerance method.

The following sections highlight some specific planning issues related to disk configuration under Windows NT, as follows:

- Partitions
- Windows NT file systems
- Windows NT fault-tolerance methods

A. Partitions

A *partition* is a logical organization of a physical disk. An operating system such as Windows NT can subdivide a disk drive into several partitions. Each partition is formatted separately. Windows NT assigns a different drive letter to each of the partitions, and users interact separately with each partition as if each partition were a separate disk drive.

Partitioning is the act of defining a partition and associating that partition with an area (or areas) of free space from a hard disk.

As you plan your Windows NT configuration, you must make some decisions about the arrangement of partitions on your disk drive, as discussed next.

1. Primary and Extended Partitions

Windows NT provides the following two types of partitions:

- **Primary partitions:** A primary partition cannot be subdivided and is capable of supporting a bootable operating system. One hard disk can contain up to four primary partitions.

- **Extended partitions:** An extended partition can be subdivided into smaller logical drives (see fig. 1.3.1). This feature enables you to assign more than four drive letters to the disk. An extended partition does not support a bootable operating system. The system partition therefore cannot reside on an extended partition (see next section). One hard disk can contain only one extended partition.

If you choose to use an extended partition on a hard disk, you are limited to three (rather than four) primary partitions for that disk.

On an Intel-based computer, one primary partition must be marked *active*. The active partition is then used to boot the computer. Because any primary partition of sufficient size can support a bootable operating system, one advantage of using multiple primary partitions is that you can isolate different operating systems on different partitions.

If you install Windows NT on a computer with another operating system in place, the active partition does not change. If you install Windows NT on a new computer, the partition created by Setup becomes the active partition.

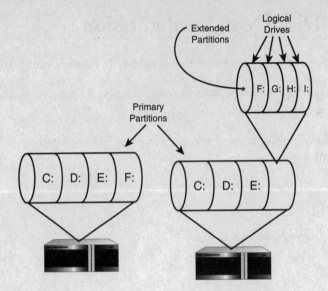

Figure 1.3.1 A physical disk can consist of up to four primary partitions or up to three primary partitions and one extended partition. An extended partition can be subdivided into logical drives.

2. Boot and System Partitions

The *system partition* is the partition that contains the files necessary to boot the operating system. The system partition does not have to be the partition on which Windows NT is installed.

The partition that holds the Windows NT operating system files is called the *boot partition*. If your system boots from drive C, and you install Windows NT on drive D, drive C is your system partition and drive D is your boot partition (see fig. 1.3.2). If you boot from drive C, and Windows NT is installed on drive C, drive C is both the system partition and the boot partition.

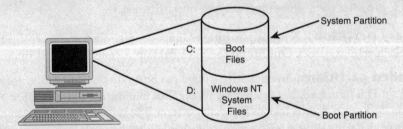

Figure 1.3.2 The partition that boots the computer is the system partition; the partition that holds the Windows NT directory is the boot partition. Note that these names are counterintuitive.

Note that the active partition is the partition used to boot the system. The system partition must therefore be the active partition.

By the way, active partitions are a relevant concept only for Intel-based computers; RISC-based computers use a hardware configuration utility to designate the system partition.

B. Windows NT File Systems

After a partition has been created, it must be formatted with a supported file system. A *file system* is a system for organizing and managing the data on a disk. Windows NT supports three file systems: FAT (File Allocation Table), NTFS (NT File System), and CDFS (Compact Disk File System). CDFS is a read-only file system for CD-ROMs, so you can immediately rule it out for hard disk partitions. Each partition must use either the FAT file system or the NTFS file system.

> **OS/2's file system HPFS (High Performance File System) is no longer supported by Windows NT 4. You have to convert HPFS-formatted partitions prior to installing NT 4.**

1. FAT

The venerable File Allocation Table (FAT) file system was originally invented for MS-DOS. FAT is now supported by Windows NT, Windows 95, and OS/2, making it the most universally accepted and supported file system (see fig. 1.3.3). For this reason alone, you should seriously consider using FAT for your partitions.

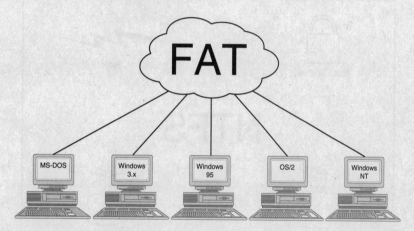

Figure 1.3.3   The FAT file system is accessible from more operating systems than NTFS, but FAT doesn't provide the NTFS advantages.

FAT has a lower overhead than its high-tech counterpart NTFS (less than 1 MB, compared to an average of 5–10 MB for NTFS), and FAT is typically the more efficient file system for small partitions (under 200 MB).

Some of the disadvantages of FAT are as follows:

- FAT is generally slower than NTFS for larger partitions. It takes longer to find and access files. For partitions greater than 200 MB, FAT performance degrades quickly.

- The maximum file, directory, or partition size under FAT is only 4 GB. Also, because Windows NT does not support any FAT compression software, including Microsoft's own DriveSpace and DoubleSpace, you cannot conserve space by compressing files on a FAT partition.

- FAT does not offer the security features offered by NTFS.

- If the power fails during a disk transaction, the FAT file system might be left with cross-linked files or orphan clusters.

You should use the FAT file system if you will be dual-booting your computer with another operating system and you want to access the partition from the other operating system.

If your Windows NT computer is a RISC-based system, your C drive needs to be FAT-formatted with at least 2 MB free space.

2. NTFS

The New Technology File System (NTFS) is designed to fully exploit the features and capabilities of Windows NT. For partitions larger than the range of 200–400 MB, the NTFS file system far outshines the FAT file system. The biggest drawback with using NTFS is that only the Windows NT operating system can access NTFS partitions (see fig. 1.3.4). If you plan to sometimes boot your computer under a different operating system, such as MS-DOS or Windows 95, you should be aware that the other operating system cannot access an NTFS partition.

Figure 1.3.4　The NTFS file system is accessible only from Windows NT—it provides a number of advantages for Windows NT users.

When partitions exceed 400 MB (on average), NTFS is your most reasonable choice. Remember that 400 MB is only an average; actual performance owes more to the number of files than to the size of the files.

NTFS is generally faster than FAT, and NTFS supports bigger partitions. (NTFS files and partitions can be up to 16 exabytes—an exabyte is one billion gigabytes, or 2^{64} bytes.)

NTFS is also safer. NTFS supports sector sparing, also known as hot fixing, on SCSI hard drives. If a sector fails on an NTFS partition of a SCSI hard drive, NTFS tries to write the data to a good sector (if the data is still in memory) and map out the bad sector so that it is not reused. NTFS keeps a transaction log while it works. Two other principal advantages of NTFS are as follows:

- **File-level security:** NTFS enables you to assign specific permissions to individual files and directories.

- **File compression:** Windows NT provides the capability to compress NTFS files. Traditional FAT compression utilities, including Microsoft's own DriveSpace and DoubleSpace, don't work under Windows NT.

You should use NTFS if you want to preserve existing permissions when you migrate files and directories from a NetWare server to a Windows NT Server system. Also, if you want to allow Macintosh computers to access files on the partition through Windows NT's Services for Macintosh, you must format the partition for NTFS.

Because NTFS has a higher overhead than FAT, somewhere between 4.5 and 10 MB for the file system itself, you cannot use the NTFS file system for floppy disks.

3. Choosing a File System

Here's a quick summary of the differences between file systems:

Feature	FAT	NTFS
File name length	255	255
8.3 file name compatibility	Yes	Yes
File size	4 GB	16 EB
Partition size	4 GB	16 EB
Directory structure	Linked list	B-tree
Local security	No	Yes
Transaction tracking	No	Yes
Hot fixing	No	Yes
Overhead	1 MB	>2 MB (avg. 4.5–10)
Required for RISC-based computers	Yes	No
Accessible from MS-DOS/Windows 95	Yes	No
Accessible from OS/2	Yes	No
Case-sensitive	No	POSIX only
Case preserving	Yes	Yes
Compression	No	Yes
Efficiency	<200 MB	>400 MB
Windows NT formattable	Yes	Yes
Convertible	To NTFS only	No

Feature	FAT	NTFS
Fragmentation level	High	Low
Floppy disk formattable	Yes	No
Extensible attributes	No	Yes
Creation/modification/access dates	Yes	Yes

Windows NT provides a utility called `Convert.exe` that converts a FAT partition to NTFS. There is no utility for directly converting an NTFS partition to FAT. To change an NTFS partition to FAT, back up all files on the partition, reformat the partition, and then restore the files to the reformatted partition.

C.   Fault-Tolerance Methods

Fundamentally, *fault tolerance* is the system's capability to compensate in the event of hardware disaster. The standard for fault tolerance is known as Redundant Array of Inexpensive Disks (RAID). RAID consists of several levels (or categories) of protection that offer a mixture of performance, reliability, and cost. One of the steps in planning your Windows NT system might be to decide on a RAID fault-tolerance method. Windows NT Server offers the following two RAID fault-tolerance methods:

- **Disk mirroring (RAID Level 1):** Windows NT writes the same data to two physical disks. If one disk fails, the data is still available on the other disk.

- **Disk striping with parity (Raid Level 5):** Windows NT writes data across a series of disks (3 to 32). The data is not duplicated on the disks (as it is with disk mirroring), but Windows NT records parity information that it can use to regenerate missing data if a disk should fail.

It is important to note that the fault-tolerance methods available through Windows NT are software-based RAID implementations. Several hardware vendors offer hardware-based RAID solutions. Hardware-based RAID solutions, which can be quite expensive, are beyond the scope of this book and beyond the scope of the Windows NT Server exam.

1. Disk Mirroring (RAID Level 1)

Disk mirroring calls for all data to be written to two physical disks (see fig. 1.3.5). A *mirror* is a redundant copy of a disk partition. You can use any partition, including the boot or system partitions, to establish a mirror.

You can measure the utilization of a fault-tolerance method by the percent of the total disk space devoted to storing the original information. Fifty percent of the data in a disk-mirroring system is redundant data. The percentage utilization is thus also fifty percent, making disk-mirroring less efficient than disk striping with parity. The startup costs for implementing disk mirroring are typically lower, however, because disk mirroring requires only two (rather than 3–32) physical disks.

Disk mirroring slows down write operations slightly (because Windows NT has to write to two disks simultaneously). Read operations are actually slightly faster, because NT can read from both disks simultaneously.

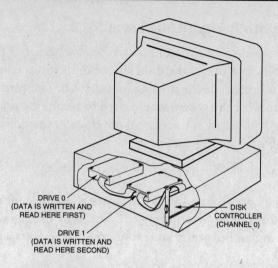

Figure 1.3.5 How disk mirroring works.

In a typical disk mirroring scenario, a single disk controller writes to both members of the mirror set. If a mirrored disk fails, the user can keep working. If the disk controller fails, however, Windows NT cannot access either disk.

Disk duplexing is a special kind of disk mirroring that provides a solution for this potential pitfall. In a disk duplexing system, each of the mirrored disks has its own disk controller. The system can therefore endure either a disk failure or a controller failure. Disk duplexing also has some performance advantages, because the two disk controllers can act independently (see fig. 1.3.6).

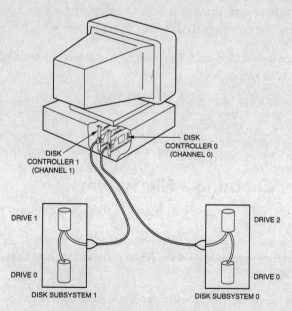

Figure 1.3.6 Disk duplexing.

2. Disk Striping with Parity (RAID Level 5)

A stripe set with parity writes information in *stripes* (or rows) across 3 to 32 disks. For each stripe, there is a parity stripe block on one of the disks. If one of the disks fails, Windows NT can use the parity stripe block to regenerate the missing information. The parity stripe block is the only data that is additional to what the system would need to record the original data without fault tolerance. Disk striping with parity is therefore more efficient than disk mirroring. The percentage of disk space available for storing data is:

```
% Utilization = (no. of disks - 1) / no. of disks x 100%
```

If you have five disks, eighty percent of your disk space is available for storing data. This compares with fifty percent in a disk mirroring system. The more disks you add, the more efficient your fault tolerance becomes. But at the same time, your setup costs also increase as you add more disks.

Windows NT must perform the parity calculations as it writes data to a stripe set with parity. Write operations therefore take three times as much memory if you are using a stripe set with parity.

Any partition except the boot partition and the system partition can be part of a stripe set with parity, provided you have enough other partitions on 3–32 other physical disks.

1.3.1   Exercise: Calculating the Percentage of Available Disk Space when Using Stripe Sets with Parity

The purpose of this exercise is to show you how to calculate how much space (in a percentage) is available for storing data when using RAID level 5, stripe sets with parity.

1.   Determine the number of hard disks you want to add to a stripe set. This example assumes that you are adding 10 disks to a stripe set.

2.   To calculate the percentage of available hard disk space for data, use the following formula:

```
% Utilization = (no. of disks - 1) / (no. of disks) x 100%
```

3.   With 10 disks, you can use ninety percent of the disk space for storing data.

1.3.2   Exercise: Choosing a File System

The purpose of this exercise is to show you how to choose a file system for NT computers.

1.   First of all, you must decide whether this computer will be used with NT only or be dual-booted with another operating system like DOS. When you need to dual-boot, you are limited to FAT for the system partition.

2.   Decide whether you will be storing sensitive information on this computer. If so, only NTFS enables you to secure the sensitive information. You need to go with NTFS on at least a single partition.

3.   If you are expecting high-volume transactions on the file system for this computer, you are also better off with NTFS because of its transaction based file system that can recover in case of unexpected system crash.

1.3   Practice Problems

1. Which of the following statements is true? Select two:

   A. The system partition contains the NT operating system.

   B. The boot partition contains the NT operating system.

   C. The system partition contains the files necessary to load the operating system.

   D. The boot partition contains the files necessary to load the operating system.

2. Which of the following statements is true? Select the best answer:

   A. There can be up to four primary partitions on a disk, or one primary and one extended partition.

   B. There can be one primary partition on a disk, or one primary and one extended partition.

   C. There can be up to four primary partitions on a disk, or three primary partitions and on extended partition.

   D. There can be up to four primary partitions on a disk, or one primary and three extended partitions.

3. Which fault-tolerant RAID levels are supported by Windows NT Server? Select the best answer:

   A. Levels 2 and 5

   B. Levels 0 and 5

   C. Levels 0 and 1

   D. Levels 1 and 5

4. Which of the following file systems are supported by Windows NT? Select all that apply:

   A. FAT

   B. FAT32

   C. HPFS

   D. CDFS

5. Your company is running legacy DOS applications that were tuned heavily and access hardware directly. Because you cannot run these applications from within NT, you have to set up these computers for dual boot. Which of the following statements is true in this situation?

   A. You have to format the system partition with FAT.

   B. You have to format the boot partition with FAT.

   C. You have to format the system partition with NTFS.

   D. You have to format the boot partition with NTFS.

6. You have decided to use NTFS on all computers in your network. Which of the following statements about NTFS are true? Select all that apply:

   A. Required on RISC computers

   B. Low overhead

   C. Accessible from OS/2

   D. Hot fixing implemented

7. What are the advantages of using a stripe set with parity? Select all that apply:

   A. Disk read operations can occur simultaneously.

   B. The boot and the system partition can be part of a stripe set.

   C. Recovery from disk failure is very rapid.

   D. Cost is lower than for a mirror set.

8. What are the advantages of using a mirror set? Select all that apply:

   A. Disk read operations can occur simultaneously.

   B. The boot and the system partition can be part of a mirror set.

   C. Recovery from disk failure is very rapid.

   D. Cost is lower than for a stripe set with parity.

9. Which of the following statements is true about disk duplexing? Select the best answer:

   A. Disk duplexing uses one SCSI controller and two hard disks.

   B. Disk duplexing uses two SCSI controllers and four hard disks.

   C. Disk duplexing uses two SCSI controllers and two hard disks.

   D. Disk duplexing isn't supported by Windows NT.

10. Which of the following statements is true about stripe sets with parity and mirror sets? Select the best answer:

   A. Mirror sets can be created with two disks; a stripe set with parity needs at least five disks.

   B. Mirror sets can be created with two disks; a stripe set with parity needs at least two disks and can employ a maximum of 32 disks.

   C. Mirror sets can be created with two disks; a stripe set with parity needs at least three disks and can employ a maximum of 32 disks.

   D. Mirror sets can be created with up to four disks; a stripe set with parity needs at least three disks and can employ a maximum of 32 disks.

1.3 Answers and Explanations: Practice Problems

1. **B, C**   The NT operating system is located on the boot partition and is loaded from the system partition.

2. **C**   There can be up to four primary partitions on a disk, or three primary partitions and on extended partition.

3. **D**   Only levels 1 and 5 of supported RAID levels are fault tolerant.

4. **A, D**   HPFS is no longer supported by NT and FAT32 introduced with Windows 95b isn't supported (yet).

5. **A**   To run DOS, you need to format the system partition using FAT.

6. **D**   Disk errors can be corrected automatically when using NTFS as your file system.

7. **A, D**   Stripe sets with parity allow for simultaneous read operations and are cheaper than mirror sets.

8. **A, B, C**   Mirror sets can be used for system and boot partition, recovery is very fast, and read operations can occur simultaneously.

9. **C**   Disk duplexing uses two SCSI controllers and two hard disks.

10. **C**   Mirror sets can be created with two disks, a stripe set with parity needs at least three disks and can employ a maximum of 32 disks.

1.3 Key Words

Boot partition   CDFS
Compression   Disk duplexing
Disk mirroring   Extended Partition
FAT   Fault tolerance
Hot fixing   HPFS
NTFS   Partition
Primary partition   RAID
Stripe set with parity
System partition

1.4   Choosing a Windows NT Network Protocol

Microsoft lists the following objective for the Windows NT Server exam: Choose a protocol for various situations. Protocols include TCP/IP, NWLink IPX/SPX Compatible Transport, and NetBEUI.

A network protocol is a collection of rules and procedures governing communication among the computers on a network. In a sense, a protocol is a language your computer uses when speaking to other computers. If two computers don't use the same protocols, they cannot communicate.

The three principal Windows NT networking protocols are as follows:

- **TCP/IP:** A widely used, routable protocol that is the basis for communication on the Internet.

- **NWLink IPX/SPX Compatible Transport:** Microsoft's rendition of Novell's proprietary IPX/SPX protocol suite. NWLink is a routable protocol designed to enable Windows NT computers to interoperate with Novell NetWare networks.

- **NetBEUI:** A very fast but non-routable protocol used on Microsoft networks. Because NetBEUI is non-routable, it is suitable only for Local Area Networks (LANs).

You should learn the advantages and disadvantages of each of these protocols and understand when to use each.

A.   TCP/IP

Transmission Control Protocol/Internet Protocol (TCP/IP) is the default protocol for the Intel version of Windows NT. TCP/IP is the only protocol supported on the Internet (which is why it is rocketing toward becoming a global standard protocol).

Windows NT's version of the TCP/IP protocol, Microsoft TCP/IP, is a 32-bit native suite of protocols. It requires more configuration than other protocols, but Microsoft also provides some excellent configuration tools. The result is a cross-platform, industry-standard, routable network implementation that you can expect only to grow in popularity.

The important things to remember about TCP/IP are as follows:

- TCP/IP is routable. Because TCP/IP packets can be forwarded through routers, you can use TCP/IP on Wide Area Networks (WANs). (The NetBEUI protocol, by contrast, can only be used on Local Area Networks.)

- TCP/IP is the language of the Internet. If your Windows NT computer will be connected to the Internet, you need to use TCP/IP.

- TCP/IP is a widely accepted standard. You can interconnect with more networks worldwide if you are using TCP/IP.

- TCP/IP accommodates a wide range of network hardware, operating systems, and applications.

You implement TCP/IP on your network with the help of three important services:

- **Dynamic Host Configuration Protocol (DHCP):** Dynamically assign ("leases") IP addresses to DHCP clients.

- **Domain Name System (DNS):** Maps IP addresses to human-readable computer names.

- **Windows Internet Name Service (WINS):** Maps IP addresses to NETBIOS computer names.

The Internet Protocol (the IP in TCP/IP) sends packets using a computer's IP Address—a unique 32-bit binary number that no other computer on the network can possess. (More precisely, it is not every computer, but rather every network adapter card, that requires its own IP Address.)

The 32-bit IP address usually is expressed as four octets, or 8-bit numbers, which then are represented in decimal form. An 8-bit number can have a value of anywhere from 0 to 255, so an IP address consists of four numbers between 0 and 255 separated by decimal points (for example, 111.12.3.141).

Every computer on a TCP/IP network must have an IP address. You can configure a permanent IP address for each computer, or you can configure each computer to receive a dynamically assigned IP address from a Dynamic Host Protocol (DHCP) server. A DHCP server is assigned a range of IP addresses. The DHCP server then "leases" (assigns for a limited duration) these IP addresses to DHCP clients in the subnet.

The Domain Name System (DNS) is a feature of TCP/IP networks that enables you to map an IP address to an alphanumeric name that is theoretically even easier for humans to remember than the decimal octet. (Internet domain names, such as `newriders.mcp.com`, are now easily recognizable in this age of e-mail.) Windows NT Server's Microsoft DNS Server service can map IP addresses to domain names on a TCP/IP network.

Windows NT's WINS service is similar to DNS except that, rather than mapping IP addresses to domain names, WINS maps IP addresses' NetBIOS names. NetBIOS names are used to identify resources on Microsoft networks. NetBIOS names follow the familiar Universal Naming Convention (UNC) format you use to locate resources from the Windows NT command prompt:

```
\\computername\sharename\path
```

The WINS service is also dynamic. Whereas DNS requires a static listing of all domain name-to-IP-address mappings, the WINS service can automatically associate NetBIOS names with IP addresses.

B. NWLink

The primary purpose of Microsoft's NWLink/SPX Compatible Transport protocol is to provide connectivity with the many thousands of Novell NetWare networks. NWLink is, however, a fully functional and fully routable protocol. Because TCP/IP is Internet-ready (and more universally accepted) and NetBEUI is faster and simpler for Microsoft LANs, however, chances are good that if you are using NWLink you will be connecting to NetWare.

NWLink provides compatibility with IPX/SPX-based networks, but NWLink alone does not necessarily enable a Windows NT computer to interact with NetWare networks. Some important points to remember are as follows:

- The NWLink protocol provides compatibility with Novell NetWare IPX/SPX networks.

- A Windows NT Workstation computer running Client Services for NetWare (CSNW) and the NWLink protocol or a Windows NT Server computer running Gateway Services for NetWare (GSNW) and the NWLink protocol can connect file and print services on a NetWare server.

- A Windows NT computer using the NWLink protocol can connect to client/server applications on a NetWare server (without requiring additional NetWare-connectivity services).

- Any Microsoft network client that uses Server Message Block (Windows NT, Windows 95, or Windows for Workgroups) can access NetWare resources through a NetWare gateway on a Windows NT Server computer running Gateway Services for NetWare. The NetWare resources appear to the Microsoft network client as Windows NT resources.

C.   NetBEUI

NetBEUI is the fastest protocol that comes with Windows NT, but it cannot be routed. This means that the NetBEUI protocol is generally only useful for what Microsoft calls "department-sized LANs." The recent emphasis on internetworking means that, in all but the smallest and most isolated networks, NetBEUI is usually not the ideal choice for a primary network protocol. That is why NetBEUI has not been a default protocol for Windows NT since version 3.1.

You cannot use NetBEUI with a router, but you can use a bridge to connect LAN segments operating with the NetBEUI protocol.

NetBEUI was designed by IBM in 1985, and one of the advantages of NetBEUI is that it enables Windows NT machines to interact with older Microsoft network machines that use NetBEUI (for instance, Windows for Workgroups 3.1 or Microsoft LAN Manager).

NetBEUI is also extremely easy to implement. It is self-tuning and self-configuring. Because NetBEUI was designed for an earlier generation of lower-performance computers, it also comes with a smaller memory overhead.

The speed and simplicity of NetBEUI comes with a downside, however: NetBEUI relies heavily on network broadcasts, which can degrade performance on large and busy subnets.

D.   Planning for Network Clients

The Windows NT CD-ROM includes client software for a number of operating systems that are not as naturally networkable as Windows NT or Windows 95. Some of those client software packages are as follows:

- Microsoft Network 3.0 for MS-DOS
- LAN Manager 2.2c for MS-DOS client
- LAN Manager 2.2c for OS/2 client

Microsoft Network Client 3.0 for MS-DOS enables MS-DOS machines to participate in Windows NT networks. An MS-DOS client using Microsoft Client 3.0 for MS-DOS configured with the full director can perform the following tasks on a Windows NT network:

- Log on to a domain
- Run logon scripts
- Access IPC mechanisms, such as RPCs, named pipes, and WinSock
- Use RAS (version 1.1)

A Microsoft Client 3.0 for MS-DOS client cannot browse the network unless a Windows NT computer or a Windows for Workgroups computer is in the same workgroup.

The Windows NT CD-ROM also includes a pair of network client packages that help connect LAN Manager 2.2c systems with Windows NT. Those client packages are LAN Manager 2.2c for MS-DOS client and LAN Manager 2.2c OS/2 client. The LAN Manager 2.2c for MS-DOS client includes some features not found in the OS/2 version, including support for the Remoteboot service and the capability to connect to a NetWare server.

Table 1.4.1 describes which network protocols and which TCP/IP services each of the client systems supports.

Table 1.4.1   Network Protocol and TCP/IP Service Support for Various Windows NT Client Systems

Network Protocol	TCP/IP Service	IPX-Compatible	IPX/SPX Compatible	NetBEUI	TCP/IP	DLC	DHCP	WINS	DNS
Network Client for MS-DOS	X	X		X	X	X			
LAN MAN 2.2c for MS-DOS	X			X	X	X			
LAN MAN 2.2c for OS/2	X			X					
Windows 95	X		X	X		X	X	X	
Windows NT Workstation	X		X	X	X	X	X	X	

1.4.1   Exercise: Choosing a Network Protocol

The purpose of this exercise is to show uses for the three different network protocols NetBEUI, IPX/SPX, and TCP/IP.

1. If you are running a LAN, need no connectivity to NetWare servers, and have no routers, your best choice is NetBEUI.

2. If your network has NetWare servers and also remote locations connected with routers, IPX/SPX is your best choice when clients connect directly to the NetWare servers. If they use gateway services on a Windows NT Server machine, only this computer must run IPX/SPX additionally, and TCP/IP can be used as primary protocol.

3. If your network is connected to the Internet, there is only one protocol of choice: TCP/IP.

1.4.2   Exercise: Testing Your TCP/IP Setup

This exercise is intended to show you the basics of TCP/IP and how it works with routers and Internet addresses.

1. Make sure TCP/IP is installed on your network.

2. Choose Start, Programs, Command Prompt.

3. From the command prompt, type **IPCONFIG**. The IPCONFIG command tells you the IP address, subnet mask, and default gateway for all network adapters to which TCP/IP is bound.

4. If TCP/IP is working properly on your system, the IPCONFIG utility outputs the IP address, subnet mask, and default gateway for your network adapter(s). If your computer obtains an IP address from a DHCP that is not working at this time—for instance, if you have a dial-up adapter that you use to access the Internet with an Internet service provider and you are not presently connected—the IP address and subnet mask appears as 0.0.0.0. If you have a duplicated IP address, the address appears, but the subnet mask appears as 0.0.0.0. Write down your IP address.

5. Type **PING 127.0.0.1**. The Ping utility (Packet INternet Groper) tests your TCP/IP connection. You can specify the IP address of another computer with the command, and Ping makes sure your connection with the other computer is working. The format for the Ping command is:

```
ping <IP address>
```

The address you just typed (127.0.0.1) is a special address called the *loopback address*. The loopback address verifies that TCP/IP is working correctly on your system.

6. Ping the IP address of your own computer. This confirms that your IP address is configured correctly and informs you as to whether any duplicate IP addresses are on your network.

7. Ping the address of another computer on your subnet. If a system has a default gateway (see step 4), it is a common practice to ping the default gateway to ensure that your connection to the gateway is working.

8. If you know the IP address of a computer beyond the gateway, ping the IP address of the remote to ensure that you can connect to remote resources.

1.4 Practice Problems

1. Which of the following protocols is mainly used to connect to Novell NetWare servers? Select the best answer:

    A. IPX/SPX

    B. TCP/IP

    C. NetBEUI

    D. AppleTalk

2. Which of the following protocols are routable? Select all that apply:

    A. IPX/SPX

    B. TCP/IP

    C. NetBEUI

    D. NetBIOS

3. For which of the following operating systems are implementations of TCP/IP available? Select all that apply:

    A. MS-DOS

    B. Windows 3.11 for Workgroups

    C. Windows 95

    D. Windows NT

4. Your network is a collection of Windows NT machines, Windows 95 machines, and MS-DOS machines running LAN MAN 2.2c Client for MS-DOS. The network, which uses the NetBEUI protocol, used to perform reasonably well, but you recently added additional nodes and noticed a sharp decline in performance. Now you are planning to add to the network again. Which of the following steps might improve network performance?

    A. Keep NetBEUI, but subdivide the network using a bridge

    B. Switch to NWLink

    C. Switch to TCP/IP

    D. A or C

    E. All of the above

5. Users on your Windows NT network occasionally have to exchange messages with users on a Novell NetWare 4.0 network via the Internet. You must use which protocol?

    A. TCP/IP

    B. NWLink

    C. Both A and B

    D. None of the above

6. Your boss is calling you. She has read about the exciting new features of the Internet, and wants the company connected to it. Which protocol do you need to install in order to make your computers Internet-ready? Select the best answer:

    A. IPX/SPX

    B. TCP/IP

    C. NetBEUI

    D. AppleTalk

7. What are the advantages of NetBEUI? Select all that apply:

    A. It can be used on networks with bridges.

    B. It can be used on networks with routers.

    C. It comes with a small memory overhead.

    D. It relies on network broadcasts.

8. Which of the following services is required for NetBIOS name resolution with TCP/IP? Select the best answer:

    A. DNS

    B. WINS

    C. DHCP

    D. RAS

1.4 Answers and Explanations: Practice Problems

1. **A** IPX/SPX is the primary protocol of NetWare servers.

2. **A, B** Only TCP/IP and IPX/SPX are routable.

3. **A, B, C, D** TCP/IP is available with all.

4. **D** You can switch to TCP/IP or subdivide your network using a bridge.

5. **A** The Internet uses TCP/IP.

6. **B** The Internet uses TCP/IP.

7. **A, C** NetBEUI has small memory overhead and can be used in networks that are connected with bridges.

8. **B** WINS allows for NetBIOS name resolution.

1.4 Key Words

Bridge	CSNW
DNS	DHCP
GSNW	Internet
IPX/SPX	NetBEUI
NetBIOS	Novell NetWare
NWLink	Router
TCP/IP	WINS

Practice Exam: Planning

Use this practice exam to test your mastery of Planning. This practice exam is 13 questions long, so you should try to finish the test within 24 minutes. Keep in mind that the passing Microsoft score is 76.4 percent. There will be two types of questions:

- Multiple Choice—Select the correct answer.

- Multiple Multiple Choice—Select all answers that are correct.

Begin as soon as you are ready. The answers follow the test.

1. Sally needs to enable Mac users from the Sales department to share files with PC users. Which operating systems support file shares for both Macintosh and PC users? Select all that apply:

    A. Windows 95b

    B. Windows NT Server

    C. You have to buy MS MacShare for Windows NT Server

    D. Windows NT Workstation with Macintosh shares

    E. None of the above

2. Which of the following statements is *not* true? Choose all that apply:

    A. NT Server is designed to operate as a network server and domain controller.

    B. NT Workstation, like Windows 95, is designed to serve as a network client and desktop operating system.

    C. Windows NT Workstation can serve as a stand-alone operating system.

    D. The most striking difference between Windows NT Workstation and Windows 95 is Workstation's client capabilities.

    E. All of the above are true.

3. How is NWLink defined? Choose all that apply:

    A. IPX/SPX-compatible transport that provides support for TCP/IP sockets and various APIs.

    B. IPX/SPX-compatible transport that provides support for IPX/SPX Sockets and NetBIOS APIs.

    C. TAPI-compliant protocol that supports Windows Sockets and NetBIOS APIs.

    D. NetBEUI protocol which can be used on networks with bridges.

    E. None of the above.

4. Which of the following statements about workgroups is *not* true?

    A. A Windows NT Server acting as a client can participate in workgroups.

    B. A workgroup is easier to install than a domain.

    C. A workgroup does not require an NT Server machine acting as a domain controller.

    D. A workgroup is simpler than a domain.

5. Which of the following statements about partitions is *not* true? Choose all that apply:

    A. If you choose to use an extended partition on a hard disk, you are limited to three primary partitions for that disk.

    B. A primary partition can be subdivided, as long as one of the divisions is the bootable OS.

C. An extended partition can be subdivided into smaller logical drives.

D. One hard disk can contain four extended partitions.

E. One hard disk can contain up to four primary partitions.

6. With which of the following systems is Windows NT Server compatible? Choose all that apply:

A. MS-DOS 5.0

B. Windows 3.1x

C. OS/2 1.x

D. POSIX-based applications

7. What are the advantages of NetBEUI? Choose all that apply:

A. It can be used on networks with bridges.

B. It comes with a small memory overhead.

C. It is used on LANs and WANs.

D. It is easily routable.

8. Which statements are true about TCP/IP?

A. TCP/IP is routable.

B. TCP/IP is the language of the Internet.

C. You can interconnect with more networks if you are using TCP/IP.

D. TCP/IP accommodates a wide range of network hardware, operating systems, and applications.

E. All of the above are true.

9. Which of the following statements is/are *not* true about the FAT file system? Choose all that apply:

A. FAT is typically the more efficient file system for small partitions.

B. FAT is generally faster than NTFS.

C. You cannot conserve space by compressing files on a FAT partition.

D. FAT is more secure than NTFS.

E. Use the FAT file system if you will be dual-booting your computer with another operating system and you want to access the partition from the other operating system.

10. Which of the following statements is *not* true about the NTFS file system? Choose all that apply:

A. The biggest drawback with using NTFS is that only the Windows NT operating system can access NTFS partitions.

B. When partitions are under 400 MB (on average), NTFS is your most reasonable choice.

C. You cannot conserve space by compressing files on a NTFS partition.

D. NTFS supports bigger partitions than FAT.

E. NTFS supports sector sparing, also known as hot fixing, on SCSI hard drives.

11. How is fault tolerance defined?

A. A system's capability to enable disk mirroring.

B. A system's capability to duplicate data during backup procedures.

C. A system's capability to compensate in the event of hardware disaster.

D. A system's capability to enable disk striping with parity.

12. Which of the following statements about disk mirroring is *not* true?

    A. Disk mirroring is RAID Level 1.

    B. In disk mirroring, Windows NT writes the same data to two physical disks.

    C. In disk mirroring, Windows NT records parity information that it can use to regenerate missing data if a disk should fail.

    D. All of the above are true.

13. Which of the following statements about the performance differences between Windows NT Workstation and Server is/are *not* true? Choose all that apply:

    A. Windows NT Workstation preloads a Virtual DOS Machine (VDM), the 32-bit MS-DOS emulator that supports legacy applications.

    B. Caching is handled differently on workstations and servers, enabling better network throughput on Windows NT Server and better local disk access time on Windows NT Workstation.

    C. Windows NT Workstation includes a configurable server service that enables you to tune the server as an application server or as a file/print server.

    D. The server files system driver used in both Windows NT Workstation and Server (SRV.SYS) is more subject to paging under Windows NT Workstation than under Windows NT Server.

    E. C and D are not true.

Answers and Explanations: Practice Exam

1. **B** NT Server offers Services for Macintosh, which enable file shares for Mac and PC users.

2. **D** The most striking difference between Windows NT Workstation and Windows 95 is security. Windows NT Workstation is an extremely secure operating system.

3. **B** NWLink is defined as the IPX/SPX-compatible transport that provides support for IPX/SPX Sockets and NetBIOS APIs.

4. **A** Unless a Windows NT Server computer is configured as a stand-alone server, it cannot participate in a workgroup.

5. **B, D** Primary partitions cannot be subdivided; one hard disk can contain only one extended partition.

6. **A, B, C, D** Windows NT Server is compatible with all aforementioned systems.

7. **A, B** NetBEUI has small memory overhead and can be used in networks that are connected with bridges.

8. **E** TCP/IP is routable, widely used, flexible, and the Internet-standard protocol.

9. **B, D** FAT is generally slower and significantly less secure than NTFS.

10. **B, C** When partitions are over 400 MB (not under), NTFS is your most reasonable choice. Windows NT provides the capability to compress NTFS files.

11. **C** Fault tolerance is the system's capability to compensate in the event of hardware disaster.

12. **C** In disk striping with parity (not disk mirroring), Windows NT records parity information that it can use to regenerate missing data if a disk should fail.

13. **C** Windows NT Workstation does not provide the configurable server service because it is limited to 10 inbound sessions.

CHAPTER 2

Installation and Configuration

2.1 Installing Windows NT Server on Intel-Based Platforms

The following Microsoft test objectives are covered in this chapter:

- Install Windows NT Server on Intel-based platforms.

- Install Windows NT Server to perform various server roles, including primary domain controller, backup domain controller, and member server.

- Install Windows NT Server by using various methods, including CD-ROM, over the network, Network Client administrator, and express versus custom.

- Install protocols and protocol bindings. Protocols include TCP/IP, NWLink, IPX/SPX compatible transport, NetBEUI.

- Configure network adapters. Considerations include changing IRQ, I/O base, memory address, and configuring multiple adapters.

- Configure Windows NT Server core services, including Directory Replicator, License Manager, and other services.

- Configure peripherals and devices, including communications devices, SCSI devices, tape device drivers, UPS service, mouse drivers, display drivers, and keyboard drivers.

- Configure hard disks to meet various requirements. Requirements include allocating disk space capacity, providing redundancy, improving performance, providing security, and formatting.

- Configure printers. Tasks include adding and configuring a printer, implementing a printer pool, and setting print priorities.

- Configure a Windows NT Server computer for various types of client computers. Client computer types include Windows NT Workstation, Windows 95, and Microsoft MS-DOS-based.

A. Hardware Requirements

Hardware requirements are dependent on the processor type. Intel-based machines have the following requirements:

Intel Processor

80486/33 or higher

16 MB of RAM

125 MB hard disk space

Hard drive may be FAT or NTFS

VGA Display or better

3.5 inch drive required

Note that all hardware must be on a current Hardware Compatibility list (available at www.microsoft.com/ntserver/hcl/hclintro.htm), or the manufacturer must supply an updated driver compatible for NT 4.0. It is possible that a device may be compatible with another driver.

B. Installation Location

Windows NT can be installed alongside other operating systems on the same machine. In this multiboot environment, each OS would be installed in its own subdirectory. The default directory for the system files of NT is WINNT.

Windows NT requires a boot partition, typically the active drive, and a system partition. The boot partition contains information about the platform. The system partition contains the source files for the OS. These can be the same or different partitions.

C. WINNT Switches

The following switches enable you to customize how WINNT.EXE begins the setup process:

/b	No boot floppies
/s	Source file location. Syntax is: WINNT.EXE /s: <path of source files>
/U	Unattended installation
/UDF	Tailored, unattended installation for installation on multiple machines
/T:drive_letter Temporary drive	Tells WINNT or winnt32 to put the installation files on the specified drive
/OX	Creates just the three boot disks
/F	Do not verify files as they are copied to hard disk
/C	Do not check for free space

D. Installation Phases

Microsoft divides the installation into four phases:

Phase 0: Preinstallation

Phase 1: Gathering information about your computer

Phase 2: Installing Networking

Phase 3: Finishing setup

1. Phase 0: Preinstallation

During preinstallation, Setup copies the necessary files to your hard drive and assembles the information it needs for the install based on the hardware detected in your machine. It is during this phase that the three setup disks are created.

- **Setup Disk 1.** When booting from disk 1, the MBR (Master Boot Record) passes control to NTLDR. NTLDR loads the kernel (NTKRNLMP.EXE). Then the HAL (Hardware Abstraction Layer) is loaded.

- **Setup Disk 2.** This disk contains a minimal version of the registry. This simple registry instructs WINNT to load the main installation driver and generic hardware drives for keyboard, floppy, video, and the driver for the FAT file system. In addition, there is provision for SCSI port drivers.

- **Setup Disk 3.** This disk contains additional SCSI drivers, the driver for the NTFS file system, and drivers for various hard disks.

During this process, the setup routine has loaded the minimal drivers for the hardware, and for the file systems. WINNT then begins user interaction by confirming hardware-related information.

a. Mass Storage Devices

Setup asks the user if it should attempt to detect mass storage devices. Upon completion of the detection, a confirmation screen appears with information WINNT has retrieved. The user may press Enter to confirm what Setup has detected or press S to specify additional devices.

b. Hardware and Components

Setup presents a list of detected hardware (mouse, keyboard, and video) and waits for a user confirmation or any changes to the list.

c. Partitions

Setup needs to know where it should install the Windows NT source files. The default directory is WINNT. The user is given the opportunity to change this directory name and to specify in which partition NT should be installed.

Setup also gives the opportunity to create a partition in unpartitioned space.

Setup then presents the following information:

- Format the partition using FAT.

- Format the partition using the NTFS file system.

- Convert the partition to NTFS.

- Leave the current file system intact.

> **NTFS is designed for NT. It is not accessible from other operating systems including Windows 95 and DOS. If the conversion to NTFS is selected, the conversion does not happen until after setup has been completed. If dual booting is planned for the machine, the active partition must remain as FAT. If it is a RISC-based machine a minimum 2 MB FAT partition is required. This is due to the firmware on RISC-based machines.**

Setup examines your hard disk for corruption. Setup allows for an exhaustive examination or a minimal exam. Choose S to skip the exhaustive examination.

Finally, Setup copies the source files to the hard disk; this will take several minutes. When Setup is complete a message appears asking that the floppy be removed and then to press Enter to restart your computer.

2. Phase 1: Gathering Information

After the computer restarts, setup displays the licensing agreement for approval and begins copying files from the CD-ROM or the Network site to the root directory.

The Setup Wizard appears announcing the remaining stages of the setup process:

- Gathering information about your computer

- Installing Windows NT Networking

- Finishing setup

- Name and Company Name

For legal and registration reasons, Setup asks for a name and company name. The Name field must be completed but the Company Name field may be left blank. Setup requires the product ID to continue.

a. Server Licensing Mode

NT Server requires a licensing mode for network connections. There are two types of licensing:

- **Per Server license.** For each per server license you purchase, one concurrent network connection is allowed access to the server. When the maximum specified amount of concurrent connections is reached, NT returns an error to a connecting user and prohibits access. An administrator, however, can still connect to the server to increase the amount of per server licenses.

- **Per Seat license.** Clients are free to connect to any server, and there are unlimited connections to the server. Each client participating in the network must have a per seat license.

Both modes of licenses are on an honor system.

b. Computer Name

Every networked Windows NT–based computer must have a unique NetBIOS computer name. A NetBIOS name may be up to 15 characters. Workgroup and domain names are also NetBIOS names so the computer name must be unique among these as well.

c. Server Type

Windows NT Server is allowed to be a PDC, a BDC, or a Member Server.

d. Administrator Password

Setup asks for an administrator account password. This password is limited to 14 characters and is case-sensitive.

e. Emergency Repair Disk

This is essentially a clone of the information stored in the \REPAIR directory in case of corruption on your hard disk.

f. Optional Components

Setup asks what additional components should be installed for the server.

3. Phase 2: Installing NT Networking

The Wizard announces that it is ready to install the networking portion of the install.

a. Network Participation

The Setup Wizard asks whether this machine will participate on the network. Setup needs to know whether participation will occur via a network card, modem, or both. If No is selected, the Setup Wizard will proceed to Phase 3, "Finishing Setup."

b. Internet/Intranet Service

Windows NT Server 4.0 comes with IIS (Internet Information Server). The Setup wizard will ask if this should be installed. If you choose Yes, the wizard will walk you through the getting started phases of IIS setup. If you choose No, an icon will be displayed on the desktop for future installation.

c. Network Adapter Card

Setup will ask if it should search for a network adapter card. Setup stops after it finds the first adapter card and the Start Search button changes into a Find Next button.

The user may also choose the option to select a network adapter card from a list. The have disk button is used to install a driver provided by an OEM. Setup may display a dialog box asking the user to confirm the network card's settings. Networking services can be installed on top of NT's RAS to use the services via a modem.

d. Network Protocols

Setup gives the user the option to install TCP/IP, NWLink, and NetBEUI. In addition, other protocols such as AppleTalk, DLC, Point to Point Tunneling Protocol, and others may be installed. TCP/IP and NWLINK IPX/SPX protocols are selected by default on Intel-based machines. NT Servers may be clients of DHCP.

e. Network Services

Setup asks what additional services should be installed. If you add to your configuration *after* setup, you may do so through Control Panel, Network.

f. Network Components

Setup completes the networking installation phase by presenting several options, including DHCP participation, IP information, modems installed, and the choice to change any settings created so far.

NT Server must be either a member of a Domain (PDC or BDC) or a member server in a workgroup or a domain. It cannot be a member in both a workgroup and a domain. NT Servers that are joining domains must have a computer account created for them before they join the domain. There are two ways to create a computer account:

- The administrator must manually add the computer account through Server Manager.

- The user adding the workstation must be a member of the Administrators group, or have the user right to "Add workstations to a domain."

4. Phase 3: Finishing Setup

After completing the networking components, setup then finishes its routine with the following steps:

- **Time Zone.** Setup requests the current date and time information during the final phase of setup. NT has an option to account for daylight savings time.

- **Exchange Configuration.** If Microsoft Exchange was selected as an optional component in Phase 1, setup requests information to configure Exchange.

- **Display Settings.** Setup detects the video display adapter.

    If the adapter uses a chipset for which NT includes a driver, it displays that information in the dialog box.

    Setup requires that the settings be tested before installation can continue.

- **Pentium Patch.** If setup detects the presence of the Intel Pentium floating point division error, Setup asks if you want to disable the floating point hardware and enable floating point emulation software.

    Disabling the hardware makes the floating-point calculations much more accurate at the expense of performance.

- **Emergency Repair Disk.** During the final phase, Setup creates a \REPAIR directory in the Windows NT root directory. This directory contains a backup of the current registry in use by NT.

If Setup was told to generate an Emergency Repair Disk, it will request a floppy at this point. Setup will format the floppy and prepare it as an Emergency Repair Disk.

2.1.1   Exercise: Installation Requirements and Procedures

This is a paper-based exercise. The information in this exercise may be applied to an actual install of Windows NT Server 4.0.

Answer the following questions based on your knowledge of the NT Server installation program:

Installation Requirements

Hardware Requirements:

1. What processor type is required?

2. What is the minimum amount of RAM required?

3. What is the minimum amount of hard disk space required?

Installation Procedures:

1. How do you dual boot between 95 and NT?

2. What is the fastest way to install NT?

3. What should you do if you have to install NT many times?

4. How can you avoid using the three setup disks?

5. What does HAL do?

6. How do you specify additional storage devices?

7. Define a Boot partition.

8. Define a System partition.

9. What are two advantages of using NTFS?

10. What are two disadvantages of using NTFS?

11. What is the default root directory of NT?

Gathering Information

1. Why is the Name field required?

2. What does Per server licensing mean?

3. What does Per seat licensing mean?

4. How many characters is the computer name limited to?

5. Why must the computer name be unique?

6. What are the roles the NT Server can play in the domain?

7. How many characters is the administrator password limited to?

Installing NT Networking

1. What does NT need to participate on the network?

2. What can you do to make NT a Web server?

3. How can NT find multiple adapter cards?

4. What is the default protocol for NT Server?

Network Components:

1. What is a domain?

2. In what two network environments will an NT member server take part?

3. What rights do you have to have to join a domain?

4. To join a domain, the computer must:

2.1   Practice Problems

1. Your supervisor would like you to install NT Server on the following machines. Based on your knowledge, which configurations would allow you to install NT Server 4.0?

   A. 16 MB RAM, 500 MB hard drive, 3.5 inch floppy, CD-ROM, and a Super VGA monitor.

   B. Pentium 200, 32 MB RAM, 4 GB SCSI hard drive, 3.5 inch floppy, CD-ROM drive, and a VGA monitor.

   C. 12 MB RAM, 1 GB hard drive, 3.5 inch floppy, and a VGA monitor.

   D. 32 MB RAM, 500 MB hard drive, 3.5 inch floppy, and a VGA monitor.

2. Your company has purchased new Ethernet network cards that are not on the HCL for NT. You should:

   A. Contact Microsoft's 800 number for unsupported hardware.

   B. Visit Microsoft.com and download all Ethernet drivers.

   C. Contact the OEM and ask for an available drive for the cards.

   D. Do not install Windows NT Server.

3. You would like to dual boot NT with Windows 95 for testing and evaluating software. You can configure this by (choose the best answer):

   A. Having two hard drives with NT on disk 0, and having Windows 95 on Disk 1.

   B. Install NT and 95 on the same hard drive, but in different partitions.

   C. Install NT and 95 in separate directories.

   D. This cannot be done.

4. The setup program for installing NT Server 4.0 is called:

   A. Setup.exe

   B. WINNT.EXE

   C. VMM32.exe

   D. WINCOM

5. Windows NT requires a boot partition. Choose the best description of a boot partition:

   A. The location of the WINNT directory where all boot and system information is stored.

   B. The partition that holds the Windows NT operating system files.

   C. Master Boot Record and NT source files.

   D. The WINNT directory must be on the active partition.

6. You would like to upgrade your NT Server 3.51 so that you do not lose your current settings. How can you do this? (Choose the best answer.)

   A. Run WINNT from the run command inside of NT Server 3.51.

   B. Run WINNT32 from the run command inside of NT Server 3.51.

   C. Run WINNT.EXE /upgrade at the DOS prompt.

   D. You must reinstall Windows NT Server 4.0, as there is no upgrade available due to registry difference of NT 3.51 and NT 4.0.

7. You have 100 workstations on which to install Windows NT Workstation 4.0. What is the easiest method to do this? (Choose the best answer.)

   A. You must visit each workstation and install NT from the CD-ROM.

B. You can share out the WINNT directory from another workstation and then connect to this through DOS.

C. You can share out the entire CD-ROM from another workstation and then connect to this through DOS.

D. You can share the entire CD-ROM from an NT Server and then connect to this through DOS.

8. You are installing NT Server 4.0 and do not want the boot diskettes generated by the setup program. How can you disable this portion of the setup program? (Choose the best answer.)

A. Windows NT Server 4.0 requires the setup disks to install.

B. Start setup with the following syntax: WINNT.EXE /b.

C. Start setup with the following syntax: WINNT.EXE /f.

D. Start setup with the following syntax: WINNT32.EXE.

9. You are installing NT server as a PDC on an Intel-based machine. When you try to designate your password for the administrator's account, you are not allowed to enter the password "Windows NT is Great." Why is this? (Choose the best answer.)

A. Passwords are limited to 14 characters.

B. Passwords cannot contain spaces.

C. Passwords cannot contain the words NT.

D. Windows NT requires that you enter your password twice to verify all settings. You are probably not typing the password identically in each field.

10. When booting from setup disk 1 during the install phase of NT Server, what role

does the HAL play? (Choose the best answer.)

A. HAL, the Hardware Abstraction Layer, is responsible for hiding the hardware from the operating system. This is what makes NT portable between RISC and Intel-based machines.

B. HAL, the Hardware Arbitration Layer, is responsible for assigning hardware resources such as IRQs.

C. HAL passes control to the NTKRNLMP.exe, which allows access to the processor(s).

D. HAL allows Direct Memory Access for the setup program to access areas of memory directly.

11. Setup Disk 2 instructs the setup program to (choose the best answer):

A. Scan the hard disk for errors.

B. Load a minimal file system to begin the file transfer process.

C. Begin building the registry based on hardware detected.

D. Load generic drivers for keyboards, floppy, video, and the drivers for the FAT file system.

12. On Setup Disk 2 and Setup Disk 3 there are SCSI port drivers available to setup. Why is this important? (Choose the best answer.)

A. 16-bit drivers are not compatible with Windows NT.

B. Setup needs these drivers to compare to any config.sys settings to determine if there are SCSI controllers installed in the machine.

C. RISC-based systems require a SCSI drive for the hard drive.

D. Setup might need these drivers to access a SCSI CD-ROM during setup.

13. During NT installation, NT asks you to confirm detected mass storage devices. You discover, however, that setup did not find all of the hard drives in your computer. You should (choose the best answer):

    A. Press escape and then F5 to force setup to look again for mass storage devices.

    B. Simply press F5. This will cause setup to search for mass storage devices.

    C. Press **S** to specify mass storage devices that setup could not recognize.

    D. You need a bus enumerator from the OEM to continue.

14. Setup presents a list of detected hardware including mouse, keyboard, and video settings. If the list is incorrect you should (choose the best answer):

    A. Start setup again using the /m switch for manual detection of devices.

    B. Press F5 to force setup to detect devices again.

    C. Use the arrow keys to select the device that is incorrect and press F8 to see alternatives.

    D. Use the arrow keys to select the device that is incorrect, and press Enter to see alternatives.

15. Setup asks you where it should install Windows NT Server. The default directory is what? (Choose the best answer.)

    A. NTSRV

    B. WINNT

    C. WINNT40

    D. NTSRV40

16. You are installing Windows NT Server 4.0 on a RISC-based machine. You would like to change the partition and the

directory in which NT will be installed. (Choose the best answer.)

    A. Change the directory name from NTSRV to whatever you like. Then arrow up or down to choose the correct partition on which the source files should be placed.

    B. Change the directory name from WINNT to whatever you like. Then arrow up or down to choose the correct partition on which the source files should be placed.

    C. Change the directory name from NTSRV40 to whatever you like. Then arrow up or down to choose the correct partition on which the source files should be placed.

    D. This cannot be done because RISC-based machines require that the source files be located on the active partition.

17. You are installing NT Server on an Intel-based machine. During installation, you realize that, although you have a 4GB SCSI drive, you have only partitioned 250 MB of the drive. You would like to dual boot with 95 and NT. What configuration should you choose? (Choose all that would work.)

    A. During setup, choose the option to create a partition in unused space. Create a 2 GB partition, format it with NTFS and install NT onto that partition.

    B. Install NT into the same partition as 95, but in separate directories.

    C. Install NT into the same partition as 95, but in separate directories. Then convert the drive to NTFS.

    D. Exit the setup program, and then use FDISK to create a new partition. Format this new partition, and then run WINNT.EXE again.

18. During setup, you have chosen the option to create a new partition onto which to

install the NT source files. What choices
do you have after designating this new
partition? (Choose all that apply.)

A. Format the partition as FAT.

B. Format the partition as NTFS.

C. Convert the partition to NTFS.

D. There is no available choice. Setup
automatically formats this partition
as NTFS.

19. You are installing NT Server and you
would like to take advantage of NTFS for
security. However, your supervisor is
worried about compatibility of NT with
other operating systems on the network.
Is this a valid concern? (Choose the best
answer.)

A. Yes, it is a valid concern because
NTFS is not compatible with any
other operating system except for NT.

B. No, it is not a valid concern because
NTFS is compatible with all
operating systems.

C. No, it is not a valid concern because
NTFS partitions are not accessible
by other operating systems only if
those operating systems are on the
same machine.

D. Yes, but only because NTFS
supports long filename support and
other operating systems might not
have long filename support.

20. You are installing Windows NT Server
onto an Intel-based machine. Currently
on this machine you have Windows 95.
You would like to dual boot between 95
and NT so you are certain to install NT
in a separate directory than 95. Upon
completion of NT setup you have no
ability to boot into 95. What went
wrong? (Choose the best answer.)

A. You must edit the boot.ini to reflect
the location of the 95 source files.

B. You told setup to convert the active
partition to NTFS.

C. You must add the line to 95's
MSDOS.SYS, BootMulit=1 to dual
boot with NT.

D. You need to use the Boot Manager
in the Administrative Tools folder
to setup dual-boot ability with
other operating systems.

21. During setup you told NT to format a
new partition you created with NTFS.
The setup program does this when?
(Choose the best answer.)

A. Immediately.

B. After the registry is built.

C. When NT is completely installed
and NT reboots for the first time.

D. The first time you open Disk
Administrator, a macro runs that
performs the conversion.

22. During installation, Setup must examine
your hard drives for any corruption. You
are confident that your hard drives are
okay and would like to skip any exhaustive exams. How can you do this?
(Choose the best answer.)

A. Setup requires an exhaustive exam
of all media before installation can
continue.

B. Press Shift+F8 to skip the exam.

C. Press Escape to skip the exam.

D. Press B to bypass the exam.

23. You are a consultant hired by a company
to install NT Server 4. You do not want
to put a name in the Name field, as you
are not an employee for your client. How
can you bypass this field? (Choose the
best answer.)

A. Click on the skip button to continue.

B. A value is required to continue.

C. Click on the cancel button to continue.

D. Enter a value now; but later, through Add/remove programs, take out your name.

24. You are a consultant hired by a company to install NT Server. When you get to the product identification field it asks you for a CD Key. Your client tells you this is unavailable. What should you do? (Choose the best answer.)

A. Call Microsoft's support for a CD key.

B. Insert a CD Key from another CD.

C. Stop installation until the original CD key is available.

D. Choose Continue and enter the CD key later, through the registry.

25. You and an associate are installing NT Server and your associate is confused about per server versus per seat licensing agreements. Which would best describe per server? (Choose the best answer.)

A. Per server enables all clients to connect as often as they want.

B. Per server allows for a predetermined amount of concurrent connections.

C. Per server allows for unlimited connections to any server available.

D. Per server allows for a limited number of connections within a 24-hour period.

26. You and an associate are installing NT Server, and your associate is confused about per server versus per seat licensing agreements. Which would best describe per seat? (Choose the best answer.)

A. Per seat allows an unlimited number of concurrent network connections.

B. Per seat allows for a limited number of connections within a 24-hour period.

C. Per seat allows for an unlimited number of concurrent network connections within 30, 60, or 90 day increments.

D. Per seat is only available if you have more than one Domain Controller.

2.1   Answers and Explanations: Practice Problems

1. **A, B, D**   The minimum requirements to install NT server on an Intel-based machine are: 80486/33 or higher, 16 MB of RAM, 125 MB hard disk space, VGA or better, and 3.5 inch floppy drive.

2. **C**   You should contact the Original Equipment Manufacturer for an updated driver for Windows NT Server. Another possibility is to check whether the network card emulates another card for which there is an NT 4 driver on the NT Server CD.

3. **C**   After you have installed Windows 95, followed by Windows NT, you can then choose MS-DOS from the OS Loader menu, or you can edit the boot.ini to create a separate entry for Windows 95.

4. **B**   To install Windows NT, run WINNT.exe from a command prompt, or from within Windows for Workgroups. Within previous versions of Windows NT or from within Windows 95, you may run the 32-bit version of the setup program called WINNT32.exe.

5. **B**   The partition that holds the Windows NT operating system is called the boot partition. The system partition is the partition that contains the files necessary to boot the operating system. The system partition does not have to be the partition where the operating system is installed.

6. **B**   WINNT32.EXE is the command to upgrade from a previous version of NT Server.

2

7. **D** By sharing out the CD-ROM from a server rather than a workstation, you bypass NT Workstation's limit of 10 concurrent connections. Server connection is limited only by the licensing agreement you have chosen during the install.

8. **B** You should use WINNT /b to disable the generation of floppies during setup. The WINNT /f command is used to disable file verification, as they are copied to the hard disk.

9. **A** Your logon password is limited to 14 characters.

10. **A** The Hardware Abstraction Layer is responsible for hiding the hardware from the OS.

11. **D** These generic drivers are needed so that user interaction can occur throughout the setup phase.

12. **D** Setup will need access to the SCSI CD-ROM drive if one exists so that it can transfer data from the CD-ROM to the hard drive.

13. **C** Press **S** to specify mass storage devices.

14. **D** Use the arrow keys to select the device that is incorrect, and press Enter to see alternatives.

15. **B** During the installation of Windows NT, the setup program recommends that you install Windows NT into the directory called WINNT. You may change this to a new name if you want.

16. **B** You are allowed on Intel or RISC-based computers to rename the directory name and to specify where the directory will be located.

17. **A, B, D** During setup you will have the opportunity to create a new partition. NT and 95 can coexist on the same partition as long as they are in separate directories. You can exit the setup program, create a new partition, and start over with WINNT; but there is no real reason to follow this method because you are able to create partitions from within the text-based setup program.

18. **A, B** During setup you have created a new partition. Because this new partition is unformatted, Setup allows you to format the partition at this time. You can format the partition with FAT or you with NT's filing system, NTFS.

19. **C** NTFS is not accessible by any other operating system that is dual booting on the same machine. Across the network, NT is compatible with most major operating systems.

20. **B** If you told Setup to convert the active partition to NTFS, 95 will be unable to boot because 95 requires a FAT partition.

21. **C** The partition is first formatted with FAT and is marked to be converted to NTFS when NT is rebooted.

22. **C** You are allowed to skip the exhaustive exam.

23. **B** The name field must be completed, the company field may be ignored.

24. **C** The product id is required to continue installation.

25. **B** Per server allows for a limited number of concurrent network connections.

26. **A** Per seat allows for an unlimited number of concurrent network connections.

2.1 Key Words

Protocol

Boot partition

System partition

NTFS

2.2 Windows NT Server 4.0 Server Roles

Windows NT Server plays one of three roles in a network environment:

Role	Characteristics
Primary Domain Controller (PDC)	First server installed in a domain Contains master copy of user database Only one PDC per domain.
Backup Domain Controller (BDC)	Maintains a copy of the domain's user account database Shares logon authentication workload with PDC May be promoted to a PDC should the PDC be taken offline A domain may have more than one BDC.
Member Server	Does not maintain a copy of the user accounts database May serve as a file, print, or application server May be a member of a domain or workgroup Cannot be promoted to domain controller without reinstalling NT server There may be multiple member servers in a domain or workgroup.

A. Domain Attributes

A *domain* is a collection of computer accounts. Only NT Workstations and servers can be true members of a domain.

Windows 95 machines, Windows for Workgroups, and DOS-based machines are not members of a domain, they are clients of the domain. Users are validated by a domain controller through a secure network channel. The NT service responsible for validation is the Netlogon service. The first server online in a domain must be the Primary Domain Controller.

1. Primary Domain Controllers

The PDC maintains a centralized database of all user account information. The PDC is responsible for validating users on the domain.

A PDC may also act as a file, print, or application server. There may be only one PDC in a domain at any given time. The PDC is where all administration of user accounts, and computer accounts should occur. The PDC will synchronize its account database to the Backup Domain Controller.

2. Backup Domain Controllers

The Backup Domain Controllers are responsible for validating user logon requests in conjunction with the PDC. They share the workload of validating user logon requests.

Backup Domain Controllers receive updates of the Domain Account Database in regular intervals, or synchronization sessions from the Primary Domain Controller.

A BDC may also act as a file, print, or application server. There is no limit to how many BDCs are in a domain.

B. Member Servers

Member Servers are NT Servers that act only as a file, print, or application servers. Member Servers may be either a member of a workgroup or a domain. Member servers do not validate user logon requests.

C. Server Maintenance

BDCs may be promoted to a PDC through Server Manager. Only an administrator can perform this function. Promotion is useful if the PDC must be taken down, or goes offline.

Promotion is a manual process; it does not happen automatically. There is no way to promote a Member Server to a Domain Controller without reinstalling NT Server.

Account synchronization may be forced through Server Manager or by typing the command NET ACCOUNTS /SYNC at the command prompt. Accounts can be synchronized throughout the entire domain or through one BDC at a time.

There is no way to move a domain controller from one domain to another without reinstalling NT Server. This is due to the SID of the domains.

There is no way to install a BDC without the presence of a PDC. To join a domain a computer must have a computer account. There are two methods of creating a computer account:

- An administrator adds the computer account through Server Manager before the computer joins the domain.

- If it is NT Server, you may select the option to create a computer account during installation. An Administrators group username and password are required.

It is possible to change the domain name by using the Control Panel network. You can also change the NetBIOS name of the server through this applet. A Domain controller can validate logon requests from any of the following clients:

- Windows NT
- Windows 95
- Windows for Workgroups
- Microsoft LAN Manager
- MS-DOS clients with the enhanced redirector installed

Domain Controller and Member servers have the following features:

- RAS support for up to 256 simultaneous connections
- Fault tolerance
- Internet Information server
- Gateway Services for Netware
- Macintosh file and print services

2.2.1   Exercise: Promoting a BDC to a PDC

This exercise requires two domain controllers. You need to log on to a domain controller with administrative rights.

To promote the BDC to a PDC:

1. Logon as administrator if you have not done so already.
2. Start the Server Manager tool from the Administrative Tools group.
3. Choose the BDC from the list of available computers.
4. What do you notice about the icons of the computers?
5. From the Computer menu, choose Promote to PDC.
6. What does this mean?
7. What messages appear during the promotion?
8. Why would this process be useful?
9. Reverse the roles back to their original setting.

2.2.2   Exercise: Synchronizing the Directory Accounts Database

1. In Server Manager, choose a BDC.
2. From the computer menu, choose Synchronize with the Primary Domain Controller.
3. What does this command mean?
4. Now choose the Primary Domain Controller.
5. From the Computer Menu, choose Synchronize the entire domain.
6. What does this command mean?
7. Exit Server Manager.

2.2   Practice Problems

1. You are the administrator for a network consisting primarily of Windows for Workgroups and Windows 95 clients. You have decided to install Windows NT Server. As you are installing NT Server 4.0, you choose to make this machine a member server because you already have a workgroup in place. With this configuration, what can your clients now do? (Choose all that apply.)

   A. Log onto the domain for centralized security.

   B. Use NT Server as a file, print, and application server.

   C. Store their work on the server for consistent backups.

   D. Your 95 clients can now use user-level security.

2. Your company has three domains: SALES, MARKETING, and AC-COUNTING. You would like to create a new domain for your office in New York to be called NEW YORK. The SALES domain has three BDCs, so you decide to move one BDC to the NEW YORK domain. To make this BDC from SALES a PDC for NEW YORK, what must you do? (Choose the best answer.)

   A. Change the domain name in the Control Panel Network to NEW YORK.

   B. Promote the BDC to a PDC through Server Manager.

   C. Reinstall Windows NT Server 4.0.

   D. Change the domain name in the Network applet to NEW YORK, and change the administrator's password.

3. You are adding a BDC to your current domain. You tell the setup program that this machine should be a BDC in the Domain called CALIFORNIA but it

responds with the message, "No domain controller could be found." You verify that the domain name is spelled correctly, that you are connected to the network, and that your PDC is online. What do you suspect is the problem? (Choose all that apply.)

   A. You do not have administrative rights to add a BDC to the domain.

   B. The BDC is not using the same protocol as the PDC.

   C. Your network card has problems.

   D. You are obtaining your IP address via DHCP, and the DHCP server is currently out of IP addresses.

4. You want to create a BDC for your client in Idaho. You decide that you will install NT Server at your office and then ship the finished server to the client. However, when you install NT Server, it will not allow you to create a BDC without the presence of a PDC. Why is this? (Choose the best answer.)

   A. A PDC must establish a secure network channel with the BDC to determine that you are using a legal copy of NT.

   B. A PDC must be present to alert the BDC that a Master Browser is already in place on the network.

   C. The PDC must be available so that the account database can be synchronized to the BDC.

   D. You can make a server a BDC before the PDC. You must, however, start the installation as WINNT.EXE /BDC from a DOS prompt.

5. Your company has just purchased a RISC-based machine that has four processors, 2 4 GB hard drives, 128 MB of RAM, and an external CD-ROM tower. Your domain, MIS, currently has a less attractive NT 3.51 server acting as a

PDC. It is your intention to make your new RISC machine your PDC and demote the 3.51 server to a BDC. What is the correct procedure to do this? (Choose the best answer.)

A. Take the 3.51 server offline, install NT Server 4.0 on the RISC-based machine, and mark it as the PDC. Then bring the 3.51 server back online and demote it through server manager to a BDC.

B. Install NT Server 4.0 as a BDC in your current domain. Then promote the BDC to a PDC in your domain.

C. You must first upgrade the 3.51 server to NT Server 4.0. Install NT Server 4.0 as a BDC in your current domain. Then promote the BDC to a PDC in your domain.

D. This cannot be done without reinstalling NT Server 4.0 on both machines.

6. Your supervisor is concerned about creating a PDC before a BDC. How would you explain the proper order of creating a domain? (Choose the best answer.)

A. You must have a BDC before a PDC because the backup domain controller is there for backup and safety, in case something happens during the installation of the PDC.

B. A PDC is always the first server online during the creation of a domain.

C. A PDC is not required to be the first server online as long as the BDC has the same domain name as the PDC.

D. The BDC can be installed first as long as the Directory Replicator service has been installed during the initial installation.

7. You are installing NT Server as a PDC for network. You currently have a workgroup called DALLAS. You would like your NT domain to be called TEXAS and your PDC to be called DALLAS. However, when you enter the server name of DALLAS, Setup will not allow you to use that name. Why? (Choose the best answer.)

A. The server name must be at least 15 characters long.

B. The server name must contain numbers and letters for security reasons.

C. The server name must be unique from any other resource on the network.

D. You must confirm the server name. You are probably not correctly typing in DALLAS in each field.

8. You are installing NT Server as a BDC. You would like to name the domain controller "Backup Domain Controller 101." The setup program will not allow you to use this name. Why? (Choose the best answer.)

A. You are already using this name somewhere else on the network.

B. Server names cannot contain spaces.

C. Server names must have letters and number for security.

D. Server names are limited to 15 characters.

9. You have accidentally installed NT Server 4.0 as a member server. You were supposed to install NT as a BDC in the domain SALES. How can you change the status of this server? (Choose the best answer.)

A. Use Server Manager to promote the member server to a BDC.

B. Run WINNT32.EXE /BDC to promote the server to a BDC.

C.   You must reinstall NT Server.

D.   Use the Control Panel's network program to change the machine to a BDC.

10.   You are the administrator for a 95 workgroup. You have decided to install NT Server as a PDC to move into a domain environment. During install you would like to use the password "AcmeSalesSupport" for the Administrator's account, but the setup program will not allow you to use this password. Why not? (Choose the best answer.)

    A.   Administrators' passwords must always be alphanumeric.

    B.   You must confirm your password, as passwords are case-sensitive and you might not be entering the same case each time.

    C.   Passwords are limited to 14 characters.

    D.   The administrators' password must match the CD-Key.

11.   You are installing NT Server as a BDC. You have a DHCP server located available to this machine. How can you configure this machine to be a client of a DHCP server? (Choose the best answer.)

    A.   This cannot be done. Domain Controllers must have static IP addresses.

    B.   You must edit the IPCONFIG.SYS file and add the line of DHCP=1.

    C.   During IP Configuration, choose to participate in DHCP.

    D.   After installation, change the DHCP participation option in the Network Applet.

12.   You are installing NT server as a BDC in your domain. During installation, Setup will not allow you to create this machine

as a BDC in the domain NEW YORK. You confirm that both machines are using the same protocol. The network card and wire is fine, and the name of the server is not in use anywhere else in the domain. What do you suspect is the problem? (Choose the best answer.)

    A.   You did not select the machine to be a BDC, but a PDC.

    B.   You are not spelling the Domain name correctly.

    C.   You do not have a computer account created for the server.

    D.   You do not have the same version of NT on both the PDC and the BDC.

13.   You are about to install NT as a BDC. You know that you must have a computer account for the BDC to join the domain. What are two ways you can create this account? (Choose two.)

    A.   Use Server Manager on the PDC and add the computer account.

    B.   Use User Manager for Domains and add the computer account.

    C.   Add the account during installation of the BDC.

    D.   Run WINNT.EXE /BDC to add the BDC account to the domain.

14.   You are trying to add an additional PDC to the domain called MARKETING. What is the correct procedure to do this? (Choose the best answer.)

    A.   During setup, make this machine a PDC in the MARKETING domain.

    B.   Use Server Manager to create a PDC account for the MARKETING domain.

    C.   You cannot do this.

    D.   Run WINNT.EXE /pdc2 switch.

15. You and a colleague are adding a BDC to your domain. Your colleague is confused by you needing another domain controller instead of just a member server. You give several reasons for installing a BDC, including which of the following? (Choose all that apply.)

    A. A BDC can be a file, print, and application server.

    B. A BDC can also validate user logon requests

    C. A BDC can be a RAS Server.

    D. A BDC can be a DHCP server.

    E. A BDC can provide backup in case the PDC fails.

16. You have a Windows 95 workgroup called XYZ. You would like to add a server to this workgroup, but your supervisor is uncertain if it should be a PDC or just a member server. You identify several key attributes of a member server, including which of the following? (Choose all that apply.)

    A. A member server can be a file, print, or application server.

    B. A member server can be a member of both a domain and a workgroup at the same time.

    C. A member server can validate logon requests from clients

    D. A member server can be a RAS server.

17. You have a Windows 95 workgroup called XYZ. You would like to add a server to this workgroup, but your supervisor is uncertain if it should be a PDC or just a member server. You identify several key attributes of a PDC, including which of the following? (Choose all that apply.)

    A. A PDC can be a file, print, or application server.

    B. A PDC can validate logon requests from clients.

    C. A PDC can be a RAS Server.

    D. A PDC can be an Internet Information Server.

18. Your domain consists of a PDC, a BDC, and a member server. You want to take the PDC down to add a hard disk, but you are worried about not having a PDC online during the maintenance. What should you do? (Choose the best answer.)

    A. Do nothing. The BDC will promote itself automatically when it detects that the PDC is offline.

    B. Manually promote the BDC to a PDC.

    C. Manually promote the BDC to a PDC, and then promote the member server to a PDC.

    D. There is no real solution. No PDC will be available during maintenance.

19. Your domain consists of a PDC and a member server. As your domain grows, you realize that your PDC is very busy validating user logon requests. To change the member server to a BDC, you do what? (Choose the best answer.)

    A. Promote the member server to a BDC.

    B. Reinstall NT Server on the member server, and tell it to be a BDC during install.

    C. Run WINNT32.EXE.

    D. Use Server Manager to add a BDC computer account to the domain, and give this computer account the same NetBIOS name of the member server.

20. Your supervisor is unclear as to why your Windows 95 machines show up in a workgroup in Network Neighborhood, but your NT Workstations show up in the Domain. You explain that only certain machines are allowed to be domain

members. Choose from the following all
that are allowed to be domain members:

    A. Windows 95

    B. Windows NT Workstations

    C. Windows NT BDCs

    D. Windows NT member servers

21. A domain controller is responsible for
validating user logon requests. The NT
Service that is responsible for logon
validation is what? (Choose the best
answer.)

    A. Netlogon service

    B. Server service

    C. Security Accounts Manager service

    D. RPC Mailslots

22. Your domain consists of one PDC and
four BDCs. Your domain is still growing,
and you would like to add another BDC.
However, you are worried about the
number of domain controllers a domain
can have. What is the best solution?
(Choose the best answer.)

    A. You are limited to five domain
controllers in a domain at a time.

    B. There is no limit to the number of
PDCs or BDCs a domain may
have.

    C. A domain may have only one PDC,
but may have many BDCs.

    D. The number of BDCs allowed
depends on the number of user
accounts in your domain. You are
limited to one domain controller
for every 120 user accounts.

23. You are planning on taking your PDC
offline to add more memory. You would
like to promote the BDC to a PDC
through Server Manager. However, when
you try to complete this task, you are not
allowed to do so. You suspect the problem
is what? (Choose the best answer.)

    A. You have accidentally selected the
PDC in Server Manager.

    B. You do not have sufficient privileges
to promote or to demote computer
accounts.

    C. You do not have a BDC, but a
member server.

    D. You must complete this command
at the machine you are promoting.

24. You would like to change the name of
your domain from XYZ to SALES. How
can you do this? (Choose the best
answer.)

    A. Server Manager at the PDC

    B. Server Manager at the BDC

    C. The network applet

    D. WINNT.EXE

25. You have successfully changed your
domain name from XYZ to SALES, but
now none of your 95 clients is able to
logon to the domain. You suspect the
problem is what? (Choose the best answer.)

    A. The Windows 95 clients are still
trying to be validated by the old
domain name. You must visit each
95 machine and change the NT
Domain name there as well.

    B. During the domain name change,
the Netlogon service has paused.
You must restart the PDC to restart
the Netlogon service. All clients will
need to restart as well.

    C. Your PDC needs to synchronize the
entire domain. You can force
domain synchronization through
Server Manager.

    D. Your Windows 95 machines must
reboot and log on to the domain
again.

26. A domain controller can validate user
logon requests from any of the following.
(Choose all that apply.)

A. Windows NT

B. OS/2 1.x or greater

C. Microsoft LAN Manager

D. MS-DOS Clients with the enhanced redirector installed

E. Windows for Workgroups

27. You are responsible for maintaining two domains. One domain is in California and the other is in New York. These domains are not connected by any means. To make things simpler, you decide to name both domains CORPORATE. The California domain has four BDCs, whereas the New York domain has only two. You decide to move a BDC from California to New York, yet when you add the BDC from California it will not recognize the PDC on the domain. You suspect the problem is what? (Choose the best answer.)

A. The time difference between New York and California has thrown off the synchronization updates of the BDC and PDC. You must use the net time command.

B. You cannot move a domain controller from one domain to another.

C. The IP Address of the BDC is incorrect because it is now in a different subnet.

D. The BDC does not have a computer account in the domain. You must add the computer account through Server Manager so that the BDC can join the domain.

28. You want to set up a RAS Server for a member server but are uncertain how many connections are allowed via RAS. How many connections are allowed via RAS? (Choose the best answer.)

A. 1

B. 250

C. 256

D. Unlimited

2.2 Answers and Explanations: Practice Problems

1. **B, C, D** A 95 workgroup would be able to use the NT Member Server as a file, print, and application server; the workgroup would have a network site to store work, and could then use the Member Server to use user-level security.

2. **C** You are not allowed to move a Domain Controller from one domain to another. This is due to uniqueness of the Domain's SID (Security Identifier).

3. **A, B** You must have administrative rights to add a BDC to a domain. If you chose not to use the same protocol as the PDC, there will be no communication between the two machines. Although a network card problem can limit your access to the PDC, you would have received a message stating that the network was unable to start. If you chose to use TCP/IP via DHCP, and there are no IP addresses available, you would have received a message stating that a DHCP server was not attached.

4. **C** If the BDC cannot locate the BDC to synchronize the account database, it will not be able to continue the installation.

5. **B** If you were to take the PDC offline and install NT Server 4.0, you would in effect be creating a new domain. There is no real reason to upgrade the 3.51 server to complete this task.

6. **B** NT requires that a PDC be the first server online during installation. You cannot add a BDC before a PDC.

7. **C** NetBIOS names must be unique from all other resources on the network.

8. **D** Server names are limited by NetBIOS to 15 characters.

9. **C** There is no way to change a member server to a BDC without reinstalling NT.

10. **C** Passwords are limited to 14 characters.

11. **C** All servers may be clients of DHCP.

12. **C** Before an NT machine can join a domain, it must have a computer account created for it.

13. **A, C** You can use Server Manager on the PDC and add the computer account, or you can add the account during installation of the BDC.

14. **C** A domain may have only one PDC at any given time.

15. **A, B, C, D, E** A BDC is capable of serving as a file, print, and application server; it can also validate user logon requests; it can be a RAS Server; it can be a DHCP server; and it can provide backup in case the PDC fails.

16. **A, D** A member server can be a file, print, or application server. A member server can be a RAS Server. A member server cannot validate users. A member server is not allowed to be a member of both a domain and workgroup at the same time.

17. **A, B, C, D** A domain controller may be all of these.

18. **B** You must promote the BDC to a PDC. This will ensure that there is always one PDC available for account maintenance.

19. **B** You must reinstall NT Server and designate during setup that this machine will be a BDC in your domain.

20. **B, C, D** A domain is a collection of computer accounts. Only NT Workstations and Servers are true members of a domain. If you wanted to get the Windows 95 machines to show up in the Domain list in Network Neighborhood, set the Workgroup name to the same as the Domain name.

21. **A** The Netlogon service is responsible for accepting logon validation requests.

22. **C** You are limited to the number of PDCs. BDCs, however, are unlimited.

23. **B** You must belong to the Administrators or Server Operators local groups to promote or demote domain controllers.

24. **C** You can change your domain name through the network applet.

25. **A** If you change the domain name, you must manually change the domain name for your Windows 95 clients as well.

26. **A, C, D, E** Windows NT domain controllers can validate users from NT, LAN Manager clients, MS-DOS, and Windows for Workgroups, as well as Windows 95.

27. **B** You cannot move a domain controller from one domain to another because of the domain SID associated with the domain controller. Even though the names of the domain are the same, it is the SID that differentiates between the two domains. You must reinstall NT Server.

28. **C** 256 simultaneous RAS connections are allowed on NT Server.

2.2 Key Words

Domain

Per Server licensing

Per Seat Licensing

WINNT.exe

WINNT32.exe

Primary Domain Controller (PDC)

Backup Domain Controller (BDC)

Member Server

2.3 NT Server 4.0 Installation Methods

The following are two possible sources of Windows NT 4 installation files:

- The Windows NT Installation CD-ROM (with three setup floppies)
- A network sharepoint (with three setup floppies)

Most installation procedures consist of two distinct phases:

- File copying: This phase takes place under a minimal text-mode version of Windows NT.
- Configuration: This phase runs under the full GUI Windows NT Setup wizard.

A. CD-ROM Installation

Using the Windows NT Installation CD-ROM is the easiest and most common method for installing NT. By booting with the three startup floppy disks that come with Windows NT, you load the necessary drivers for you CD-ROM and can proceed with the installation.

You also can begin the installation by starting the CD-ROM (from within your existing operating system) and double-clicking on Windows NT Setup.

B. Network Installs

A network install is really a CD-ROM install; an initial preinstallation phase is added in which the contents of the CD-ROM are copied across the network from the server to the client computer.

You can use Windows NT's Client Administrator application to create a network installation startup disk that will enable you to boot the client machine and connect to the shared directory with the installation files.

> **To improve performance, copy the contents of the CD-ROM to the hard drive and share the hard disk's copy rather than the CD's. Hard disks are much faster than CD-ROM drives.**

To start an installation across the network, you must first redirect an MS-DOS drive letter to the network sharepoint containing the installation files. Depending on the client you use the following:

- NetWare clients use the MAP command to connect to a Netware server located in the installation directory.
- Windows 95 clients map a drive through the Network Neighborhood.
- MS-DOS clients should use the NET USE command.
- Windows for Workgroups clients use Disk, Connect Network Drive in File Manager.

C. Client Administrator Installation Aids

The Network Client Administrator application, in the Administrative Tools group, lets you configure your Windows NT Server system to assist you with the process of installing client machines on the network. The first two options are designed to help with installing network clients, as follows:

- **Make Network Installation Startup Disk.** Shares the client installation files on the network and creates an installation startup disk you can use to connect to the server from the client machine and to download the installation files.

- **Make Installation Disk Set.** Creates a set of floppies you can use to install network client software on a client computer.

1. Network Installation Startup Disk

The Make Network Installation Startup Disk option in the Network Client Administrator enables you to set up a share containing installation files and then a create a network startup floppy disk that enables you to connect to the installation files from the client machine.

An MS-DOS system disk is required as a startup disk. You can use this option to create a network startup disk for any of the following operating systems:

- Windows NT Server v3.5, 3.51, 4.0

- Windows NT Workstation v3.5, 3.51, 4.0

- Windows 95

- Windows for Workgroups v3.11

- Microsoft Network Client for MS-DOS v3.0

You must purchase a license agreement for each NT, 95, or Windows for Workgroup client you install. The Make Installation Disk Set radio button in the Network Client Administrator dialog box enables you to create a set of floppy installation disks you can use to install the following network client packages:

- Microsoft Network Client 3.0 for MS-DOS and Windows

- Microsoft LAN Manager 2.2c for MS-DOS

- Microsoft LAN Manager 2.2c for OS/2

- Microsoft Remote Access Service Client v1.1 for MS-DOS

- Microsoft TCP/IP for Windows for Workgroups

2. Creating the Startup Disks

Follow these steps:

1. Select the Make Installation Disk Set radio button and click on Continue. The Share Network Client Installation Files dialog box appears.

2. After that, you'll see the Make Installation Disk Set dialog box. Choose the network software you want to install on the client, choose a destination drive, and click on OK.

The floppies used with Network Client Administrator must be formatted before creating the disk set. The Windows NT Server and Workstation startup disks work only for Intel computers.

D. Installation Types

Windows NT Server and Workstation differ in the setup options. NT Server uses the Custom setup option only. The available setup options for Windows NT are:

- **Typical.** Ideal for most installations. Portable installs accessibility options, Accessories, Communication programs, and Multimedia.

- **Portable.** Designed for notebook and other portable computers. Setup installs accessibility options, all Windows NT accessories except for Desktop wallpaper and Mouse Pointers, all communication programs, and all multimedia components supported by the hardware.

- **Compact.** Designed to conserve hard disk space. Only components required by Windows NT are installed.

- **Custom.** Useful when the user installing Windows NT needs to choose individual components that are not available through one of the express setup options.

2.3.1   Exercise: Creating a Network Installation Startup Disk

To create a network installation startup disk:

1. Select the Make Network Installation Startup Disk radio button in the Network Client Administrator dialog box. The Share Network Client Installation Files dialog box appears.

2. You can either copy the files to your hard disk and share them, or share them directly from the Windows NT Server CD-ROM.

3. The Share Files radio button shares the files directly from the CD-ROM, which doesn't require any hard disk space. Choose Copy Files to a New Directory, and then Share radio button to copy the files to your hard disk—you'll need 64 MB of hard disk space.

4. The Use Existing Shared Directory radio button tells Client Administrator to set up the installation disk to use an existing share. You can specify a server name and a share name.

5. When you have configured the location of the installation files, click on OK.

6. The Target Workstation Configuration dialog box appears. Specify the size of the floppy disk, the type of network client software, and a network adapter card for the client machine. Click on OK.

7. The Network Startup Disk Configuration dialog box appears. Specify a computer name, user name, domain, and network protocol for the client machine, plus any TCP/IP settings. The Destination Path is the path to the floppy drive.

8. Insert a formatted, high-density MS-DOS system disk in the destination drive and click on OK.

9. You now can use the network installation startup disk to boot the client machine and connect to the installation files.

2.3.2 Exercise: Creating an Installation Disk Set

The Make Installation Disk Set radio button in the Network Client Administrator dialog box enables you to create a set of floppy disks you can use to install the following network client packages:

- Microsoft Network Client 3.0 for MS-DOS and Windows

- Microsoft LAN Manager 2.2c for MS-DOS

- Microsoft LAN Manager 2.2c for OS/2

- Microsoft Remote Access Service Client v1.1 for MS-DOS

- Microsoft TCP/IP for Windows for Workgroups

To create an installation disk set, follow this procedure:

1. The floppies must be pre-formatted before making the installation disk set. As you select different clients, the dialog box will instruct on the number of floppies required for that client. Select the Make Installation Disk Set radio button and click on Continue. The Share Network Client Installation Files dialog box appears.

2. After that, you'll see the Make Installation Disk Set dialog box. Choose the network software you want to install on the client, choose a destination drive, and click on OK.

2.3 Practice Problems

1. Most installation procedures consists of two distinct phases, which are what? (Choose two answers.)

   A. File copying phase

   B. Registry assembly phase

   C. An .inf file assembly phase

   D. System configuration phase

2. The most practical way of installing NT Server is (choose the best answer):

   A. CD-ROM

   B. Over the network

   C. Floppies

   D. Copy the i386 directory from the CD-ROM to the hard disk and then run WINNT.EXE

3. To start the setup program inside Windows 95, a user can do what? (Choose all that apply.)

   A. Run WINNT.EXE from the Start menu.

   B. If autorun is enabled for the CD-ROM, insert the NT 4.0 CD, and then choose the button for NT setup.

   C. Run WINNT32.EXE from the Start menu.

   D. Map a drive to the network share of NT and double-click on the WINNT.EXE.

4. You would like to do a network install for NT Server 4.0 because the Intel machine you are setting up as a BDC does not have a CD-ROM. You notice, however, that this method takes somewhat longer than when you installed the server locally on your PDC. Why is this? (Choose the best answer.)

   A. BDC must synchronize with the PDC, which takes 20–30 minutes longer.

   B. Setup is doing an exhaustive hardware search looking for a CD-ROM drive on your machine.

   C. Setup must copy the files across the network.

   D. Setup must replicate the account database with the PDC to ensure you have rights to join the domain.

5. What NT tool allows you to create a network installation startup disk? (Choose the best answer.)

   A. NT Disk Administrator

   B. Server Manager

   C. Network Client Administrator

   D. Add/Remove Programs

6. A network client startup disk does what? (Choose the best answer.)

   A. Enables a DOS machine to connect to the server and login as administrator

   B. Enables a RISC-based machine to connect to the server and install the network client software across the network

   C. Enables an Intel-based machine to connect to the server and install the network client software across the network

   D. Enables an Administrator to start an over-the-network installation of a PDC

7. A network client startup disk enables you to do what? (Choose the best answer.)

   A. Connect to a PDC and log on as Administrator.

   B. Connect to an NT Server and start the installation of a network client from a network source file location.

C. To have an OS/2 machine join a domain.

D. To have a Windows 95 or Windows NT Workstation client switch between membership in a domain and a workgroup.

8. What must be done to the floppy to be used as the network client startup disk? (Choose all that apply.)

    A. It must be formatted in Windows NT.

    B. It must be formatted in the same operating from which you will be installing (95, DOS, OS/2).

    C. It must be a DOS system disk.

    D. It must be an unformatted disk.

9. To improve performance of the network install, you should do what? (Choose the best answer.)

    A. Buy a faster CD-ROM drive.

    B. Use 3.5-inch floppies rather 5.25-inch floppies.

    C. Copy the contents of the CD-ROM to the server rather than sharing out the CD-ROM.

    D. Give users full control of the CD-ROM when you share it out at the server.

10. You have shared out the source files for NT Server 4.0. You are ready to begin the network installation of NT Server. To start an installation over the network, you must first do what on the client side? (Choose the best answer.)

    A. Confirm that the client is not logged into any domain or workgroup.

    B. Map a drive to the shared site on the server.

    C. Assign the client an IP address of 127.0.0.1.

D. Assign the client the same IP address of the server.

11. On your BDC called NT4BDC, you have shared out the i386 directory of the CD-ROM as i386 so that you can install NT Server across the network. The machine on which you would like to install NT Server is using DOS 6.22, and you have the full redirector installed. What is the proper command to connect to the server to begin the installation? (Choose the best answer.)

    A. net use \\nt4bdc\i386

    B. net use W: \\i386\nt4bdc

    C. net use W: //nt4bdc/i386

    D. net use W: \\nt4bdc\i386

12. You are trying to install NT Server on a Windows 95 machine and would like to map a drive to the shared site on your server. How would you do this? (Choose the best answer.)

    A. Restart the machine in DOS and use the NET command.

    B. Open a DOS prompt and in Windows 95 and use the NET command.

    C. Map a drive through Network Neighborhood.

    D. Create a batch file to connect to the share site.

13. The Network Client Administrator enables you to do what? (Choose the best answer.)

    A. Add computer accounts to your domain.

    B. Add user accounts to your domain.

    C. Create a Network Installation Startup Disk.

    D. Manage which clients are allowed to connect to resources on your server.

14. The Network Client Administrator enables you to do what? (Choose the best answer.)

    A. Make an Installation Disk Set.

    B. Create shares on other domain controllers.

    C. Stop sharing resources on your servers.

    D. Add computer accounts to your domain.

15. You can use the Network Client Administrator to create a Network Installation Startup Disk for what operating systems? (Choose all that apply.)

    A. NT Server v3.5, 3.51, 4.0

    B. Windows NT Workstation v3.5, 3.51, 4.0

    C. Windows 95

    D. OS/2

16. On the NT Server 4.0, the source files for what clients are included? (Choose all that apply.)

    A. Windows 95

    B. Microsoft Bob

    C. Windows for Workgroups

    D. MS DOS 6.22

17. The Windows NT Server and NT Workstation startup disks will work on RISC-based machines if you (choose the best answer):

    A. Do nothing. They work already on RISC and Intel-based platforms.

    B. These startup disks will not work on RISC-based machines.

    C. Specify in the Network Client Administrator that the target machine is a RISC-based computer.

    D. Format the floppy with NTFS.

18. You are creating a network installation startup disk. You can't decide if you should copy the files to your hard drive and share them out, or share them directly from the CD-ROM. Two factors may affect your decision, they are:

    A. If you copy the files to your hard drive, the access time will be faster than the CD-ROM.

    B. If you copy them to your hard drive, it will use approximately 64-MB hard disk space.

    C. If you copy the files to your hard drive, only an administrator will have rights to them.

    D. If you copy the files to your hard drive, everyone will have full control to the resource.

19. During the creation of a Network Startup Disk, the target workstation dialog box requests three pieces of information. They are:

    A. The size of the floppy disk

    B. The protocol to be used during installation

    C. The type of client software

    D. The network adapter card

20. During the creation of a Network Startup Disk, the Network Startup Disk Configuration dialog box requests specific information to be used during the install. The information requested is what? (Choose all that apply.)

    A. Computer name

    B. User name

    C. Domain name

    D. Network protocol to be used

21. The Network Client Administrator enables you to create an installation disk set to install what network client packages from floppies? (Choose all that apply.)

A. Windows 95

B. Network Client 3.0 for DOS

C. Microsoft TCP/IP for Windows for Workgroups

D. Microsoft LAN Manager for OS/2

22. The Network Client 3.0 for DOS and Windows allows a DOS machine to do what? (Choose the best answer.)

A. Participate in server announcements.

B. Receive Exchange email.

C. Map drives to network resources.

D. Participate in domain synchronization.

23. You would like to install NT Workstation on 100 Intel-based computers. You do not want to install from CD-ROM at each machine. What is the best method of installation? (Choose the best answer.)

A. Use the Disk Administrator to create a network startup disk to automatically connect to a server to begin the install.

B. Use Server Manager to create a network startup disk to automatically connect to a server to begin the install.

C. Use the Network Client Administrator to create a network startup disk to automatically connect to a server to begin the install.

D. Map a drive through DOS to the client share site and run WINNT.EXE across the network.

24. You and an assistant are installing NT Workstation. Your assistant is uncertain why you should use the typical install. You identify several key reasons why you are using the Typical install method, including what? (Choose the best answer.)

A. Typical installs accessibility options, Accessories, Communication programs, and Dial Up Networking.

B. Typical installs accessibility options, Accessories, Communication programs, and Multimedia.

C. Typical installs Accessories, Communication programs, and Peer Web Services.

D. Typical installs all Accessories, Communication programs, and Peer Web Services.

25. You and an assistant are installing NT Workstation. You have opted to use the portable option because you are installing NT on a laptop. What features are included with the portable install? (Choose all that apply.)

A. Accessibility options

B. All accessories

C. All accessories except for wallpaper and Mouse Pointers

D. All Communication Programs

E. None of the above

26. You and an assistant are installing NT Workstation. You have opted to use the compact option because you are installing on a computer with very limited hard disk space. Why is this a good solution for your environment? (Choose the best answer.)

A. NT installs all accessories except for games.

B. NT installs only the most common components.

C. Only components required by Windows NT are installed.

D. Only accessories required by NT are installed.

27. You are installing NT Server. What install methods do you have? (Choose all that apply.)

    A. Typical

    B. Portable

    C. Compact

    D. Custom

2.3   Answers and Explanations: Practice Problems

1. **A, D**   Windows NT first copies the needed files to a temp directory on your system through a minimal text mode version of Windows NT. Setup then moves into the system configuration phase through the Windows NT Setup Wizard.

2. **A**   The CD-ROM method is the most practical way to install NT Server.

3. **A, B, D**   Answer C is not acceptable because WINNT32.EXE is for upgrading from a previous version of Windows NT.

4. **C**   When installing over the network, Setup adds an additional preinstallation phase of copying the source files across the network.

5. **C**   The Network Client Administrator enables you to create a network client startup disk.

6. **C**   The Network Client Administrator creates a network startup disk for Intel-based machines only.

7. **B**   The Network Client administrator enables you to connect to a shared site on the server and start the installation process of network client software.

8. **C, D**   The Network client startup disk must be a bootable disk. It can be formatted using MS-DOS or Windows 95.

9. **C**   You will want to copy the contents of the CD-ROM to hard disk space rather than share out the CD-ROM because hard drives are faster than CD-ROM drives.

10. **B**   Before you can start the install, you must map a drive to the server's share site.

11. **D**   You use the UNC syntax of \\servername\sharename to map a drive to the shared site.

12. **C**   By navigating through the Network Neighborhood to the shared sight on your server, you can right-click the share and choose Map Network Drive.

13. **C**   The Network Client Administrator enables you to create a Network Startup disk to install client files across the network.

14. **A**   The Network Client Administrator enables you to create an Installation Disk Set to install client files through a floppy disk rather than across the network.

15. **A, B, C**   You are not allowed to create an startup disk for OS/2 through the Network Client Administrator.

16. **A**   Windows for Workgroups is not included with Windows NT 4.0. It was included with Windows NT 3.5x CDs. The Windows 95 client software is included on the CD, but you must purchase a client license for any systems onto which you install Windows 95. DOS 6.22 is not included with Windows NT 4.0. This software must be purchased separately.

17. **B**   The Windows NT Server and NT Workstation startup disks will not work on RISC-based computers.

18. **A, B**   Hard disks are faster than CD-ROMs. The source files will use 64 MB of hard disk space.

19. **A, C, D**   These three pieces of information are required to continue with the network startup disk.

20. **A, B, C, D**   The Network Startup Disk Configuration dialog box needs the information to complete the Network Startup Disk.

21. **B, C, D**   The Network Client Adminis-
    trator enables you to create an installation
    disk set to install the Network Client for
    DOS, TCP/IP for Windows for
    Workgroups, and LAN Manager for OS/2.

22. **C**   The Network Client 3.0 for DOS
    and Windows will allow a DOS client to
    have Microsoft networking functions.

23. **C**   The Network Client Administrator is
    used to create a network startup disk to
    install over the network.

24. **B**   Typical is ideal for most scenarios.

25. **A, C, D**   Portable install is to be used
    when you are installing onto a laptop or
    other mobile type computer.

26. **C**   When you are installing the compact
    method, only the components that NT
    requires are installed.

27. **D**   With NT Server, you can only
    perform a Custom install.

2.3   Key Words

Network install

Network sharepoint

Disk set

Client Administrator

2.4   Configuring Protocols and Network Bindings

The Control Panel Network application is a central spot for entering and altering network configuration information. The five tabs of the Network application are as follows:

- **Identification.** The Identification tab specifies the computer name for the computer and the domain to which it belongs.

- **Services.** The Services tab lets you add, remove, or configure network services.

- **Protocols.** The Protocols tab lets you add, remove, and configure network protocols.

- **Adapters.** The Adapters tab lets you add, remove, and configure network adapter cards. Click on Add to view a list of available network adapter card drivers. The Properties button lets you configure the IRQ and the Port address for the adapter.

- **Bindings.** Network Bindings are software interfaces between network cards, protocols, and services; the bindings tab enables you to tweak the arrangement of Bindings to increase performance on your NT machine.

A.   Installing and Configuring NWLink

NWLink is the Microsoft 32-bit version of IPX/SPX. To connect to NetWare servers, NWLink is required. To install the NWLink protocol, open Control Panel's Network applet, choose the Protocols tab and click on the Add button. From the list of available protocols, choose the NWLink protocol.

NWLink alone will not allow an NT Server to connect to a NetWare Server. IN addition the Gateway Services for NetWare (GSNW) is required. GSNW allows a computer running Windows NT to access file and print resources on a NetWare server.

GSNW also acts as a gateway to the NetWare servers so that the resources on the NetWare server can appear to be shared off of the NT Servers.

GSNW may be installed through Control Panel, Network, Add a Service.

1. Frame Type

If you know which frame type is in use on your network, you can use this dialog box to manually set Windows NT to match it. By default, Windows NT is configured to detect the frame type automatically, which it does by sending out a Routing Information Protocol (RIP) request on all frame types when NWLink is initialized. One of the following scenarios will occur:

- **No response from any of the frame types.** NWLink uses the default frame type, which is 802.2 when Windows NT is first installed.

- **A response from one of the frame types.** NWLink uses this frame type, which also becomes the default protocol the next time autodetection occurs.

- **Multiple responses are received.** NWLink steps through this list (in order) until it finds a frame type that was one of the multiple responses. After it finds a frame type, it stops searching for additional frame types:

- Ethernet 802.2
- Ethernet 802.3
- Ethernet II
- SNAP

NT Workstation and Windows NT Server can be configured for multiple frame types, but you can use Control Panel Network to do so only for Server. If you want Windows NT Workstation to use multiple frame types, you must edit the registry directly with the Registry Editor (RegEdt32.exe).

An incorrect frame type can cause an immense slowdown in network performance. IPXROUTE CONFIG command from the command prompt will generate a report of what frame type is currently in use. The following table shows which frame types particular servers use.

802.2	802.3
Windows NT Workstation 3.5x	Windows NT 3.1
Windows NT Server 3.5x	Windows NT Advanced Server 3.1
NetWare 4.x	NetWare 3.11 and below
NetWare 3.12	Windows for Workgroups 3.x retail
Windows for Workgroups 3.11 from the Windows NT Server CD	
Microsoft Network Client 3.0	

2. Internal Network Number

The Internal Network Number is similar to a subnet address on a TCP/IP network. It determines which servers are considered "local" and which ones are considered "remote."

B.   Using TCP/IP

TCP/IP is quickly becoming the industry standard protocol. It is considered an open protocol in that no one company owns the protocol.

1. IP Addresses

The Internet Protocol sends packets using a network interface card's (NIC) IP Address (a unique 32-bit binary number that no other computer on the network can possess). Each NIC requires its own IP address.

An IP Address is a unique 32-bit addressed associate with NIC's Media Access Control (MAC) layer, or serial number of the NIC. No other host on the network can have the same IP address. A typical IP address is 131.107.5.21. Each number separated by a period is called an *octet*.

2. Subnet Mask

Subnet masks are used to mask a portion of the IP address so that the TCP/IP protocol can distinguish the host id from the network id. A Subnet mask is dependent on the class of IP addresses in use on the network. The three classes of IP addresses are:

- **Class A.** The first octet belongs to the net id and the others to the host id. Class A net ids can range from 0 to 127.

- **Class B.** The first two octets define the net id, and the next two octets define the host id.

- **Class C.** The first three octets define the net id, and the last octet is the host id.

Depending on the class of IP address in use, a subnet mask appears as follows:

Class A 255.0.0.0

Class B 255.255.0.0

Class C 255.255.255.0

3. Default Gateway

A default gateway is a *router,* a device that sends packets on to a remote network. A router can be a device created for that purpose, such as Cisco or 3Com makes, or it can be a Windows NT–based computer that has at least two network cards (for spanning two networks) and has IP Routing enabled.

C. TCP/IP Standards

Follow these guidelines for TCP/IP:

- Host ids cannot be set to all zeros or all ones, because 0 refers to the local network, whereas 255 refers to broadcast. An easy rule of thumb is to stay away from 0 and 255 when assigning octets.

- Don't use 127 as a net id. When 127 is used as the first octet of a net id, TCP/IP recognizes the address as a special diagnostic address called the *loopback address,* so called because any message to this address is returned to its sender.

- All net ids on a subnet must match. If an NIC doesn't have the same net id as the rest of the NICs on its subnet, the host can't communicate with the other hosts on the Subnet.

- All NICs must be assigned a unique ID. If two NICs have the same IP Address assigned to them, unpredictable results may happen.

D. Installing TCP/IP

To install TCP/IP, start from the Control Panel Network application. Choose the Protocols tab and click on the Add button. Select TCP/IP Protocol. Choose OK.

You can install TCP/IP in two ways:

- **Installing TCP/IP with DHCP.** When installing TCP/IP setup asks if Dynamic Host Configuration Protocol (DHCP) should be used for dynamically assigning IP addresses. A DHCP server leases addresses to clients when they join the network.

- **Installing and Configuring TCP/IP manually.** To install TCP/IP manually, you must supply the IP address and subnet mask for each NIC in the computer. In addition, the IP addresses of the default gateway, WINS servers, and DNS servers are required if you intend to use these features.

E. Windows Internet Name Service

WINS is a service that runs on NT Server. It is responsible for resolving NetBIOS names to IP addresses. It is similar to the LMHosts file except that it dynamically registers the IP address of hosts and the services that they are providing if they are participating in WINS.

More than WINS server may be added in the TCP/IP properties in the Network Applet. There are three WINS addressing parameters:

- **Enable DNS for Windows Resolution.** Selecting this check box instructs Windows NT to look up NetBIOS names against a Domain Name Server, which is usually a service running on Windows NT Server, or a daemon running on UNIX.

- **Enable LMHOSTS Lookup.** This check box incorporates a text database mapping of NetBIOS names to IP addresses into the name resolution process.

- **Scope ID.** Enables administrators to create logical IP networks that are invisible to each other. Hosts must belong to the same NetBIOS scope before they can communicate.

F. DNS

DNS servers are used to resolve Fully Qualified Domain Names (FQDN) to IP addresses.

To configure DNS, select the DNS tab in the Microsoft TCP/IP Properties dialog box. Enter your domain name. Click on the Add button under the DNS Service Search Order dialog box and enter the addresses of the DNS servers on your network.

G. TCP/IP Diagnostics

A host of TCP/IP utilities are included with Windows NT. Some of the more useful ones are IPCONFIG, PING, and TRACERT.

- **IPCONFIG.** IPCONFIG displays the TCP/IP configuration parameters of the local host. The /ALL switch can be used to display every field, including DHCP and WINS information.

- **PING.** PING is a diagnostic utility used to test the connection between two hosts on an Internetwork. The syntax for ping is as follows:

  ```
  PING 131.107.2.200
  ```

- **TRACERT.** The TRACERT utility traces the hops (number of routers crossed) that packets take on their way from the local host to a remote host.

H. NetBEUI

NetBEUI is a fast non-routable protocol. It is primarily used for small LAN. To install NetBEUI, start from the Control Panel Network application. Choose the Protocols tab and click on the Add button. Select the NetBEUI Protocol. Choose OK.

I. Protocol Bindings

To bind a protocol to a network interface card is to create a direct connection between the hardware and the transport protocol. An administrator can change the bindings for network adapter cards as well as services.

To configure network bindings, choose the Bindings tab on the Network applet in Control Panel. There are several options to adjust on the Bindings tab. The following table list the configuration options.

Option	Action
Show Bindings for	Views bindings for adapters, protocols, and services on the network
Enable	Enables the selected bindings path
Disable bindings	Disables the selected bindings path
Move Up	Moves the selected bindings up
Move Down	Moves the selected bindings down

2.4.1 Exercise: Installing and Configuring TCP/IP

This lab assumes you have an NT Server 4.0 installed. You might need your CD-ROM to install the source files for TCP/IP.

To install TCP/IP:

1. Open Control Network.

2. Choose the protocol tab.

3. Click on the Add button.

4. Choose TCP/IP from the list of available protocols and click on OK.

5. NT will prompt you to use DHCP. Choose No.

6. At this point, NT will ask for the install files for TCP/IP. Map NT to the appropriate location of the i386 directory.

To configure TCP/IP:

1. If you know a valid IP address for your network, enter that IP address. If not, enter the IP address of 131.107.2.200.

2. If you have entered a valid IP address for your network, enter the corresponding subnet mask. If you entered 131.107.2.200, use the subnet mask of 255.255.255.0.

3. If your network has a router and you know the IP address of the router, enter that information now. Otherwise, leave this field blank.

4. Choose the DNS tab.

5. If you have a DNS server, enter that information now. If you are uncertain about this information, leave this field blank.

6. Choose the WINS Address tab.

7. If you have a WINS Server, enter the IP address now. If you are uncertain about the IP address of your WINS server, or you do not have it, leave this information blank.

8. Choose OK to finish the TCP/IP install. NT will need to reboot to configure your TCP/IP bindings.

2.4.2 Exercise: Testing Your IP Address with PING

This exercise assumes you have completed Exercise 2.4.1 or already have an IP address on your NT machine. To test your IP address with PING:

1. Start a DOS prompt.

2. Type in the following command: PING 127.0.0.1.

3. What is the reply you receive?

4. PING the IP address of your machine.

5. What is the reply you receive?

6. If you know the IP address of another NIC on your network, PING that address now.

7. PING an IP address that you know is incorrect. For example, PING 131.107.127.127.

8. What response do you receive?

2.4 Practice Problems

1. The primary location to add or configure network protocols is: (Choose the best answer.)

    A. Control Panel's Protocols applet

    B. Server Manager

    C. Control Panel's Network applet

    D. Network Client Administrator

2. You would like to change the name of your domain from SALES to MARKETING. Where are you allowed to do this? (Choose the best answer.)

    A. The Network Applet's Identification tab.

    B. Server Manager for Domains.

    C. You must use the Registry Editor.

    D. You are not allowed to change domains names due to the SID associated with the domain controllers.

3. You would like to add the Gateway Services for NetWare. Where do you add this service? (Choose the best answer.)

    A. Choose Services for NetWare from the Administrative tools group.

    B. You do not have to add this service. It is installed by default in the Control Panel as GSNW.

    C. Add the service through the Network applet, Services tab.

    D. Add the service through the Control Panel's Add/Remove programs.

4. Your network spans multiple states, and you are primarily using TCP/IP. You have decided that you do not need to use NetBEUI. How do you remove this protocol? (Choose the best answer.)

    A. Choose Network, Protocols, choose NetBEUI and remove.

    B. Choose Network, Protocols, choose remove all inactive transport services.

    C. Use the Add/Remove programs tab.

    D. You cannot remove NetBEUI. NT server requires NetBEUI because of the NetBIOS Name Servers Service.

5. Your network is primarily Ethernet, you do however, have a small subnet of Token Ring adapter cards. To provide connectivity for these users, you have added a Token Ring network card to your server. NT, however, has not detected this new hardware at startup time. How can you add the card? (Choose all that apply.)

    A. Using the Add New Hardware in Control Panel.

    B. Using the Network Applet in Control Panel.

    C. Run NTDETECT.COM from a DOS prompt.

    D. Run the NT hardware qualifier from the NT Server CD-ROM.

6. You are responsible for integrating NT Server and your NetWare servers for your company. You have successfully installed NT Server, but NT cannot access any of your NetWare servers. What do you suspect is the problem? (Choose all that apply.)

    A. Your NetWare servers are NetWare 3 servers, which are not compatible with NT Server 4.0.

    B. You need to add the NWLink protocol to your NT servers.

    C. You need to add the Gateway Service for NetWare.

    D. You need to purchase Client 32 for NetWare.

7. You are responsible for integrating NT Server and your NetWare servers for your

company. You have successfully installed NT Server, with the NWLink protocol, but NT cannot access any of your NetWare servers. What do you suspect is the problem? (Choose the best answer.)

A. You need to designate NT to participate in SAP announcements.

B. You need to configure the correct frame type for your NT Server to match the NetWare servers.

C. You need to add the Gateway Service for NetWare.

D. NT cannot participate in RIP, so therefore it cannot access the NetWare servers.

8. You have NetWare 4 servers and NetWare 3 servers that use different frame types. Because NT is using the autodetect method, you are uncertain which frame type NT is using. How can you detect which frame type NT is using? (Choose the best answer.)

A. Use the IPXROUTE CONFIG command from a DOS prompt.

B. Use the IPXROUTE /ALL command from a DOS prompt.

C. Locate the IPFRAME setting in HKEY_LOCAL_MACHINE in the registry. The frame type will be located at this setting.

D. NT defaults to 802.2 if it is using the autodetect frame type.

9. You have NetWare 4 servers and NetWare 3 servers that use different frame types. How can you add additional frame types to your NT server so that it will access both NetWare 4 and NetWare 3 servers? (Choose the best answer.)

A. You are only allowed one frame type per server.

B. You must add an additional network card and assign a frame type to each card.

C. You must edit the registry to add additional frame types.

D. Use the Control Panel Network to add additional frame types.

10. You and an associate are installing NT Server with Gateway Services for Netware and the NWLink protocol so that you can access your NetWare servers. Your associate is confused about how NT can autodetect the frame type. You describe the process by stating what? (Choose the best answer.)

A. NT uses SAP to determine which frame type is in use.

B. NT sends a NetBIOS announcement over IPX/SPX and evaluates the returned packets to determine what frame types are in use.

C. NT uses the Routing Information Protocol (RIP) to determine what frame types are in use.

D. NT simply defaults to 802.2 if autodetect is chosen.

11. Your NT Workstation is currently using the Client Services for Netware and you have NWLink installed so that you can connect to your Netware server's resources. You would like to add additional frame types to your NT Workstation so that it can communicate with multiple servers on your network. How can you do this? (Choose the best answer.)

A. Use the Control Panel Network.

B. Use autodetect for the properties of NWLink.

C. You must edit the registry to add additional frame types.

D. You must add an adapter card for each frame type you would like to use.

12. What protocols ship with Windows NT Server? (Choose all that apply.)

A. NWLink

B. DLC

C. NetBEUI

D. ARCNET v2.x

13. You have installed NT Server as a member server in your NetWare environment. You would like your Windows 95 clients to access resources on your member server. How can this be done? (Choose the best answer.)

A. Windows 95 can access both an NT member server and a NetWare server through the Microsoft Clients for NetWare and Microsoft Networks available through 95's Network applet.

B. You need to add the Gateway Services for NetWare.

C. You need to add the NWLink protocol to your member server.

D. You need to change your broadcast types from Microsoft browsing to SAP.

14. During installation of NWLink, you access the setting for the internal network number on the properties of NWLink. What does this internal network number do? (Choose the best answer.)

A. Specifies what frame type will be used with NWLink.

B. Allows for boot/p to work with NT Server.

C. Determines which servers are considered local and which are considered remote.

D. Specifies what version the NetWare server is.

15. Your network consists of NetWare 3.51 servers and NT 4.0 servers, along with Windows 95 clients. You would like your Windows 95 clients to logon to both your NT Domain and your NetWare servers. How can this be done? (Choose the best answer.)

A. Add the Microsoft Client for Microsoft Networks and the Microsoft Client for NetWare Networks on the 95 machines. Specify what servers they are to log into and what domains they are to log into.

B. Add NWLink to your 95 and NT Servers.

C. Add the Client32 from Novell.

D. This cannot be done. Windows 95 clients are restricted to logging into either Windows 95 machines or NT Servers. They are not allowed to log into both.

16. You would like to add the TCP/IP protocol to your NT server. How can this be done? (Choose the best answer.)

A. TCP/IP can be installed during setup because it is the default protocol on NT machines.

B. TCP/IP can be installed in the Control Panel Add/Remove Programs.

C. Run WINNT32.EXE from a DOS prompt.

D. Do nothing. TCP/IP is required by NT Server.

17. You would like to add TCP/IP to your NT Domain. Your supervisor is concerned that you will have to purchase IP addresses. He does not want to spend the additional dollars at this time, so he is encouraging you to stay with NetBEUI. Is the supervisor's argument valid? (Choose the best answer.)

A. Yes. To use TCP/IP you must purchase a class of IP address from the InterNIC.

B. Yes. To use TCP/IP you must purchase IP addresses from the InterNIC, and you have to purchase a router, or default gateway.

C. No. The IP addresses are free of charge; no one company owns the TCP/IP protocol.

D. No. You need to purchase IP addresses from the InterNIC only if your company is planning to have Internet connectivity, such as a Web server. Otherwise, you can create your own IP addresses.

18. You are installing NT Server as a BDC. You have elected to use TCP/IP as this server's only protocol. You decide not to use DHCP, so you manually enter the IP address of this machine. You discover, however, that another computer is currently using the IP address you specified. Why is this a concern? (Choose the best answer.)

A. It is not a concern because NT Server has precedence over another machine with the same IP address. If the same machine is an NT Server, they will share the IP address.

B. Because the IP addresses correlate to the MAC layer of the NIC, the IP address may be used by one machine at a time.

C. IP addresses require a subnet mask. You need to configure a different subnet mask in order to use this IP address.

D. You need to add the User Datagram Protocol (UDP) through services to allow more than one machine to have the same IP address.

19. You are examining your IP addresses. You realize that IP addresses, such as 131.107.2.21, are broken down by periods. The number between the periods is called what? (Choose the best answer.)

A. Octave

B. Octet

C. Octon

D. Octove

20. You are installing NT Server as a BDC. Your domain is currently using TCP/IP. You decide to manually configure the IP address of this machine. What components of TCP/IP are mandatory? (Choose all that apply.)

A. IP Address

B. Default Gateway

C. WINS

D. Subnet Mask

21. You are installing NT Server. You decide to use TCP/IP in your domain. You do have a DHCP server available to you. What does DHCP do? (Choose the best answer.)

A. DHCP checks for duplicate IP addresses on the subnet to ensure, via ICMP, that no two addresses are the same.

B. DHCP uses ARP, the address resolution protocol, to associate your IP address with the NIC's MAC layer.

C. DHCP automatically assigns you an IP address along with any IP information previously established on the DHCP server.

D. NT Servers cannot be participants of DHCP.

22. You and a colleague are installing NT Server. You are uncertain if you should participate in WINS. What is WINS? (Choose the best answer.)

A. WINS, the Windows Internet Name Service, maps Fully Qualified Domain Names to IP Addresses. You need this service only if you have also installed IIS and are using it as an Internet server.

B. WINS, the Windows Internet Name Service, maps NetBIOS names to IP addresses. You can use this service to reduce network traffic.

C. WINS, the Windows Internet Name Service, creates http names for your NT Server. You need this service only if you have installed IIS.

D. WINS, the Windows Internet Name Service, maps IP addresses to serial card numbers of NICs.

23. You are installing TCP/IP on your NT Workstation. You are using DHCP, but have been instructed to manually enter the DNS IP addresses manually. What is DNS? (Choose the best answer.)

A. DNS maps FQDN to IP addresses for Internet connectivity.

B. DNS maps NetBIOS names to IP addresses.

C. DNS merges NetWare TCP/IP clients with NT's directory services.

D. DNS generates Domain Names for IIS.

24. You are installing NT Server as a BDC. Your domain is currently using TCP/IP. You decide to manually configure the IP address of this machine, but are uncertain what a subnet mask does. What is a subnet mask? (Choose the best answer.)

A. Subnet masks enable you to segment your DHCP client with scope options set in the DHCP server.

B. Subnet masks are used to mask your NetBIOS name so that your machine can participate in WINS.

C. Subnet masks are used to mask a portion of the IP address so that the transport protocol can differentiate between the host id and the network id.

D. Subnet masks enable an administrator to use an IP address more than once in a domain.

25. You have installed NT Workstation on your computer. Everyone else on the network has access to the Internet, you, however, do not. You verify that your IP address and subnet mask are correct. What do you suspect is the problem? (Choose all that apply.)

A. You have not specified a DNS Server.

B. You have not specified a WINS Server.

C. You have not specified the IP Address of the default gateway.

D. You have not specified the IP address of your domain controller.

26. You have installed NT Workstation and are using TCP/IP. You are obtaining your IP address from a DHCP server. How can you find out what IP address has been assigned to your machine? (Choose the best answer.)

A. Go to the DHCP Server and access the DHCP Manager tool.

B. Go to your WINS Server and access the WINS Manager.

C. Use the IPCONFIG utility.

D. If you are using DHCP, there is no way to determine what IP address has been assigned to your computer.

27. You are troubleshooting an IP address of a user. What tool should you use from your desk to check the status of the user's IP address? (Choose the best answer.)

A. PING

B. IPCONFIG /all

C. TRACERT

D. Network Monitor

28. You have a small workgroup of NT
Workstations. What protocol should you
use? (Choose the best answer.)

A. NWLink

B. TCP/IP

C. NetBEUI

D. DLC

29. Your domain spans two states. Your
supervisor has read about the fast and
easy-to-configure protocol NetBEUI. He
would like you to use this protocol
instead of TCP/IP. What would you tell
him? (Choose the best answer.)

A. NetBEUI packets will not pass over
routers.

B. NetBEUI will work fine in your
environment.

C. NetBEUI is not supported with
NT.

D. NetBEUI is very hard to configure
and install.

30. What is a protocol binding? (Choose the
best answer.)

A. The process of installing a protocol.

B. The process of associating a service
or network adapter card with a
protocol.

C. The process of adding a third-party
protocol.

D. The process of configuring a
protocol to ignore network packets
from other services on the network.

2.4 Answers and Explanations: Practice Problems

1. **C** All protocol management is done
through the Network applet in the
Control Panel.

2. **A** You are allowed to change domain
names through the Network applet.

3. **C** You add all services through this tab.

4. **A** You can add or remove protocols
through this tab.

5. **B** This is the method used to add
adapter cards to your network.

6. **B, C** To connect to NetWare, you need
to add the NWLink protocol and
Gateway Services for NetWare.

7. **C** GSNW is required to access NetWare
resources from an NT Server.

8. **A** The IPXROUTE CONFIG command will tell you what frame type NT
has detected on the network and is
currently using.

9. **D** NT Server enables you add additional frame types through the Control
Panel Network. NT Workstation,
however, requires that you add additional
frame types through the registry.

10. **C** NT takes advantage of RIP to
determine what frame type(s) are in use.

11. **C** On Windows NT Workstation, you
must edit the registry to add multiple
frame types.

12. **A, B, C** NWLink, DLC, and NetBEUI
ship with Windows NT Server.

13. **A** Your Windows 95 machines would
use the Client for Microsoft Networks
and the Client for NetWare networks.

14. **C** The internal network number is
similar to TCP/IP's subnet mask.

15. **A** Windows 95 machines are allowed to
log on to NetWare servers and Windows
NT Servers.

16. **A** TCP/IP is the default protocol for NT servers.

17. **D** You need only purchase IP addresses if your company is planning Internet connectivity. Otherwise, you may follow a set of rules for IP address creation.

18. **B** Only one machine can have a given IP address.

19. **B** The number between the periods is called an octet.

20. **A, D** The IP address, and Subnet masks field must be completed. WINS, the default gateway, and DNS are optional components of TCP/IP.

21. **C** Dynamic Host Configuration Protocol automatically assigns IP Address to computers, including NT Server.

22. **B** WINS maps NetBIOS names to IP addresses.

23. **A** Your DNS servers IP addresses are required so that you can have Internet connectivity using Fully Qualified Domain Names (FQDN) for browsing.

24. **C** Subnet masks are used to mask a portion of the IP address so that the transport protocol can differentiate between the host id from the network id.

25. **A, C** You need the IP address of your DNS server to have access to the Internet. You need the IP address of the default gateway to get access to the Internet.

26. **C** The IPCONFIG command tells you all about your IP address. Answer A and B will work, but they are too impractical.

27. **A** PING is the tool used to test the validity of IP addresses.

28. **C** NetBEUI is the fastest protocol for this environment and requires no configuration after installation. Although TCP/IP or NWLink would work, NetBEUI is the best answer.

29. **A** NetBEUI packets will not pass over routers. TCP/IP was designed for networks that cross routers.

30. **B** Protocol may be bound to network cards or services.

2.4   Key Words

NWLink	NetBEUI
Bindings	DLC
TCP/IP	PING

2

2.5   Configuring Network Adapters

The Adapters tab of the Control Panel Network application lets you add and configure network adapters for your system. You have several options to install the Network adapters:

- **Installing an adapter after setup.** Open Control Panel Network and click on the Add button. The Select Network Adapter dialog box that appears lets you select an adapter from a list. To install an adapter that isn't on the list, click on Have Disk.

- **Installing Multiple adapters during setup.** During the NT installation, setup can detect your network adapter card. Setup stops after it finds the first card and the Start Search button changes into a Find Next button.

- **Installing Multiple adapters after setup.** Open Control Panel Network and click on the Add button. The Select Network Adapter dialog box that appears lets you select an adapter from a list. To install an adapter that isn't on the list, click on Have Disk.

A.   Assigning Resources to Network Adapter Cards

There are three resources to consider for your Network Adapter Card. They are:

- **IRQ.** This is the interrupt request. Interrupts are requests for the CPU to process the data in the NIC before the buffer is cleared by new data from the LAN.

  IRQ are set either by manually assigning the IRQ by setting jumpers on the NIC; running a setup program from the OEM; or by changing the IRQ setting on the properties of NIC in the Control Panel Network.

- **I/O address.** I/O addresses are the electronic location of the Network adapter card in the system. I/O must be unique for each device so instructions sent to the device will be sent to the correct location.

  I/O addresses are set in the properties of the network adapter card in Control Panel Network.

- **Transceiver Type.** The transceiver Type is used to determine what type of cabling you are using on your network.

2.5.1   Exercise: Adding a Network Adapter Card

To add a Network Adapter card, follow these steps:

1. Open the Control Panel Network.

2. Choose the Adapters tab.

3. Click on the Add button one time.

4. The select Network Adapter dialog box appears. Choose the 3COM Etherlink III ISA Adapter.

5. Setup will prompt you for your Windows NT Server CD-ROM.

6. Enter the path to your CD-ROM and to the i386 directory (or to the appropriate RISC directory if you are not on an Intel-based machine).

7. Note the I/O address, the default IRQ, and the Transceiver type.

8. Choose OK.

2.5.2   Exercise: Removing the Network Adapter Card

To remove a Network Adapter card, follow these steps:

1. Open the Control Panel Network if it is not already open.

2. Choose the Etherlink Network Adapter card installed in Exercise 2.5.1.

3. Choose the Remove button.

4. Exit the Control Panel Network.

2

2.5   Practice Problems

1. You are installing NT Server as PDC on an Intel-based machine. You have two network cards in the machine—an Ethernet card and a Token Ring card. During installation, the Setup program only finds one card. What should you do to make NT find the second card? (Choose the best answer.)

   A. Setup will automatically stop after finding the first network card. The search button will then change to a Find Next button. You should click on this button.

   B. You must press Shift+F3 to force setup to detect any additional cards.

   C. You cannot allow setup to automatically detect the cards. It is only capable of finding one card. You must choose the Specify button and then choose both network cards from the list.

   D. During setup you can only detect one card. To add additional cards, you must finish setup and use the network applet to add additional cards.

2. You are installing NT on an Intel-based machine. You have a network card that is not on NT's Hardware Compatibility list. You do, however, have the driver on a floppy from the OEM. How can you add the adapter during setup? (Choose the best answer.)

   A. Copy the contents of the floppy to the active partition before installing NT. This will force NT to discover the card during the network install portion.

   B. Choose the Have Disk button during the network card installation phase to provide the driver.

   C. Create a protocol.ini that references the location of the network card driver.

   D. You must complete setup without the card, and then add it through the Network applet.

3. You would like to check the IRQ of your network adapter card. You can do this using which method(s)? (Choose all that apply.)

   A. Using the Device Manager

   B. Using the Control Panel Network and checking the properties on the card on the Adapters tab

   C. Typing IRQCONFIG at the DOS prompt

   D. Using the Windows NT Diagnostics utility

4. An IRQ is what? (Choose the best answer.)

   A. An interrupt of the network card to signify it has received packets.

   B. An interrupt of the network card to an area of memory so the Virtual Memory will clear address space for the protocol packets.

   C. An interrupt of the network card to the processor to signify it has data in the buffer. The processor must evaluate the data before the network buffer is flushed for new packets delivered.

   D. A number assigned to a device to signify what the device is.

5. What is an I/O address? (Choose the best answer.)

   A. The electronic location of a device in the system

   B. The number assigned to a device to signify what the device is in the system

   C. An area of memory used for file I/O

D. A setting used to interrupt the I/O Manager to signify that new data is available to be saved to the hard disk from the device's buffer

2.5   Answers and Explanations: Practice Problems

1. **A**   Allow setup to find the next card by clicking the Find Next button.

2. **B**   Setup allows for drivers to be added during the detection of network cards.

3. **B, D**   You may check the IRQ status of the networks card through Control Panel Network.

4. **C**   An interrupt request tells the processor it has information to process now.

5. **A**   An I/O address is the electronic location of a device in the system. It allows information sent to the device to be delivered.

2.5   Key Words

Client Services for NetWare

Gateway Services for NetWare

Regedt32.exe   DHCP

IP address   WINS

Subnet mask   IPCONFIG

2

2.6   Windows NT Core Services

A service is a built-in application that provides support for other applications or other components of the operating system. Examples of Windows NT services include:

- Windows Internet Name Service (WINS), which maps IP addresses to NetBIOS names.

- UPS service, which interacts with an Uninterruptible Power Supply system to prevent your system from abruptly shutting down.

- Server service, which accepts I/O requests from the network and routes the requested resources back to the client.

- Workstation service, which accepts I/O requests from the local system and redirects the requests to the appropriate computer on the network.

Services are background processes that perform specific functions in Windows NT. Typically, services don't interact with the user interface in any way.

A.   The Services Application

The Control Panel Services application manages the services on your system. Note that the Services dialog box also includes buttons that stop a service, pause a service, or continue a service that has been paused. Pausing a service causes the service to continue handling the processes it's currently serving, but not take on any new clients.

To enable a service for a given hardware profile, click on the HW Profiles button in the Services dialog box, select a profile, and click on OK. The logon account defines a security context for the service. Because services are Win32 programs, they must run under the aegis of a user account. Here are two options:

- **System Account.** An internal account, called SYSTEM, can be used either by the operating system or by the service. This method isn't recommended, however, because you can't fine-tune rights and permissions without possibly affecting the performance and stability of the operating system and other services that may use this account.

- **This Account.** You may designate any user account from your account database here. You should create a separate account for each service for which you want to configure rights and permissions.

B.   Network Services

The Services tab of the Control Panel Network application lets you add, configure, and remove services that support network functions.

Some of the services in the Network Services list are configurable through the Network application and some are not. Select a service and click on the Properties button to open a configuration dialog box for the service.

DHCP, WINS, DNS, RAS, and Gateway Services for NetWare are actually services that, although often configured elsewhere, can still be added, started, stopped, and managed through the Network Services tab and the Control Panel Services application.

C. Directory Replication

Directory Replication is a facility that lets you configure Windows NT Servers to automatically transmit updated versions of important files and directories to other computers on the network.

The purpose of Directory Replication is to simplify the task of distributing updates for logon scripts, system policy files, Help files, phone lists, and other important, generally read-only, files. The network administrator updates the file(s) on a single server (called the *export server*) and the export server automatically distributes the file(s) to other network servers or even to network workstations. The computer receiving the update is called the *import computer*. A Windows NT Server, a Windows NT Workstation, or a LAN Manager OS/2 server can act as an import computer.

The parameters for the Directory Replicator service are found in the Registry key:

```
HKEY_LOCAL_MACHINE\SYSTEM\CurrentControlSet\Services\Replicator\Parameters
```

Most of the parameters in the previous Registry key can be configured within Server Manager. Two important exceptions are:

- **Interval.** A REG_WORD value that defines how often an export server checks for updates. The range is from one to 60 minutes and the default is five minutes.

- **GuardTime.** A REG_WORD value that defines how long a directory must be stable before its files can be replicated. The range is 0 to one half of the Interval value.

The export directory on the export server holds the files and directories are replicated across the network. The default export directory is

```
\<winnt_root>\System32\Repl\Export
```

When the Directory Replicator service starts, NT shares the export directory with the share name Repl$. Each import computer has a directory called the import directory, and the default directory is

```
\<winnt_root>\System32\Repl\Import
```

The Directory Replicator service copies designated directories and their contents from the export server's export directory to the import directories of the import computers. In addition to copying files, the Directory Replicator service automatically creates any necessary subdirectories in the import directory so that after each replication the directory structure of the import directory matches the export directory's directory structure.

The process occurs as follows:

1. The export server periodically checks the export directory for changes and, if changes have occurred, sends update notices to the import computers.

2. The import computer receives the update notices and calls the export computer.

3. The import computer reads the export directory on the export server and copies any new or changed files from the export directory to its own import directory.

1. Troubleshooting Directory Replication

The Status parameter in the Manage Exported Directories and the Manage Imported Directories dialog boxes gives the status of the directory replication for a subdirectory. The possible values are as follows:

- **OK.** The export server is sending regular updates, and the import directory matches the export directory.

- **No Master.** The import computer isn't receiving updates, which means the export server may not be running, or the Directory Replicator service on the export server may not be running.

- **No Sync.** The import directory has received updates, but the data in the updates isn't what it should be, which means there could be an export server malfunction, a communication problem, open files on either the import of the export computer, or a problem with the import computer's access permissions.

- **(Blank).** Replication has never occurred. The cause could be improper configuration on either the import or the export computer.

2. Directory Replication Errors

When the Directory Replication service generates an error, check Event Viewer to learn what you can about the cause. Microsoft recommends the following solutions for some common replication errors:

- **Access Denied.** The Directory Replicator service might not be configured to log on to a specific account.

- **Exporting to Specific Computers.** Designate specific export servers for each import server and specific import computers for each export server.

- **Replication over a WAN link.** When transmitting replication data across a WAN link, specify the computer name rather than just the domain name when you click on the Add button in the Directory Replication dialog box.

- **Logon Scripts for Member Servers and Workstations.** NT Workstations and non-controller NT Servers must use the default logon script directory:

  ```
  C:\<winnt_root>\System32\Repl\Import\Scripts
  ```

D.   Windows NT Client Licenses

Microsoft requires that every client accessing a resource on a computer running Windows NT Server have a Client Access License (CAL). Microsoft provides two options for purchasing Client Access Licenses, as follows:

- **Per Server mode.** Client Access Licenses are assigned to each server. A Windows NT Server might be licensed for, say, 10 simultaneous client connections. No more than 10 clients will be able to access the server at one time—additional clients will not be able to connect.

- **Per Seat mode.** Client Access Licenses are assigned to each client machine. You purchase a CAL for every client computer on the network.

Microsoft allows a one-time switch from Per Server to Per Seat licensing mode. If your network has only one server, Microsoft recommends that you choose Per Server licensing mode. If you have more than one server on your network, Microsoft suggests the following formulas:

A=Number of servers

B=number of simultaneous connections to each server

C=total number of seats (clients) accessing computers

If A * B < C use Per Server licensing. Number of CALs=A*B

IF A * B > C use Per Seat licensing. Number of CALs=C

1. The Licensing Application

The Control Panel Licensing application opens the Choose Licensing Mode dialog box. The Choose Licensing Mode dialog box lets you add or remove client licenses or switch from Per Server to Per Seat licensing mode.

License replication is a convenient feature that lets individual servers send their licensing information lists to a master server. The master server creates and updates a database of licensing information for the entire network.

2. License Manager

License Manager, a tool in the Administrative Tools program group, displays licensing information for the network. You can maintain a history of client licenses, examine your network's Per Server and Per Seat licenses by product, and browse for client license information on particular network clients.

You also can use License Manager to add or edit license groups. A license group is a group of users mapped to a group of Per Seat licenses. License groups are a means of tracking per seat license usage in situations where an organization has more users than computers (or in some cases, more computers than users).

E.   Computer Browser Service

The Computer Browser service oversees a hierarchy of computers that serve as browsers for the network. A browser is a computer that maintains a central list of network servers.

That list then becomes available to clients who are "browsing" the network looking for remote computers, printers, and other resources. The list that appears when you open the Network Neighborhood application, for instance, comes from a network browser list. In a Windows NT domain, each computer assumes one of five browser roles:

- **Master browser.** Each workgroup or domain subnet must have a master browser. At startup, all computers running the Server service (regardless of whether they have resources available for the network) register themselves with the master browser.

- **Domain master browser.** The domain master browser requests subnet browse lists from the master browsers and merges the subnet browse lists into a master browse list for the entire domain. This computer is always the Primary Domain Controller.

- **Backup browsers.** The backup browser gets a copy of the browse list from the master browser (on the subnet) and distributes the browse list to subnet clients who request it.

- **Potential browser.** A potential browser is a computer that isn't presently acting as a browser but can become a browser at the request of the master browser or as a result of a browser election.

- **Non-browser.** A non-browser is a computer that cannot act as a browser.

The first time a client computer attempts to access the network, it obtains a list of backup browsers for the subnet or workgroup from the master browser. It then asks a backup browser for a copy of the browse list. If a master browser fails, a new master browser is chosen automatically in what is known as a *browser election*. A browser election can occur if a client or backup browser cannot access the master browser. Some of the criteria used in a browser election are as follows:

- **Operating system.** Windows NT Server gets a higher score than Windows NT Workstation, which gets a higher score than Windows 95.

- **Version.** Windows NT Server 4 gets a higher score than Windows NT Server 3.51, and so forth.

- **Present browser role.** A backup browser scores higher than a potential browser.

You can configure a Windows NT computer to always, never, or sometimes participate in browser elections, using the MaintainServerList parameter in the registry key:

```
HKEY_Local_Machine\System\CurrentControlSet\Services\Browsr\Parameters
```

The possible values are as follows:

- **Yes.** Always attempt to become a browser in browser elections (default for Windows NT Server domain controllers).

- **No.** Never attempt to become a browser in browser elections.

- **Auto.** The Auto setting classifies the computer as a potential browser (default for Windows NT Workstations and Windows NT Servers that aren't acting as domain controllers).

2.6.1 Exercise: Configuring Directory Replication

This exercise requires two computers that network together. One computer must be an NT Server and the other can be Windows NT Server or NT Workstation.

To set up the export server for directory replication:

1. Verify that the Registry is okay. Specifically, unless you have added SP1 or SP2, you must manually edit the registry to force Directory Replication to work. The next six steps walk you through the process of correcting the registry entry.

2. Run Regedt32.exe. From the Options menu verify that you are not working in Read Only Mode.

3. Open this key: HKEY_LOCAL_MACHINE\SYSTEM\CurrentControlSet\Control\SecurePipeServers\winreg\AllowedPaths.

4. Double-click on Machine:REG_MULTI_SZ. The Multi-String Editor dialog box opens.

5. In the Data field, add an entry by pressing your arrow key down to clear anything that might be highlighted, and then pressing Enter.

6. Type the following exactly as it appears without the period at the end: System\CurrentControlSet\Services\Replicator.

7. Click on OK, exit the Registry Editor, restart your machine, and then log back on as an administrator.

8. Create a new account for the Directory Replicator service. The Directory Replicator account must be a member of the Backup Operator group and the Replicator group for the domain. When you set up the new account, be sure to enable the Password Never Expires option and disable the User Must Change Password at Next Logon option. Also, make sure the account has logon privileges for all hours.

9. Assign the new account the User Right "Log on as a Service."

10. In the Control Panel, double-click on the Services applet. Select the Directory Replicator Service from the list and click the Startup button. Change the Startup type to Automatic and configure the Log on as section to use the account that you created in step 2 with the password you set.

11. Start the Server Manager application in the Administrative Tools program group. Server Manager is a tool for managing network servers and workstations from a single location.

12. In the Server Manager, double-click on the export server to open the Server Properties dialog box

13. Click on the Replication button to open the Directory Replication dialog box.

> **A Windows NT Server can serve as an export server, an import computer, or both.**

14. In the Directory Replication dialog box, select the Export Directories radio button. The default path to the export directory appears in the From Path box. Click on the Add button to open the Select Domain dialog box. Click on a domain to select it. Double-click on a domain to display the computers within that domain. If you select a whole domain, all import servers in the domain receive the replicated data. If you choose a specific computer, only that computer receives the replicated data. You can choose any combination of domains and specific computers.

15. Click on the Manage button to open the Manage Exported Directories dialog box. Subdirectories within the export directory appear in the Sub-Directory list. You can add or remove subdirectories from the list by clicking on the Add or Remove buttons. By default, the Scripts subdirectory appears.

    Note the check boxes at the bottom of the screen. Enabling the Wait Until Stabilized check box tells the Directory Replicator service to wait at least two minutes after any change to the selected subdirectory tree before exporting. Enabling the Entire Subtree check box tells the Directory Replicator service to export all subdirectories beneath the selected subdirectory. The Add Lock button lets you lock the subdirectory so it can't be exported. More than one user can lock a subdirectory. (Consequently, a subdirectory can have more than one lock.) To remove a lock, click on the Remove Lock button.

16. If you do not see a dialog box stating that the Directory Replicator service is starting, you need to start the Directory Replicator service yourself. In Server Manager, select the Export Computer in the list of computers, and select the Services option from the Computer menu. Select the Directory Replicator service and click on the Start button to start the Directory Replicator service.

2.6.2   Exercise: Configuring the Import Computer

To set up the import computer for directory replication:

1. Verify that Registry is okay. Specifically, unless you have added SP1 or SP2, you must manually edit the registry to force Directory Replication to work. The next six steps will walk you through the process of correcting the registry entry.

2. Run Regedt32.exe. From the Options menu, verify that you are not working in Read Only Mode.

3. Open this key:
   HKEY_LOCAL_MACHINE\SYSTEM\CurrentControlSet\Control\SecurePipeServers\winreg\AllowedPaths.

4. Double-click on Machine: REG_MULTI_SZ. The Multi-String Editor dialog box opens.

5. In the Data field, add an entry by pressing your down arrow key to clear anything that might be highlighted, and then pressing Enter.

6. Type the following exactly as it appears without the period at the end:
   System\CurrentControlSet\Services\Replicator.

   Click on OK, exit the Registry Editor, restart your machine, and then log back on as an administrator.

7. Double-click on the Services icon in the Control Panel. Select the Directory Replicator service and click on the Startup button to open the Service dialog box.

8. In the Startup Type frame, select the Automatic radio button. Select the This Account radio button and enter a username and password for the replicator account you created on the export server.

9. Start Server Manager, select the computer you're now configuring, and click on the Replication button in the Properties dialog box. The Directory Replication dialog box appears. This time, you're concerned with the import side (the right side) of the dialog box, but the configuration steps are similar to steps for configuring the export side. The default import directory appears in the To Path box. Click on the Add button to add a domain or a specific export server. Click on the Manage button to open the Manage Imported Directories dialog box, which lets you manage the import directories.

10. In the Manage Imported Directories dialog box, click on Add or Remove to add or remove a subdirectory from the list. Click on Add Lock to add a lock to the subdirectory.

11. If you do not see a dialog box stating that the Directory Replicator service is starting, you need to start the Directory Replicator service yourself. In Server Manager, select the Import Computer in the list of computers, and select the Services option from the Computer menu. Select the Directory Replicator service and click on the Start button to start the Directory Replicator service.

2.6 Practice Problems

1. In Windows NT, a service is what? (Choose the best answer.)

    A. A network share site

    B. The component of NT that creates the UNC names

    C. A built-in application that provides support for other applications

    D. A component that allows for more than 10 concurrent connections

2. The WINS service does what for Windows NT?

    A. Allows 16-bit Windows applications to run on NT

    B. Translates 16-bit calls from a Windows application and converts them into 32-bit calls for NT

    C. Maps NetBIOS names to IP addresses

    D. Maps IP addresses to Network card's MAC addresses

3. The DHCP service does what for Windows NT?

    A. Allows 16-bit Windows applications to run on NT

    B. Translates 16-bit calls from a Windows application and converts them into 32-bit calls for NT

    C. Maps NetBIOS names to IP addresses

    D. Assigns IP addresses to clients automatically

4. Your server shows up in the network neighborhood, and others can connect to your server's shares. However, when you try to connect to another resource on the network you cannot. What do you suspect is the problem? (Choose the best answer.)

    A. You have a real mode driver for your network card and you need a 32-bit protected mode driver.

    B. The server service has been paused or stopped.

    C. The Workstation service has been paused or stopped.

    D. The Network protocol in use has been disabled.

5. You have an NT Server that is a backup domain controller. You previously had several shares but now all of the sharing symbols in Explorer are gone and no one can connect to your machine. What is the problem?

    A. The PDC is down.

    B. You are not logged on as the administrator.

    C. The server service has been stopped.

    D. Someone has the same NetBIOS name as your server.

6. Your boss has asked you to pause a service, as she is trying to troubleshoot a problem on your network. You would do this using:

    A. The Devices Applet in Control Panel

    B. The Services applet in Control Panel

    C. The NET STOP command

    D. The NET PAUSE command

7. Which service is responsible for printing?

    A. Spooler

    B. WINS

    C. SERVER

    D. PRINT Redirector

8. You would like to enable the Gateway Services for NetWare at different times throughout the day on your test NT server. What are the methods to enable GSNW to start only when you want it to?

    A. Create a Hardware Profile that matches up with the services you would like to run at startup.

B. Configure the Service applet to start only specified services at boot. Then when you need GSNW, start it manually.

C. You cannot do this. GSNW must be running at all times when NT Server is installed on the machine.

D. Create a batch file with NET STOP and NET START commands to stop and start the GSNW service. Then use the AT scheduler to run the batch file at different times throughout the day.

9. You are configuring a service and are uncertain why you need to specify a logon account for the service. The reason is because:

A. No object can access the registry without a logon id.

B. The logon account determines in what security context the service will run.

C. Enables auditing of a service.

D. Services, part of the operating process, will generally run in real time. By specifying the service as a user, the threads will lose thread priority and will be more secure with the system.

10. You are configuring a service to use the SYSTEM account. You have heard that this isn't a wise thing to do. Why not? (Choose the best answer.)

A. The System account may only be used by the Security Accounts manager.

B. The System Account is to be used as a backup administrator account. The password is blank.

C. The System account is a default user account used to validate remote clients.

D. The System account is used by many services and by the Operating System. Any security changes to this account might have detrimental effects on the OS.

11. You and a colleague are installing Windows NT Server 4.0 as a BDC. Your colleague is unclear on why you have decided to use the Directory Replicator service. The primary purpose of the Directory Replicator service is:

A. To automate the installation on NT Server 4.0.

B. To replicate an exact configuration on Widows NT Server 4.0 to another machine.

C. To replicate directories containing logon scripts, system polices, and crucial, read-only information.

D. To allow users to be validated by this BDC. The account database on the server must be replicated to this machine on a regular basis.

12. A computer running this OS can act as an import computer. (Choose all that apply.)

A. Windows NT Server

B. Windows NT Workstation

C. LAN Manager

D. Windows 95

13. You are allowed to edit the parameters for Directory Replication through what? (Choose the best answer:)

A. Control Panel System.

B. Control Panel Devices.

C. The registry editor.

D. You cannot change a value on this service.

14. What is the Interval value and what does it do for Windows NT? (Choose the best answer.)

A. A registry setting that monitors how often NT checks the export directory for changes

B. A registry setting that monitors how often a client checks export directory for changes

C. A service that synchronizes the account database to other domain controllers

D. A service that synchronizes the browse list with other browsers in the network

15. You have configured directory replication on your export server. You decide, however, that you would like to increase the GUARDTIME to ensure stabilization of your directories before they replicate. You can do this by doing what? (Choose the best answer.)

A. Changing the GUARDTIME value in the Server Manager utility.

B. Changing the GUARDTIME value in the Registry.

C. Using the GUARDTIME= command at a DOS prompt.

D. You cannot change the GUARDTIME value anywhere in the system.

16. What is the default directory for exporting data to other computers on your network?

A. \<winnt root>\System32\REPL

B. \<winnt root>\System32\REPL\EXPORT

C. \<winnt root>\System32\REPL\SCRIPTS

D. \<winnt root>\System32\REPL\IMPORT

17. You have configured Directory Replication on your export server and would like to check the status of replication on your import computer. You can do this through which method? (Choose the best answer.)

A. The Registry Editor

B. Server Manager

C. Network Client Administrator

D. The NET=Replication command

18. You have configured Directory replication on your server. However, when you check the status of Directory Replication on the import computer, you receive a message that says "No Master" under the status field. This means what? (Choose the best answer.)

A. There is no Master Domain Controller available.

B. There is no Master Browser.

C. The import computer is not receiving updates from the export server.

D. The import server has not been identified on the export server.

19. You have configured Directory Replication on your server to replicate directories to an NT Server in another domain. However, when you check the status of the directories in the other domain, you receive a "No Master" message. Why is this happening? (Choose all that apply.)

A. You must specify the computer name instead of the domain name when replicating between domains in a trust relationship.

B. You must first create a trust relationship between the domains to establish directory replication between the two domains.

C. Your REPL account must have the same username and password in both domains.

D. You must add the REPL user to the Domain Admins group in both domains.

20. You are about to create a single-server domain and your supervisor asks you why you have chosen to use per server instead of per seat licensing. You would respond with what? (Choose the best answer.)

A. Per server licensing is needed because you do not have enough clients to justify the cost of buying per seat.

B. Per server licensing is needed because you have only one domain controller at this time.

C. Per server licensing is needed because you are integrating with NetWare servers.

D. Per server licensing is needed because Microsoft requires you to purchase per server when you first install NT Server.

21. You have installed NT Server as a PDC with 25 Client Access Licenses. Your company has hired 20 additional users that need access to your server. To allow these clients access to your server, you must do what? (Choose the best answer.)

A. Reinstall NT and specify the additional 20 users.

B. Purchase per seat licenses and use the Control Panel Licensing application.

C. Purchase additional per server Client Access Licenses and add the additional licenses through the Admin Tools.

D. Purchase additional per server Client Access Licenses and add the additional licenses through the Control Licensing application.

22. You have a Windows NT Server that is a member server. You would like to configure this machine so that it is never a browser in your domain. You can do this how? (Choose the best answer.)

A. Through the Control Panel to Network, set the Browsing parameter under services to No.

B. Through the Control Panel to services. Choose Configure on the Browser service and set the value to No.

C. Through the Control Panel to services. Stop the browser service.

D. By editing the registry to change the role of a browser on NT Server.

E. You cannot do this after the initial server installation.

23. Your NT Domain is segmented into three subnets. You have a backup domain controller on two subnets and a PDC on one subnet. The roles these machines play in browsing are what? (Choose the best answer.)

A. The PDC is the Domain Master Browser. The two BDCs are clients of the Domain Master Browser.

B. The PDC is the Domain Master Browser. The two BDCs have no role in browsing.

C. The PDC and the two BDCs act as backup Master Browsers because the network is segmented.

D. The PDC is the Domain Master Browser and the BDCs are Master browsers because the network is segmented.

24. You are testing a PDC. During the testing phase you have to reboot the machine several times. Each time you check the Event Viewer and you notice that the Browser service has forced an election. Why is this happening? (Choose the best answer.)

A. If you have the Browser Service enabled, all NT machines will force an election to determine who is the Browser.

B. Browser elections happen each time a server comes onto the network.

C. Browser elections are forced each time the Primary Domain Controller reboots because the PDC must be the Domain Master Browser.

D. Browser election happen every fifteen minutes on an NT Domain.

25. Based on the previous question, how could you stop these elections from happening each time you reboot the machine? (Choose the best answer.)

A. You cannot stop the elections from happening.

B. You must disable the server service.

C. You must edit the registry and configure the PDC not to maintain a Server List.

D. You must edit the properties of the Browser service through Control Panel Services.

26. You have a Windows NT Server that you are testing as a PDC. You are rebooting this machine every 30 minutes or so due to tests on your system. You notice that after each boot, the Event Viewer has a message that states it is initializing a browser election on your network. Why is this so? (Choose the best answer.)

A. Browser elections happen every 28 minutes regardless of whether they are needed.

B. Browser elections happen every 30 minutes regardless of whether they are needed.

C. The PDC is required, by default, to be the Domain Master Browser. By rebooting, you are forcing a browser election in your domain.

D. The Browser election is a default entry in Event Viewer. No election is actually happening on your network.

2.6 Answers and Explanations: Practice Problems

1. **C** In Windows NT, a service provides support for other applications and components of the operating system.

2. **C** The WINS service maps NetBIOS names to IP address.

3. **D** The DHCP service assigns IP addresses to clients automatically.

4. **C** The Workstation service has been paused or stopped.

5. **C** If the server service is stopped, shares are not available to anyone.

6. **B** Pause the DHCP service using the Control Panel, Services applet.

7. **D** Pausing a service keeps all current connections but does not add any additional clients.

8. **A, D** A hardware profile enables you to configure a service at startup as would using a batch file in conjunction with the AT scheduler.

9. **B** The logon account provides the security context for the service.

10. **D** The System account is used by many services and by the operating system. Any security changes to this account could have detrimental effects on the OS. Instead, you should configure a service to use an account created and configured specifically for that service.

11. **C** The primary purpose of the Directory Replicator service is to replicate directories containing logon scripts, system polices, and crucial, read-only, information.

12. **A, B, C** Windows 95 cannot act as an import computer.

13. **B** You edit the parameters for Directory Replication through the Registry editor. The key for the service is: HKEY-LOCAL MACHINE\SYSTEM\Current ControlSet\Services\Replicator\Paramters.

14. **A**   The Interval value is a registry setting that monitors how often NT checks the export directory for changes.

15. **B**   You can change the GUARDTIME value only in the Registry editor.

16. **B**   The \<winnt root>\System32\REPL\EXPORT directory is the default directory for exporting data to other computers on your network.

17. **B**   To check Directory Replication status, use the Server Manger, Directory Replication command.

18. **C**   The import computer is not receiving updates from the export server.

19. **A, C**   To replicate directories to an NT Server in another domain, you must specify the computer name in addition to the domain name when replicating over a WAN link.

20. **A**   Per server licensing is needed because you have only one server in small domain. As your domain grows, you are allowed a one-time conversion of per server to per seat.

21. **D**   To allow 20 additional clients access to your server, you must purchase additional per server Client Access Licenses and add the additional licenses through the Control Licensing application.

22. **D**   You must edit the Registry to change the role of a browser on NT Server.

23. **D**   Each subnet must have a Master Browser; the PDC is always the Domain Master Browser.

24. **C**   The PDC is always the Domain Master Browser. Because the machine is being rebooted often, it is announcing its presence to the network.

25. **C**   To stop the elections from happening each time you reboot the machine, you have to edit the registry and change the value of the PDC to non-browser.

26. **C**   The NT Server PDC is required, by default, to be a browser server. By rebooting, you are forcing an election in your domain for your NT Server.

2.6   Key Words

Directory Replication

Per Server licensing

Per Seat license

Domain master browser

Backup browsers

AT.EXE

Hardware Profile

GuardTime

Interval

2.7 Configuring Peripherals and Devices

Control Panel includes several applications that help you install and configure peripherals and devices.

A. Devices

The Devices application (SRVMGR.CPL) writes to

```
HKEY_LOCAL_MACHINE\SYSTEM\CurrentControlSet\Services.
```

You can start, stop, or disable device drivers in this Control Panel applet. The three columns in the Control Panel Devices main display area are labeled Device, Status, and Startup. The Device column identifies the name of the device driver as it appears in the Registry; the Status column reads "Started" if the driver is active, and otherwise appears blank; the Startup column denotes when each driver is configured to initialize.

Choose one of the following Startup types:

- **Boot.** These devices start first, as soon as the kernel is loaded and initialized
- **System.** These devices start after the boot devices and after the HKEY_LOCAL_MACHINE subtree has begun to be built.
- **Automatic.** These devices start late in the boot process, after the Registry is almost entirely built, just before the Winlogon screen appears.
- **Manual.** These devices are never started without administrator intervention.
- **Disabled.** These devices cannot be started at all unless their startup types is changed to something other than Disabled.

To start a device that isn't active, select the device and choose the Start button. To stop a device that's active, select the device and choose the Stop button. To enable or disable a device for a given hardware profile, select the device, click on HW Profiles, select enable or disable to change to the desired status, and click on OK.

B. Multimedia

The Multimedia application (MMSYS.CPL) writes to

```
HKEY_LOCAL_MACHINE\SYSTEM\CurrentControlSet\Services.
```

Multimedia device drivers are added and configured from this Control Panel applet.

C. Ports

The Ports application (PORTS.CPL) writes directly to the following key:

```
HKEY_LOCAL_MACHINE\SYSTEM\CurrentControlSet\Services\Serial
```

This Control Panel interface lists only the serial ports that are available but not in use as serial ports.

If you need an additional port for use under Windows NT, choose the Add button. You may assign a different COM port number, base I/O port address or IRQ, or enable a First In-First Out (FIFO) buffer for that port.

1. UPS

The UPS application (UPS.CPL) writes to the following key:

```
HKEY_LOCAL_MACHINE\SYSTEM\CurrentControlSet\Services\UPS
```

If your computer is equipped with a Universal Power Supply (UPS), Windows NT can be configured to communicate with it. Armed with the correct information, Windows NT can recognize the following:

- **Power failure signal.** The point when an event is logged and the Server service paused. No new connections to this server can be made, but existing connections still function.

- **Low battery signal at least two minutes before shutdown.** As the name implies, Windows NT recognizes when the UPS battery is about to be exhausted.

- **Remote UPS Shutdown.** Signals Windows NT that the UPS is shutting down.

The Execute Command File option enables an administrator to specify a batch or executable file that runs immediately preceding a shutdown.

If no Low Battery Signal is configured, the administrator can enter the Expected Battery Life and the Battery Recharge Time Per Minute of Run Time in the lower-left corner of the dialog box.

After the initial PowerOut alert is raised (the power failure signal has been received), Windows NT waits until the Time Between Power Failure and Initial Warning Message has elapsed, and then sends an alert to all interactive and connected users.

2. SCSI Adapters

This application is one of the great misunderstandings in Windows NT. As it suggests, this application opens the SCSI Adapters dialog box, which is used to install SCSI adapter drivers. However, this dialog box also is used to install and remove IDE CD-ROM drivers as well as drivers for CD-ROM drives that use proprietary interfaces, such as Mitsumi or Panasonic drives.

IDE drivers are added through this applet because they are ATAPI drivers, which are a subset of the SCSI drivers. To add a SCSI adapter or CD-ROM device driver, follow these procedures:

1. Double-click the SCSI Adapters application in the Control Panel.

2. In the SCSI Adapters dialog box, choose the Drivers tab and click on the Add button.

3. Select the driver from the list of available drivers in the Install Driver dialog box. If your driver isn't listed but you have a disk from the manufacturer with a Windows NT driver, click on the Have Disk button.

4. Choose OK. You must point Windows NT toward the original installation files (or the disk that contains the driver) and restart the computer in order for the new driver to initialize.

To remove a SCSI adapter or CD-ROM device driver, perform these instructions:

1. Select the Drivers tab in the SCSI Adapters dialog box.

2. Select the driver you want to remove.

3. Choose the Remove button.

3. Tape Devices

To add a tape drive device driver, follow these steps:

1. Double-click on the Tape Devices icon in Control Panel.

2. Select the Drivers tab.

3. Click on the Add button.

4. Select the driver from the list of available drivers. If your driver isn't listed but you have a disk from the manufacturer with a Windows NT Driver, click on the Have Disk button.

5. Choose OK. You must point Windows NT toward the original installation files (or the disk that contains the driver) and restart the computer in order for the new driver to initialize.

To remove a tape drive device driver, follow these steps:

1. Select the driver from the list of installed drivers in the Tape Devices dialog box of the Drivers tab.

2. Choose the Remove button.

4. PC Card (PCMCIA)

The PC Card application helps you install and configure PCMCIA device drivers. A red X next to a device in the PC card list indicates that NT doesn't support the device.

5. Modems

The Modems application enables you to add or remove a modem. To add a modem:

1. Double-click on the Modems application in the Control Panel.

2. Click on Add in the Modem Properties dialog box.

3. In the Install New Modem dialog box, click on Next if you want NT to try to detect your modem. If you want to select your modem from the list, or if you're providing software for a modem not listed, enable the check box and then click on Next

4. Select a manufacturer and a model, and click on Next. Or click on the Have Disk button if you're installing software for a modem not shown on the list.

5. Select a port for the modem, or select All ports. Click on Next.

Select a modem in the Modems list and click on Properties to change the parameters for that modem. The Telephony Modem dialog box opens, with two tabs, General and Connection. The General tab enables you to set the port number and the maximum speed.

The Dialing Properties button in the Modem Properties dialog box calls up the My Location tab, which is also in the Telephony application. The My Locations tab enables you to set the dialing characteristics for the modem. To add a new location, follow these steps:

1. Click on the New button at the top of the My Locations tab. (NT announces that a new location has been created.)

2. The new location has the name New Location (followed by a number if you already have a location called New Location). Click on the name and change it if you want to give your location a different

name. (NT might not let you erase the old name completely until you add your new name. Add the new name and then backspace over the old text if necessary.)

3. Change any dialing properties. The new properties will apply to your new location.

6. Keyboard

The Keyboard application opens the Keyboard Properties dialog box, which enables the user to set the keyboard repeat rate, the repeat delay, the cursor blink rate, and the keyboard layout properties.

7. Mouse

The values for this key control the mouse speed, sensitivity, and left- or right-handedness. The one new setting added to this dialog box's Win3.x predecessor is the Snap to Default option in the Motion tab, which instantly positions the pointer over the default button in the active dialog box.

8. Display

The Display application configures the values in the following key, including the video driver, screen resolution, color depth, and refresh rate:

```
HKEY_LOCAL_MACHINE\SYSTEM\CurrentControlSet\Services\<video_driver>\Device0\
```

The five tabs of the Display Properties dialog box are as follows:

- **Background.** Defines the wallpaper for the Desktop.
- **Screen Saver.** Defines the screen saver for the Desktop.
- **Appearance.** Defines window properties.
- **Plus!.** The Visual Enhancements tab from the Microsoft Plus! package for Windows 95 lets you configure the desktop to use custom desktop icons or stretch the wallpaper to fit the screen.
- **Settings.** Defines desktop colors, refresh frequency, and other screen-related settings.

You should always test new display settings before making changes permanent. Although Windows NT can detect the capabilities of your video card, it can't do the same with your monitor.

Windows NT can change video resolution on the fly as long as the color depth does not change. To change the video display adapter:

1. Start the Control Panel Display application and click on the Settings tab.

2. Click on the Display Type button. The Display Type dialog box appears.

3. Click on the Change tab in the Adapter Type frame. The Change Display dialog box appears. Select an adapter from the list and click on OK. Or, if you have a manufacturer's installation disk, click on Have Disk.

2.7   Practice Problems

1. You have opened the Control Panel, Ports to see what ports are on your NT computer. However, Com1 does not appear in the list of ports. Why is this?

    A. Com1 never appears in the list of Ports because it is reserved for the OS.

    B. Com1 is not supported under Windows NT 4 due to the HAL limitations on some computers.

    C. Com1 is in use.

    D. You need to press the refresh button to see the available ports.

2. You have added a UPS to your NT server. The UPS initiates a power failure signal, yet all users stay connected to their home directories on the server. Why is this?

    A. The UPS saves power by disconnecting users that are inactive. All users are currently active on the server.

    B. The UPS saves power by disconnecting users that are active. All users are currently inactive on the server.

    C. The UPS cannot disconnect users to the server, because it would interfere with the NT security model.

    D. Current users will stay connected; however, any new users will not be allowed to connect.

3. You would like to add an IDE CD-ROM device to your NT server. You cannot find an appropriate setting to add this device. Where do you add the IDE CD-ROM driver?

    A. Add the Hardware. NTDETECT.Com will find the device and request the driver from you.

    B. Add the Hardware. NTDETECT.com will automatically pull the driver from its library of IDE devices.

    C. Add the Hardware. Then use the IDE Hardware applet in Control Panel.

    D. Add the Hardware. Then use the SCSI applet in Control Panel.

4. What can you configure in the Keyboard applet? (Choose all that apply.)

    A. Repeat rate

    B. Function key settings

    C. Cursor blink rate

    D. Num lock on or off at startup

5. You have just changed the resolution from 640×480 to 800×600 on your NT machine. Now you must do what to put the settings into effect?

    A. Reboot.

    B. Reboot and choose VGA mode and the reboot as normal.

    C. Press F5 to refresh the screen.

    D. Test your settings and then exit Display.

6. In Control Panel, Devices you have what choices to configure startup for system devices? (Choose all the apply.)

    A. Boot

    B. System

    C. Automatic

    D. Manual

7. The Control Panel, Multimedia enables you to do what?

    A. Adjust system sound

    B. Add video cards

    C. Change video resolution

    D. Add device drivers

    E. All of the above

8. You have added a UPS to your NT
    Server. The Remote UPS Shutdown does
    what to Windows NT?

    A. Tells Windows NT Clients that the
        server will be shutting down

    B. Receives a command from Win-
        dows NT that the server has been
        properly shutdown

    C. Receives a command from Win-
        dows NT that the server has been
        improperly shutdown

    D. Tells Windows NT that the UPS
        will be shutting down

9. You have added a UPS to your NT
    Server. The power failure signal affects
    Windows NT Server in what way?

    A. Tells Windows NT that there has
        been a power surge

    B. Tells Windows NT that there has
        been no interrupt in power as the
        power signal has been constant to
        NT in 30-second pulses

    C. The point where the server service
        is paused and an event is logged

    D. Emits a whistle through NT's
        sound system to alert the adminis-
        trator that there has been an error
        on the system

10. You would like to schedule a .bat file to
    run before NT is shut down by the UPS.
    How can you do this?

    A. You must use the AT scheduler
        command.

    B. You must use the NET start
        /interactive command.

    C. You must create a Hardware Profile
        that specifies the .bat file to run
        before shutdown.

    D. You must supply the path to the file
        in the Execute Command File
        option in the UPS dialog box.

11. You have installed a UPS on your server.
    During a power failure, when does NT
    send an alert to all connected users?

    A. After the initial PowerOut message
        has been received by the server, NT
        waits until the time between power
        failure and the initial warning
        message has elapsed before sending
        a message.

    B. After the second PowerOut message
        has been received by the server, NT
        waits until the time between power
        failure and the initial warning
        message has elapsed before sending
        a message.

    C. After the initial PowerOut message
        has been received by the server, NT
        sends a message to all connected
        users.

    D. Two minutes before remote
        shutdown of the UPS.

12. You would like to add an IDE CD-ROM
    drive to your NT Server configuration.
    How can you do this?

    A. Add the hardware and reboot.
        NTDETECT.COM will find the
        hardware and install the necessary
        drivers.

    B. Use the Controllers applet in
        Control Panel.

    C. Use the SCSI applet in Control
        Panel.

    D. Use the Add New Hardware Wizard
        in Admin Tools.

13. You have received an updated driver for
    your SCSI controller for NT server 4.0.
    Where do you add this new driver?

    A. Control Panel, Add new Programs,
        use Windows NT setup.

    B. Control Panel, System, Device
        Manager.

    C. Run Setup from the floppy or
        CD-ROM.

D. Use the Control Panel, SCSI to update the drivers.

14. You have added a tape device to your system; however, it does not show up as a drive letter in Explorer. How do you configure and manage this tape drive?

  A. You have incorrectly installed the tape drive. Tape drives always show up as a drive in Explorer.

  B. You must use the Control Panel, Backup to configure the device.

  C. You must use the Control Panel, Tape Drive to configure the device.

  D. You must use the Control Panel, SCSI to configure the device.

15. You have installed an internal modem in your system, but you are uncertain as to where you should configure this device. How can you configure the modem?

  A. Use the RAS server service in Control Panel services.

  B. Use the RAS Admin tool in the Admin tools folder.

  C. Use the modem applet in Control Panel.

  D. Use the Dial-up Networking applet in Control Panel.

16. You have installed Windows NT Server 4.0 on your Intel-based machine. You would like to check the configuration of current ports installed on your service. You must use what to determine the ports available on your server?

  A. Locate the HKEY LOCAL MACHINE\SYSTEM \CurrentControlSet\Services\Ports in the registry.

  B. Use the Device applet in Control Panel.

  C. Use the Ports applet in Control Panel.

  D. Use the Ports /* command from the DOS prompt.

17. You decide to check the status of your ports by using the Control Panel, Ports applet. When you open the application, you discover that COM1 is missing from the list of installed ports. Why is this?

  A. COM1 is reserved for NT under Windows NT Server 4.0.

  B. COM1 is currently in use by a hardware device.

  C. Your registry has become corrupt and you must use the ERD to restore it.

  D. None of the above.

18. You would like to add an additional port to your computer. How can you change the IRQ of this port?

  A. You must use the setup program that came with the new hardware.

  B. You can use the Ports applet in Control Panel.

  C. You must use the Device Manager.

  D. You can edit the registry entry of HKEY LOCAL MACHINE\HARDWARE|PORTS.

2.7 Answers and Explanations: Practice Problems

1. **C** The port application will show only the ports that are available, and Com1 is not available.

2. **D** During a power failure signal, current users stay connected; any new users, however, cannot connect.

3. **D** In addition to adding SCSI devices with the SCSI applet in the Control Panel, you also can add and remove IDE CD-ROM drivers with this applet.

4. **A, C** From the Keyboard applet, you can configure repeat rate and cursor blink rate. You cannot configure Function key settings and Num lock on or off at startup because these options do not exist in this applet.

5. **D** After changing the resolution, you should test your settings and then exit Display.

6. **A, B, C, D** Choosing Control Panel, Devices enables you to choose from all these choices.

7. **D** You can add device drivers from Control Panel, Multimedia.

8. **D** The remote UPS Shutdown tells Windows NT that the UPS will be shutting down.

9. **C** The power failure signal affects Windows NT Server to the point where the server service is paused and an event is logged.

10. **D** To schedule a .bat file to run before NT is shut down by the UPS, supply the path to the file in the Execute Command File option in the UPS dialog box.

11. **A** NT sends an UPS alert to all connected users after the initial PowerOut message has been received by the server. NT then waits until the time between power failure and the initial warning message has elapsed before sending a message.

12. **C** Use the SCSI applet in Control Panel to add an IDE CD-ROM drive to your NT Server configuration.

13. **D** Use the Control Panel, SCSI to update all drivers.

14. **C** You must use the Control Panel, Tape Drive to configure the tape drive.

15. **C** Use the modem applet in Control Panel to configure your internal modem.

16. **C** You can check all available ports in the Control Panel, Ports applet.

17. **B** COM1 is currently in use by a hardware device. The Ports applet shows you only the available ports in your computer.

18. **B** You can use the Ports applet in Control Panel to change the IRQ of a port.

2.7 Key Words

Devices

Multimedia

Ports

UPS

SCSI adapters

PC Cards

Modems

2.8   Configuring Hard Disks with Disk Administrator

Disk Administrator is Windows NT's disk utility. To access Disk Administrator, you must be using an administrator account. To start the Disk Administrator, choose Start, Programs, Administrative Tools (common), Disk Administrator.

When using the Disk Administrator for the first time, a message box appears, telling you the following:

```
No signature found on Disk 0. Writing a signature is a safe operation and
will not affect your ability to access this drive from other operating
systems, such as DOS.

If you choose not to write a signature, the disk will be marked OFF-LINE and
will be inaccessible to the Windows NT Disk Administrator program.

Do you want to write a signature on Disk 0 so that Disk Administrator can
access the drive?
```

If you choose not to write a signature, the disk will be inaccessible to the Windows NT Disk Administrator program. Do you want to write a signature on Disk 0 so that the Disk Administrator can access the drive?

Choosing Yes creates a 32-bit signature that uniquely identifies the disk written to the primary partition. This function makes possible recognition of the disk as the original, even if it is has been used with a different controller or its identification has changed.

A.   Customizing the Display

The status bar at the bottom of the Disk Administrator's main window displays basic disk information. Along with the status bar, a color-coded legend displays the different representations for partition colors and patterns.

You also can set different colors and patterns to distinguish between different disks and disk characteristics for the primary partition, logical drive, mirror set, and volume set.

Initially, each disk represented in the display window is sized proportionately. By choosing Options, Region Display, you get several choices in the Region Display Options dialog box for customizing the appearance of each region.

B.   Partitioning

Partitioning refers to the method in which hard disks are made usable. To create primary partitions using the Disk Administrator, follow these steps:

1. Select an area of free space on a disk.

2. Choose Partition, Create.

    A message box appears indicating the possible minimum and maximum sizes for a new primary partition.

3. In the Create Primary Partition dialog box, enter the size of the partition you want to create and choose OK.

To create an extended partition using the Disk Administrator, follow these steps:

1. Select an area of free space on a disk.

2. Choose Partition, Create Extended.

    A message box appears indicating the possible minimum and maximum sizes for a new extended partition.

3. In the Create Extended dialog box, enter the size of the extended partition you want to create and choose OK.

To create a logical drive within an extended partition, select the extended partition and choose Partition, Create.

To create a volume set using the Disk Administrator, follow these steps:

1. Select the areas of free space you want to include with a volume set.

2. Choose Partition, Create Volume Set.

    A message box appears indicating the possible minimum and maximum sizes for a new extended partition.

3. In the Create Volume Set dialog box, enter the size of the volume set you want to create and choose OK.

After you create a volume set, you must format it before you can use it (NTFS and FAT are both supported). To format the new volume, you must save the changes by choosing Partition menu, Commit Changes Now, or by responding to the prompts when exiting the Disk Administrator. The only differences between configuring volume sets and ordinary partitions are as follows:

*   The system and boot partitions cannot be part of a volume set.

*   You can extend an NTFS volume set (but not a FAT volume set) by selecting the volume set in Disk Administrator and simultaneously selecting at least one area of free space (hold down the Ctrl key to select more than one area at a time). Choose the Partition, Extend Volume Set to get a chance to enter a new size for the volume set.

*   A volume set can be made up of two to 32 areas of disk space. More than one area can be used on a physical disk.

*   You can never shrink a volume set; after creating or extending it, it's set in stone. You can delete the entire volume set, but not any individual area within it.

If you choose to implement a volume set, be aware of the following drawbacks and dangers:

*   Only Windows NT supports volume sets; if you're booting between Windows NT and Windows 95, MS-DOS, or another operating system, your volume set is inaccessible if Windows NT isn't active.

*   Your volume set will break because all drives fail sooner or later, and combining free space from multiple drives increases the chances of a disaster.

To extend a volume set, both the existing set and the volume you're adding must be formatted with NTFS. To extend a volume set using the Disk Administrator, follow these steps:

1. Select an NTFS volume, and then select the area(s) of free space you want to add. (Hold down the Ctrl key while you select the areas of free space.)

2. Choose Partition, Extend Volume Set.

   A dialog box appears indicating the possible minimum and maximum sizes for the creation of an extended partition.

3. In the Create Extended Volume Set dialog box, enter the total size for the volume and choose OK.

C. Creating Stripe Sets

Stripe sets differ from volume sets in that the free space areas must all be equally sized areas from 2 to 32 physical disks.

Data is read from and written to the stripe set in 64 KB blocks, disk by disk, row by row. If multiple controllers service your stripe set, or if your single controller can perform concurrent I/O requests, you can improve performance dramatically because you can then use multiple drives simultaneously. Be careful, however—not only do the same dangers apply to stripe sets as apply to volume sets, the potential disaster is even more dire. If any single member of a stripe set fails, the entire volume becomes inaccessible to the point that—because your data is contiguous only for 64 KB at a time—not even a disk editor can help you. Windows NT Server has a more robust method of improving performance while maintaining fault tolerance, called stripe sets with parity. Use a stripe set with parity if you really want the performance boost from striping.

If you're using Windows NT Workstation rather than Server, you don't have that option, but you can go with a hardware implementation of striping that offers some method of parity maintenance. This fault tolerant technology is called Redundant Array of Inexpensive Disks (RAID).

The same rules apply for both stripe sets and volume sets—no limits on drive types, no limit for the file system, and no system and boot partitions. You cannot extend a stripe set the way you can volume sets, however, and you cannot shrink one either.

> **A stripe set can support IDE, EIDE, and SCSI drive types.**

When creating a stripe set, the space on each disk must be the same size. To create a stripe set using the Disk Administrator, follow these steps:

1. Select at least two areas of free space on different hard drives.

2. Choose Partition, Create Stripe Set.

   A dialog box appears indicating the possible minimum and maximum sizes for the creation of an extended partition.

3. In the Create Stripe Set dialog box, enter the total size of the stripe set you want to create and choose OK.

As with a volume set, you must format the stripe set before you can use it.

D. Marking Partitions as Active

On a disk(s) using a Windows NT computer, the areas that contain the startup files are called the system and boot partitions.

The system partition contains the boot files, and the boot partition contains the system and support files. These notations appear backwards by conventional terminology, but they accurately describe Windows NT.

With an I386 computer, the system partition is located on the first disk, is marked active, and is designated as the primary partition. You can have only one active partition at a time. To boot between multiple operating systems, you must set the partition as active before restarting the computer.

On RISC-based systems, hard disks aren't marked as active; rather, a manufacturer-supplied hardware configuration utility controls them. To mark a partition as active using the Disk Administrator, follow these steps:

1. Select a primary partition that contains startup files for a particular OS you want to make active.

2. Choose Partition, Mark Active.

    A dialog box appears indicating that the new partition is active and will be used on startup.

3. Choose OK in the Disk Administrator dialog box.

Notice the asterisk that now appears in the color bar of the new active partition.

E. Committing Changes

After you create a partition, you may format it from within Disk Administrator, but only if you choose Partition, Commit Changes Now. Until you commit changes, your commands aren't actually carried out, so you can change your mind if necessary.

F. Deleting Partitions

You can delete any partition except for the system and boot partitions (and you can't delete those because Windows NT is using them) from Disk Administrator. Simply select the partition you want to delete, then choose Partition, Delete. Confirm your action to officially remove the partition from the interface. Again, until you commit changes, nothing officially happens.

G. Saving and Restoring Configuration Information

The Configuration command on Disk Administrator's Partition menu enables you to save or restore a disk configuration using a floppy disk. You can save the disk configuration to a blank floppy, a floppy with a previous disk configuration, or an emergency repair disk.

Microsoft recommends that you save a copy of your disk configuration before upgrading Windows NT. The Configuration Restore option restores a saved disk configuration from a floppy.

Both the Restore and Search options come with a warning that you are about to overwrite your disk configuration. The Restore and Search operations don't create or delete partitions, but they do affect drive letters, volume sets, stripe sets, parity stripes, and mirrors.

H. Using Other Disk Administrator Options

The Disk Administrator Tools menu provides some options for further defining and protecting hard disks.

1. Format

A hard disk is divided into logical sections that enable a disk to locate data in a systematic fashion. This process is called formatting. To format a partition using the Disk Administrator, follow these steps:

1. Select the newly created partition you want to format.

2. Choose Partition, Commit Changes Now. Click on Yes to save the changes.

3. Choose Tools, Format.

4. In the Format dialog box, enter the volume label to identify the partition.

5. Select the type of file system to use, and then choose OK.

    If you enable the Quick Format check box, the Disk Administrator doesn't scan for bad sectors during the format process. This option isn't available when you format mirror sets or stripe sets with parity.

6. Choose Yes from the Confirmation dialog box to begin the process.

You also can format partitions from the command prompt using this syntax:

```
FORMAT <drive_letter>: /FS:FAT[vb]NTFS
```

2. Assigning a Drive Letter

Normally, Windows NT assigns drive letters starting with the first primary partition on the first physical drive, followed by the logical drives, and finally the remaining primary partitions. After Disk 0 is complete, Windows NT begins assigning drive letters to the partitions on the next physical drive in the same fashion.

If you want to override the normal drive-naming algorithm, choose Tools, Assign Drive Letter. You may change the drive designation to any other unused letter, or you may simply remove the drive letter altogether. The latter option may seem of dubious value, but it allows an administrator to "hide" a partition and its files by not providing the computer a "handle." To change a drive letter using the Disk Administrator, follow these steps:

1. Select the partition or logical drive that you want to assign a drive letter.

2. Choose Tools, Assign Drive Letter.

    A message box appears indicating the remaining drive letters for assignment.

3. In the Assign Drive Letter dialog box, select the letter to use and choose OK.

3. Properties

If you click on a volume and choose Tools, Properties, the Volume Properties dialog box appears. (The Volume Properties dialog box is the same dialog box that will appear if you right-click on the disk in Explorer and choose Properties.)

To check for disk problems from Disk Administrator, select the partition you want to check, choose Tools, Properties, and select the Tools tab from the Properties dialog box. Click on the Check Now button to open the Check Disk dialog box, which offers the following options:

- Automatically fix file system errors
- Scan for and attempt recovery of bad sectors

Choose either or both options and click on the Start button to begin checking the partition.

I. Fault Tolerance

Fundamentally, fault tolerance is the system's ability to recover in the event of hardware disaster.

The standard for fault tolerance is known as Redundant Array of Inexpensive Disks (RAID). The two RAID fault-tolerance methods available with Windows NT are as follows:

- Disk Mirroring
- Disk Striping with Parity

1. Creating a Mirror

Disk mirroring is a RAID level 1 fault tolerance method. A mirror is a redundant copy of another disk partition, and it uses the same or a different hard disk controller. To create a mirror using the Disk Administrator, follow these steps:

1. Select at least two areas of free space on different hard drives or you may select an existing partition on one physical disk and an area of free space of equal or greater size on another physical disk.

2. Choose Fault Tolerance, Establish Mirror.

The Disk Administrator then creates spaces of equal size on both disks and assigns a drive letter to them.

2. Creating a Stripe Set with Parity

A stripe set with parity is considered RAID 5. A stripe set with parity ensures fault tolerance because the data is written to 2 to 32 physical disks in 64K segments with parity information written to each drive in rotation. The parity information that spans all drives regenerates data if a drive fails.

To create a stripe set with parity, follow these steps:

1. Select between 3 and 32 areas of free disk space on separate physical disks.

2. Choose Fault Tolerance, Create Stripe Set with Parity.

   A dialog box appears indicating the possible minimum and maximum sizes for a new extended partition.

3. In the Create Stripe Set with Parity dialog box, enter the size of the stripe set to create and choose OK.

The Disk Administrator calculates the stripe set with parity's total size, based on the number of disks selected, and creates a space that is equal on each disk.

As you must with other new volumes, you must format the stripe set before it can be used. To format the new volume, save the changes by choosing Partition, Commit Changes Now or answer the prompts when exiting the Disk Administrator. You also must restart the system before formatting.

J. Securing System Partition on RISC Machines

The system partition on a RISC computer must be a FAT partition. Because Windows NT cannot provide the same security for a FAT partition that it provides for an NTFS partition, the RISC version of Windows NT includes a special Secure System Partition command that provides an extra layer of security for RISC-based system partitions.

2.8.1 Exercise: Creating a Partition

This exercise requires free space on a fixed disk. To format a partition using the Disk Administrator, follow these steps:

1. Select the newly created partition you want to format.

2. Choose Partition, Commit Changes Now. Click on Yes to save the changes.

3. Choose Tools, Format.

4. In the Format dialog box, enter the volume label to identify the partition.

5. Select the type of file system to use, then choose OK.

    If you enable the Quick Format check box, the Disk Administrator doesn't scan for bad sectors during the format process. This option isn't available when you format mirror sets or stripe sets with parity.

6. Choose Yes from the Confirmation dialog box to begin the process.

You also can format partitions from the command prompt using this syntax:

```
FORMAT <drive_letter>: /FS:FAT[vb]NTFS
```

2.8   Practice Problems

1. You would like to add a partition to your NT Server. To do this you must use what utility?

   A. FDISK

   B. Server Manager

   C. Disk Administrator

   D. CHECKDISK

2. To add a partition to NT Server you must be logged on as what?

   A. A member of the Power Users Group

   B. A member of the Administrators Group

   C. A member of the server Operators group

   D. A member of the Domain Users group

3. The first time you start Disk Administrator you receive a message telling you that Disk Administrator will be writing a signature to the disk. What does this mean?

   A. This allows NT to access the FAT file system on the active partition.

   B. This allows NT to have complete access beyond any security set on the system.

   C. This writes a 32-bit signature that identifies the disk as the original.

   D. This writes a 16-bit signature that identifies the disk as the original so NT can boot up through real mode phases into protected mode.

4. Which of the following can be created in Disk Administrator for NT Workstation?

   A. Stripe sets

   B. Stripe sets with parity

   C. Fat extended volume sets

   D. Mirror sets

5. Which of the following can be created in Disk Administrator for NT Server? (Choose all that apply.)

   A. Stripe sets

   B. Stripe sets with parity

   C. Fat extended volume sets

   D. Mirror sets

6. How many primary partitions can you create in Windows NT on one physical drive?

   A. 1

   B. 2

   C. 3

   D. 4

7. What types of file systems are you allowed to format with NT 4? (Choose all that apply.)

   A. NTFS

   B. HPFS

   C. FAT

   D. FAT32

8. You have created a new partition in Windows NT but you cannot see the partition when you reboot to DOS. What is the likely cause of the problem?

   A. You have formatted the partition with FAT32.

   B. You have formatted the partition with NTFS.

   C. Your BIOS has 1024 cylinder limit so your drive is not completely accessible through DOS.

   D. You are not logged on as Administrator.

9. You have just created a new partition but the format command is grayed out in Disk Administrator. What must you do to format the drive?

A. Reboot the machine.

B. Use the convert.exe command.

C. Commit changes now.

D. Format the drive from a DOS prompt.

10. You would like to delete a partition, but when you press Delete on the keyboard, nothing happens to the selected partition. How can you remove the partition from your system?

A. The Delete Key does not work on the keyboard; you must use the Delete command from the Partition menu.

B. You are not logged on as administrator. Only an Administrator can delete partitions.

C. You must commit changes first and then delete the partition

D. You must use the DelPart utility.

11. You would like to extend a volume set that you created and formatted. However, the command to extend the volume set is grayed out. Why can't you extend the volume set?

A. You do not have administrative rights.

B. Items on the volume set are currently in use.

C. The volume set must be formatted with NTFS to be extended.

D. You cannot extend any volume set on NT.

12. You would like to create a volume set. What is the minimum areas of free disk space required?

A. 1

B. 2

C. 3

D. 4

13. You would like to create a volume set. What is the maximum areas of free disk space allowed?

A. 4

B. 8

C. 12

D. 32

14. You would like to create a stripe set. What is the minimum number of hard disks required?

A. 1

B. 2

C. 3

D. 4

15. You would like to create a stripe set. What is the maximum number of hard disks allowed?

A. 4

B. 8

C. 12

D. 32

16. How can stripe sets be dangerous to data?

A. Data can become corrupted easier on the drives.

B. The FAT table cannot keep track of data files larger than 1 GB.

C. There is no fault tolerance on the stripe sets.

D. Stripe sets cannot be backed up by most backup software.

17. You have four hard disks that are configured as follows: Disk 0 has 400 MB of free space; Disk 1 has 150 MB of free space; Disk 2 has 500 MB of free space; and Disk 3 has 200 MB of free space. What is the largest stripe set you can create using any combination of hard disks?

2

A. 600 MB

B. 800 MB

C. 1350 MB

D. You cannot make a stripe set as you need 32 drives to make a stripe set.

18. Data is read and written to the stripe set in what size?

    A. 4 KB

    B. 16 KB

    C. 32 KB

    D. 64 KB

19. A colleague is trying to create a stripe set. He is using IDE, SCSI, and SyQuest drives. He is not allowed to create the stripe. Why not?

    A. All drives must be SCSI.

    B. All drives must be IDE.

    C. You cannot include removable media in stripe sets.

    D. Your colleague is not an administrator.

20. In Disk Administrator you can tell which partition is currently active in what way?

    A. Choosing Partition to Find Active...

    B. Choosing Tool to Find Active...

    C. Looking for the Asterisk in the title bar of the active partition.

    D. Looking for partition that reads 1381 on the title bar.

21. You and a colleague are making several changes to your hard disk configuration. As a safety method, you would like to save your current configuration before you begin. How can you do this?

    A. Run the rdisk utility.

    B. Save the registry file to floppy.

    C. Choose export configuration from the Partition menu.

D. Copy the Clone directory of the registry to a floppy.

22. You would like to change the drive letter of the CD-ROM drive to W. How can you do this in Disk Administrator?

    A. Choose Partition, change drive letter.

    B. Choose Tools, change drive letter.

    C. Choose Partition, Properties, Advanced, change drive letter.

    D. You cannot change drive letters in Disk Administrator, they can only be changed through Computer policies.

23. You would like to create a mirror set on NT Workstation. How can this be done with Disk Administrator?

    A. Choose Fault Tolerance, create mirror set.

    B. Choose Partition, create mirror set.

    C. Choose Partition, properties, Advance, mirror set.

    D. This cannot be done on Workstation.

24. What is the maximum number of drives that can be in a mirror set?

    A. 1

    B. 2

    C. 3

    D. 4

25. Which are attributes of a mirror set? (Choose all the apply.)

    A. Areas of two separate drives must be of equal size.

    B. You cannot mirror the system or boot partition.

    C. You can mirror the system and boot partition.

    D. You can create mirror sets only on Disk Administrator.

26. You would like to create a stripe set with parity on your NT Workstation. How can this be done?

    A. Choose Fault Tolerance, create stripe set.

    B. Choose Partition, create stripe set.

    C. Choose Partition, properties, Advance, stripe set.

    D. This cannot be done on Workstation.

27. Your machine is configured as follows: Disk 0 has 150 MB of free space; Disk 1 has 300 MB of free space; Disk 2 has has 500 MB of free space; Disk 3 has 650 MB of free space. What is the largest stripe set with parity you can create using any combination of disks?

    A. 800 MB

    B. 900 MB

    C. 1000 MB

    D. 1,650 MB

28. With the answer from the above question, what is the total area of hard disk space used for parity?

    A. 150 MB

    B. 300 MB

    C. 600 MB

    D. 900 MB

29. How do you mark a partition as Active on a RISC based machine?

    A. Choose Partition, mark as active.

    B. Choose Tools, mark as active.

    C. Choose the partition area, and press Shift+F5.

    D. You do not mark partitions as active on RISC machines.

2.8 Answers and Explanations: Practice Problems

1. **C**   Use Disk Administrator to add a partition to your NT Server.

2. **B**   To add a partition to NT Server, you must be logged on as a member of the Administrators local Group.

3. **C**   The message telling you that Disk Administrator will be writing a signature to the disk means that this writes a 32-bit signature that identifies the disk as the original.

4. **A**   Stripe Sets can be created in Disk Administrator for NT Workstation.

5. **A, B, D**   Stripe sets, stripe sets with parity, and mirror sets can be created in Disk Administrator for NT Server.

6. **D**   You can create four primary partitions in Windows NT on one physical drive.

7. **A, C**   NT allows both NTFS and FAT file systems.

8. **B**   If you cannot see a newly created partition when you reboot to DOS, you probably have formatted the partition with NTFS. NTFS partitions are not accessible through any OS other than NT.

9. **C**   To format a new partition, choose Commit changes now from the Partition menu.

10. **A**   To delete a partition, you must use the Delete command from the Partition menu. The Delete key doesn't work.

11. **C**   The volume set must be formatted with NTFS to be extended.

12. **B**   The minimum areas of free disk space required to create a volume set is two.

13. **D**   The maximum areas of free disk space allowed to create a volume set is 32.

14. **B**   Two hard disks are required for a stripe set.

15. **D**   The maximum number of hard disks allowed to create a stripe set is 32.

16. **C**   Stripe sets can be dangerous to data because there is no fault tolerance on them.

17. **B**   800 MB is the largest stripe set you can create. Use the 400 MB on Drive 0, plus 400 from Disk 2.

18. **D**   Data is read and written to the stripe set in 64 KB sizes.

19. **C**   You cannot include removable media in stripe sets

20. **C**   To tell which partition is currently active in Disk Administrator, look for the asterisk in the title bar of the active partition.

21. **C**   To save your current hard disk configuration, choose Export Configuration from the Partition menu.

22. **B**   Choose Tools, Change Drive Letter to change the drive letter of the CD-ROM drive in Disk Administrator.

23. **D**   This cannot be done on Workstation.

24. **B**   The maximum number of drives in a mirror set is two.

25. **A, C, D**   You can use a mirror set to mirror the system or boot partitions.

26. **D**   You cannot create a stripe set with parity on your NT Workstation.

27. **D**   900 MB. Because three drives are required with stripe sets with parity, you can use the 300 MB from Disk 1, 2, 3 for a total of 900 MB.

28. **B**   300 MB, because three drives are the equivalent of one drive and will be devoted to parity information.

29. **D**   You do not mark drives as active on RISC based machines.

2.8   Key Words

Partitioning

Disk Administrator

Stripe set

Stripe sets with parity

Mirror sets

Volume sets

RAID

Boot partition

System partition

2.9   Configuring Printing

In Windows NT the term printer refers to the software that controls a specific printing device or devices.

Windows NT uses the term printing device to refer to the hardware that produces the actual output. Windows NT also uses the term print queue, but in NT, a print queue is simply the list (queue) of documents waiting to print.

A.   Windows NT Printing Architecture

You should become familiar with the components of the Windows NT printing process for the MCSE exam. The process goes roughly as follows:

1. When an application on an NT client sends a print job, Windows NT checks to see if the version of the printer driver on the client is up-to-date with the version on the print server. If it isn't, Windows NT downloads a new version of the printer driver from the print server to the client.

2. The printer driver sends the data to the client spooler. The client spooler spools the data to a file, and makes a remote procedure call to the server spooler, thus transmitting the data to the server spooler on the print server machine.

3. The server spooler sends the data to the Local Print Provider.

4. The Local Print Provider passes the data to a print processor, where it's rendered into a format legible to the printing device. Then, if necessary, the Local Print Provider sends the data to a separator page processor, where a separator page is added to the beginning of the document. The Local Print Provider lastly passes the rendered data to the print monitor.

5. The print monitor points the rendered data to the appropriate printer port and, therefore, to the appropriate printing device.

1. Printer Drivers

In the first step of the printing process, Windows NT checks to see if the printer driver on the print client is current; if it isn't, Windows NT downloads a new copy of the printer driver from the print server.

When you set up a Windows NT printer, the Setup wizard asks for the operating systems and hardware platforms of all client machines that are going to access the printer. The wizard then places the appropriate printer drivers on the server so they will be available for downloading.

The Windows NT printer driver is implemented as a combination of two dynamic link libraries (or DLLs) and a printer-specific minidriver or configuration file.

Typically, Microsoft supplies the two dynamic link libraries with Windows NT, and the original equipment manufacturer of the printer supplies the minidriver or configuration file. The following list describes these three files:

- The Printer Graphics Driver DLL. This dynamic link library consists of the rendering or managing portion of the driver; it's always called by the Graphics Device Interface.

- The Printer Interface Driver. This dynamic link library consists of the user interface or configuration management portion of the printer driver; it's used by an administrator to configure a printer.

- The Characterization File. This component contains all the printer-specific information, such as memory, page protection, soft fonts, graphics resolution, paper orientation and size, and so on; it's used by the other two dynamic link libraries whenever they need to gather printer-specific information.

These three components of a printer driver (printer graphics driver, printer interface driver, and configuration file) are all located in the following directory, according to their Windows NT platforms (w32x86, w32mips, w32alpha, and w32ppc) and version numbers (0 = version 3.1, 1 = version 3.5x, 2 = version 4.x):

```
winnt_root\system32\spool\drivers.directory
```

The printer driver is specific to both the operating system and the hardware platform.

2. Spooler

The Spooler is a Windows NT service that operates in the background to manage the printing process.

The NT Spooler service must be running on both the client and the print server machines for the printing process to function properly. By default, the spool file folder is the winnt_root\system32\spool\PRINTERS directory. You can change the spool folder by using the Advanced tab of the printer server Properties dialog box.

In the event that a print job gets stuck in the spooler to the point that an administrator or print operator cannot delete or purge it, you can stop the Spooler service and restart it using the Control Panel Service application.

You also can start or stop the Spooler service using the following commands at the command prompt:

```
net start spooler
net stop spooler
```

3. Router

The print router receives the print job from the spooler and routes it to the appropriate print processor.

4. The Print Processor

The process of translating print data into a form that a printing device can read is called rendering. The rendering process begins with the printer driver. The print processor is responsible for completing the rendering process. The tasks performed by the print processor differ depending on the print data's data type. The primary Windows NT print processor is called WINPRINT.DLL, and is located in

```
winnt_root\system32\spool\prtprocs\platform
```

WINPRINT.DLL recognizes the following data types:

- Raw data. Fully rendered data that is ready for the printer.

- Windows NT Enhanced Metafile (EMF). A standard file format that many different printing devices support. Instead of the raw printer data being generated by the printer driver, the Graphical Device Interface generates NT EMF information before spooling. After the NT EMF is created, control returns to the user.

- TEXT. Raw text with minimal formatting. The TEXT data type is designed for printing devices that don't directly accept ASCII text.

5. Print Monitors

Print Monitors control access to a specific device, monitor the status of the device, and communicate this information back to the spooler, which relays the information via the user interface.

To install a new print monitor, click on Add Port in the Ports tab of the printer Properties dialog box. Click on the New Monitor button in the Printer Ports dialog box that appears. In addition, the print monitor has the following duties:

- Detect unsolicited errors (such as Toner Low).

- Handle true end-of-job notification. The print monitor waits until the last page has been printed to notify the spooler that the print job has finished and can be discarded.

- Monitor printer status to detect printing errors. If necessary, the print monitor notifies the spooler so that the job can continue or be restarted.

Windows NT provides some standard print monitors. These include print monitors for the following:

- Local output to LPTx, COMx, remote printer shares and names pipes (\WINNT_ROOT\SYSTEM32\LOCALMON.DLL).

- Output to Hewlett-Packard network interface printing devices (\WINNT_ROOT\SYSTEM32\HPMON.DLL), which can support up to 225 (configured for 64) Hewlett-Packard network interface printing devices. This print monitor requires the DLC protocol.

- Output to Digital network port printers (DECPSMON.DLL), supporting both TCP/IP and DECnet protocols. The DECnet protocol doesn't ship with Windows NT.

- Output to LPR (Line Printer) Ports (LPRMON.DLL), allowing Windows NT to print directly to UNIX LPD print servers or network interface printing devices over the TCP/IP protocol.

- Output to PJL Language printing device (PJLMON.DLL).

- Output to Apple Macintosh postscript printers (SFMMON.DLL), for Windows NT servers with services for the Apple Macintosh installed.

B. Printers Folder

The Printers folder is the Windows NT printing system's primary user interface. From the Printers folder, you install, configure, administer, and remove printers. You also supervise print queues; pause, purge and restart print jobs; share printers; and set printer defaults.

You can install printers on your Windows NT workstation in two ways: install a printer on your own workstation, or connect to a remote printer. From the Printers folder, double-click on the Add Printer icon to open the Add Printer Wizard.

The first screen of the Add Printer Wizard asks if the new printer will be attached to your computer (the My Computer option) or connected to another machine and accessed via the network.

The My Computer option requires Administrator, Print Operator, Server Operator or Power User rights, whereas the Network printer server option does not; you don't have to be an Administrator or a Power User to connect to a shared printer on another machine.

C.   Adding a Printer on Your Own Machine

If you select the My Computer option from the Add Printer Wizard screen, and then click on Next, the Wizard asks you what port you want to use. The next screen asks you to specify the manufacturer and model of the new printer.

The next screen asks for a printer name, and whether you want the printer to become the default printer for Windows-based programs. As with all objects in Windows NT, a printer requires a name. The printer name can be as long as 32 characters and doesn't have to reflect the name of the driver in use.

The next screen asks if you want to share the printer. If you want to share the printer with other computers on the network, you must also specify a share name (the default share name is the first eight characters of the printer name specified in the preceding screen). The wizard also asks you to specify the operating systems of all computers that will be sharing the printer. Your only choices are Windows 95 and a number of NT versions and platforms.

The Add Printer Wizard then attempts to install the printer driver. You may be asked to supply the Windows NT installation disk. (If you designate Windows 95 as the operating system of a computer sharing the printer, you may also be prompted to supply the location of the Windows 95 Printer INF files.) The wizard then asks if you want to print a test page.

D.   Adding a Network Print Server

If you choose the network printer server option in the first screen of the Add Printer Wizard, the Wizard opens the Connect to Printer dialog which asks for the name of the shared printer to which you want to connect.

The Wizard then asks if you want the printer to serve as a default printer, and completes the installation. If the installation is successful, the icon for the printer appears in the Printers folder.

Almost all the configuration settings for a printer in Windows NT 4 are accessible through following three options of the Printers folder File menu:

- Document Defaults
- Server Properties
- Properties

You also use the Sharing option in the File menu for configuration; specifically, to set up the printer as a shared printer on the network. It's actually just a different path to the Sharing tab of the Properties dialog box.

1. Document Defaults

Choose File, Document Defaults to open the Default Document Properties dialog box. The Default Document Properties dialog box contains document settings for the documents that are to print on the selected printer.

The Page Setup tab defines the Paper Size, Paper Source, and Orientation options for controlling settings for the document you want to print.

2. Server Properties

Choose File, Server Properties to open the Print Server Properties dialog box.

a. Forms

The Forms tab of the Print Server Properties dialog box defines the print forms available on the computer. Think of a print form as a description of a piece of paper that might be in a printer tray. A print form tells NT the size of the paper and where to put the printer margins. You can create your own print forms from within the Forms tab. To create your own form, follow these steps:

1. Click on an existing form in the Forms On list.
2. Select the Create a New Form check box.
3. Change the name of the form, and change the form measurements to the new settings.
4. Click on the Save Form button.

b. Ports

The Ports tab of the Printer Server Properties dialog box maintains a list of available ports. You can add, delete, or configure a port.

c. Advanced

The Advanced tab of the Printer Server Properties dialog box provides the location of the spooler and an assortment of logging and notification options.

3. Properties

You can find most of the printer configuration settings in the printer Properties dialog box. To open the printer Properties dialog box, select a printer in the Printers folder and choose File, Properties, or right-click on the printer and choose Properties.

a. The Printer Properties General Tab

The General tab lets you install a new driver for the printer. The Print Test Page button provides a convenient method for testing whether a printer connection is working.

b. Separator File

By default, Windows NT doesn't separate print jobs with even a blank sheet of paper; to print a separator page between print jobs, you must configure a separator file, of which three are included with Windows NT.

You may use one of these or create your own:

- SYSPRINT.SEP. Prints a separator page for PostScript printers; stored in the \<winnt_root>\SYSTEM32 directory.

- PSCRIPT.SEP. Switches Hewlett-Packard printers to PostScript mode for printers incapable of autoswitching; located in the \<winnt_root>\SYSTEM32 directory.

- PCL.SEP. Switches Hewlett-Packard printers to PCL mode for printers not capable of autoswitching (and prints a separator page before each document); located in the \<winnt_root>\SYSTEM32 directory.

You also may choose to design your own separator page. If so, use a text editor and consult the escape codes listed in table 2.1. The escape codes are special symbols that prompt Windows NT to replace them with specific pieces of data.

Table 2.9.1   Windows NT Printing Escape Codes

Code	Instruction for Windows NT
\<number>	Skip specified number of lines (0–9).
\B\M	Print text in double-width block mode.
\B\S	Print text in single-width block mode.
\D	Print current date using Control Panel International format.
\E	Eject the page.
\F<filename>	Print a file.
\H<code>	Send printer-specific hexadecimal ASCII code.
\I	Print job number.
\L<text>	Print the specified text (use another escape code to end).
\N	Print username of job owner.
\T	Print time the job was printed. Use Control Panel International format.
\U	Turn off block mode (see \B\M and \B\S).
\W<width>	Set width of the page (<=256).

c. Print Processor

The print processor is the component of the printing subsystem that actually performs the rendering. Typically, WINPRINT.DLL performs the print processor functions. If it becomes necessary to replace it, Windows NT does it for you.

WINPRINT.DLL supports the following five data types:

- Raw Fully rendered data ready for printing.

- RAW (FF appended).

- RAW (FF auto).

- NT EMF (enhanced metafile format) A device-independent file format. An EMF file can be spooled directly to the print server and rendered at the server into the correct print format.

- TEXT Raw, unformatted ASCII text ready for printing as is.

d. Printer Properties Ports Tab

The printer Properties Ports tab lets you select a port for the printer, and add or delete a port from the tab. The Configure Port button allows you to specify the Transmission Retry time (the amount of time that must elapse before NT notifies you that the printing device isn't responding). The Transmission Retry setting applies not just to printer you selected but to all printers that use the same driver.

e. Printer Properties Scheduling Tab

The printer Properties Scheduling tab lets you designate when the printer is to be available, and to set the printer priority. It also displays some miscellaneous settings that define how the printer processes print jobs. Table 2.9.2 describes the options in the Printer Properties Scheduling tab.

Table 2.9.2 Options in the Printer Properties Scheduling Tab

Option	Description
Available	The Available setting lets you limit the availability of a printer to a specific period of time.
Priority	The default priority for a printer is 1, but it can be set as high as 99. Changing this setting from its default of 1 is useful in situations in which you have more than one printer printing to the same printing device, in which case the printer with higher priority (99 being the highest) prints before printers of lower priority (1 being the lowest).
Spool Print Documents	If you spool print documents, the computer and the printer don't have to wait for each other.
Hold Mismatched Documents	In other Windows-based operating environments, improperly configured print jobs—a print job, for example, requesting a paper tray that isn't present—can be sent to a printer, which usually causes the printer to hang with an error message. But with the Hold Mismatched Documents option selected, Windows NT examines the configuration of both the print job and printer to make sure that they are in agreement before it sends the job.
Print Spooled Documents First	Ordinarily, Windows NT prints documents on a first-come, first-served basis; the document at the top of the queue prints before the documents below it. If the document at the top of the queue takes a long time to

continues

Table 2.9.2   Continued

Option	Description
	spool, and if the Job Prints While Spooling option isn't selected, you might want to enable the Print Spooled Documents First setting. Windows NT always prints the first available completely spooled print job.
Keep Post-Print Documents	Windows NT cleans up after itself as it finishes printing each job. If you enable the Keep documents after they have printed option, however, Windows NT keeps the print document after it prints.

> Under the Spool print documents option, there are two other options:
> - **Start printing after the last page is spooled.**
> - **Start printing immediately.**

f. The Printer Properties Sharing Tab

The Sharing tab lets you share the printer with other computers on the network. To share a printer, follow these steps:

1. Select Sharing tab in the printer Properties dialog box.

2. Specify a share name (or accept the default, which is the first eight characters of the printer name).

3. Specify what operating systems the other workstations will be using (so NT can automatically download the necessary print drivers to the connecting computers).

4. Click on OK.

You access the Sharing tab directly by clicking on a printer and choosing File, Sharing in the Printers folder, or by right-clicking on a printer and choosing Sharing.

g. The Printer Properties Security Tab

The Security tab lets you configure permissions, auditing, and ownership for the printer

Windows NT printers are Windows NT resources, and Windows NT resources are Windows NT objects. Windows NT objects are protected by the Windows NT security model. To set or change permissions, a user must be the owner, an Administrator, a Power User, a Server Operator, a Print Operator, or a user who has Full Control permissions on the printer's ACL.

The four possible permission levels are as follows:

- No Access. Completely restricts access to the printer.
- Print. Allows a user or group to submit a print job, and to control the settings and print status for that job.

2

- Manage Documents. Allows a user or group to submit a print job, and to control the settings and print status for all print jobs.

- Full Control. Allows a user to submit a print job, and to control the settings and print status for all documents as well as for the printer itself. In addition, the user or group may share, stop sharing, change permissions for, and even delete the printer.

These permissions affect both local and remote users. By default, permissions on newly created printers comply with the following scheme:

Administrators	Full Control
Creator/Owner	Manage Documents
Everyone	Print
Power Users (workstations only)	Full Control
Print Operators (domain only)	Full Control
Server Operators (domain only)	Full Control

To change the permission level for a group, select the group in the Name list and enter a new permission level in the Type of Access combo box, or open the Type of Access combo box and select a permission level.

h. Printer Properties Device Settings Tab

The printer Properties Device Settings tab maintains settings for the printing device. These settings differ depending on your printing device.

> As you install a new printer, you can designate as a printer to share over the network.

E.   Setting Up a Printer Pool

A printer pool is essentially a single logical printer that prints to more than one printing device; it prints jobs sent to it to the first available printing device (and therefore provides the throughput of multiple printing devices with the simplicity of a single printer definition).

Printer pools are an extremely efficient way of streamlining the printing process, although they don't necessarily fit every environment. Before your network can use a printer pool, it must meet the following criteria:

- You must have at least two printing devices capable of using the same printer driver because the entire pool is treated as a single logical device, and is managed by a single printer driver.

- The printing devices should be adjacent to each other. Users aren't notified of the actual device that prints their job; users should be able to check all the printing devices rapidly and easily.

To create a printer pool, configure the printer to print to more than one port, and make sure a printing device is attached to each of the ports that the printer is using.

When creating a printer pool, it's essential to choose the ports in order of fastest to slowest speed, as that is the order the print jobs are routed through.

F. Printing from MS-DOS Applications

MS-DOS applications provide their own printer drivers and automatically render printer data to the RAW data type or to straight ASCII text.

The MS-DOS application typically isn't equipped to process UNC names, so if it is printing to a remote printer, you should map a physical port to the remote printer, as follows:

```
net use LPTx: \\pserver\printer_share_name
```

Because the application itself renders the printer data, an MS-DOS application that prints graphics and formatted text must have its own printer driver for the printing device. An MS-DOS application can print ASCII text output without a vendor-supplied printer driver.

2.10 Configuring Windows NT Server for Client Computers

The Windows NT CD-ROM includes client software to assist with networking certain common operating systems with Windows NT. Chapter 1 discusses some of the client software packages included with Windows NT Server. When you are configuring networking protocols on your Windows NT Server system, it is important to remember that all these software packages don't support all the native Windows NT network protocols and network services.

Table 2.10.1 describes which network protocols and which TCP/IP services each of the client systems supports. This table also appears in Chapter 1, in the section entitled "Choosing a Windows NT Network Protocol." You must ensure that the Windows NT configuration provides the appropriate protocols for whatever client systems you'll have running on your network. For more on these client systems, see Chapter 1.

Table 2.10.1   Network Protocol and TCP/IP Service Support for Various Windows NT Client Systems

Network Protocol TCP/IP Service

	Net-BEUI	Com-patible	Com-patible	TCP/IP	DLC	DHCP	WINS	DNS
Network Client for MS-DOS	X	X	IPX	X	X	X		
LAN MAN 2.2c for MS-DOS	X		IPX/SPX	X	X			
Lan MAN 2.2c for OS/2	X			X				
Windows 95	X		X	X		X	X	X
Windows NT Workstation	X		X	X	X	X	X	X

2.9 and 2.10   Practice Problems

1. What is the difference between a printer and a printing device?

    A. A Printer is where the document's final output is.

    B. A Printing device is where the document's final output is.

    C. A Printer refers to a shared queue.

    D. A Printing device refers to a shared queue.

2. What will NT do if you are printing a network printer and the local driver does not match the driver on the server?

    A. NT will generate error 5738—network printing error.

    B. NT will not respond and your job will not print out on the device.

    C. NT will download the driver from the server to the local machine.

    D. Your document will likely be printed as many pages of code.

3. The Windows NT component is largely responsible for printing is what?

    A. GDI

    B. ActiveX

    C. Preemptive threads

    D. I/O Manager

4. What is the spooler's primary job?

    A. To hold the print job until a printer is available

    B. To hold the print job until the application has relinquished control of the data

    C. To receive notifications from the printer that the job has been finished

    D. To transfer the print file from the local machine to a print server

5. What is the print processor's primary function?

    A. To render the job into a language the printing device can understand

    B. To forward jobs from the GDI to the print spooler service

    C. To handle threads from the spooler service

    D. To monitor all aspects of the print process

6. What is the print monitor's primary function?

    A. To allow user management of print job

    B. To point the data to the appropriate port so the job will be printed on the printing device

    C. To manage the flow of data between clients and servers

    D. To manage the creation of the EMF and RAW data during the print process

7. When you install a printer on Windows NT, why does it ask you what other Operating Systems will be connecting to the shared printer?

    A. For security reasons

    B. To create the NetBIOS share name

    C. To enable EMF printing over the network

    D. To install the drivers needed by those Operating Systems so that they can be downloaded from the server

8. What three components constitute a Windows NT print driver?

    A. The Graphics Driver DLL

    B. The Graphics Device Interface

    C. The Printer Interface Driver

    D. The Characterization File

9. What does the Graphics Driver DLL do?

    A. It handles all communication between the NT executive services and the hardware.

    B. It is the rendering and managing portion of the driver.

    C. It is the communication and query portion of the driver.

    D. It generates information from the printer device to the NT executive services.

10. What does the printer interface driver do?

    A. Handles all communication between the NT executive services and the hardware

    B. Handles the communication and query portion of the driver

    C. Generates information from the printer device to the NT executive services

    D. Handles the user interface and configuration management portion of the driver

11. What does the Characterization File do?

    A. Contains all printer specific information

    B. Manages all postscript and true type fonts

    C. Handles the processing of converting True Type fonts into bitmap images on the printer

    D. Manages postscript conversion to bitmap images for the printer

12. The spooler service does what?

    A. Sends data across the network to print servers

    B. Receives data from network interface printing devices

    C. Operates in the background to manage the printing process

    D. Receives true end of job notification

13. If a document will not print what can you do to resume printing?

    A. Reinstall the printer.

    B. Choose the stalled document individually and cancel the document.

    C. Choose Purge Print Jobs from the Printer menu.

    D. Restart the server.

14. If you have tried to purge the printer, but the document will not purge, what should you do next?

    A. Restart

    B. Reinstall NT server

    C. Reinstall the printer

    D. Stop and restart the spooler service

15. What two ways can you use to stop the spooler service?

    A. Reboot the server.

    B. Use Control Panel, Services.

    C. Use the net stop spooler command.

    D. Use the net stop services command.

16. The print router does what?

    A. Accepts print jobs and routes them to the appropriate print processor.

    B. Accepts print job from clients across WAN links.

    C. Routes job from a client machine to a network interface printing device.

    D. Routes job from a client machine to a shared printer.

17. The primary Windows NT print processor is called what?

    A. NTPRINT.DLL

    B. WINPRINT.DLL

    C. WINCOM.DLL

    D. NTWIN4.DLL

18. The advantage of using Enhanced Metafile Spooling is what?

    A. Faster printing on the printing device.

    B. Guaranteed updates of print drivers.

    C. Security.

    D. Returns control back to the application faster than RAW.

19. What are functions of a print monitor? (Choose all that apply.)

    A. Detects unsolicited error messages.

    B. Handles true end of job notification.

    C. Handles entries on the Access Control Lists with the Local Security Authority.

    D. Monitors printers for error messages.

20. What can you do from the printers folder in Windows NT?

    A. Install printers

    B. Configure Printers

    C. Administer printers

    D. Delete printers

21. The printer name in Windows NT can be how long?

    A. 255 character

    B. 254 characters

    C. 32 characters

    D. 15 characters

22. You are configuring a network printer. You would like to specify a new form for a printer. The page size is 8 inches by 10 inches. How can you create this in Windows NT?

    A. You must specify this in each application.

    B. You must use the Device Manager.

    C. Use the Forms tab on the Server Properties.

    D. Use the Advanced tab on the Server Properties.

23. Your company recently added an NT Server to your NT Workstation workgroup. During installation, you configured the server to be a Windows NT Server Primary Domain Controller (PDC). After installing the server, your NT Workstations can see the PDC in Network Neighborhood, however, the machines are still logging into a workgroup. What do you suspect is(are) the problem(s)? Choose all that apply:

    A. You have not created user accounts for your domain.

    B. You have not added the correct protocol on your PDC.

    C. You have not added computer accounts for the NT Workstations through Server Manager.

    D. You have not configured the NT Workstations to log into the domain.

24. Your company recently added an NT Server to your NT Workstation workgroup. During installation, you configured the server to be a Windows NT Server Primary Domain Controller (PDC). The protocol used on the server is TCP/IP. You have created all users and computer accounts on the server, however, when attempt to configure the NT Workstations to log into your domain, you are unsuccessful. What do you suspect is the problem? Choose the best answer:

    A. You do not have rights to add a computer to the domain.

    B. You do not have the TCP/IP installed on the workstations.

    C. Your Server needs service pack 3 to continue.

D. Your workstation must be rein-
stalled and then configured to log
onto the domain because workstations are not allowed to migrate
from workstations to domains with
reinstalling.

25. You would like your Windows 95 users to
log into your Windows NT domain.
How can this be accomplished?

A. You cannot do this unless you have
administrative rights.

B. You cannot do this unless you have
a computer account created for you
in the domain by the administrator.

C. Through Control Panel's Network
applet, and then configure File and
Print sharing for Microsoft Networks to log into the domain.

D. Through Control Panel's Network
applet, and then configure the
Client for Microsoft Networks to
log into the domain.

2.9 and 2.10 Answers and Explanations: Practice Problems

1. **B, A**   A printing device is where the
document's final output is.

2. **C**   NT will download the driver from
the server to the local machine.

3. **A**   GDI is largely responsible for
printing.

4. **D**   The spooler's primary job is to
transfer the print file from the local
machine to a print server.

5. **A**   The print processor's primary
function is to render the job into a
language the printing device can understand.

6. **B**   The print monitor's primary function
is to point the data to the appropriate
port so the job will be printed on the
printing device.

7. **D**   It asks what other operating systems
will be connecting to the shared printer in
order to install the drivers needed by
those operating systems so that they can
be downloaded from the server.

8. **A, C, D**   The three components that
constitute a Windows NT print driver are
the Graphics Driver DLL, the Printer
Interface Driver, and the Characterization
File.

9. **B**   It is the rendering and managing
portion of the driver.

10. **D**   It is the user interface and configuration management portion of the driver.

11. **A**   The Characterization File contains all
printer-specific information.

12. **C**   The spooler service is a service that
operates in the background to manage the
printing process.

13. **B**   Try to cancel the single document
first. If that does not work, then you
should try to purge all of the print jobs.

14. **D**   Stop and restart the spooler service.

15. **B, C**   Using Control Panel, Services and
using the net stop spooler command are
the two ways can stop the spooler service.

16. **A**   The print router accepts print jobs
and routes them to the appropriate print
processor.

17. **B**   The primary Windows NT print
processor is called WINPRINT.DLL.

18. **D**   Enhanced Metafile Spooling returns
control to the application faster than
RAW.

19. **A, B, D**   The print monitor detects
unsolicited error messages, handles true
end of job notification, and monitors
printers for error messages.

20. **A, B, C, D**   You can do all of the above
from the printers folder in Windows NT.

21. **C**   The printer name in Windows NT
can be 32 characters long.

22. **C** To create a new form for a printer, use the Forms tab on the server properties.

23. **A, C, D** You must create user accounts in User Manager for Domains; you must create computer accounts through Server Manager; and you must configure the NT Workstations to log into the domain.

24. **B** Your workstations cannot see the server because they do not have TCP/IP installed, or configured properly.

25. **D** The Client for Microsoft Networks must be configured to log into the domain.

2.9 and 2.10   Key Words

Printer

Printing device

Printer Graphics Driver DLL

Printer Interface Driver

Characterization File

Spooler service   client computer

Printer Pool   domain

Print Processor   PDC

Print Router

Practice Exam: Installation and Configuration

Use this practice exam to test you mastery of "Installation and Configuration." This practice exam is 20 questions long. The passing Microsoft score is 764 out of 1,000. There will be two types of questions:

- Multiple Choice—Select the correct answer.

- Multiple Multiple Choice—Select all answers that are correct.

1. You have installed NT Server and you are using the per seat licensing agreement. You have purchased 50 client access licenses. The server has reached 50 network connections; what will happen when the 51st person tries to connect? (Choose the best answer.)

   A. The person that has been connected the longest will be disconnected so that the new connection can be established.

   B. The person that has been idle the longest will be disconnected so that the new connection can be established.

   C. NT will evaluate users according to their SID to determine their ranking. The person with lowest network ranking will be disconnected so that the new connection can be established.

   D. The 51st user will not be allowed to connect.

2. You have decided to use per server licensing. Where in Server do you enter the registration numbers for the licensing agreements? (Choose the best answer.)

   A. Control Panel to Licensing

   B. Network Client Administrator

   C. Licenser Manager

   D. There is no requirement to add licensing numbers to NT

3. You have successfully installed Windows NT Server. However, when you go to logon as Administrator for the first time, you are not allowed to logon. You entered you password as "Gun-shy" but you still cannot logon. What could be wrong? (Choose the best answer:)

   A. Gun-shy is not a valid password for NT server.

   B. NT did not confirm your password as Gun-shy, so it substituted your password with the default of "password."

   C. Passwords are case-sensitive. Make certain that your caps lock is not on.

   D. You must logon as Admin instead of Administrator. Admin is the initial administrative account. Administrator is a system account reserved for the OS.

4. You have designated NT to create an Emergency Repair Disk during install. What information is copied to this Emergency Repair Disk? (Choose the best answer.)

   A. A compressed version of the setup files.

   B. The contents of \REPAIR directory.

   C. The SID of the Administrative account.

   D. The Registry Editor.

5. Windows NT Server ships with the Internet Information Server. During setup, you choose not to install this component as part of the NT Server install. After setup, you decide that you would like to install IIS. How can you do this? (Choose the best answer.)

   A. Double-click on the Install IIS Icon on the desktop.

B. Run WINNT32 and choose to only install IIS.

C. Use the Add/remove programs applet in Control Panel.

D. Run IISSetup.exe from the NT Server CD ROM.

6. During the final phase of installation, setup asks for the date and time of your location. You realize that your state participates in daylight savings time and the time change will happen in two weeks. You want to save yourself the trouble of having to change the time in two weeks. What should you do? (Choose the best answer.)

A. Go ahead and change the time to match the daylight savings time in two weeks.

B. Use the option to account for daylight savings time.

C. Use the AT command to schedule a time change.

D. Reset the CMOS to update the time in military standards.

7. You have installed NT Server as a PDC. During installation, you asked that NT create an Emergency Repair Disk. When NT prompted you for a floppy, you inserted a floppy that contained a README.TXT file that you created for future reference. When setup was finished creating the Emergency Repair Disk, you noted that the README.TXT was no longer on the floppy. Why? (Choose the best answer.)

A. The Emergency Repair Disk deletes all files not marked as read only on the floppy.

B. No text files are allowed on the Emergency Repair Disk.

C. Setup formats the floppy before generating the Emergency Repair Disk.

D. All original files on the floppy are now marked as hidden.

8. Domain Controllers and member servers have the following in common. (Choose all that apply.)

A. May be RAS servers

B. May logon users to the domain

C. May have unlimited network connections

D. Offer Macintosh file and print services

9. You are the administrator for three domains. Each domain has a PDC, three BDCs, and five member servers. Your TEXAS domain needs another member server, whereas your UTAH domain doesn't really need one of their member servers. To move the member server from the UTAH domain to the TEXAS domain you must do what? (Choose the best answer.)

A. Reinstall NT Server 4.0

B. Add a computer account for the member server and tell it to join the TEXAS domain

C. Run the convert.exe program

D. Promote the member server to a BDC in the TEXAS domain

10. The install program for Windows NT Server is called WINNT.EXE. Where on the CD-ROM is this executable located? (Choose the best answer.)

A. At the root directory

B. In the \Admin\nettools directory

C. In the \i386 directory

D. In the \WINNT\setup directory

11. Where do you configure protocol bindings? (Choose the best answer.)

A. Control Panel, Add New Hardware

B. Control Panel, Devices

2

C. Network Protocol tab

D. Network Binding tab

12. You have an NT Workstation that not only shares out resources for TCP/IP clients, but also connects to resources on a NetWare server. What would be the most effective way to configure the bindings on this machine? (Choose the best answer.)

A. Disable the NWLink protocol on the server service, and disable the TCP/IP protocol on the workstation service.

B. Disable the NWLink protocol on the workstation service, and disable the TCP/IP protocol on the server service.

C. Disable the NWLink protocol on the server service only.

D. You cannot disable bindings on Window NT Workstation.

13. You are installing NT Server on an Intel-based machine. What protocol(s) is/are installed by default? (Choose all that apply.)

A. TCP/IP

B. TCP/IP, NetBEUI

C. TCP/IP, IPX/SPX

D. IPX/SPX

E. IPX/SPX, NetBEUI

14. An I/O address is what? (Choose the best answer.)

A. The electronic location of a device in the system.

B. The number assigned to a device to define the device in the system.

C. An area of memory used for file I/O.

D. A setting used to interrupt the I/O Manager to signify new data is available to be saved to the hard disk from the device's buffer.

15. You network is segmented into three parts. How is the list of resources from each segment replicated to all other segments? (Choose the best answer.)

A. Each segment has a master browser. The master browser for each segment sends its browse list to all other segments.

B. Each segment has a master browser. The master browser for each segment sends its browse list to the Domain Master Browser, which merges the list and then sends it to each of the segment master browsers.

C. Being segmented does not affect your browsing scheme. All machines send their resource lists to the Domain Master Browser.

D. You must use directory replication to force synchronization of browsers across WAN links.

16. You have added an UPS to your NT Server system. You would like to configure NT to run a batch file at shutdown. How can you do this?

A. Using the Execute Command File option in the UPS applet.

B. Using the Execute Command File option in the HKEY LOCAL MACHINE\HARDWARE/UPS setting in the registry.

C. Using the AT Scheduler.

D. Creating a UDF file for the UPS warning and identifying this UDF through the registry setting of HKEY LOCAL MACHINE\HARDWARE\UPS.

17. You would like to add an IDE CD-ROM device to your server, but you cannot find a setting to do this anywhere in Control Panel. You can add this device by:

A. Using the Add New Hardware Wizard.

B. Doing nothing. NTDETECT.COM will detect the device upon rebooting the machine.

C. Using the SCSI adapters applet in Control Panel.

D. Using the setup program that came with the new hardware.

18. What are attributes of a software-based stripe set with parity on Windows NT Server? (Choose all the apply.)

A. Requires between three and 32 hard disks.

B. You cannot stripe the boot or system partition.

C. You can stripe the boot or system partition.

D. Parity information is written across all drives in rotation.

19. How does Windows NT separate print jobs by default?

A. With a blank sheet of paper.

B. With a sheet of paper containing the name, date, and current document title.

C. With a sheet of paper containing the name, date, current document title, and number of pages.

D. NT does not separate print jobs.

20. The print processor does what?

A. Handles all threads of the printing process between the application in User mode and the Microkernel in Executive Services

B. Generates all threads of the printing process between the application in User mode and the Microkernel in Executive Services

C. Renders the job for the final destination

D. Handles true end-of-job notification

Answers and Explanations: Practice Exam

1. **D** The 51st user will not be allowed to connect. Administrators, however, will be allowed to override this restriction so that they can increase the number of network connections.

2. **D** All Client Access Licenses are done on the honor system.

3. **C** Passwords are case-sensitive.

4. **B** The contents of \REPAIR directory is copied to the Emergency Repair Disk.

5. **A** If you choose not to install the Internet Information Server during install, the Setup program will add the icon directly to your desktop.

6. **B** NT includes an option to account for daylight savings time.

7. **C** Setup formats the floppy to ensure validity of the floppy, and to make certain enough room is available on the floppy for the required files.

8. **A, C, D** NT Server, domain controllers, or member servers can be RAS servers, have unlimited network connections, and offer services for Macintosh.

9. **B** Member servers are allowed to migrate from domain to domain as long as they have a computer account in the domain to which they are migrating.

10. **C** Each platform, RISC or Intel, has a corresponding directory on the CD-ROM.

11. **D** You configure protocol bindings in the Network Binding tab.

12. **A** By disabling the NWLink protocol on the server service, only TCP/IP will be bound to that service. If you disable the TCP/IP on the workstation service, NWLink will be the only protocol used for that service.

2

13. **C** TCP/IP and IPX/SPX are the selected protocols by default on an NT server installation.

14. **A** An I/O address is the electronic location of a device in the system. It allows information sent to the device to be delivered.

15. **B** The list of resources from each segment is replicated to all other segments because each segment has a master browser. The master browser for each segment sends its browse list to the Domain Master Browser, which merges the list, and then sends the merged list back to each of the segment master browsers.

16. **A** Use the Execute Command File option in the UPS applet to configure NT to run a batch file at shutdown.

17. **C** Use the SCSI adapters applet in Control Panel to add an IDE CD-ROM device to your server.

18. **A, B, D** Your machine is configured as follows: Disk 0 has 200 MB of free space; Disk 1 has 300 MB of free space; Disk 2 has 500 MB of free space; and Disk 3 has 650 MB of free space.

19. **D** NT does not separate print jobs.

20. **C** Print Processor renders the job for the final destination.

CHAPTER 3

Managing Resources

This chapter helps you prepare for the "Managing Resources" section of Microsoft's Exam 70-67, "Implementing and Supporting Microsoft Windows NT Server 4.0." Microsoft provides the following objectives for the "Managing Resources" Section:

- Manage user and group accounts. Considerations include Managing Windows NT groups, managing Windows NT user rights, administering account policies, and auditing changes to the user account database.

- Create and manage policies and profiles for various situations. Policies and profiles include local user profiles, roaming user profiles, and system policies.

- Administer remote servers from various types of client computers. Client computer types include Windows 95 and Windows NT Workstation.

- Manage disk resources. Tasks include copying and moving files between file systems, creating and sharing resources, implementing permissions and security, and establishing file auditing.

3.1 Managing User and Group Accounts

Microsoft lists the following objective for the Windows NT Server exam: Manage user and group accounts.

Considerations include: managing Windows NT groups, managing Windows NT user rights, managing Windows NT account policies, and auditing changes to the user account database.

Windows NT users get their rights and permissions in either of two ways:

- They are explicitly assigned a right or permission through their accounts.

- They are members of a group that has a right or permission.

An administrator creates an account (maybe more than one) for each person who uses the system. When prompted by WinLogon, the user enters the username and password to log on. Windows NT then checks the user's credentials against the list of valid users and groups for each object to which he or she requests access.

A.   Users and Groups

Windows NT administrators can create two types of accounts:

User account	Belongs to one person only; rights and permissions assigned to user accounts affect only the person who uses the account to log on.
Group account	A collection of users that holds common rights and permissions by way of its association with the group. The number of people in a group is unlimited, and all members enjoy the rights and permissions assigned to the group.

In practice, a group is a vehicle for assigning rights and permissions to an individual user. If you determine that a certain group of users in your environment requires a specific set of rights and permissions, you can create a group that has those rights and permissions and add the users to the new group. It is important to note that there is no order of precedence among user and group accounts. No one group takes priority over any other group, and groups do not take priority over user accounts (or vice versa).

For management purposes, it is easier to use group accounts when assigning rights and permissions. First, it's cleaner: users can be members of as many groups as desired, and group names can be more descriptive than usernames. Second, it's simpler: if you need to give a user the right to back up files and directories, you can find a built-in group, called Backup Operators, specifically designed for that purpose. In fact, you rarely have to create a new group because Windows NT has built-in groups for almost anything anyone needs to do on the system.

Windows NT has three types of groups:

Local	Used to assign rights and permissions to resources on the local machine. Remember that these resources consist of drive space and printers on that specific computer. That local group exists only on that computer. This changes slightly at the domain level—a local group created on a domain controller (either PDC or BDC) appears on all domain controllers within that domain.
Global	A collection of user accounts within the domain. These global groups have no power by themselves—they must be assigned to local groups to gain access to the local resources. You use a global group as a container of users that you then can add to local groups.
Special	Generally used for internal system access to resources and permissions. Special groups cannot be added or deleted—they contain predefined sets of users.

When a Windows NT workstation becomes part of a domain, the built-in domain global groups (described later in this chapter) join the corresponding local groups in the workstation's local security database. Each user account in the domain database is a member of an appropriate global group. By nesting global groups in the local groups of individual machines, Windows NT provides users with seamless access to resources across the domain.

A global group must be a member of a local group, but a local group cannot be a member of a global group, nor can a global group be a member of another global group. A global group can contain only user accounts. A local group can contain user accounts and global groups, but putting users in local groups is not good domain management.

1. Built-In Local Groups on Domain Controllers

Windows NT domain controllers oversee eight built-in local groups and three built-in global groups. The Windows NT domain local groups are as follows:

- Administrators
- Users
- Guests
- Backup Operators
- Replicator
- Account Operators
- Print Operators
- Server Operators

a. Administrators

Administrators is the most powerful group. Because Administrators has complete control over the entire Windows NT environment, use caution when adding users to this group. If you are the administrator for a Windows NT machine, consider creating an ordinary user account as well for safety reasons. Use administrator-level accounts only when necessary. In the following situations, it is necessary to use administrator-level accounts:

- To create other administrator-level accounts
- To modify or delete users, regardless of who created them
- To manage the membership of built-in groups
- To unlock workstations, regardless of who locked them
- To format a hard disk
- To upgrade the operating system
- To back up or restore files and directories
- To change the security policies
- To connect to administrative shares

b. Users

By default, new accounts become members of the Users group. The Users group provides users everything needed to run applications safely and to manage their local environment—local to the user, that is, not the computer. Users can:

- Run applications
- Manage their own files and directories (but not share them)
- Use printers (but not manage them)
- Connect to other computers' directories and printers
- Save their settings in a personal profile

Assign the Users account unless you need to perform a task that only an administrator or power user has the right to do.

c. Guests

Because Windows NT Workstation requires accounts for anyone who accesses the system, you can use the relatively powerless Guest group (described later in this chapter) to allow limited access to users who don't possess an account on your computer. Because the default Guest account does not require a password, it poses a security risk. The extent of the access provided to the Guests group depends on how you implement it. If you are concerned about security, disable the Guest account.

d. Backup Operators

Members of the Backup Operators group have a singular purpose: to back up files and directories and to restore them later. Although standard users can back up and restore files to which they have been granted permissions, backup operators can override the security on resources, but only when using the NTBackup program.

Backup operators have the following rights:

- Back up and restore files
- Log on locally
- Shut down the server

e. Replicator

The Replicator group is a special group used by the Directory Replication Service. See Chapter 2, "Installation and Configuration," for information.

f. Account Operators

Account Operators group members can create, delete, and modify users, global groups, and local groups. However, they cannot modify the Administrators or Server Operators group.

g. Print Operators

Members of the Print Operators group waive the following rights:

- Create, manage, and delete print shares
- Log on locally
- Shut down the server

h. Server Operators

The Server Operators group has the power to administer primary and backup domain controllers. It can perform the following actions:

- Log on at servers
- Lock and unlock servers
- Backup and restore servers
- Shut down servers
- Manage network shares
- Format the server's hard disk

2. Built-In Global Groups on Domain Controllers

Windows NT domain controllers also oversee the following three global groups:

Domain Admins	Global group of administrator accounts. It is a member of the Administrators local group for the domain, and is, by default, a member of the local group for every computer in the domain running Windows NT Server or NT Workstation. A domain administrator, therefore, can perform administrative functions on local computers.
Domain Users	Global group of user-level accounts. During setup, the domain's Administrator account is part of the Domain Users global group. All new domain accounts are automatically added to the Domain Users group.
Domain Guests	Global group for users with guest-level accounts. The Domain Guest group is automatically a member of the domain's Guest group.

3. Built-In Special Groups on Windows NT Server

Windows NT Server computers have the following built-in special groups:

Creator/Owner	Includes the user account that created or took ownership of a resource.
Everyone	Automatically includes every user who accesses this computer, either locally or remotely.
Interactive	Includes the user who logs on locally to a machine.
Network	Contains all users connected to a shared resource over the network.

4. Built-In Groups on Workstations and Member Servers

Windows NT Server member servers (servers that are not domain controllers) and Windows NT Workstations have the following built-in local groups:

- Administrators
- Backup Operators
- Power Users
- Guests
- Replicator
- Users

The descriptions for these groups are the same as the descriptions for their domain-controller counterparts, except for the Power User group, which is not a built-in group on Windows NT domain controllers.

Power users have considerably more power than ordinary users, but not nearly the amount of control that an administrator has. Take care when using or giving out Power User accounts. They are ideal for the following types of tasks:

- Sharing (and revoking) directories on the network

- Creating, managing, and sharing printers

- Creating accounts (but not administrator-level)

- Modifying and deleting accounts (but only the accounts that the power user has created)

- Setting the date and time on the computer

- Creating common program groups

Power users cannot touch any of the security policies on a Windows NT system, and their powers are limited in scope. Use a Power User account rather than an Administrator account if you can accomplish what you need to as a power user.

Windows NT member servers and workstations don't control any global groups, because global groups can be created and administered only on domain controllers. Global groups nevertheless play an important part in assigning local rights and permissions to server and workstations resources.

5. Member Server and Workstation Accounts

Windows NT Server machines acting as member servers maintain local account databases and manage a set of local accounts and groups independent of any domain affiliations. To access a Windows NT system, a user must provide credentials even if that system is not attached to a domain, or even if it has never been attached to a domain. The local account information controls access to the machine's resources.

Domain users can access resources on server and workstation machines logged into the domain because (by default) each domain user is a member of the global group Domain Users, and the global group Domain Users is a member of the machine's local group Users. In the same way, domain administrators are part of the global group Domain Admins, which is part of the machine's local Administrator's group.

6. Hard-Coded Capabilities

So far, only the hard-coded characteristics (ones which cannot be modified) of the Windows NT built-in groups have been discussed. Users cannot, for example, share directories, and power users cannot be prevented from sharing directories (to which they have access, of course).

You cannot modify hard-coded capabilities, but you can change user rights. An administrator can grant or revoke a user right at any time. Only administrators have the hard-coded capability to manage this policy. At this point, it is important to clearly distinguish between user rights and resource permissions. *User rights* define what a user can and cannot do on the system. *Resource permissions* establish the scope where these rights can be used. In other words, user rights are stuff you can do, and resource permissions control where you can do it.

7. Built-In User Accounts

Groups are the center of power in Windows NT, but groups need members to have any effect at all. At least two accounts are created when you install Windows NT:

- Administrator

- Guest

a. Administrator

The Administrator account, the first account created during an installation, is a member of the Administrators group. The Administrator account is permanent—you cannot disable or delete it, although it might not be a bad idea to rename it for security purposes.

b. Guest

The Guest account is another permanent account. It is a member of the Guests group, but this affiliation can be changed. Like the Administrator account, the Guest account itself has no inherent power or lack thereof; it is the group membership for the account that establishes its scope.

You can disable the Guest account. You might want to disable the account if you are in a secure environment; otherwise, users who don't have an account on your system can log on as guests. At the very least, consider adding a password to the Guest account.

B.   User Manager for Domains

Windows NT Server includes this tool, which you can use to administer User and Group accounts. User Manager for Domains is similar to the User Manager tool available with Windows NT Workstation, but, whereas User Manager is primarily designed to oversee local Workstation accounts, User Manager for Domains includes additional features that enable it to manage accounts at the domain level and even interact with other domains.

To reach User Manager for Domains, choose Programs in the Start menu, choose Administrative Tools (Common), and then select User Manager for Domains.

> **User Manager for Domains enables you to administer any domain over which you have administrative rights. The Select Domain option in the User menu enables you to choose a different domain.**

User Manager for Domains enables you to:

- Create new user and group accounts.

- View and configure the properties of user and group accounts.

- Add and remove members.

- View and configure account policy restrictions.

- Add user rights to users and groups.

- Audit account-related events.

- Establish, view, and configure trust relationships.

You can find most administration and configuration options on the User and Options menus.

1. Creating a User

To create a new user account, choose the New User command in the User menu in User Manager for Domains. The New User dialog box opens.

Only two pieces of information are mandatory to create an account:

Username	The username is a short "handle" used to identify the user to the system. The name in the Username field must be unique. The username can be as long as 20 characters and is not case-sensitive—however, you cannot use the following characters: -"/\[]:;|=,+*?<>.
Password	The password is proof that the user account actually belongs to the person attempting to use it. The password entered in the Password field is case-sensitive and cannot exceed 14 characters. The Password field can also be left blank (although not recommended for obvious reasons). The password must be confirmed to make certain that you did not mistype a character.

The other parameters in this dialog box are optional but useful. These parameters are:

- **Full Name field:** The Full Name is a free text field that can be used for the full name, including spaces and initials, for a particular user. Having both a username and a full name enables users to log on quickly (using the username) but still be listed and available by their full name.

- **Description field:** This field is also free text. Use it to track the department to which a user belongs, or maybe a location or project team.

- **User Must Change Password at Next Logon field:** Because a new account has a preset password picked by the administrator, this option forces the user to change the password immediately after logging on the first time after setting this option. When the user attempts to log on, the message You are required to change your password at first logon appears. After the user dismisses the message, a Change Password dialog box appears.

- **User Cannot Change Password field:** Enabling this check box prevents users from making any change to their password at any time. You might want to use this for the Guest account and any other account that several people might share.

- **Password Never Expires field:** Enabling the Password Never Expires check box overrides any blanket password expiration date defined in the Account policy. Again, the Guest account is a likely candidate for this option.

- **Account Disabled field:** To turn off a specific account but not to remove it from the database, enable this check box. In general, you should disable rather than remove user accounts. If a person leaves the organization and then later returns, you can reactivate the account. If the user never returns, you can rename the account and reactivate it for the new person replacing the former user. All rights and permissions for the original user are transferred to the new user.

a. Advanced User Properties

Clicking on the six buttons at the bottom of the New User dialog box opens the following corresponding dialog boxes:

Groups	Add and remove group memberships for the account.
Profile	Add a user profile path, a logon script name, and a home directory path to the user's environment profile.
Hours	Define specific times when the users can access the account. (The default is always.)
Logon To	Specify the workstations to which the user can log on. (The default is all workstations.)
Account	Provide an expiration date for the account. (The default is never.) You also can specify the account as global (for regular users in this domain) or local.
Dialin	Specify that the user can access the account via a dial-up connection. You also can assign call back Properties.

Don't confuse a domain local account with a local group membership or a local account on a workstation. A domain local account is designed to enable individual users from untrusted domains to access to this domain. Unless a domain local account is explicitly granted logon permission, the user must log on normally to a workgroup or domain where he or she has a valid account and then connect to the domain controller that is home to the domain local account.

b. User Environment Profiles

The Profile button invokes the User Environment Profile dialog box, where you can specify the following important user settings:

- User profile path
- Logon script name
- Home directory

Figure 3.1.1 shows how the User Environment Profile dialog box for a new user account can be filled in.

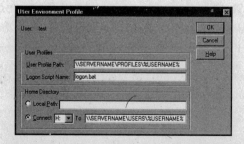

Figure 3.1.1   The User Environment Profile dialog box.

The User Profiles section of the User Environment Profile dialog box enables you to specify the user profile path and the logon script name. The user profile path is for cases in which a roaming or mandatory profile for the user will reside on another computer (as shown for this user in fig. 3.1.1). If the user will log on to both Windows NT 3.x and Windows NT 4 computers, include the user profile file name in the user profile path. If the user will use only a computer running Windows NT 4, the user profile path should point to the user profile directory and should not include the file name. If the directory does not exist, Windows NT creates it when the roaming profile is created, but note that the local machine must have access to the roaming profile directory by way of a network share.

The Logon Script Name text box enables you to specify a logon script for the user. *Logon scripts* are CMD or BAT files that contain a series of valid Windows NT commands. A logon script might re-establish a series of network drive connections or display a welcome message. Notice that the dialog box asks only for the name, not the full path. Windows NT already has a directory for logon scripts, but it is buried pretty deep:

```
<winnt_root>\SYSTEM32\REPL\IMPORT\SCRIPTS
```

The Home Directory section of this dialog box is used whenever a user opens or saves a file in an application, or when the user opens a command prompt window. The default home directory is \USERS\DEFAULT; if a workstation will support more than one user, consider establishing separate home directories for each user. Note that users are not restricted to or from these home directories (unless you establish that security separately); this is just where they start by default when working with documents.

User Manager will create the home directory automatically as long as you have it create a single directory at a time. You might have User Manager create a home directory called c:\ken, for example, but it cannot create c:\ken\home if the \KEN directory did not already exist. That is just a limitation of User Manager.

Click on the Local Path radio button to specify a local path for the home directory. To specify a home directory on the network, click on the Connect radio button, select a drive letter from the drop-down list, and enter the network path in the To box.

> **Here's a tip for home directory creation: If you would like the home directory name to be the same as the user's username, you can use a special environment variable in this dialog box: %USERNAME% (as shown in fig. 3.1.1). The actual username replaces %USERNAME% after the account is created. This is not really any faster than just typing in the actual username, but it can really save time when copying accounts.**

When you use User Manager for Domains to create a user's home directory on an NTFS partition, the default permissions for that directory grant that user Full Control and restrict access to all other users.

2. Creating a Group

You can create new global and local groups by using the New Global Group and New Local Group options on the User Manager for Domains User menu. The following rules apply to global groups and their creation:

- By default, the Administrator account is automatically a member of the new group.

- Only user accounts can be members of a global group.

To add a member to the new global group, select a user in the Not Members list and click on the Add button to add the user to the Members list. Click on the Remove button to remove a user account from the Members list.

The New Local Group dialog box differs slightly from the New Global Group dialog box (fig. 3.1.2 shows the New Local Group dialog box). To add additional members to the new local group, click on the Add button. In contrast to global groups, individual users and global groups both can join a local group.

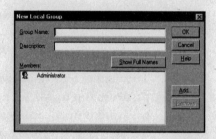

Figure 3.1.2   The New Local Group dialog box.

If you select one or more users in the User Manager for Domains main screen up front creating a new group, those users automatically appear in the membership list for the new local or global group.

After you create your local groups, you can manage them much as you manage your user accounts. You should, however, be aware of the following idiosyncrasies concerning local groups:

- You cannot rename a group after it has been created.

- You cannot disable a group after it has been created.

- If you do want to delete a group, just select the group in User Manager and choose Delete from the User menu. Be aware that you are deleting only the group itself, not the users within the group.

- You can add and/or remove members from the group by selecting the group in User Manager and choosing User, Properties.

3. User and Group Properties

The Properties command on the User menu of the User Manager opens a Properties dialog box for the selected object. The User Properties dialog box resembles the New User dialog box except that all the information is filled in. Use the User Properties dialog box to edit user properties after creating an account.

4. Administering Account Policy

If you need to administer anything related with passwords (expiration, password length, account lockout and more), go to Account in the Policies menu. The Account Policy dialog box opens.

The Account Policy dialog box is pretty busy; the options you can set in this dialog box are described in Table 3.1.1.

Table 3.1.1   Options in the Account Policy Dialog Box

Option	Description
Maximum password age	Setting a maximum password age forces users to choose a new password periodically. Users get a warning 14 days before the password is about to expire.
Minimum password age	The default, Allow Changes Immediately, enables users to change back to a favorite, if overused, password. Allow Changes In x forces users to wait anywhere from 1–999 days before making changes.
Minimum password length	Setting a minimum password length forces users to choose longer passwords. Although you can require up to 14 characters, using 6 to 8 usually suffices.
Password uniqueness	This setting tells Windows NT to remember each old password (up to 24). As long as a password is in a user's password history cache, the user cannot reuse it. A Remember setting of 24 combined with a Minimum Password Age of 7 days forces users to wait almost six months before reusing a password.
Account lockout	Windows NT will lock out an account after a certain number of bad logon attempts (that is, an incorrect password for a valid username) within a certain period of time. You can enable this feature by choosing the Account lockout radio button and filling in the appropriate parameters.
Forcibly disconnecting users	To have the system forcibly disconnect users when their logon hours have expired, enable this check box.
Password change policy	When a user's password nears expiration, the user is prompted at each logon to change it. If the user declines and the password age is exceeded, the user cannot log on until the password is changed. If this selection is cleared (the default), the user is presented with the Change Password dialog box and not allowed to proceed until changing the obsolete password.

5. Assigning Rights to Groups

User or group rights cannot be viewed as properties for a user account or group. Instead, you must choose a right from the drop-down list in the User Rights Policy dialog box so that you can view the users assigned to this specific right. You can access this dialog box via the User Rights command on the policies menu.

Whereas a *permission* is targeted at a specific object (such as a directory or file), the term *right* refers to a general right to take a particular action on the system. Some Windows NT rights are as follows:

- Log on locally
- Shut down the system
- Back up files and directories
- Restore files and directories
- Take ownership of files or other objects

The built-in groups described earlier in this chapter are automatically assigned appropriate user rights. Choose Restore files and directories from the Right combo box in the User Rights Policy dialog box. You will see that Administrators, Backup Operators, and Server Operators all have the right to restore files and directories.

6. Auditing Account-Related Events

The Auditing option in the User Manager for Domains Policy menu invokes the Audit Policy dialog box, which enables you to track certain account-related events. You can track either the success or the failure of the following events:

- Logon and Logoff
- File and Object Access
- Use of User Rights
- User and Group Management
- Security Policy Changes
- Restart, Shutdown, and System
- Process Tracking

The event information is stored in the security log. You can view the security log by using Event Viewer.

7. Trust Relationships

The Trust Relationships option on the User Manager for Domains Policy menu enables you to set up and modify trust relationships for the domain.

A trust relationship is a relationship between different domains in which one domain, the *trusting* domain, relinquishes control of its account database to another domain, called the *trusted* domain. Trust relationships are commonly used in Wide Area Network (WAN) situations, and you will get a heavy dose of them if you ever decide to prepare for the Windows NT Server Enterprise exam.

C. Account Administration Tasks

An administrator's job does not end after creating the accounts; in fact, it just begins. Changes and modifications inevitably are necessary in day-to-day operations. You can review the properties of any user account by double-clicking on the username in User Manager for Domains or by selecting the username and choosing User, Properties.

Although you can change most things about a user in the User Properties dialog box, you should be aware of a few separate commands that are available only from the User menu, outlined in Table 3.1.2.

Table 3.1.2   Account Administration Tasks

Option	Description
Copy	If you need to create many users at one time, consider creating a template account and copying it. When you copy an account by choosing User, Copy in the User Manager, you must enter a new username, full name, and password, but the other properties are retained, including the description, group memberships, and profile information. The only exception is the Account Disabled check box, which is cleared automatically.
Delete	Windows NT tracks user accounts internally with a Security Identifier (SID), which is used to track user rights and permissions on resources (the username is never used for this purpose). The SID is unique in the entire system and is never reused again even when the corresponding user has long been deleted.
Rename	The User Properties dialog box shows that although you can change a user's full name at any time, the username is fixed. To change the username (remember, the username is the logon name), you must choose User, Rename in the User Manager for Domains. Remember that the Security Identifier (SID), which, once created, never changes, even if the account is renamed.

3.1.1   Exercise: Adding a New Account Operator User

The purpose of this exercise is to create a new user AccOp that is added to the Account Operators group.

1. Open User Manager for Domains and choose New User in the User menu.

2. The New User dialog box opens. Enter AccOp as the username and a password. All other entries are optional.

3. Click on the Groups button to open the Group Membership dialog box.

4. Select "Account Operators" in the "Not Member of" listbox and click Add to make the new user a member of this group. Click OK when done.

5. Now you can click Add to create the user account.

3.1.2   Exercise: Setting Account Policy

This exercise will give you practice setting account policy. The policy that is set in this example includes setting a maximum password age (25 days), password history (5), and minimum password length (6 characters).

1. Open User Manager for Domains and choose Account in the Policies menu.

2. Enable the Expires In radio button and set Days to 25.

3. Go to Password Uniqueness frame and enable Remember passwords and enter 5.

4. Finally, go to the Minimum Password Length frame and enable the At Least radio button and enter 6 as the minimum password length. Click OK to let your changes take effect.

3

3.1   Practice Problems

1. You are the administrator of MegaCorp, which is running a Windows NT Domain named MEGANET. You are responsible for all tasks, including user management, but you are short on time. You want to temporarily assign Dan, who is working for finance, the right to administer user accounts. How can you achieve this? Select the best answer:

   A. Assign the right "Administer Accounts" to Dan's account.

   B. Add Dan to the Domain Admins group.

   C. Add Dan to the Account Operators group.

   D. Add Dan to the Power Users Operators group.

2. Dan is now managing user accounts and calls you one day, telling you that he has deleted an account for an employee that had signed off that day, but the employee returned a few days later. Dan tells you that he has created a new account with the same name, but the employee complains that he isn't able to access his files any more. What has happened? Select the best answer:

   A. Someone has taken ownership of the files.

   B. Dan forgot to assign the employee's account to groups that had access permissions.

   C. Accounts are identified by a SID that is unique for every account throughout the system, and simply recreating an account with the same name doesn't bring back the SID.

   D. The employee has entered an incorrect password when he logged on to his workstation.

3. Your account operator, Dan, is facing a new problem: Your company is hiring summer interns that need to have read access to specific resources on your system. How can you achieve maximum security? Select the best answer:

   A. Create a user account for every summer intern, and set the account to expire at the end of summer. Assign the accounts to the project's group in which they are working, giving them full access to all resources.

   B. Create one user account for all summer interns, and set the account to expire at the end of summer. Assign the accounts to the project's group in which they are working, giving them full access to all resources.

   C. Create a user account for every summer intern and set the account to expire at the end of summer. Assign the accounts to a new group, SummerIntern, and grant this group appropriate permissions to the resources they need.

   D. Simply rename a user account of an employee that is currently on vacation and tell the password to the summer interns.

4. You suspect that users are simply recycling their old passwords when the system asks them to change it every 30 days. To prove this, you are running a brute force password cracker program using the Administrator account every 30 days to see which passwords are used throughout the system. You are right, passwords are recycled, some users even use their username as password or simply have a blank password. How can you prevent all of this? Choose the correct answer(s):

   A. Set a minimum password length.

   B. Set the minimum password age.

   C. Keep a password history.

   D. You can't prevent this.

5. You consider the built-in Administrator account a security risk because everyone knows half the information necessary to break into your system. How can you reduce or even eliminate this risk? Select the best answer:

   A. Delete the Administrator account.

   B. Disable the Administrator account.

   C. Choose an impossible-to-guess password for the account.

   D. Rename the Administrator account and assign a hard-to-guess password.

6. The finance division has twenty computers. They have hired two summer interns and want them to be able to use all workstations with exception of the computer named SECUREFIN (running NT Workstation). Both summer interns are using the same account (defined in the domain). How can you achieve this? Select the best answer:

   A. Select the summer interns account, and select "Logon To" and set "Logon to all workstation, except" to SECUREFIN.

   B. Select the summer interns account and select "Logon To," then set "User may logon to these workstations" and enter all other nineteen computers of FINANCE.

   C. You cannot do this.

7. You want to allow members of the finance division to log on to your network only between 8 a.m. and 6 p.m. on workdays. How can you achieve this? Select two:

   A. Specify logon hours for every user.

   B. Enable "Forcibly disconnect remote users from server when logon hours expire."

   C. Enable Auditing of logon and logoff events.

   D. You cannot do this.

8. You suspect that a member of the finance division is working on the weekend using the SECUREFIN computer. How can you prove this? Select the best answer:

   A. Enable auditing for the users of the finance division and check the security log on Monday using Event Viewer to see if someone logged in to the SECUREFIN computer on the weekend.

   B. Enable auditing of logon and logoff events, and check the security log on Monday using Event Viewer to see if someone logged in to the SECUREFIN computer on the weekend.

   C. Audit Process tracking, and check the security log on Monday using Event Viewer to see if someone logged in to the SECUREFIN computer on the weekend.

   D. Enable auditing of logon and logoff events, and check the system log on Monday using Event Viewer to see if someone has logged in to the SECUREFIN computer on the weekend.

9. Which of the following statements is true about security identifiers (SID)? Select the best answer:

   A. A SID is created using a one-time hash function, and thus you can recreate a SID by reentering the same username.

   B. A SID is a unique identifier that is recycled after a certain amount of time, however, you cannot assign a SID to a specific user account.

   C. A SID is a unique identifier for user accounts, it is never recycled and used by Windows NT to track a user internally.

   D. A SID is used to track Windows NT file shares.

10. Which rights do members of the Backup operators group own? Select all that apply:

   A. Back up files.

   B. Restore files.

   C. Log on locally.

   D. Shut down the server.

11. Which of the following groups are available on domain controllers? Select all that apply:

   A. Server Operators.

   B. Power Users.

   C. Domain Admins.

   D. Interactive.

12. A user tells you that he cannot log on to his workstation. After walking to the site and talking to the user, you find out that he changed his password yesterday when he was forced to do so because you set a maximum password age. What can you do to get this user logged on? Select the best answer:

   A. Disable the maximum password age setting, and let the user log on with the old password.

   B. Create a new user account for the user with Password Never Expires enabled, and let the user log on.

   C. In User Manager, assign a new password to the user's account and require "Change Password at next Logon" to be shown at logon. Tell the user to log on with the new password and this time, and to remember the password.

   D. Tell the user to log on as Administrator using his old password.

13. A new department with 120 workers is added to your network. You need to set up 120 identical accounts with home directories for each. How can you achieve this most effectively? Select the best answer:

   A. Create a single user account, assign it to all appropriate groups and assign the home directory to \\MEGASERVER\USERHOME\ Template. Copy the user account 120 times and you are done.

   B. Create a single user account, assign it to all appropriate groups, and assign the home directory to \\MEGASERVER\USERHOME\ %USERID%. Copy the user account 120 times and you are done.

   C. Create a single user account, assign it to all appropriate groups and assign the home directory to \\MEGASERVER\USERHOME\ %USERNAME%. Copy the user account 120 times and you are done.

   D. You have to create every single account by assigning groups and home directories yourself.

14. Your network has a PDC and two BDCs. There are also 5 NT Server computers that have no domain role associated with them. You want to assign Becky the task of a backup operator on all these machines. How can you achieve this? Select the best answer:

   A. Add Becky to the Domain Admins group.

   B. Add Becky to the Backup Operators group.

   C. Create a new global group, Domain Backup Operators, and add this group to the local Backup Group on the domain controllers and servers. Add Becky to the Domain Backup Operators group.

   D. Create a new local group, Domain Backup Operators, and add this group to the local Backup Group on the domain controllers and servers. Add Becky to the Domain Backup Operators group.

15. Some users are going to leave for three months for holidays. As you are concerned about security, you want to prevent abuse of these accounts during this time period. How can you achieve this? Select the best answer:

    A. Revoke the right to log on locally for these user accounts.

    B. Select "User may log on to these workstations" in User Manager for these accounts, but don't select any workstations.

    C. Disable the accounts for these users.

    D. Delete the accounts for these users.

16. If you are logged on to a Windows NT computer, of which group do you automatically become a member? Select the best answer:

    A. Power User

    B. Interactive

    C. Everyone

    D. Network

17. Name the four special groups of Windows NT. Select the best answer:

    A. Global, Interactive, Creator Owner, Local

    B. Interactive, Power Users, Global, Local

    C. Network, Creator Owner, Interactive, Everyone

    D. Everyone, Global, Local, Personal

18. Which local user groups are granted the right to shut down a domain controller by default? Select all that apply:

    A. Users

    B. Administrators

    C. Backup Operators

    D. Server Operators

    E. Print Operators

    F. Account Operators

19. Your company has hired a new accountant who is working for a trial period of two months. You need to assure that the account for this new user can be used only two months. How can you achieve this? Select the best answer:

    A. Set the password expiration to two months.

    B. Set the Account Expires option for this user account to a date that is two months away.

    C. Create a logon script that checks the date and automatically logs off the user when the end of the trial period is reached.

    D. You cannot set an account to expire.

20. You have established account lockout after 5 unsuccessful logins with duration Forever selected. On Monday mornings you often get calls from users saying they cannot logon to the computer at the first attempt and the system tells them that the account is locked. They also tell you that they could logon successfully on Friday. What is the most likely cause for this happening? Select the best answer:

    A. They have accumulated five unsuccessful logon attempts in the last few days and now the system locks them out.

    B. One of the users is fooling you: He simply enters five password guesses for a user account he knows in order to stop others from getting to work on Monday morning.

    C. The users have changed their password on Friday, because you have set the password expiration period to seven days and they no longer remember the passwords they have chosen.

    D. A Backup Operator has made a restore on the weekend, including the registry of the PDC.

3

21. Please refer to question 3.1.20—how could you detect from where these unsuccessful logon attempts were made? Select the best answer:

   A. Audit successful logon attempts.

   B. Audit Use of user Rights.

   C. Audit successful and failed logon attempts.

   D. Audit failed logon attempts.

22. Who has the right to backup and restore files? Select the best answer:

   A. Server Operators, Account Operators, Backup Operators

   B. Administrators, Server Operators, Replicator

   C. Backup Operators, Server Operators, Administrators

   D. Replicator, Backup Operators, Administrators

23. Built-in local groups can be (select all that apply):

   A. Renamed

   B. Deleted

   C. Disabled

   D. Copied

24. Which of the following statements is true?

   A. Local groups and user accounts can be contained in a global group.

   B. Global groups and user accounts can be contained in a local group.

   C. Only user accounts can be contained local groups.

   D. Only local groups can be contained in global groups.

25. Which kinds of groups are known to Windows NT? Select all that apply:

   A. Global

   B. Personal

   C. Local

   D. Special

26. A user is complaining that the time displayed on his computer is incorrect, and that the system keeps telling him that he hasn't got sufficient rights to change it. What action can you take as an administrator to allow the user to change the system time himself? Select the best answer:

   A. Temporarily add the user to the Server Operators group.

   B. Tell him the Administrator password so he can logon as Administrator and change the time.

   C. Add the user the "Change the system time" right.

   D. You have to change the time yourself.

27. When you are connecting to a shared directory on a NT Server, of which group do you automatically become a member? Select the best answer:

   A. Interactive

   B. Local

   C. Network

   D. Creator Owner

28. You are creating a new user account in the domain MEGACORP. By default, of which group is this new user a member? Select the best answer:

   A. Local

   B. Everyone

   C. Domain Users

   D. Domain Guests

29. What is the difference between a locked out user account and a disabled user account? Select the best answer:

    A. A locked out user account does not retain its SID, whereas a disabled user account does.

    B. A system administrator can lock out a user account, but he cannot disable a user account.

    C. A system administrator can disable a user account, but he cannot lock out a user account.

    D. A disabled user account does not retain its SID, whereas a locked out user account does.

3.1 Answers and Explanations: Practice Problems

1. **C** Account Operators are able to manage user accounts without the additional power that is inherent to the Domain Admins group.

2. **C** NT tracks only the SID for resource permissions, therefore, when the account is deleted and with it the SID, simply recreating the username isn't sufficient as the SID isn't reused.

3. **C** Managing permissions with groups is easier than assigning each account the desired permission.

4. **D** You can't restrict users from using their usernames as passwords unless you install specific software to prevent this.

5. **D** Renaming is your only option.

6. **C** You can restrict logon only to eight workstations.

7. **A** Logon hours are used to specify a time period when a specific user is allowed to log on.

8. **B** Auditing allows you to track security and object usage.

9. **C** SIDs are unique in NT and represent a user account.

10. **A, B, C, D** All answers are correct because of the task of backing up and restoring a local computer.

11. **A, C** Only Domain Admins and Server Operators are available for administration on domain controllers.

12. **C** The Administrator has to set a new password.

13. **C** Use templates for creating identical user accounts.

14. **C** You need to create a new global group and add it to local Backup Operators.

15. **C** Disabling prevents anyone from using the account, however, any permissions are retained.

16. **B** You automatically become a member of the Interactive group.

17. **C** Network, Creator Owner, Interactive, and Everyone are the four special groups of Windows NT.

18. **B, C, D, F** Users and Print Operators must not log on to a domain controller.

19. **B** Account expiration is the way to assure that the account for this new user can be used for only two months.

20. **B** When a username is known, everyone can try to figure the password for this account.

21. **D** Auditing can track user logons.

22. **C** The Backup Operators, Server Operators, and Administrators have the rights to backup and restore files.

23. **D** Only copying is allowed for local built-in groups.

24. **B** Only global groups and user accounts can be members of a local group.

25. **A, C, D** Personal is not a group known to NT.

3

26. **C**   Users and groups can be assigned rights.

27. **C**   Everyone connecting to a share automatically becomes member of the special Network group.

28. **C**   Domain Users is the default group, however, you can remove the user from this one.

29. **C**   Lockouts occur when you specified security policy to lock out an account after specified number of retries.

3.1   Key Words

User	Group
Local groups	Global groups
Creating users	Deleting users
Disabling users	Creating groups
Renaming users	Deleting groups
User rights	Auditing
Account policy	Account lockout
Built-in groups	Special groups
Backup Operators	
Server Operators	
Print Operators	
Administrators	Guests
Account Operators	
Power Users	
Replicator	Interactive
Network	Everyone
Creator Owner	Domain Guests
Domain Admins	Domain Users
User Manager	Event
ViewerMember Server	
Logon scripts	

3.2   Managing Policies and Profiles

Policies and profiles are two powerful methods for defining the user environment. Microsoft lists the following objective for the Windows NT Server exam: Create and manage policies and profiles for various situations. Policies and profiles include local user profiles, roaming user profiles, and system policies.

A.   User Profiles

A user profile is the entire collection of configuration data that applies to a specific user and only to that user. Because profiles are maintained for each individual user, users can change their own environment without affecting the environment of other users. Profiles contain quite a number of items, including the following:

- Settings for the user-specific Control Panel entries
- Persistent network drive connections
- Remote printer connections
- Personal program groups
- User environment variables
- Bookmarks in Help
- Preferences for Win32 applications
- Most recently accessed documents in Win32 applications

The user's profile subdirectory generally consists of

- an ntuser.dat file (containing Registry information)
- a transaction log file called ntuser.dat.log (which provides fault tolerance for ntuser.dat)
- and a series of folders containing other items such as shortcuts and application-specific profile data

Windows NT provides two types of user profiles:

- **Local Profiles:** Because a local profile resides on the local machine, it does not follow the user if the user logs on to the network from a different machine.
- **Roaming Profiles:** A profile that can follow the user to other computers on the network because it is stored at a central location.

1. Local Profiles

Unless you specify a roaming profile (see the following section), Windows NT obtains user-specific settings from a local user profile on the workstation the user is currently using. You can find a local user profile subdirectory for each workstation user in the <winnt_root>\profiles directory.

When a user logs on for the first time, the Windows NT logon process checks the user account database to see whether a roaming profile path has been specified for the account (see the following section). If the accounts database doesn't contain a profile path for the user, Windows NT creates a local user profile subdirectory for the user in the <winnt_root>\profiles directory and obtains initial user profile information from the local default user profile, which is stored in the subdirectory:

```
<winnt_root>\profiles\Default User
```

Windows NT saves all changes to the user profile in the new local user profile. The next time a user logs on at the workstation, Windows NT accesses the local user profile and configures all user-specific settings to match the information in the profile.

2. Roaming Profiles

A *roaming profile* is a centrally located user profile that other workstations on the network can access at logon. You specify a path to a roaming profile subdirectory in User Manager.

When a user logs on to the domain, the Windows NT logon process checks to see whether the account database contains a roaming profile path for the account.

If the account database contains a path to a roaming profile, Windows NT compares the local version of the profile with the roaming profile specified in the account database. If the local version is more recent, Windows NT asks whether you would like to use the local version rather than the roaming version. Otherwise, Windows NT downloads the roaming version.

At logoff, if the user is a guest or if the profile is a mandatory profile (see next section), Windows NT doesn't save the current user profile to the user profile subdirectory. If the user is not a guest, and if the profile isn't mandatory, Windows NT saves the current profile information. If the profile type is set to Roaming, Windows NT saves the current profile information to both the local copy and the version specified in the account database.

3. Mandatory Profiles

A mandatory profile is a preconfigured roaming profile that the user cannot change. To create a mandatory profile, create a roaming profile subdirectory and specify the path to that directory in User Manager for Domains. Then, copy a user profile to the roaming profile subdirectory (using the Copy To command in the User profile tab of the Control Panel System application) and rename the ntuser.dat file to ntuser.man. The MAN extension makes the profile read-only.

4. Switching Local and Global Profiles

The User Profiles tab of the Control Panel System application will use a locally stored version of the profile, or whether the computer should download a roaming profile at logon. If you are logged on as an administrator, the user profile list in figure 3.2.1 displays all user profiles currently stored on the computer. If you are logged on as a user, the list displays only the profile you are currently using. The Change Type button enables you to specify whether to use the local version of the profile, or whether to download a roaming profile at logon. If you choose the roaming profile option, click on the box labeled Use cached profile on slow connections if you want Windows NT to use the local profile when the network is running slowly.

Click on the Copy To button box in the User Profiles tab to open the Copy To dialog box, which enables you to copy the user profile to another directory or to another computer on the network. If a different user will use the profile at its new location, you must give that user permission to use the profile. To add a user to the permissions list for the profile, click on the Change button in the Copy To dialog box.

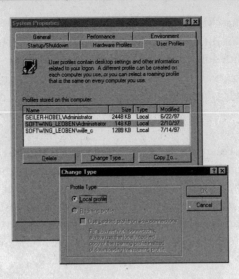

Figure 3.2.1 The System Properties User Profiles tab with the Change Type dialog box opened.

B.   Hardware Profiles

Hardware profiles, a new addition to NT, refers to a collection of information about devices, services, and other hardware-related settings. Hardware profiles were designed for portable computers. The hardware configuration of a portable computer might change each time the portable is attached or removed from a docking station. A hardware profile enables the user to define a set of hardware conditions under which the computer will operate at a given time.

If you have defined more than one hardware profile, Windows NT displays a menu of hardware profiles at startup and asks which profile you want to use. The profile you specify becomes the active hardware profile. Any changes to your hardware configuration affect the active hardware profile. You can enable or disable a device for a given hardware profile using the Control Panel Devices application. You can enable or disable a service using the Control Panel Services Application.

C.   Managing System Policy with System Policy Editor

System Policy Editor, a powerful configuration tool included with Windows NT Server, enables a network administrator to maintain these options for the entire network from a single location:

- Machine Configurations
- User Policies

System Policy Editor can operate in the following modes:

- Registry mode
- Policy File mode

The exam objectives for the "Managing Resources" section of the NT Server exam specifically mention *system policies*. This implies that, at least for the purposes of the "Managing Resources" section, the Policy File mode functions of System Policy Editor are the more significant. The Windows NT Registry, however, is an extremely important part of Windows NT, and System Policy Editor Registry mode is an able and important interface to the registry.

1. Registry Mode

In Registry mode, System Policy Editor enables whoever is using it to display and change Registry settings of either the local computer or another computer on the network. System Policy Editor does not provide the complete Registry access provided that Registry Editor affords, but it is much easier to use, and it provides powerful access to settings you cannot access via Control Panel. System Policy Editor has a hierarchical structure similar to the Registry and is remarkably simple and convenient when you consider its power. You can use System Policy Editor for the following tasks:

- Set the maximum number of authentication retries

- Prohibit NT from creating 8.3 aliases for long file names

- Define a logon banner to appear prior to logon

- Enable or disable a computer's capability to create hidden drive shares

- Hide the Network Neighborhood icon

- Remove the Run command from the Start menu

- Require a specific desktop wallpaper

- Disable Registry editing tools

The best way to get a feel for the kinds of things you set using System Policy Editor is to browse through the Properties dialog boxes yourself. As you study for the MCSE exam, spend some time familiarizing yourself with System Policy Editor settings.

You can find System Policy Editor in the Administrative Tools program group. Choose Programs in the Start menu, select Administrative Tools, and click on the System Policy Editor icon. Figure 3.2.2 shows System Policy in Registry Mode with the settings for the local computer displayed.

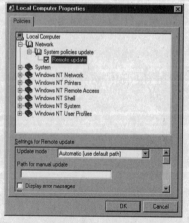

Figure 3.2.2   System Policy Editor Registry mode with the Local Computer Properties dialog box opened.

You are not limited to configuring the local computer's registry settings. You can use System Policy Editor to configure another computer on the network as well.

2. Policy File Mode

System Policy Editor's Policy File mode looks similar to Registry mode, but it is significantly different; System Policy is a kind of meta-Registry. The System Policy file can contain settings that override local Registry settings, you can therefore use System Policy Editor to impose a configuration on a user or machine that the user cannot change.

For Windows NT machines, the System Policy file is called NTConfig.pol. To enable system policy, create the NTConfig.pol file (using System Policy Editor) and place it in the \<winnt_root>\System32\Repl\Import\Scripts folder of the Domain controller's boot partition. This directory is shared as \\PDC_servername\Netlogon$. (Store system policy information for Windows 95 machines in the file Config.pol rather than NTConfig.pol.)

When a Windows NT computer attempts to log on, Windows NT looks for the NTConfig.pol file and checks NTConfig.pol for system policy information that affects the user or computer. Windows NT merges the system policy information with local Registry settings, overwriting the Registry information if necessary.

The types of settings you can define through System Policy Editor's Policy File mode are similar to the settings you can define through Registry mode, but system policy settings override Registry settings. Also, because you can apply system policy settings to groups, you can simultaneously set policies for several users, or even for an entire domain.

A complete set of all system policy information for a given configuration is stored in one big system policy file. You can create different system policy files to test different system policy configurations. The active file (for NT machines), however, must be saved as NTConfig.pol.

Windows NT Server includes some System Policy templates, which contain system policy settings and categories. The template files present on Windows NT are as follows:

- c:\<winnt_root>\inf\common.adm Settings common to both Windows NT and Windows 95 (and not present on the following two files)

- c:\<winnt_root>\inf\winnt.adm Windows NT settings

- c:\<winnt_root>\inf\windows Windows 95 settings

To add a System Policy template, choose Options, Policy Template from the System Policy Editor and choose a template from the list.

The System Policy templates are written in a proprietary scripting language. (See the Windows NT Resource kit for more information on the policy template scripting language.)

3.2.1   Exercise: Creating a New Hardware Profile

The purpose of this exercise is to create a new Hardware Profile.

1. Open Control Panel and double-click on the System application.

2. Click on the Hardware Profiles tab, which enables you to create new hardware profiles and change the order of precedence among hardware profiles. You can also specify whether Windows NT waits indefinitely for you to choose a hardware profile on startup, or whether the choice defaults to the highest-preference profile after a specific time interval.

3. To create the new hardware profile, select an existing profile and click on the Copy button. The new hardware profile will appear in the Available Hardware Profiles list in the Hardware Profiles tab.

4. Close the System application and reboot the computer; select the new profile when prompted by Windows NT during startup.

5. Back in Windows NT, you now you can start to configure this new hardware profile by enabling/disabling services and devices.

3.2.2   Exercise: Applying System Policies

The purpose of this exercise is to show you how to work with System Policy Editor to configure interesting settings of the local computer.

1. Open System Policy Editor in the Administrative Tools menu. Select Open Registry from the File menu.

2. The local registry is being opened. Double-click on Local Computer to start configuring the local machine.

3. Open Network, System Policies Update and enable the Remote Update check box. This entry is used for system policies stored on servers (ntconfig.pol) and their automatic updating on the local computer.

4. Go to Windows NT Network, Sharing and enable (depending on whether the computer is running NT Server or Workstation) the appropriate check box to create hidden administrative shares for the computer.

5. Go to Windows NT System, Logon and enable "Do not display last logged on user name" check box to automatically clear the username in the logon dialog box.

6. Go to Windows NT User Profiles and enable the deletion of cached copies of roaming profiles.

7. Click OK and select Save from the File menu to make your changes persistent.

3.2 Practice Problems

1. You are creating a policy file that is to be used by all computers and users throughout your domain. Where do you have to put this file and which name must it have? Select the best answer:

   A. Put it in <winnt_root>\System32\ Repl\Import\Scripts, and name the file config.pol.

   B. Put it in <winnt_root>\System32\ Repl\Import\Scripts, and name the file ntconfig.pol.

   C. Put it in <winnt_root>\System32\ Repl\Export\Scripts, and name the file config.pol.

   D. Put it in <winnt_root>\System32\ Repl\Export\Scripts, and name the file ntconfig.pol.

2. A user logs on to many different workstations and complains that every time he logs on that the changes he made previously to the desktop on another workstation are not available on this workstation. What is the problem? Select the best answer:

   A. The user has a mandatory profile.

   B. The user has a roaming profile.

   C. The user has a local profile.

   D. The user has a per-workstation profile.

3. How can you ensure that a user always gets his current profile independent of the workstation on which he logs on? Select the best answer:

   A. Create a mandatory profile for the user.

   B. Create a roaming profile for the user.

   C. Create a local profile for the user.

   D. Create a per-workstation profile for the user.

4. New summer interns are hired and only a single user account is created for all interns, even though they will be working on different computers. You want to ensure that no single summer intern can mess up the user profile, which means that all changes made to the profile should be ignored. What can you do to achieve this? Select the best answer:

   A. Create a mandatory profile for the interns user account.

   B. Create a mandatory roaming profile for the interns user account.

   C. Create a mandatory local profile for the interns user account.

   D. Create a mandatory per-workstation profile for the interns user account.

5. How do you create mandatory profiles? Select the best answer:

   A. Rename profile.dat to profile.man.

   B. Apply read-only permissions for the interns user account to profile.dat.

   C. Rename ntuser.dat to ntuser.man.

   D. Apply read-only permissions for the interns user account to ntuser.dat.

6. Where do you have to specify the path for roaming profiles? Select the best answer:

   A. In Control Panel, System application, tab User Profiles enter the path to the roaming profile.

   B. In User manager, User Environment Profile, enter the path to the roaming profile.

   C. Enter the information in the Registry under the key HKEY_ CURRENT_USER.

   D. Using System Policy Editor, set the path to the roaming profile for a user or an entire group.

3

7. Which statement best describes Windows 95 and Windows NT policies?

   A. Windows 95 policies can be stored only locally; Windows NT policies can reside on a server share.

   B. Windows 95 doesn't have system policies.

   C. Windows 95 and Windows NT are enforcing the same policies, and therefore they can be interchanged.

   D. The policies are not the same and cannot be interchanged.

8. The finance department was added to the domain yesterday; today all users from this department are complaining that the desktop settings they made are no longer available. What has happened? Select the best answer:

   A. The users didn't save their desktop settings before shutting down their workstations.

   B. The users are not allowed to save changes because their profiles are mandatory.

   C. You have run of licenses for desktop customization on your server.

   D. The group the users belong to doesn't have the right to save desktop settings.

9. Which of the following statements about roaming profiles is *not* true?

   A. Roaming profiles are located on a server share.

   B. Roaming profiles can be stored locally.

   C. You can switch between using roaming and local profiles.

   D. Roaming profiles can't be mandatory.

10. System policies are used to (select all that apply):

    A. Distribute mandatory user profiles.

    B. Restrict access to parts of NT.

    C. Enable administrative shares.

    D. Customize logon.

11. Your boss has bought a new laptop. At his office, he is using a docking station to connect to the LAN; at home he uses a PCMCIA card to dial the office. How can you manage the different hardware setups in NT? Select the best answer:

    A. Install a second copy of NT on the hard disk, one configured for the docking station, the other for use with the modem.

    B. Create a hardware profile for both situations, and activate the devices accordingly.

    C. You don't have to do anything—NT automatically detects docking stations and PCMCIA cards.

    D. You cannot, because NT doesn't support Plug and Play.

12. In System Policy Editor, for which objects can you set a policy? Select all that apply:

    A. Groups

    B. Users

    C. Servers

    D. Computers

3.2 Answers and Explanations: Practice Problems

1. **B** This is the location where NT computers look for policy files.

2. **C** Local profiles are created on every NT computer when a user logs on for the first time.

3. **B** Roaming profiles are stored on a server and retrieved every time a user logs on to a NT computer.

4. **B** Mandatory profiles prevent users from changing any settings.

5. **C** Renaming ntuser.dat must be done in order to make a profile mandatory.

6. **B** You have to specify roaming profiles in User manager, User Environment Profile.

7. **D** Windows 95 and NT use different policy files.

8. **B** Mandatory profiles prevent users from changing any desktop settings.

9. **D** Roaming profiles can be mandatory.

10. **B, C, D** Roaming profiles are not distributed using system policies.

11. **B** Hardware profiles are used for managing different hardware configurations.

12. **A, B, D** There is no specific notion of Servers in system policies.

3.2 Key Words

Profiles

Roaming profiles

System policy editor

Registry mode

Policy templates

Mandatory profiles

Local profiles

Policy file mode

3.3   Managing Windows NT Server from Client Machines

The Network Client Administrator tool, located in the Administrative Tools program group, makes a set of Windows NT administration tools available to Windows NT clients. The Administration tools enable you to perform network administration functions from a client machine. Microsoft lists the following objective for the Windows NT Server exam: Administer remote servers from various types of client computers. Client computer types include Windows 95 and Windows NT Workstation.

There are two packages of client-based network administration tools: one for Windows 95 clients and one for Windows NT Workstation clients. The Windows 95 client-based network administration tools are as follows:

- Event Viewer

- File Security tab

- Print Security tab

- Server Manager

- User Manager for Domains

- User Manager Extensions for Services for NetWare

- File and Print Services for NetWare

Before you can use the Windows 95 client-based network administration package, you must have a 486DX/33 or better Windows 95 computer with 8 MB of RAM (highly recommended) and a minimum of 3 MB of free disk space in the system partition. Client for Microsoft Networks must be installed on the Windows 95 computer.

The Windows NT Workstation client-based network administration tools are as follows:

- DHCP Manager

- Remote Access Administrator

- Remoteboot Manager

- Services for Macintosh

- Server Manager

- System Policy Editor

- User Manager for Domains

- WINS Manager

Before you can use the client-based network administration package, the Windows NT Workstation must be a 486DX/33 or better with 12 MB of RAM and a minimum of 2.5 MB of free disk space in the system partition. The Workstation and Server services must be installed on the Windows NT Workstation.

3.3.1   Exercise: Creating a Server Share for the Client-Based Network Administration Tools

The purpose of this exercise is to copy the client-based network administration tools to a server's hard disk and create a share for these.

1. Open Network Client Administrator from the Administrative Tools menu. Select "Copy client-based network administration tools" and click Continue.

2. In the Share Client-based Administration Tools dialog box you are presented three options: Share Files, Copy Files to a new directory and then share, as well as use existing shared directory. Select the second option and enter the path where to store the files. Leave the share name as proposed. In the path field enter the path to the source location of the tools (the NT Server CD-ROM).

3. The files are copied and the share is created automatically. You are finished with your task.

3.3.2   Exercise: Installing the Client-Based Network Administration Tools on a Windows NT Computer

The purpose of this exercise is to install the NT version of the client-based network administration tools from the server share created in Exercise 3.3.1 to a local NT workstation or server.

1. Open Windows NT Explorer or File Manager to navigate to the servershare you have previously installed the administration tools.

2. Once on the share, go to the Winnt folder and double-click on setup.bat.

3. Let the installation proceed.

4. When the installation is finished, create icons for the tools and start using them as if you were working on the remote machine.

3.3   Practice Problems

1. Which of the following are client-based administration tools for Windows 95? Select all that apply:

   A. Event Viewer

   B. Remoteboot Manager

   C. File and Print Services for NetWare

   D. User Manager for Domains

2. Which of the following are client-based administration tools for Windows NT? Select all that apply:

   A. Event Viewer

   B. Remoteboot Manager

   C. File and Print Services for NetWare

   D. User Manager for Domains

3. For which operating systems are client-based administration tools available? Select all that apply:

   A. Windows 3.x

   B. Windows 95

   C. Windows NT

   D. Apple Macintosh System 7

4. Which of the following are *not* client-based administration tools for Windows 95? Select all that apply:

   A. Server Manager

   B. Remoteboot Manager

   C. File and Print Services for NetWare

   D. System Policy Editor

5. Which of the following are *not* client-based administration tools for Windows NT? Select all that apply:

   A. Services for Macintosh

   B. Remoteboot Manager

   C. File and Print Services for NetWare

   D. System Policy Editor

3.3   Answers and Explanations: Practice Problems

1. **A, C, D** Remoteboot Manager is not available on Windows 95.

2. **A, B, D** File and Print Services for NetWare are not client-based administration tools for Windows NT.

3. **B, C** There are only client-based administration tools for NT and Windows 95.

4. **B, D** Remoteboot Manager and System Policy Editor are not part of the client-based administration tools for Windows 95.

5. **C** File and Print Services for NetWare are not part of the client-based administration tools for NT.

3.3   Key Words

Windows 95 clients

Windows NT clients

Network Client Administrator

3.4   Managing Disk Resources

A big part of an NT administrator's job is managing file resources for the network. Microsoft lists the following objective for the Windows NT Server exam: Manage disk resources. Tasks include copying and moving files between file systems, creating and sharing resources, implementing permissions and security, and establishing file auditing.

A.   Copying and Moving Files

When you copy a file within or between partitions with the Copy command, a new instance of that file is created, and the new file inherits the compression and security attributes of the new parent directory.

The same effect results if a file is moved between partitions by using the Move command. (Remember that a move between partitions is really a copy followed by a delete.) When a file is moved within a partition, the file retains its original attributes. The attributes do not change, because the file itself is never altered. Only the source and target directories change.

1. Long File Names

Although all the Windows NT-supported file systems support long file names, you should be aware of certain issues.

a. FAT Long File Names

Only 512 directory entries are permitted in the root directory of any partition. Because each long file name requires a directory entry for every thirteen characters (or portion thereof) in its name and an additional entry for its 8.3 alias, you are in danger of quickly reaching the entry limit if you use excessively long file names in a root directory.

Also, if you are dual-booting between Windows NT and Windows 95, you should be aware that although the long file names are compatible with both operating systems, Windows 95 has a path limitation of 260 characters, including the drive letter. If you use a deep hierarchy of subdirectories with long file names, therefore, you may find that Windows 95 cannot access a file buried deep within that directory tree.

The two operating systems also differ in the way they create the 8.3 alias. Both Windows NT and Windows 95 begin by taking the first six legal characters in the LFN (in other words, stripping spaces and punctuation and converting to uppercase) and following them by a tilde (~) and a number. If the first six legal characters result in a unique identifier for that file, the number following the tilde is 1. If a file in that directory already has the same first six legal characters, the numeric suffix will be 2. For an extension, Windows NT uses the first three legal characters following the last period in the LFN. To give you an idea of what this looks like, here is a sample directory listing:

```
Team Meeting Report #3.Doc        TEAMME~1.DOC
Team Meeting Report #4.Doc        TEAMME~2.DOC
Team Meeting Report #5.Doc        TEAMME~3.DOC
Team Meeting Report #6.Doc        TEAMME~4.DOC
Nov. 1995 Status Report.Doc        NOV199~1.DOC
```

Both Windows 95 and Windows NT generate aliases in this fashion until the fifth iteration of the same first six legal characters. At this point, Windows 95 continues to do so, but Windows NT does something altogether different; it takes only the first two legal characters, performs a hash on the file name to produce four hexadecimal characters, and then appends a ~5. The ~5 remains for all subsequent aliases of those same initial six characters. If additional reports were saved in the directory used in the preceding example, for example, here is how Windows 95 would and Windows NT might generate the aliases:

	Windows 95	**Windows NT**
Team Meeting	TEAMME~5.DOC	TEA4F2~5.DOC Report #7.Doc
Team Meeting	TEAMME~6.DOC	TE12B4~5.DOC Report #8.Doc
Team Meeting	TEAMME~7.DOC	TE833E~5.DOC Report #9.Doc

If you choose to disable long file name support altogether on a FAT partition, be careful when copying files from a partition that does support LFNs because both the COPY and XCOPY commands always default to using the LFN for their operations.

If you are copying from an LFN-enabled FAT partition or from an NTFS partition, you can use the /n switch with both COPY and XCOPY. The /n switch directs the command to use the alias rather than the LFN.

b. NTFS Long File Names

NTFS generates an alias for each LFN the same way that FAT does. This auto-generation takes time, however. If you won't be using 16-bit MS-DOS or Windows 3.x-based applications, you might consider disabling the automatic alias generation by adding a value called NtfsDisable8dot3NameCreation with a type of REG_DWORD and a value of 1 to HKEY_LOCAL_MACHINE\System\CurrentControlSet\Control\FileSystem. To re-enable alias generation, set the value to 0, or delete the value.

B.   Converting a FAT Partition to NTFS

You can convert a FAT partition to NTFS at any time. You cannot, however, convert an NTFS partition to a FAT partition. Therefore, if you aren't certain about what type of file system to use for a partition, you might want to start with FAT and convert after you are sure there will be no ill effects.

To convert from FAT to NTFS, issue this command from the command prompt (there is no GUI utility for this):

```
CONVERT <drive_letter>: /FS:NTFS
```

C.   NTFS Compression

Individual files and directories can be marked for compression on NTFS partitions only. (An entire drive can be compressed, too, but all you are really doing is compressing the root directory and the files within it; everything is handled at the file level.)

Compression occurs on the fly. All this is transparent to applications and the rest of the operating system. NTFS compresses each file individually, so you always know the exact amount of disk space you have. You can also choose which files to compress, so you don't have to waste time compressing the entire drive.

NTFS compression does not free up as much disk space as most MS-DOS–compatible compression products. The reason for the loose compression in Windows NT is actually to ensure that performance is not affected adversely.

Typically, disk compression products sacrifice performance for extra compression. In Windows NT, you can get a compression ratio almost as good as the MS-DOS 6.22 DriveSpace compression engine, without sacrificing any noticeable performance. When a user marks files to compress, NTFS analyzes the files to see how much disk space will be saved and the amount of time it will take to compress and decompress the file. If NTFS determines that it is not a fair trade, it does not compress the file, no matter how many times the user issues the compress command.

You can compress any file or directory on an NTFS partition, even if it is the system or boot partition. NTLDR, a hidden, system, read-only file in the root of your system partition, is the only file that you cannot compress.

1. Compressing and Uncompressing Files, Directories, and Drives

One of a few ways to compress a file or directory on an NTFS partition is to select the directories and files in File Manager, and choose File, Compress. To compress NTFS files using Explorer, follow these steps:

1. Select the files you want to compress. Use the Ctrl key to select multiple files.

2. Choose File, Properties. The Properties dialog box appears.

3. In the Attributes frame, select the Compressed check box (see fig. 3.4.1).

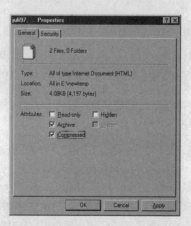

Figure 3.4.1   File Properties dialog box for a file on an NTFS partition.

If you select a directory rather than or along with a file, you are asked whether you want to compress all the files and subdirectories within that directory.

To uncompress files or directories, select them and disable the Compressed check box in the Properties dialog box.

When files and directories are compressed, a new Compression attribute is set for those objects. Note that the Compression attribute does not display for non-NTFS partitions.

The procedure for compressing a drive is similar to the procedure for compressing a file or directory. Select the drive in My Computer or Explorer, and then choose File, Properties. Select the Compress check box at the bottom of the General tab of the Properties dialog box.

2. COMPACT.EXE

You also can use a command-line utility to compress files. The COMPACT.EXE command enables a user to compress files and directories from the command prompt. The following table lists switches you can use with the COMPACT command.

Use	To
COMPACT <filelist> /C	Compress
COMPACT <filelist> /U	Uncompress
COMPACT <filelist> /S	Compress an entire directory tree
COMPACT <filelist> /A	Compress hidden and system files
COMPACT <filelist> /I	Ignore errors and continue compressing
COMPACT <filelist> /F	Force compression even if the objects are already compressed
COMPACT <filelist> /Q	Turn on quiet mode; that is, display only summary information

You also can use the COMPACT command without any switches, in which case it just reports on the compression status, size, and ratio for each file in the file list.

3. Special Notes About Compressed Directories

Directories do not truly get compressed; the Compressed attribute for a directory just sets a flag to tell Windows NT to compress all current files and all future files created in this directory.

With that in mind, it may be easier to understand that when you copy or move compressed files, the files do not always stay compressed.

When a new file is created in an NTFS directory, it inherits the attributes set for that directory. When a file is created in a "compressed" directory, for example, that file will be compressed. When a file is created in an uncompressed directory, the file will not be compressed. So when a compressed file is copied to an uncompressed directory, the new copy of the file will not be compressed. Likewise, if an uncompressed file is copied to a "compressed" directory, the copy of the file will be compressed even though the original is not.

This much probably makes sense. Windows NT includes a MOVE command, however, that, when used within a single partition, swaps directory pointers so that a single file appears to move from one directory to another. Note the word "appears." The file does not actually go anywhere;

it is the source and target directories that actually record a change. When files are moved, attributes do not change. In other words, a compressed file moved into an uncompressed directory stays compressed, and an uncompressed file moved into a compressed directory stays uncompressed.

If you don't think that is complicated enough, Windows NT enables you to use the MOVE command even when the source and target directories are on two different partitions. In this scenario, it is not possible for a directory on one partition to point to a file on another partition. Instead, Windows NT copies the file to the target partition and deletes the original file. Because the target partition now contains a brand-new file, that file inherits the attributes of its new parent directory.

When you copy a file within or between partitions, or move a file between partitions, therefore, the compression attribute of the new copy is inherited from its new parent directory. When you move a file within a single partition, the attributes on the file remain unchanged.

D.   Sharing Directories

Sharing refers to publishing resources on a network for public access. When you share a resource, you make it available to users on other network machines. The Windows NT objects most commonly shared are directories and printers. This section (and the following subsections) look at how to share directories.

If you are familiar with NetWare but not with Windows NT, you need to understand the concept that, by default, absolutely no Windows NT resources are available to remote users; resources must be explicitly published (shared) on the network to host network users.

If you are familiar with Windows for Workgroups or Windows 95 but not with Windows NT, you also should understand that Windows NT users cannot share directories on their computers; only administrators and power users have this privilege. Because shares are computer-specific, and because users cannot modify anything that affects the entire computer, shares are off-limits. This restriction is not a default; granting this capability to users is impossible, as is revoking this capability from administrators and power users.

Even if you are an administrator, you must have at least List permissions to the directory before you can share a directory. Any user who has locked you out of a share probably does not want you to publish it on the network.

Three ways to create shared directories are as follows:

- Using Explorer or My Computer (or you can still use File Manager)
- Using the command prompt
- Using Server Manager

1. Sharing with Explorer and My Computer

You can share directories in Windows NT in a number of ways. The easiest, and usually the most efficient, uses Explorer or My Computer.

Right-click on the directory you want to share and choose Sharing from the shortcut menu to open the Sharing tab of the Properties dialog box. You also can reach the Sharing tab by choosing File, Properties. Or, My Computer enables you to choose Sharing directly from the File menu after you select a directory.

The Share Name defaults to the name of the directory. You can change it; it does not affect the actual directory name at all, it just defines the way the directory appears to network users.

You should never have to change the path. As long as you select the appropriate directory before you choose the Sharing command, the Path box should be set correctly.

The comment is optional. It is nothing more than a free-text tag line that appears next to the share name when browsing in Explorer or Network Neighborhood. (Choose View, Details if you want to see the comments.)

Click on the Permissions button to open the Access Through Share Permissions dialog box, from which you can build an Access Control List for the share to prevent unauthorized network access.

The ATS permissions are completely independent from the local NTFS permissions. In fact, ATS permissions can even be applied to FAT partitions. Because they apply to the entire share, however, you cannot assign granular file-level permissions unless the partition on which the share resides is NTFS.

The ATS permissions themselves are not that granular. Here are your choices:

No Access	Users with No Access to a share can still connect to the share, but nothing appears in File Manager except the message `You do not have permission to access this directory.`
Read	Assigns R and X permissions to the share and its contents.
Change	Assigns R, X, W, and D permissions to the share and its contents.
Full Control	Assigns R, X, W, and D permissions to the share and its contents. In addition, for NTFS shares, P and O permissions are added.

Just as with local NTFS permissions, user and group permissions accumulate, with the exception of No Access, which instantly overrides all other permissions.

Remember, however, that ATS permissions are completely independent of local NTFS permissions. If both sets of permissions are assigned, only the most restrictive permissions are retained.

If you don't require security, you don't have to touch the ATS permissions. The default permissions grant the Everyone group Full Control (just as the default NTFS permissions do).

Choose the OK button to enact sharing of the directory. To modify the share configuration, right-click on the directory again and choose Sharing from the shortcut menu.

The Sharing tab looks identical to the New Share dialog box, with the addition of the New Share button. Click on the New Share button to share the directory again, with a different name and ACL. It does not remove the original share, it just shares the directory again. You can share a single directory an unlimited number of times.

2. Sharing from the Command Prompt

To share from the Windows NT command prompt, use the NET SHARE command, using this syntax:

```
NET SHARE <share_name>=<drive_letter>:<path>
```

To share the C:\PUBLIC directory as Documents, use the following command:

```
NET SHARE Documents=C:\PUBLIC
```

To add a comment for browsers, use the /REMARK switch:

```
NET SHARE Documents:=C:\PUBLIC /REMARK:"Public Documents"
```

To set the user limit to Maximum allowed, use the /UNLIMITED switch (although this is the default):

```
NET SHARE Documents:=C:\PUBLIC /REMARK:"Public Documents" /UNLIMITED
```

To set a specific user limit, use the /USERS switch:

```
NET SHARE Documents:=C:\PUBLIC /REMARK:"Public Documents" /USERS:5
```

To stop a share using the NET SHARE command, use the /DELETE switch:

```
NET SHARE Documents /DELETE
```

a. Hidden Shares

Regardless of how you created it, you can hide a share by ending the share name with a dollar sign ($):

```
NET SHARE Documents$=C:\Public
```

Users can still connect to these shares, but they must explicitly supply the entire path to do so. And of course, the shares can still be protected using Access Through Share Permissions.

b. Administrative Shares

Any Windows NT-based computer that has hard-coded ACLs that grant Full Control to Administrators and No Access to everyone else has at least the following two hidden shares:

C$	Shares the root of the computer's drive C—If other partitions exist on the drive, those partitions also will have similar shares (but not for CD-ROM or disk drives). Consequently, administrators can easily connect to other computers on the network.
ADMIN$	Shares the root of the Windows NT installation, regardless of where it may have been installed—it gives administrators easy access to the operating system directory on any Windows NT-based computer.

To permanently disable these shares, open System Policy editor in Registry mode and go to Windows NT Network, Sharing and disable the Create hidden drive shares check box.

3. Monitoring and Managing Shares

To see a list of all the shares on the system, open the Server application in the Control Panel. Although you cannot stop sharing a resource from the Server application, you can see a complete list of shared resources as well as a list of connected users and other server-related items.

The Server application is a subset of Windows NT Server's Server Manager application. It is a front end for administering connections to your computer. In the Server dialog box, you can view the Usage Summary for your server.

The Usage Summary tracks the following statistics:

Sessions	The number of computers connected to this server.
Open Files	The total number of files currently open for access by remote users.
File Locks	The total number of file locks placed against this computer by remote users.
Open Named Pipes	The total number of named pipes between this computer and connected workstations. (Named pipes are an interprocess communication (IPC) mechanism.)

The Server dialog box also acts as the launch pad for five other server-configuration dialog boxes, as follows:

Users Sessions	Shows detailed information about current user sessions on your Windows NT-based server. (Click on the Users button.)
Shared Resources	Displays detailed information about current shares on your server. (Click on the Shares button.)
Open Resources	Displays the resources of your computer currently being used by remote users. (Click on the In Use button.)
Directory Replication	You can configure the Directory Replicator service in this window. (Click on the Replication button.)
Alerts	Enables an administrator to enter a list of users or workstations to whom messages will be sent in the event of a significant server event. (Click on the Alerts button.)

To view the shared resources on your system, click on the Shares button in the Server application's Server dialog box. The Shared Resources dialog box that appears shows a list of all shares presently configured for your system and the path to each share (see fig. 3.4.2).

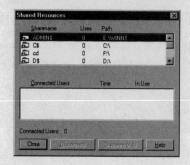

Figure 3.4.2 The Shared Resources dialog box.

Server Manager, in the Administrative Tools group, offers a similar view of shared resources on the local system and on other network computers as well. Click on a computer icon in the Server Manager main screen to open the dialog box.

In the Server Manager, not only can you view the share information for a remote PC, you can actually create a new shared directory. Select a computer in the Server Manager and choose Computer, Shared Directories. The Shared Directories dialog box then shows the shared directories for the computer you selected. Click on the New Share button to add a new share. The New Share dialog box (see fig. 3.4.3) that appears asks you to specify a share name, a path, and an optional comment that will appear in descriptions on the share. You also can limit the number of simultaneous users who can access the share. The Permissions button enables you to specify Access Through Share (ATS) permissions.

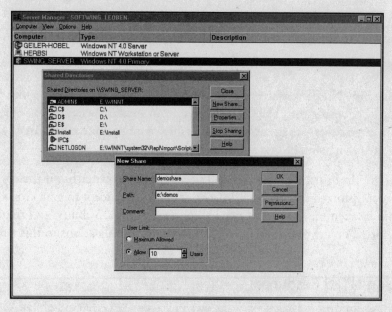

Figure 3.4.3 Server Manager with dialog boxes Shared Directories and New Share opened.

The Stop Sharing button in the Shared Directories dialog box enables you to terminate a share. The Properties button opens the Shared Properties dialog box, which is similar to the New Share dialog box.

E.   Working with NTFS File Permissions and Security

The NTFS file system supports a complex arrangement of directory and file security for which there is no equivalent in the FAT file system. The following sections examine important aspects of NTFS security:

- Ownership of NTFS Resources
- Auditing NTFS Resources
- Securing NTFS Resources

1. Ownership of NTFS Resources

Every NTFS file and directory has one account designated as its owner. The owner of a resource is the only account that has the right to access a resource, modify its properties, and secure it from outside access.

By default, the owner of a resource is the user who created the resource. Only one user can own a resource at any given time, except that a user who is a member of the Administrators group cannot be the sole owner of any resource. Any resource created by an administrator, for example, is co-owned by the entire Administrators group.

To identify the owner of any file or directory, follow these steps:

1. Select the file or directory in My Computer or Windows NT Explorer.
2. Choose File, Properties. The Properties dialog box appears.
3. Click on the Security tab.
4. Click on the Ownership button. The Owner dialog box appears.

Remember that only NTFS resources have owners. You also can take ownership away from the current owner by choosing the Take Ownership button in the Owner dialog box. Normally, only administrators can do this—they can take ownership of any resource because they have been granted the Take Ownership of File and Directories user right.

If you are not an administrator, you may still be able to take ownership if the current owner has granted you permission to take ownership. The important concept to grasp for now, however, is that ownership is taken, never given. Ownership involves responsibility, and that responsibility can never be forced on anyone, even by an administrator. Implications to this rule will surface shortly.

2. Auditing NTFS Resources

One of the most important aspects of Windows NT security is that system administrators can *audit* access to objects such as directories files. In other words, you can configure NT to track all attempts (successful or not) to access NTFS resources for various purposes. The record of all access attempts then appear in the Security log of the Event Viewer.

If you copy a file to a directory configured for auditing, the file inherits the directory's auditing configuration. If you move a file (dragging a file in Explorer to another directory in the same partition is a move), the file retains its original auditing configuration.

You can audit the following six access events for success and/or failure:

- Read

- Write

- Execute

- Delete

- Change Permissions

- Take Ownership

3. Securing NTFS Resources

The set of permissions on a file or directory is just another attribute (or stream) attached to the file, called an Access Control List (ACL). Each ACL contains a series of Access Control Entries (ACEs), and each Access Control Entry references a specific user or group SID and a type of access to grant or deny that SID.

a. Discretionary Access

Who gets to assign permissions to a resource? The owner of the resource. Who is the owner of the resource? The user who created it. In other words, unlike other operating systems, security is not the sole domain of the administrator. If you create a file, you, not the administrator, get to secure it. You can, in fact, easily lock administrators out of their resources. And that makes sense in many environments.

Because locking administrators out of files and directories is dangerous, there is a spare key. An administrator cannot be blocked from taking ownership of a resource, and after the administrator owns the resource, he or she can modify the permissions on the resource so that he or she can access it. Remember, though, that ownership can be taken but never given, and that goes for giving back too.

When the administrator owns the resource, he/she can never return ownership to the original user without that user explicitly taking ownership. And that is how it should be for legitimate situations in which a user might be absent from work when a critical file needs to be accessed. The administrator could get into a sticky situation by accessing files without a legitimate reason.

b. Permissions Versus User Rights

You may remember that resource permissions are not the same thing as user rights. User rights are tasks stored with your account information in the Registry, which you can perform on the system as a whole. NTFS permissions are stored with the resource itself, in the ACL property discussed earlier.

It is important to understand the difference between rights and permissions, because that understanding brings light to why the resource permissions assigned to a user cannot be viewed the way trustee assignments in other operating systems such as Novell NetWare are viewed. Displaying all the permissions assigned to a user requires searching all the NTFS files and directories on all the NTFS partitions on the workstation and on shared directories of any other workstation or server on the network. It also requires searching for incidence of the user's SID or group SIDs on the ACL of each of those files.

c. Directory-Level Permissions

Permissions can be placed on both directories and files. When they are, you need to resolve the permissions to figure out the effective permissions for a user.

The owner of a directory may grant a user the following permissions:

No Access	Restricts users from accessing the directory by any means. The directory appears in the directory tree, but instead of a file list, users see the message "You do not have permissions to access this directory."
List	Restricts users from accessing the directory, although they may view the contents list for the directory.
Read	Users can read data files and execute program files from the directory, but cannot make changes.
Add	Users cannot read or even view the contents of the directory, but may write files to the directory. If you write a file to the directory, you receive the message "You do not have permissions to access this directory, but you still may save or copy files to it."
Add & Read	Users may view and read from the directory and save new files into the directory, but cannot modify existing files.
Change	Users may view and read from the directory and save new files into the directory, may modify and even delete existing files, and may change attributes on the directory and even delete the entire directory
Full Control	Users may view, read, save, modify, or delete the directory and its contents. In addition, users may change permissions on the directory and its contents, even if they do not own the resource. Users can also take ownership at any time.

What actually happens with all these levels of permissions is a combination of six basic actions that can be performed against a resource:

- Read (R)
- Write (W)
- Execute (X)
- Delete (D)
- Change Permissions (P)
- Take Ownership (O)

The following table breaks down these permissions by permissions level:

Level	Directory Permissions	File Permissions
No Access	None	None
List	RX	Unspecified
Read	RX	RX
Add	WX	Unspecified
Add & Read	RXWD	RX
Change	RXWD	RXWD
Full Control	RXWDPO	RXWDPO

The two custom levels of permissions are Special Directory Access and Special File Access, both of which enable the owner (or any user granted the "P" permission) to custom build an access control entry by using any combination of the six basic actions mentioned here.

When a new directory or file is created on an NTFS partition, the resource inherits the permissions on its parent directory, the same way it inherits the compression attribute. (See the section, "NTFS File Compression," earlier in this chapter.)

d. File-Level Permissions

Although permissions for files are not as varied as they are for directories, NTFS can store permissions for files also. The owner of a file may grant users the following permissions:

No Access	Cannot access this file at all, although the file name and basic attributes still appear in File Manager.
Read	Can read this file if it is a data file, or execute it if it is a program file, but can not modify it.
Change	Can read, execute, modify, or delete this file.
Full Control	Can read or execute, write to, or delete this file, may change permissions on it, as well as take ownership away from the current owner.

The following table breaks down these file permissions:

Level	Permissions
No Access	None
Read	RX
Change	RXWD
Full Control	RXWDPO

As with Directory permissions, a Special Access level allows anyone who has the capability to change permissions to custom build an access control entry for a user or group.

e. Setting Permissions

To set permissions on a file or directory, first select the resource in Explorer or My Computer, and then choose File, Properties. Click on the Permissions button on the Security tab of the File Properties dialog box to open the File Permissions dialog box.

To remove a user or group from the ACL, select the user and click on the Remove button. To add a user or group to the ACL, click on the Add button. Clicking on the Add button opens the Add Users and Groups dialog box, which includes a list of all the groups in your account database (see fig. 3.4.4).

Figure 3.4.4   The Add Users and Groups dialog box.

If you want to grant access to a specific user, click on the Show Users button. Otherwise, only the group names are displayed. Choose the users and groups you want to add to the ACL individually or collectively and click on the Add button to enter their names in the Add Names list box at the bottom of the dialog box. Don't try to set their access level here, unless all of these accounts are going to be granted the same access level. When you click on the OK button, you get another chance to modify the permission level for each individual account on the ACL.

Setting permissions for a directory brings up a slightly different dialog box—you can set the following additional options before the new permissions are applied to the directory:

- **Replace Permissions on Subdirectories:** Modifies the permissions on all directories in the directory tree, but not on any files within those directories, even in the top-level directory.

- **Replace Permissions on Existing Files:** The permissions that apply to the directory also apply to the files within the directory, but not to subdirectories or files within subdirectories.

Selecting both check boxes applies these permissions to the entire directory tree and its contents. Enabling neither check box changes the permissions on the top-level directory only.

f. Local Groups

When working with user rights, assigning rights to user and built-in groups usually suffices. When assigning resource permissions, however, adding individual users may be too time-consuming, and adding built-in groups may be too inclusive. Imagine having a directory that contains meeting minutes for a project on which you are working. You would like to grant permissions to the people on the project team, but the team contains more than 30 people.

Assigning permissions to everybody would take a long time, and assigning permissions to the Users group would give access to too many people.

It is time to introduce local groups, a separate level of user management in Windows NT. Local groups can be created by any user for any purpose (Headquarters, Marketing, Vice Presidents, Portland, Engineering), and once created, can be reused repeatedly. By creating a local group called MyProject and including all the project team members, you need to grant only a single set of permissions for each meeting report.

g. Local Groups versus Built-In Groups

A *local group* is a group used to assign rights and/or permissions to a local system and local resources. Local groups are similar to built-in groups in that both can contain many users to address a single purpose. In fact, technically, the built-in groups in Windows NT Workstation are local groups.

Local and built-in groups also have similar structures. Both can contain local users, domain users, and global groups, and users and global groups from trusted domains. The only type of account that cannot be placed inside a local group is another local group.

The difference between local and built-in groups lies in their intended purposes. The built-in groups are predefined and preassigned to specific rights and capabilities for system management. They are not intended for use in managing access to resources. Local groups are impractical for managing the system, but are ideal for assigning permissions to files and directories.

The only other difference between the two types of groups is that built-in groups are permanent members of a computer's account database, whereas local groups can be created and deleted at will.

h. How User and Group Permissions Interact

At this point, you have probably realized that users are likely to be in many different groups. Abigail's user account, for example, may be a member of the Users group, but also the Marketing group, the Department Managers group, the Philadelphia group, and the Project X group. Each of these user and group accounts is likely to be granted permissions to resources at one time or another, and it is quite likely that some of the accounts might occasionally appear on the same Access Control List. In such scenarios, how should the permissions granted to both a user's user account and group accounts be resolved?

Quite simply, user and group permissions are cumulative; neither takes precedence over the other. If the Marketing group has Read access to a file and the Department Managers group has Change access to the same file, Abigail (a member of both groups) has both—or in other words, Change access, because Change already includes the R and X permissions that Read incorporates.

The one exception to this rule is the No Access permission. No Access overrides all other permissions granted to a user or the user's groups, regardless of where the No Access was assigned. If Abigail were granted Read access to a file but Marketing was granted No Access, for example, Abigail would not be able to access the file. You cannot—and this cannot be emphasized enough—override a No Access permission.

No Access is intended as a "negator" to remove permissions from a user or group that may already have been implicitly added to the ACL through membership in another group.

i. How Directory and File Permissions Interact

When you have permissions on both directories and files—such is the case on an NTFS partition—things get just a bit more complicated. Fortunately, you can resolve this situation pretty easily, although a few odd circumstances might surround the situation.

Simply put, file permissions override directory permissions. Likewise, it is possible to grant a user Read access to a directory and yet still grant Full Control over a single file within that directory.

This can lead to some odd scenarios. Sam may not want anyone to view the contents of his private directory, for example, so he assigns the directory this ACL:

> Sam: Full Control

If Beth tries to view this directory, she gets the You do not have permission to access this directory message. Yet Sam may still want to occasionally grant Beth access to one or two of his files. One day, he grants Beth Read access to a document in his private directory. Beth can read that file, but how can she access it? She can't view the directory contents in Explorer, and when she does a File/Open in an application, she cannot view the directory contents there either. Before she can access the file, Beth must type the full path to the file, from the application in which she wants to view it.

j. File Delete Child

Consider another odd scenario. Sam decides to grant Everyone Full Control to his private directory, and just apply Read permissions to Everyone for the individual files within the directory. Sam knows that although users might be able to copy and save files in his directory, they can't change the ones already present, because those files have only Read permissions. Sam also knows that no one else can change permissions on the existing files, because those files have only Read permissions. Sam, however, thinks that no one can delete his existing files because they only have Read permissions. On this last count, he is wrong.

In addition to the six basic permissions (RXWDPO) granted with Full Control, there is a seventh, implicit permission, called File Delete Child (FDC). FDC is included for POSIX compatibility, and it grants a user who has Full Control over a directory the capability to delete a top-level file within that directory, even if that user does not have delete permissions to the file itself! Only top-level files can be deleted, not subdirectories or files within subdirectories.

There is a workaround, but you must grant Special Directory Access before you can use it. If you grant Special Directory Access and choose all six permissions rather than grant Full Control to a directory, the user granted this level of access won't have the FDC permission. It looks like you are really just assigning the equivalent of Full Control, but you are doing so minus File Delete Child. By the way, don't waste time searching for File Delete Child in the Explorer interface—it is not there. It's an implicit permission granted only when Full Control is granted over a directory.

An even better workaround is to never grant anyone Full Control over anything, unless you grant it to yourself as the owner. After all, you probably don't want anyone else to have the power to change permissions on the file and lock you out. And you certainly don't want someone to have the capability to take ownership of the file at the same time so that you can't even change permissions back to what they were. A good rule of thumb is never to grant anyone any permissions higher than Change. That is high enough, because a user with Change access can delete the resource itself.

k. Special Considerations for the Boot and System Partitions

When you install Windows NT on an NTFS partition, it is tempting to prevent necessary files from being deleted or overwritten, to try to exclude users from accessing the Windows NT installation directory tree. If you examine the Access Control List for that directory, however, you won't see the customary Everyone/Full Control that you normally find on NTFS resources.

The critical entry on the ACL is the SYSTEM/Full Control ACE. Do not, under any circumstances, remove this ACL from the list, or modify it. Otherwise, Windows NT crashes and you cannot restart the operating system.

If this does happen, don't panic. You can use the Emergency Repair Disk to strip the permissions from the Windows NT installation directory tree.

3.4.1   Exercise: Taking Ownership

The purpose of this exercise is to show how user A, who owns a file or directory, can initiate ownership transfer to user B, who then finishes the ownership transfer by taking it.

1. User A selects the file or directory he wants to transfer ownership to user B. He opens the security tab and clicks on Permissions.

2. Once on there, he selects user B from the user list and assigns Read access. Back in the Permissions dialog box, he selects Special Access and enables Take Ownership. User A's part is finished.

3. Now user B can go to the Security tab, select Ownership and then click Take Ownership to be the new owner of the file.

3.4.2   Exercise: Configuring Auditing

The purpose of this example is to show how to configure auditing for a file using NT Explorer. Follow these steps:

1. Right-click on an NTFS file in Explorer of My Computer and choose Properties.

2. Click on the Security tab of the File Properties dialog box.

3. Click on the Auditing button. The File Auditing dialog box appears (see fig. 3.4.5). You can audit either successful or failed attempts at any of the actions listed, and you can specify which specific groups or users you want to audit.

4. Click on the Add button to add a group or user to the audit list. Click on the Remove button to delete a group or user from the audit list.

The Directory Auditing dialog box is similar. The procedure for reaching the Directory Auditing dialog box is similar to the procedure for reaching the file Auditing dialog box. Right click on a directory, choose Properties, choose the Directory Properties Security tab, then click on the Auditing button. The Directory Auditing dialog box enables you to choose whether the new auditing arrangement you are configuring will replace the auditing on subdirectories or existing files.

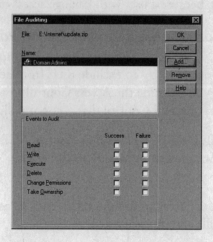

Figure 3.4.5   The File Auditing dialog box.

3.4   Practice Problems

1. You are copying a file that is compressed with permissions set to Read for Everyone to an uncompressed directory in which Everyone has Change permissions. Which of the following statements is true?

   A. The file will be compressed and Change permissions enforced for Everyone.

   B. The file will be compressed and Read permissions enforced for Everyone.

   C. The file will be uncompressed and Read permissions enforced for Everyone.

   D. The file will be uncompressed and Change permissions enforced for Everyone.

2. You are moving a file that is compressed and has permissions set to Read for Everyone to an uncompressed directory in which Everyone has Change permissions. Which of the following statements is true?

   A. The file will be compressed and Change permissions enforced for Everyone.

   B. The file will be compressed and Read permissions enforced for Everyone.

   C. The file will be uncompressed and Read permissions enforced for Everyone.

   D. The file will be uncompressed and Change permissions enforced for Everyone.

3. You are moving a file that is compressed and has permissions set to Read for Everyone to a different disk on an uncompressed directory in which Everyone has Change permissions. Which of the following statements is true?

   A. The file will be compressed and Change permissions enforced for Everyone.

   B. The file will be compressed and Read permissions enforced for Everyone.

   C. The file will be uncompressed and Read permissions enforced for Everyone.

   D. The file will be uncompressed and Change permissions enforced for Everyone.

4. Which of the following statements is true?

   A. You can convert FAT partitions to NTFS at any time using Disk Administrator.

   B. You can convert FAT partitions to NTFS at any time using the command line utility convert.exe.

   C. You can convert NTFS partitions to FAT at any time using Disk Administrator.

   D. You can convert NTFS partitions to FAT at any time using the command line utility convert.exe.

5. Which of the following statements about NTFS compression is true?

   A. Compression is only available for entire drives.

   B. Both FAT and NTFS file systems support compression.

   C. You can tune NTFS compression with Registry editor going to the HKEY_LOCAL_MACHINE\ CurrentControlSet\Services\Ntfs and setting the NtfsCompression Factor to a higher number.

   D. NTFS compression is transparent to all applications and can be used only on NTFS formatted volumes.

3

6. Which of the following command lines forces all files in the directory to be recompressed? Select the best answer:

   A. COMPACT *.* /C

   B. COMPACT *.* /F

   C. COMPACT *.* /R

   D. COMPACT *.* /S

7. You want to format a floppy disk using the NTFS file system. Select the best method of doing this:

   A. Go to Disk Administrator, select the floppy disk drive and run the Format command from the Tools menu. Specify NTFS as file system.

   B. Open File Manager and select Disk, Format NTFS. You are prompted to insert a disk.

   C. You cannot format floppy disks using NTFS.

   D. You have to use the RDISK utility to format removable disks with NTFS.

8. You have set up the computer of your boss as a Windows NT computer with drive C: formatted with NTFS. Now, he wants to test-drive Windows 95b on this computer. What would you need to do to install Windows 95b? Select the best answer:

   A. Nothing. Simply start the installation program of Windows 95b.

   B. Add an MS-DOS entry to the boot.ini file, and restart the computer. Now you can install Windows 95b.

   C. You have to backup the files, format the drive with FAT, install Windows 95b, and then install Windows NT again. Don't forget to restore the files.

   D. You cannot go with solution C because NT can't read the FAT32 entries of Windows 95b.

9. Which file systems are supported by Windows NT? Select all that apply:

   A. CDFS

   B. HPFS

   C. NTFS

   D. FAT

10. Which file systems allow to secure files with ACLs? Select all that apply:

    A. CDFS

    B. HPFS

    C. NTFS

    D. FAT

11. You have set the following permissions on a directory: Change for the Sales group, Read for the SalesManagers group, and No Access for Everyone. Ronnie is member of the SalesManagers group. What kind of access is he granted? Select the best answer:

    A. Change

    B. Read

    C. Take Ownership

    D. No Access

12. You have set the following permissions on a directory: Change for the Sales group, and Read for Ann (who is member of the SalesManagers and the Sales group). What kind of access is she granted? Select the best answer:

    A. Change

    B. Read

    C. Take Ownership

    D. No Access

13. You have created a share on a directory. The directory permissions are as follows: Change for the Sales group, and Read for Ann (who is member of the SalesManagers and the Sales group). The share has Read permission for the Sales group. What kind of access is she granted? Select the best answer:

    A. Change

    B. Read

    C. Take Ownership

    D. No Access

14. You have created a share on a directory. The directory permissions are as follows: Change for the Sales group, and Read for Ann (who is member of the SalesManagers and the Sales group). The share has Read permission for the Sales group. What kind of access has Ronnie, who is member of the SalesManager group? Select the best answer:

    A. Change

    B. Read

    C. Take Ownership

    D. No Access

15. Which of the following statements is true about the following share on the MEGAMACH server: \\MEGAMACH\machine$

    Select the best answer:

    A. It is an administrative share.

    B. It is a hidden share.

    C. The share can be accessed only from Windows NT computers.

    D. The dollar sign ($) is invalid for share names. This share cannot exist.

16. Which of the following statements is true about administrative shares?

    A. Administrative shares cannot be disabled.

    B. Administrative shares are available to Administrators, Server Operators, and Account Operators.

    C. Administrative shares can be turned off.

    D. Administrative shares are available on Windows NT Server only.

17. What are the default file and directory permissions on an NTFS partition? Select the best answer:

    A. Everyone Full Control

    B. Administrators Full Control, Everyone Read

    C. Everyone Change

    D. Everyone No Access

18. Ben has been offered a management position in another company and is about to leave the company. His replacement, Joey, asks him to turn over his project files. Which of the following is best way to achieve this?

    A. Ask the administrator to assign permissions on Ben's files to the Joey.

    B. Ben must grant Take Ownership permission to Joey on his files and then Joey must take ownership on these.

    C. Joey must execute Take Ownership from the Security tab on Ben's files and directories.

    D. None of this works. Ben has to e-mail the files to Joey.

3.4   Answers and Explanations: Practice Problems

1. **D**   When copying, the file inherits compression and permissions from the destination folder.

2. **B**   Moving on the same disk retains compression and permissions.

3. **D**   Moving to a different disk is a copy operation followed by a delete operation.

4. **B**   You can convert FAT partitions to NTFS at any time using the command line utility convert.exe.

5. **D**   NTFS compression is performed on the fly and does not warrant special attention by applications accessing the compressed files.

6. **B**   COMPACT *.* /F forces all files in the directory to be recompressed.

7. **C**   You can't format a floppy disk with NTFS because of its overhead.

8. **D**   NT currently does not support FAT32.

9. **A, C, D**   HPFS is no longer supported with NT 4.

10. **C**   Only NTFS allows you to set permissions.

11. **D**   No Access overrides all other permissions.

12. **A**   Permissions are cumulative.

13. **B**   Permissions are cumulative.

14. **D**   No Access overrides all others.

15. **B**   Trailing "$" denotes hidden shares.

16. **C**   You can only turn off administrative shares.

17. **A**   Standard installation sets permission to Everyone Full Control.

18. **B**   Take Ownership enables others to gain control over files owned by a user granting Take Ownership.

3.4   Key Words

Copying	Moving
NTFS compression	
Compact.exe	Sharing
Server managers	Share permissions
Net share	Monitoring shares
Managing shares	NTFS permissions
Take Ownership	Auditing
File Delete Child	

Practice Exam: Managing Resources

Use this practice exam to test your mastery of Planning. This practice exam is 9 questions long, so you should try to finish the test within 15 minutes or so. Keep in mind that the passing Microsoft score is 76.4 percent. There will be two types of questions:

- Multiple Choice—Select the correct answer.

- Multiple Multiple Choice—Select all answers that are correct.

Begin as soon as you are ready. Answers follow the test.

1. Which of the following groups are built-in global groups on Windows NT domain controllers? Select all that apply:

    A. Domain Users

    B. Domain Operators

    C. Domain Guests

    D. None of the above

2. You want to prevent users on your system from changing back to their original passwords right after they have been forced to change it by your account policy (password expiration set to 25 days). How can you circumvent this problem? Select the best answer:

    A. Enable Password never expires for all users.

    B. Set the maximum password age to 2.

    C. Set the minimum password age to 24.

    D. Keep a password history.

3. You are creating a single account for your summer interns. How can you prevent a single intern from changing the password for the user account? Select the best answer:

    A. Set Password Expires for this account to the amount of time this account is intended to be used.

    B. Use a blank password.

    C. Enable "User cannot change password."

    D. Revoke the right "Change password" from the account the summer interns will be using.

4. System Policy Editor comes with the following policy templates (select all that apply):

    A. common.adm

    B. winnt.adm

    C. windows.adm

    D. user.adm

5. Where are the policy template files stored by default? Select the best answer:

    A. <winnt_root>\inf

    B. <winnt_root>\profiles

    C. <winnt_root>\system32\config

    D. <winnt_root>\System32\Repl\ Import\Scripts

6. Which of the following are client-based administration tools for Windows NT? Select all that apply:

    A. Services for Macintosh

    B. Remoteboot Manager

    C. File and Print Services for NetWare

    D. System Policy Editor

3

7. You have created an application pool share named POOL. You want to audit who executes a specific setup program. How can you achieve this? Select the best answer:

    A. Enable auditing on the share for Execute events.

    B. Enable auditing for the specific Setup program for Execute events only.

    C. You cannot do this.

    D. Enable auditing for the specific Setup program for Execute and Read events.

8. Which of the following statements isn't true about account types? Choose all the apply:

    A. Windows NT administrators can create two types of accounts: user accounts and group accounts.

    B. A user account can belong to one person only.

    C. A group account is limited to 256 users.

    D. A group account is a collection of users that holds common rights and permissions by way of its association with the group.

    E. All of the above are true.

9. Windows NT users get their rights and permissions in which of the following ways? Choose all that apply:

    A. They are explicitly assigned a right or permission through user accounts.

    B. They acquire rights after the administrator manually enables such rights.

    C. They are members of a group that has a right or permission.

    D. They acquire rights from another user.

Answers and Explanations: Practice Exam

1. **A, C**   Domain Users and Domain Guests are built-in global groups on Windows NT domain controllers.

2. **D**   Password history prevents users from using old passwords.

3. **C**   You can prevent a single intern from changing the password for the user account by enabling "User cannot change password."

4. **A, B, C**   The user.adm file doesn't come with System Policy Editor.

5. **A**   <winnt_root>\inf is the default location for system policy templates.

6. **A, B, D**   File and Print Services for NetWare are not part of the client-based administration tools for NT.

7. **B**   Auditing enables you to monitor which files are accessed.

8. **C**   A group account can hold an unlimited amount of users.

9. **A, C**   Users get rights when they are explicitly assigned a right or permission through their accounts, or when they are members of a group that has a right or permission.

CHAPTER 4

Connectivity

The "Connectivity" section of the Microsoft Exam (70-67) includes the following objectives:

- Configure Windows NT Server for interoperability with NetWare servers using various tools. Tools include Gateway Services for NetWare and Migration Tool for NetWare.

- Install and configure Remote Access Service (RAS). Configuration options include configuring RAS communications, configuring RAS protocols, configuring RAS security, and configuring dial-up networking clients.

4.1 NetWare Connectivity

Microsoft Windows NT Server provides features that permit connectivity to NetWare-based systems. The following sections outline these features, which include: NetWare Gateway Service (GSNW), Client Services for NetWare (CSNW), and the Migration Tool for NetWare.

A. Gateway Services for NetWare (GSNW)

Gateway Services for NetWare (GSNW) is available only with Windows NT Server. GSNW performs the following functions:

- Enables Windows NT Server systems to access NetWare file and print resources directly.

- Enables a Windows NT Server to act as a gateway to NetWare resources. Non-NetWare clients on a Windows NT network then can access NetWare resources through the gateway as if they were accessing Windows NT resources without any need for NetWare client licensing (see fig. 4.1.1).

GSNW is a practical solution for occasional NetWare access, but is not designed to serve as a high-volume solution for a busy network. Because all Windows NT clients must reach the NetWare server through a single connection, there is potential for a bottleneck and performance diminishes considerably with increased traffic.

Network clients with operating systems that use Server Message Block (SMB)—Windows NT, Windows 95, and Windows for Workgroups—can access a share through a GSNW gateway. GSNW supports both NDS-based and bindery-based NetWare systems.

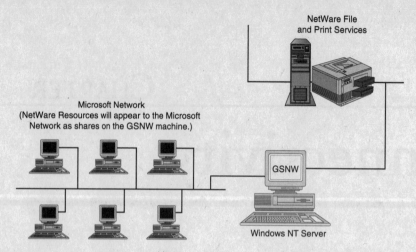

Figure 4.1.1 GSNW enables a Windows NT Server to act as a gateway to NetWare resources.

NetWare Directory Service (NDS) is a distributed database of network resources primarily associated with NetWare 4.x systems. Bindery-based NetWare networks are primarily associated with NetWare 3.x.

1. GSNW Installation and Configuration

In order to install GSNW, you must be logged on the NT Server as an Administrator. Before installing GSNW, you must remove any NetWare redirectors presently on your system (such as Novell NetWare services for Windows NT) and reboot the Server. GSNW is a network service; it is installed using the Services tab of the Control Panel Network application. To install GSNW, follow these steps:

1. Choose Start, Settings/Control Panel. Double-click on the Control Panel Network application icon.

2. In the Network application's Network dialog box, select the Services tab. Click on the Add button to open the Select Network Services dialog box.

3. Select Gateway (and Client) Services for NetWare in the Network Service list; then click on OK.

4. Windows NT prompts you for the location of the files (typically, the installation CD-ROM).

5. Windows NT asks if you want to restart your system. You must restart the system to enable the new service.

2. GSNW as a Gateway

To configure GSNW to act as a gateway to NetWare resources, you must have supervisor equivalence on the NetWare server, and perform the following steps:

1. Using NetWare's Syscon utility, create a group called NTGATEWAY on the NetWare server.

2. Using NetWare's Syscon utility, create a user account on the NetWare server for the gateway and add the gateway user account to the NTGATEWAY group.

3. Double-click on the GSNW icon in the Control Panel. The Gateway Service for NetWare dialog box appears. The Preferred Server, Default Tree and Context, Print Options, and Login Script Options frames are discussed in the following section.

4. To configure Windows NT to act as a gateway, click on the Gateway button. The Configure Gateway dialog box appears.

5. Select the Enable Gateway check box. In the Gateway Account text box, enter the name of the account you created on the NetWare server. Below the account name, enter the password for the account and retype the password in the Confirm Password text box.

GSNW essentially enables you to create a Windows NT share for a resource on a NetWare server. Microsoft network machines that use Server Message Block (SMB), such as Windows NT, Windows 95, and Windows for Workgroups, can then access the share even if they don't have NetWare client software. NetWare directories and volumes presently shared through a gateway appear in the Share name list at the bottom of the Configure Gateway dialog box.

To create a new share for a NetWare directory or volume, click on the Add button in the Configure Gateway dialog box. You are asked to enter a share name and a network path to the NetWare resource. You then can enter a drive letter for the share. The share appears to Windows NT, Windows 95, and Windows for Workgroups machines as a network drive on the gateway machine.

The Remove button in the Configure Gateway dialog box removes a gateway share. The Permissions button lets you set permissions for the share.

B. Client Services for NetWare (CSNW)

Client Services for NetWare (CSNW) enables a Windows NT Workstation to access file and print services on a NetWare server (see fig. 4.1.2). CSNW is incorporated into Windows NT Server's GSNW. GSNW and CSNW both support NDS-based and bindery-based NetWare servers. GSNW and CSNW also support Novell's NetWare Core Protocol (NCP) and Large Internet Protocol (LIP).

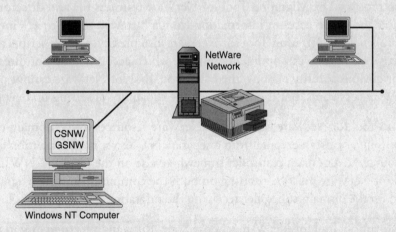

Figure 4.1.2   CSNW enables a Windows NT computer to access file and print services as a client on a NetWare network.

CSNW, like GSNW, is a network service; you install it using the Services tab of the Control Panel Network application. If you're running Windows NT Server, CSNW functions are installed automatically when you install GSNW.

The first time you log on after you install CSNW or GSNW, Windows NT prompts you to enter a preferred server and attempts to validate your credentials for the NetWare network.

The Select Preferred Server for NetWare dialog box shows the name of the user attempting to log on and a drop-down list of available NetWare servers. As implied by the username parameter, this is a per-user configuration parameter. The selected server is stored in HKEY_CURRENT_USER, not HKEY_LOCAL_MACHINE.

Choose <None> in the Select Preferred Server for NetWare dialog box if you don't want to have a preferred server authenticate your logon request. Choosing the Cancel button just defers the decision until the next time you log on.

After you select a preferred server, Windows NT always tries to have that server authenticate the user. If the server is unavailable, the user is prompted for a new preferred server. A user can change his or her preferred server at any time via the new CSNW icon in Control Panel (which was added during installation of CSNW).

Double-clicking on the GSNW icon in Control Panel opens the Gateway Service for NetWare dialog box, which lets you select a preferred server and a default tree and context for the NetWare network.

You also can choose to run a NetWare logon script. To connect to a client to a NetWare server's printer, use the Add Printer Wizard in the Printers folder as you would for any Network attached printer device.

C.   Migration Tool for NetWare

To ease the transition process from NetWare to NT Server, Microsoft provides a tool to automate the migration process. The Migration Tool for NetWare transfers file and directory information along with user and group account information from a NetWare server to a Windows NT domain controller. The Migration Tool for NetWare also preserves logon scripts and directory and file effective rights. You can optionally indicate which accounts, files, or directories you want migrated. For obvious security reasons, the Migration Tool for NetWare cannot preserve the original NetWare passwords, but it does provide the capability of setting up new passwords.

The Migration Tool for NetWare can migrate NetWare resources to the domain controller on which it is running, or it can execute from a separate NT Server or Workstation and migrate the NetWare resources to a domain controller somewhere else on the network. NWLink and Gateway Services for NetWare must be running on both the computer running Migration Tool for NetWare and on the domain controller receiving the migration.

To run the Migration Tool for NetWare, choose Start, Run, and type **nwconv** in the Run dialog box.

The Migration Tool for NetWare provides a number of options for transferring file and account information. Always migrate files and directories to an NTFS partition if possible, because NTFS file and directory permissions provide an equivalent to the trustee rights specified for these resources in the NetWare environment.

4.1.1 Exercise: Creating a Gateway to a NetWare Directory Using GSNW

Note: This exercise requires both an NT Server and a NetWare Server.

Exercise 4.1.1 examines the process of establishing a gateway to a NetWare directory using Gateway Services for NetWare.

1. Log on to the NT Server as an Administrator if you have not done so already.

2. From the Control Panel, double-click on the Network icon.

3. Choose the Services tab and click on the Add button.

4. Select Gateway (and Client) Services for NetWare in the Network Service list; then click on OK.

5. After all the required files are copied, click on Yes to restart your system.

   What new icon has been added to the NT Server's Control Panel?

6. From the NetWare server, open the Syscon utility.

7. Create a group called NTGATEWAY.

8. Create a user account for the gateway and add the gateway user account to the NTGATEWAY group.

9. Back at the NT Server, double-click on the GSNW icon in Control Panel. The Gateway Service for NetWare dialog box appears. To configure Windows NT to act as a gateway, click on the Gateway button.

   Under what circumstances would you want to utilize the Gateway Service for NetWare?

10. The Configure Gateway dialog box appears. Click on the Enable Gateway check box. In the Gateway Account text box, enter the name of the account you created on the NetWare server. Below the account name, enter the password for the account and retype the password in the Confirm Password text box.

11. To create a new share for the NetWare directory or volume, click on the Add button. You are asked to enter a share name and a network path to the NetWare resource. You then can enter a drive letter for the share.

12. From another SMB-compatible computer on the Microsoft network (Windows NT, Windows 95, or Windows for Workgroups), access the gateway computer through Network Neighborhood. Look for the drive letter you entered in step 5 for the NetWare directory. Double-click on the drive letter and browse the NetWare files.

4.1 Practice Problems

1. When using GSNW to provide access to NetWare resources for Microsoft clients, what are the NetWare licensing requirements for the clients?

   A. Each of the clients must obtain individual NetWare licensing.

   B. No additional NetWare licensing is required.

   C. You need to obtain NetWare licensing only for the maximum number of clients that will connect at any given time.

   D. None of the above.

2. After installing a NetWare gateway using GSNW, you can then create a share on the gateway machine for NetWare files using what?

   A. GSNW

   B. Control Panel

   C. Explorer or My Computer

   D. Any of the above

3. The Migration Tool for NetWare is not capable of preserving which of the following?

   A. Accounts

   B. Files

   C. Rights

   D. Directories

   E. Passwords

4. Your company currently has several thousand NT clients and several hundred NetWare clients running on separate networks. The NetWare server contains vital information that needs to be accessed continuously by everyone. The managers have requested that you provide a plan for providing equal access between these networks. What course of action would be the best solution?

   A. Install the GSNW service.

   B. Report that a solution is not possible.

   C. Purchase NetWare client licenses for all the NT side clients in order to allow them direct access to the server.

   D. Use the Migration Tool for NetWare, and convert the NetWare clients to NT.

5. How do you attach to a NetWare server's printer?

   A. Use File and Print Services for NetWare (FPNW).

   B. Use the Add Printer Wizard in the Printers folder.

   C. You cannot connect to a NetWare Server printer.

   D. Use the DLC protocol.

6. Installing what service will enable your Windows NT Server machine to access file and print resources on a NetWare server?

   A. File and Print Services for NetWare (FPNW)

   B. Client Services for NetWare (CSNW)

   C. Gateway Services for NetWare (GSNW)

   D. Directory Service Manager for NetWare (DSMN)

7. Which service must be established on an NT Server before you can share NetWare print queues?

   A. FPNW

   B. GSNW

   C. NetWare Migration Tool

   D. DLC

8. Which two statements regarding GSNW are accurate:

   A. GSNW attaches the NT Server to the NetWare server as a client.

   B. GSNW shares user account information between NetWare servers and NT Server.

   C. GSNW emulates a NetWare Server to clients using the NetWare Requester.

   D. GSNW permits NT Server to request resources from the NetWare server, and to share them with clients on the Microsoft network.

9. Some of your Microsoft network clients use an old application that does not send a proper end-of-file message to the printer on the attached NetWare server utilizing GSNW on an NT Server. What simple step could you perform to overcome this situation?

   A. Move the printer to the NT side of the network.

   B. Upgrade the application to a NetWare-aware version.

   C. Open the GSNW tool in the Control Panel and select the Add Form Feed option.

   D. Open the Printer device properties, choose the Device settings tab, and select the Add Dorm Feed option.

10. The Migration Tool for NetWare can migrate NetWare resources to which type of domain controller?

    A. Only to the domain controller on which the Migration Tool for NetWare is currently running.

    B. Besides the domain controller that is running the migration process, it can migrate NetWare resources to any available domain controller running NWLink and GSNW.

    C. Besides the domain controller that is running the migration process, it can migrate NetWare resources to any available domain controller that has an available NTFS partition.

    D. The migration process must transfer resources only to a separate domain controller running NWLink, GSNW, and has an available NTFS partition.

11. What must be running on the NT Server that is going to be receiving the migration, before using the Migration Tool for NetWare?

    A. GSNW

    B. NWLink

    C. NTFS

    D. IP

12. If your Microsoft network has a relatively small number of clients who want to be able to access resources on a NetWare server, what would be the best solution?

    A. Use floppy disks to transfer any needed files.

    B. Purchase additional NetWare client licenses as needed, and attach them to the NetWare server.

    C. Use the NWCONV tool to migrate the NetWare server resources to an NT Server.

    D. Install and configure GSNW.

13. When using the Migration Tool for NetWare, why is it preferable to migrate the NetWare resources to an NT Server utilizing NTFS?

    A. Using a non-NTFS partition will cause significant performance problems.

    B. There is no choice; you must use an NTFS partition during the migration process.

4

C. NTFS file and directory permissions provide an equivalent to the trustee rights specified in the NetWare environment.

D. NTFS is the only way to properly transfer account password information to the NT Server.

14. Which Microsoft network clients can access NetWare resources through a NetWare gateway on a Windows NT Server?

A. Currently, Windows 95 and Windows NT are supported.

B. Any Microsoft client that uses Server Message Blocks: WFWG, Windows 95, and Windows NT.

C. Any client using Microsoft's NWLink IPX/SPX protocol stack.

D. MS-DOS, Windows 3.x, LAN Manager, WFWG, Windows 95, NT Workstation, and Macintosh.

15. What command is used in the Run box to start the Migration Tool for NetWare?

A. CONVNW.EXE

B. MTNW.EXE

C. CONVNW.COM

D. NWCONV.EXE

16. What tool must be used on the NetWare server to create the necessary group and account on the NetWare server to facilitate the installation of GSNW on a NT Server?

A. SYSCON

B. PCON

C. User Manager

D. DSMN

17. After installing GSNW and rebooting the NT Server, you are prompted to choose a preferred server. Which server option should you choose in the Select Preferred Server for NetWare dialog box if you don't want to have a preferred server authenticate your logon request?

A. <None>

B. The NetWare server with the least amount of activity

C. The name of the NetWare server that was initially established during the installation of GSNW

D. <All>

18. What is the primary purpose of GSNW?

A. GSNW essentially enables you to create a Windows NT share for a resource on a NetWare server.

B. GSNW provides an essential component utilized by the Migration Tool for NetWare.

C. GSNW provides an economical alternative to purchasing NetWare client licensing.

D. A and C.

19. During the installation of GSNW, which tab of the Network application's dialog box is utilized?

A. Identification

B. Services

C. Protocols

D. Adapters

E. Bindings

20. A GSNW gateway can provide Windows NT networks with convenient access to NetWare resources, but isn't an appropriate solution under which of the following circumstances?

A. Serving as a high-volume Microsoft client to NetWare resource solution for a busy network.

B. Sharing multiple NetWare resources with Microsoft clients.

C. Providing an economical solution when only a nominal number of Microsoft clients will be accessing NetWare resources.

D. When reducing administrative overhead is desirable.

4.1   Answers and Explanations: Exercises

The Gateway Services for NetWare icon is the new icon added to the NT Servers Control Panel in step 5.

In step 9, you would want to utilize the Gateway Service for NetWare to permit SMB-compatible computers on the NT network (Windows NT, Windows 95, or Windows for Workgroups) access to resources on the NetWare server.

4.1   Answers and Explanations: Practice Problems

1. **B** It is not necessary for clients accessing the NetWare server through the NT GSNW service to have NetWare client licensing (just the NT Server itself).

2. **A** To create a new share for a NetWare directory or volume, click on the Add button in the Configure Gateway dialog box within the GSNW application.

3. **E** For security reasons, the Migration Tool for NetWare cannot preserve the original NetWare password, but it provides you with the capability of setting a new password from within the tool.

4. **D** Under this scenario, the best option is to use the Migration Tool for NetWare and convert all users to an NT environment. Otherwise, there is tremendous potential for a bottleneck at the GSNW NT server.

5. **B** The connection to a NetWare server's printer is relatively transparent. Simply use the same basic procedures you use to connect to any network attached printer device.

6. **C** GSNW provides access to file and printer resources on a NetWare server.

7. **B** GSNW provides accessibility to NetWare printer queues in addition to file resources.

8. **A** As far as the NetWare server is concerned, the NT Server running GSNW is just another client. The NT Server can then share the NetWare resources among the Microsoft network.

9. **C** By using the Form Feed option, you can often overcome such printing issues.

10. **B** The Migration Tool for NetWare can migrate NetWare resources to the domain controller on which it is running, or it can execute from a separate NT Server or Workstation and migrate the NetWare resources to a domain controller somewhere else on the network. Both the domain controller running the migration process and the domain controller receiving the migration process resources must be running NWLink and GSNW.

11. **A, B** GSNW and the NWLink protocol stack must be running before the Migration Tool for NetWare will function properly.

12. **D** GSNW is a practical solution unless you have a busy, high-volume network with a substantial number of clients who want to utilize the GSNW.

13. **C** Although it is not necessary to migrate NetWare resources to an NTFS partition, it is always the preferred method in order to preserve equivalent rights.

14. **B** Clients must support Server Message Blocks (SMB) in order to access a share through a GSNW gateway.

15. **D** The executable filename is NWCONV.EXE, and is located in the %SYSTEMROOT%\SYSTEM32 directory.

16. **A** NetWare's SYSCON is utilized to create and manage groups and accounts on a NetWare server.

17. **A** If you do not want to have a specific NetWare server assigned as a preferred server, choose the <none> option. This permits any available NetWare server to authenticate your logon request.

18. **A**   GSNW essentially enables you to
create a Windows NT share for a resource
on a NetWare server. By attaching an NT
Server to NetWare resources utilizing
GSNW, the NT Server can then share the
attached resources as needed.

19. **B**   The GSNW service, as well as all
other network services, is installed under
the Services tab within the Network
application in the Control Panel.

20. **A**   Should the situation indicate that a
high volume of traffic is orchestrated
through the GSNW, it is advisable to seek
an alternative solution, such as migrating
the NetWare server resources to NT using
the Migration Tool for NetWare.

4.1   Key Words

Gateway Services for NetWare

Client Services for NetWare

Server Message Block

Preferred Server

Migration Tool for NetWare

NetWare Directory Service (NDS)

4.2   Remote Access Service (RAS)

Windows NT *Remote Access Service* (RAS) provides the technology to permit an NT-based computer to connect to a remote network via a dial-up connection and fully participate in the network as a network client. RAS also enables your Windows NT computer to receive dial-up connections from remote computers.

RAS supports SLIP and PPP line protocols, and NetBEUI, TCP/IP, and IPX network protocols. Because so many Internet users access their service providers using a phone line, RAS often serves as an Internet interface.

The dial-up networking application (in the Accessories program group) lets you create phonebook entries, which are preconfigured dial-up connections to specific sites. The Telephony application in the Control Panel enables the remote user to preconfigure dialing properties for different dialing locations.

RAS can connect to a remote computer using any of the following media:

- **Public Switched Telephone Network (PSTN).** (Also known as the phone company.) RAS can connect using a modem through an ordinary phone line.

- **X.25. A packet-switched network.** Computers access the network via a Packet Assembler Disassembler device (PAD). X.25 supports dial-up or direct connections.

- **Null modem cable.** A cable that connects two computers directly. The computers then communicate using their modems (rather than network adapter cards).

- **ISDN.** A digital line that provides faster communication and more bandwidth than a normal phone line. (It also costs more—that's why not everybody has it.) A computer must have a special ISDN card to access an ISDN line.

Windows NT 4 also includes a new feature called Multilink. Using Multilink, a Windows NT computer can form a RAS connection using more than one physical pathway. One Multilink connection, for example, can use two modems at once (or one modem line and one ISDN line) to form a single logical link. By using multiple pathways for one connection, Multilink can greatly increase bandwidth. Of course, the computer has to have access to more than one pathway (that is, it must have two modems installed) or you can't use it.

A.   RAS Security

Like everything else in Windows NT, RAS is designed for security. Here are some of RAS' security features:

- **Auditing.** RAS can leave an audit trail, enabling you to see who logged on when and what authentication they provided.

- **Callback security.** You can enable RAS server to use callback (hang up all incoming calls and call the caller back), and you can limit callback numbers to prearranged sites that you know are safe.

- **Encryption.** RAS can encrypt logon information, or it can encrypt all data crossing the connection.

- **Security hosts.** In case Windows NT isn't safe enough, you can add an extra dose of security by using a third-party intermediary security host—a computer that stands between the RAS client and the RAS server and requires an extra round of authentication.

- **PPTP filtering.** You can tell Windows NT to filter out all packets except ultra-safe PPTP packets (described in the section "PPTP").

B.   RAS Line Protocols

RAS supports the following line protocols:

- SLIP

- PPP

- PPTP

1. SLIP

Serial Line Internet Protocol (SLIP) is a standard protocol for serial line connections over TCP/IP networks. SLIP is relatively old for the computer age—it was developed in 1984—and lacks some of the features that are available in PPP. SLIP operates only with older modems and will not operate at speeds greater than 19.2 baud. Each node in a SLIP connection must have a static IP address; that is, you can't use Windows NT features such as DHCP and WINS. Unlike PPP, SLIP does not support NetBEUI or IPX; you must use TCP/IP with SLIP. Also, SLIP cannot encrypt logon information.

2. PPP

Point-to-Point Protocol (PPP) was originally conceived as a deluxe version of SLIP. Like SLIP, PPP is an industry standard for point-to-point communications, but PPP offers several advantages over SLIP. Most notably, PPP isn't limited to TCP/IP. PPP also supports IPX, NetBEUI, and several other network protocols, such as AppleTalk and DECnet.

Because PPP supports so many protocols, it allows much more flexibility in configuring network communications. Windows NT automatically binds RAS to TCP/IP, NetBEUI, and IPX if those protocols are installed at the same time as RAS.

Another advantage of RAS is that it supports encrypted passwords.

3. PPTP

Point-to-Point Tunneling Protocol (PPTP) is related to PPP, but is different enough, and important enough, to deserve its own section. PPTP is a protocol that lets you transmit PPP packets over a TCP/IP network securely. Because the Internet is a TCP/IP network, PPTP enables highly private network links over the otherwise highly public Internet. PPTP connections are encrypted, making them a nearly impenetrable to virtual voyeurs.

In fact, PPTP is part of an emerging technology called Virtual Private Networks (VPNs). The point of VPN is to provide corporate networks with the same (or close to the same) security over the Internet that they would have over a direct connection.

Another exciting advantage of PPTP (and another reason that it fits nicely into the scheme of the virtual private network) is that PPTP doesn't discriminate among protocols. Because PPP supports NetBEUI, IPX, and other network protocols, and because a PPTP operates on PPP packets, PPTP actually lets you transmit non-TCP/IP protocols over the Internet.

Because PPTP provides intranet privacy over the open Internet, it can significantly reduce costs in some situations. Networks that once would have depended on extravagant direct connections now can hook up via a local Internet service provider.

C. Routing with RAS

RAS comes with a NetBIOS gateway. A RAS client using the NetBEUI protocol can connect to a RAS server and, using the NetBIOS gateway on the RAS server, can gain access to the remote LAN beyond the gateway regardless of what protocol the LAN is using (see fig. 4.2.1).

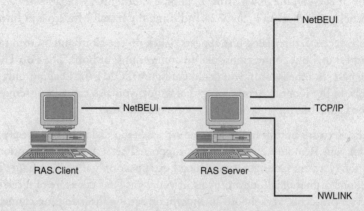

Figure 4.2.1   RAS can act as a NetBIOS gateway, connecting NetBEUI clients with networks using other protocols.

RAS can act as a TCP/IP or IPX router. RAS also is capable of serving as a Service Advertising Protocol (SAP) agent. (*SAP* is a NetWare protocol that lets servers advertise their services to the network.)

D. The Telephony API

The *Telephony Application Program Interface* (TAPI) provides a standard interface with telephony applications. (Telephony applications are applications that enable a computer to interact with telephone services, such as a network fax service or an online answering machine). TAPI oversees communication between the computer and the phone system, including initiating, answering, and ending calls. In effect, TAPI is a device driver for the phone system.

Windows NT's basic TAPI settings are set up in the Dialing Properties dialog box. The Dialing Properties dialog box maintains location and area code settings, as well as calling card settings and a setting for the dialing type (tone or pulse). The first time you run a TAPI-aware application, you have a chance to set dialing properties. Or, you can reach the Dialing Properties dialog box directly in several ways, including through the Control Panel Telephony and Modems applications.

E.   Installing and Configuring RAS

RAS is a network service, and, like other network services, is installed and removed using the Services tab of the Control Panel Network application. Install RAS as follows:

1. In the Control Panel, double-click on the Network application icon.

2. In the Network dialog box that appears, click on the Services tab and then click on the Add button. The Select Network Service dialog box appears.

3. In the Select Network Service dialog box, choose Remote Access Service from the Network Service list and click on OK. Windows NT prompts you for the path to the Windows NT Installation CD-ROM.

4. Windows NT prompts you for name of an RAS-capable device and an associated communications port. A modem installed on your system typically appears as a default value. Click on OK to accept the modem, or click on the down arrow to choose another RAS-capable device on your system. You also can install a new modem or an X.25 Pad using the Install Modem and Install X25 Pad buttons.

5. The Remote Access Setup dialog box appears. Click on the Configure button to specify whether to use the port for dial-out connections, dial-in connections, or both. The Port Usage options apply only to the port. In other words, you could configure COM1 for Dial out only and COM2 for Receive only. In the Remote Access Setup dialog box, you also can add or remove a port entry from the list. The Clone button lets you copy a port configuration.

6. Click on the Network button in the Remote Access Setup dialog box to specify the network protocols for your Remote Access Service to support. The Server Settings options in the lower portion of the Network Configuration dialog box appear only if you configure the port to receive calls. Select one or more dial-out protocols. If you want RAS take care of receiving calls, select one or more server protocols, and choose an encryption setting for incoming connections. You also can enable Multilink. Multilink allows one logical connection to use several physical pathways.

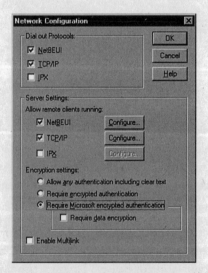

Figure 4.2.2   The Network Configuration dialog box.

Note in figure 4.2.2 that a Configure button follows each of the Server Settings protocol options. Each Configure button opens a dialog box that enables you to specify configuration options for the protocol, as follows:

- The RAS Server NetBEUI Configuration dialog box lets you specify whether the incoming caller will have access to the entire network or to only the RAS server.

    By confining a caller's access to the RAS server, you improve security (because the caller can access only one computer), but you reduce functionality because the caller can't access information on other machines.

- The RAS Server TCP/IP Configuration dialog box lets you define how the RAS server assigns IP addresses to dial-up clients (see fig. 4.2.3). You can use DHCP to assign client addresses, or you can configure RAS to assign IP addresses from a static address pool. If you choose to use a static address pool, input the beginning and ending addresses in the range. To exclude a range of addresses within the address pool, enter the beginning and ending addresses in the range you're excluding in the From and To boxes, then click on the Add button. The excluded range appears in the Excluded ranges box.

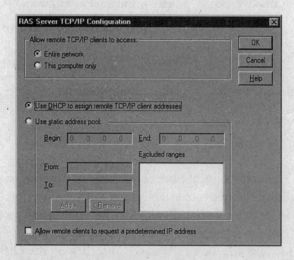

Figure 4.2.3   The RAS Server TCP/IP Configuration dialog box.

The RAS Server TCP/IP Configuration dialog box lets you specify whether a client can access the entire network or only the RAS server. By confining a caller's access to the RAS server, you improve security (because the caller can access only one computer), but you reduce functionality because the caller can't access information on other machines.

- The RAS Server IPX Configuration dialog box lets you specify how the RAS server assigns IPX network numbers.

    You also can specify whether a client can access the entire network or only the RAS server. By confining a caller's access to the RAS server, you improve security (because the caller can access only one computer), but you reduce functionality because the caller can't access information on other machines.

7. After you define the RAS settings to your satisfaction, click on OK.

8. The Network application's Services tab appears in the foreground. You should see Remote Access Service in the list of services. Click on the Close button.

9. Windows NT asks whether you want to Restart your computer. Choose Yes.

F.   Changing the RAS Configuration

To view or change your RAS configuration, follow these steps:

1. Double-click on the Network icon in the Control Panel and select the Network application's Services tab.

2. Select Remote Access Service from the services list and click on the Properties button.

3. The Remote Access Setup dialog box appears. Specify your new RAS configuration as described in steps 5 to 7 in the preceding section.

G.   Dial-Up Networking

The Dial-Up Networking application lets you establish remote connections with other computers. The most common uses for Dial-Up Networking are as follows:

- Accessing an Internet service provider
- Accessing a remote Windows NT computer or domain

You can open the Dial-Up Networking application as follows:

1. Choose Start, Programs, Accessories.

2. Click on the Dial-Up Networking icon.

Dial-Up Networking maintains a list of phonebook entries. A *phonebook entry* is a bundle of information that Windows NT needs to establish a specific connection. You can use the Dial-Up Networking application to create a phonebook entry for your access provider, your Windows NT domain, or any other dial-up connection. When it's time to connect, select a phonebook entry from the drop-down menu at the top of the screen and click on the Dial button. If you access the phonebook entry often, you can create a Desktop shortcut that lets you access the phonebook entry directly.

You can create a new phonebook entry as follows:

1. Click on the New button in the Dial-Up Networking dialog box to open the New Phonebook Entry dialog box.

2. In the New Phonebook Entry Basic tab, specify a name for the entry, an optional comment, and the phone number you want Windows NT to dial to make the connection. The Alternates button beside the phone number box lets you specify a prioritized list of alternative phone numbers. You also can specify a different modem or configure a modem from the Basic tab.

3. In the New Phonebook Entry Server tab, specify the communications protocol for the dial-up server (in the Dial-up server type combo box) and the network protocol. If you select the TCP/IP network protocol, click on the TCP/IP Settings button to configure TCP/IP settings.

4. The New Phonebook Entry Script tab defines some of the connection's logon properties. You can tell Windows NT to pop up a terminal window after dialing or to run a logon script after dialing. A terminal window enables you to interactively log on to the remote server in terminal mode. The Run this script radio button option automates the logon process. For more information on dial-up logon scripts, click on the Edit script button, which places you in a file that provides instructions and sample logon scripts, called SWITCH.INF. The Before dialing button lets you specify a terminal window or a logon script to execute before you dial.

5. In the New Phonebook Entry Security tab, you can require encrypted authentication, or you can elect to accept any authentication including clear text. You also can specify data encryption.

6. The New Phonebook Entry X.25 tab serves only for X.25 service. Select an X.25 access provider from the Network combo box and enter the requested information.

7. After you make changes to the New Phonebook Entry tab, click on OK. The new phonebook entry appears in the Dial-Up Networking dialog box.

1. Editing a Phonebook Entry and Other Options

The More button in the Dial-Up Networking dialog box offers several options. Figure 4.2.4 shows the More menu.

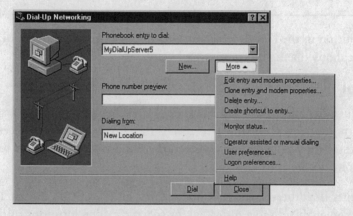

Figure 4.2.4 The Dial-up Networking More menu.

The following list describes the More menu options.

- **Edit entry and modem properties.** Returns you to the setup tabs you configured in the preceding section.

- **Create shortcut to entry.** Creates a shortcut to the active phonebook entry.

- **Monitor status.** Opens the Control Panel Dial-Up Networking Monitor.

- **User preferences.** Opens a User Preferences dialog box that presents the following four tabs:

  - **Dialing.** Lets you specify dialing options, such as the number of redial attempts and the time between redial attempts. You also can use the Dialing tab to enable or disable Autodial (see the following section).

  - **Callback.** Tells Windows NT what to do if the server you connect to offers callback. You can specify a number, you can elect to skip callback, or you can tell NT to prompt at the time callback is offered.

  - **Appearance.** Offers some dial-time interface options.

  - **Phonebook.** Lets you specify a Dial-Up Networking phonebook. Phonebook entries are stored in a file with the .pbk extension. The default phonebook is the system phonebook. Using the Phonebook tab, you can place an entry in your personal phonebook (a user-specific phonebook), or you can choose a different phonebook.

- Logon preferences. Configures Dialing, Callback, Appearance, and Phonebook settings for a remote Windows NT logon. The Logon preferences options are very similar to the User preferences options in the previous discussion. The difference is that the User preferences options apply to a user who is already logged on to Windows NT and is trying to connect to a remote machine. The Logon preferences apply to a user who isn't yet logged on to Windows NT and wants to log on directly to a Windows NT domain via a remote connection. The Windows NT Ctrl+Alt+Del logon dialog box includes the Logon using dial-up networking check box. If you enable this check box and log on using Dial-Up Networking, the preferences you set in the Logon preferences dialog box apply.

> **The Logon preferences dialog box doesn't appear unless you log on as an Administrator.**

The Location button in the Dial-Up Networking dialog box lets you set a dialing prefix or suffix or specify a Telephony dialing location.

2. AutoDial

Windows NT includes a feature called AutoDial. AutoDial automatically associates network connections with Phonebook entries. This means that if you attempt to access a file or directory that can be accessed only via a dial-up connection, Windows NT attempts to make the dial-up connection automatically.

AutoDial supports IP addresses, Internet host names, and NetBIOS names. By default, AutoDial is enabled. You can enable/disable AutoDial for specific calling locations using the Dialing tab of the User Preferences dialog box.

4.2.1   Exercise: Using Windows NT RAS and the AutoDial Feature

Exercise 4.2.1 outlines the process of establishing a RAS connection from a remote client to an NT domain and demonstrates the use of the AutoDial feature.

1. Log on to a Windows NT domain using dial-up networking. (Check the Logon using Dial-up Networking check box below the domain name in the Windows NT Logon dialog box.) Make sure that you are not connecting to the network locally.

   What step should you take to ensure that your network connection is truly remote?

2. Locate a text file or a word processing document on a shared directory somewhere on the domain using Network Neighborhood icon in Explorer. (Use a file type that your computer is configured to recognize automatically—click on Options in the Explorer View menu and choose the File Types tab for a list or registered file types. A .txt file or a Write file should work.) If Explorer can't find the other computers in the domain, pull down the Explorer menu and click on Find with the Computer option. Enter the name of the computer with the shared directory you want to access in the Find: Computer dialog and click on the Find Now button. The computer will appear as an icon in the Find:Computer dialog box. Double-click on the icon for a list of shared resources.

3. When you've located a file on the remote share, right-click on the file and choose Create Shortcut from the shortcut menu that appears. Create a shortcut to the file and drag the shortcut to the Desktop on your own computer.

4. Double-click on the shortcut to make sure it opens the file.

5. Shut down your system.

6. Log on again; this time, don't use dial-up networking. (Deselect the Logon Using Dial-up Networking check box.) You might get a message that says Windows NT could find the domain controller and logged you on using cached account information. Click on OK.

7. Wait until the logon process is finished. Double-click on the shortcut to the file on the remote domain.

8. If you selected the Always prompt before auto-dialing check box in the Appearances tab of the Dial-up Networking User Preferences dialog box, Windows NT will ask if you want to initiate a connection with the remote file. Click on Yes. AutoDial will automatically dial the remote network and attempt to initiate a connection to the file referenced in the shortcut.

4

4.2   Practice Problems

1. You want remote TCP/IP RAS clients to have access to the entire TCP/IP network, but right now they can only connect to the RAS server machine. What will enable the client to reach the network?

    A. The Entire Network check box in the Server tab of the Dial-up Networking Edit Phonebook Entry dialog box.

    B. The Entire Network radio button in the Remote Access Permissions dialog box of the Remote Access Admin application.

    C. The Entire Network radio button in the TCP/IP Configuration dialog box accessible via the Network button in the Remote Access Setup dialog box.

    D. A, B, and C are all necessary.

2. You have several salespeople who dial in to your network via RAS. How can you configure the security options in RAS so the users can minimize long-distance phone charges?

    A. Configure the user's Dial-Up Networking software to use PPTP, which bypasses the PSTN billing computers, thus giving the users free long-distance service.

    B. Configure the RAS service to perform a callback based on the number specified by the user dialing in to the RAS server. The server authenticates the logon and then disconnects and calls the user back at the specified number.

    C. Issue the users long-distance calling cards and have their RAS calls billed directly to the company.

    D. Make sure the users are calling only from public telephones and are making collect calls to the RAS server. Then configure the RAS server to accept collect calls.

3. Which types of communication-interface hardware can be utilized with RAS?

    A. Modem

    B. Network Interface Card (NIC)

    C. Null modem cable via serial ports

    D. ISDN card

4. A user is trying to dial in to the NT Server-based RAS server. The user is connecting, but is disconnected immediately and receives a message that says he or she isn't an authorized dial-in user. What is the first thing you should do?

    A. Restart the NT Server, because one of the modems must be disabled.

    B. Change the security configuration options on the RAS server to enable any authentication method including clear text.

    C. Check to make sure the user has dial-in permissions in User Manager for Domains.

    D. Tell the user to restart his/her remote system and try again.

5. What's the name of the feature that lets RAS use more than one communication channel at a time for the same connection?

    A. Multinet

    B. Multilink

    C. ISDN

    D. Multichannel

6. What is the primary use of RAS?

    A. To provide a method for connecting a remote client to the network via a dial-up connection and fully participate on the network.

    B. To provide permanent leased line links between LANs.

    C. For Network administrators to establish remote network management capability.

    D. To provide essential prerequisites for DSU/CSU connections.

7. If you're having problems with the RAS server, what can you do to have NT create a log?

    A. Under Remote Access Administrator, configure the logging option.

    B. Under Control Panel, Network, Services, configure RAS to write all connection information to the System log.

    C. In the Registry, set the parameter Logging under the following key to 1 to create a PPP.LOG file in the <winnt root>\system32\Ras directory: `HKEY_LOCAL_MACHINE\ System\CurrentControlSet\Services \Rasman\ PPP\`.

    D. Run the program Raslog.exe to create a RAS log in the <winnt root>\system32\Ras directory.

8. You want to let users connect to your local area network using the Internet; however, you're concerned that security might be a problem. Which protocol should you use to ensure a reliable connection and a secure transmission of information?

    A. PPP

    B. SLIP

    C. IEEE 802.2

    D. PPTP

9. What is the name of the utility that enables remote users to access the network through an NT Workstation or Server?

    A. Remote Control

    B. Remote Access Service

    C. Remote Network Service

    D. The Internet

10. Which of the following serial protocols supports the NetBEUI, IPX/SPX, and TCP/IP transport protocols over RAS?

    A. PPP

    B. SLIP

    C. PPTPS

    D. IEEE 802.2

11. The type of connections that RAS supports is/are (select all that apply):

    A. PSTN (Public Switched Telephone Network)

    B. X.25

    C. IEEE X.400

    D. Null Modem Cable

    E. ISDN

    F. RadioLan

12. Identify the two serial protocols that RAS supports.

    A. IEEE 802.2 and X.25

    B. Ethernet and Token Ring

    C. SLIP and PPP

    D. ESLIP and PPTP

13. Your management is concerned that accessing the network via RAS might open up security problems. What features does RAS support that help alleviate some of these concerns?

    A. RAS supports the U.S. Government DES (Data Encryption Standard) and encrypts all data going across the communication channel.

    B. RAS, in fact, can be more secure than a LAN connection because of the Callback security, Encryption of userid and password information, and PPTP features.

    C. RAS is not secure over standard PSTN connections unless data scrambling equipment is used on both ends of the connection.

    D. You can obtain a C2 level version the RAS product that meets U.S. Government standards for security.

4

14. A user calls you and states that she's getting connected to the NT Workstation via RAS, but cannot see any resources on the network. What could be causing the problem?

    A. The user is using a userid that isn't configured to have network access via RAS.

    B. She's dialing in with a protocol configured for "This computer only" when it needs to configured for "Entire network."

    C. She needs to use a different protocol. NetBEUI isn't routable, so she can't see any other devices on the network if she's using it as the dial-in protocol.

    D. She needs to configure her RAS server to use ISDN because the PSTN can support only a limited amount of bandwidth.

15. You're trying to run a program from a NetWare server over your RAS connection. You have installed the NWLink-compatible transport protocol at your remote computer, but you still cannot connect to the NetWare server. What did you forget to do?

    A. You need to install the Client Service for NetWare (CSNW) so you can access a NetWare server using file and print services.

    B. You need to install the FPNW (File and Print Services for NetWare) on the RAS Server to gain access to the NetWare servers.

    C. You must dial in to the NetWare server directly.

    D. You have to change your protocol to TCP/IP and install TCP/IP on the NetWare server.

16. Users would like to be able to connect to the Internet using the company's T1 connection from home. You configure RAS to allow your users to dial in. What protocol must they use to dial in to the RAS server?

    A. IEEE 802.2

    B. Ethernet

    C. NetBEUI

    D. TCP/IP

17. Which statement below correctly identifies the differences between the RAS software running on Windows NT Workstation and RAS software running on Windows NT Server?

    A. When RAS is running on NT Workstation, you can access only the shared resources on that machine. When it is running on NT Server, you can access resources on the entire network.

    B. When RAS is running on NT Workstation, you can access shared resources on the entire network, except for resources on NetWare Servers. Before you can do so, you must be running RAS on Windows NT Server.

    C. RAS running on Windows NT Workstation supports only one simultaneous connection whereas, if it is running on NT Server, it can support up to 256 connections.

    D. RAS running on Windows NT Workstation supports up to 256 simultaneous connections, whereas if it is running on NT Server, it can support only one simultaneous connection, because the server is running other services that tie up the CPU.

18. Which feature of RAS enhances security and billing situations by calling back the client computer after the client computer initiates a call to the RAS server to request a network connection?

    A. CHAP

    B. Leased links

    C. autodial

    D. callback

19. Which of the following security features are incorporated into RAS?

    A. RAS can leave an audit trail, enabling you to see who logged on when and what authentication they provided.

    B. There is a multilink requirement, forcing the remote user to utilize more than one link.

    C. The callback feature that hangs up the incoming caller and calls back at a predetermined number.

    D. Encryption of the logon process and or all data transferring over the RAS connection.

20. With which protocol can RAS perform routing capabilities?

    A. TCP/IP

    B. NetBEUI

    C. IPX

    D. DLC

4.2 Answers and Explanations: Exercises

In order to ensure that your network connection is truly remote, you must disconnect the cable from the network card. This ensures that you are not connecting to the network locally.

4.2 Answers and Explanations: Practice Problems

1. **C** By default, only the local server can be accessed from RAS clients. You must select the Entire Network option in order to allow RAS clients to browse all of the available network resources.

2. **B** The callback option provides not only the capability to reduce phone use charges, but also increases security by ensuring that the RAS client is legitimate.

3. **A, C, D** A NIC is not supported or utilized by RAS.

4. **C** It is vital to ensure that all RAS clients have the dial-in permissions option selected within the User Manager for Domains.

5. **B** Multilink enables a single logical connection to use several physical pathways, such as two modems.

6. **A** The primary use of RAS is to provide a means for remote, or traveling clients, to connect to the NT Server on an occasional basis. It is not intended for heavy traffic or permanent connections.

7. **C** By changing the registry entry value to True (1), you can create and update the PPP.LOG file for both troubleshooting and additional security auditing purposes.

8. **D** PPTP is a protocol that transmits PPP packets over a TCP/IP network securely.

9. **B** Remote Access Service provides remote connectivity.

10. **A** PPP is not restricted to TCP/IP; it also supports IPX, NetBEUI, and other network protocols.

11. **A, B, D, E** PSTN, X.25, Null Modem Cable, and ISDN are media types that RAS can utilize.

4

12. **C**   SLIP and PPP are the two types of serial protocols that RAS supports.

13. **B**   Callback, encryption, and PPTP features ensure a secure connection to the NT Server under RAS.

14. **B**   By default, only the local server can be accessed from RAS clients. If no resources are on the local server, you must select the Entire Network option in order to permit RAS clients access to network resources.

15. **A**   Client Service for NetWare has to be installed in order to access the NetWare resources.

16. **D**   TCP/IP is utilized in conjunction with the T1 link.

17. **C**   Whereas NT Workstation supports only a single RAS connection, Windows NT Server supports up to 256 simultaneous RAS connections with the appropriate hardware and licensing.

18. **D**   The callback option provides a means of controlling phone bills by calling back the clients at an assigned number. This can be especially economical if your company has a decent long-distance phone rate. The callback option also provides great security from hackers. If hackers obtain a username and password, they are still prevented access to the network because the NT server will disconnect them and try to call them back at a predetermined number.

19. **A, C, D**   Multilink option enables one logical connection to use several pathways if they are available.

20. **A, C**   RAS can act as a TCP/IP or IPX router. However, the NT Server running RAS comes with a NetBIOS gateway. A RAS client using the NetBEUI protocol can connect to a RAS server and, using the NetBIOS gateway on the RAS server, can gain access to the remote LAN beyond the gateway, regardless of what protocol the LAN is using.

4.2 Key Words

Remote Access Service (RAS)

Integrated Services Digital Network (ISDN)

Serial Line Internet Protocol (SLIP)

Point-to-Point Protocol (PPP)

Point-to-Point Tunneling Protocol (PPTP)

Telephony Application Program Interface (TAPI)

Callback   Phonebook entries

AutoDial   Multilink

Service Advertising Protocol (SAP)

Practice Exam: Connectivity

Use this practice exam to test your mastery of Connectivity. This practice exam is made up of 10 questions. Keep in mind that the passing Microsoft score is 76.4 percent. There will be two types of questions:

- Multiple Choice—Select the correct answer.

- Multiple Multiple Choice—Select all answers that are correct.

Begin as soon as you are ready. Answers follow the test.

1. Your manager has requested that you provide existing NetWare server resource accessibility to a small team of engineers that are Windows 95 clients currently attached to an NT Server. Choose the best course of action:

    A. Install a new NetWare server exclusively for the engineering team.

    B. Install GSNW on the NT Server.

    C. Purchase the necessary NetWare licensing for the team of engineers.

    D. Migrate the NetWare server over to an NT domain server.

2. What two components that must be running on an NT domain server in order to execute the Migration Tool for NetWare?

    A. NWLink

    B. NTFS

    C. RAS

    D. GSNW

3. For what purpose is NetWare's Syscon utility utilized during the installation of GSNW?

    A. To establish the proper rights and permissions for the NT Server to properly use GSNW.

    B. NetWare Syscon tool is not used during the setup and configuration of GSNW.

    C. To establish a user account on the NetWare server to enable GSNW to act as a gateway to NetWare resources.

    D. To establish a group and user account on the NetWare server to enable GSNW to act as a gateway to NetWare resources.

4. How do you create a new share for a NetWare directory or volume on the NT Server running GSNW?

    A. By using the Explorer tool on the NT Server.

    B. With the GSNW tool initial dialog box, which provides the buttons to add, remove, and set Permissions for NetWare directories and volumes.

    C. The shares are determined by the NetWare server.

    D. With the GSNW tool's Gateway button that launches the Configure Gateway dialog box, which in turn provides the buttons to add, remove, and set Permissions for NetWare directories and volumes.

5. Which two of the following must both the local NT Server and remote NT Server using RAS have in order to take advantage of the Multilink option?

    A. Both must have access to more than one physical pathway, such as two modems.

    B. Both must have the Multilink option selected.

    C. Both must be running ISDN compatible hardware.

    D. One of the two must have the Multilink option selected.

4

6. Which of the following network protocols are supported by RAS?

   A. TCP/IP

   B. NetBEUI

   C. DLC

   D. IPX

7. When is encryption used with a RAS connection (choose three)?

   A. When used with the SLIP protocol.

   B. During the logon process.

   C. Optionally, all data can be set to be encrypted.

   D. In conjunction with the PPTP protocol, which encrypts PPP packets.

8. Which of the following does the AutoDial feature *not* support?

   A. IP addresses

   B. NetBIOS names

   C. MAC addresses

   D. Internet host names

9. Which of the following statements about Server Message Block (SMB) is *not* true?

   A. It is jointly developed by Microsoft, Intel, and IBM.

   B. It is a file-sharing protocol.

   C. It specifies a series of commands utilized to pass information between computers using four message types.

   D. All of the above are true.

10. RAS can connect to a remote computer using which of the following media?

   A. Public Switched Telephone Network (PSTN)

   B. X.25

   C. Null modem cable

   D. ISDN

Answers and Explanations: Practice Exam

1. **B** GSNW is an ideal solution in circumstances where network traffic is minimal through the gateway.

2. **A, D** NWLink and GSNW must be installed and running for the NetWare Migration tool to run.

3. **D** NetWare's Syscon utility is used to establish user groups and accounts on the NetWare server, both of which are required to set up the GSNW gateway.

4. **D** You must use the GSNW tool to establish shares for the gateway connected NetWare resources. This is done with the GSNW tool's Gateway button, which launches the Configure Gateway dialog box (which in turn provides the buttons to add, remove, and set Permissions for NetWare directories and volumes).

5. **A, B** In order to establish a Multilink between two NT Servers, they must both have access to two or more modems or ISDN channels, and both must have the Multilink option selected.

6. **A, B, D** TCP/IP, IPX, and NetBEUI are all network protocols supported with RAS.

7. **B, C, D** Encryption is always used during the logon process, and RAS can optionally be set to use data encryption at all times. If PPTP is used, it encrypts PPP packets. The outdated SLIP protocol does not support encryption.

8. **C** IP addresses, NetBIOS names, and Internet host names can all be used by the AutoDial feature of RAS.

9. **D** All the statements about Server Message Block (SMB) are true.

10. **A, B, C, D** RAS can connect to a remote computer using all of the aforementioned media.

CHAPTER 5

Monitoring and Optimization

The performance of your applications on Windows NT depends on the combination of hardware and software on your system. Microsoft provides the following objectives for the "Monitoring and Optimization" section of the exam, as follows:

- Monitor performance of various functions by using Performance Monitor. Functions include processor, memory, disk, and network.

- Identify performance bottlenecks.

5.1 Performance Optimization

Optimal performance means getting the best results with the hardware and software you have. Optimization of a task consists of measuring and analyzing the resource demands of the task to determine what can be done to make it finish in a shorter period of time.

A. Performance Objectives

Performance objectives vary depending on the role of the computer in the network.

After you optimize performance of your application the next question is whether that level of performance meets your business goals. You may have the best performance possible with your existing system, but to get adequate performance you may need to upgrade one or more components, such as memory, disk, network card, or processor.

The best way to know what you can do to improve performance is to measure it. Gathering data on how your system performs under various circumstances gives you the information you need to make appropriate changes to your system.

B.   Windows NT Tunes Itself

One of Microsoft's design goals for Windows NT was that it should not require a user to make changes to Registry settings to get good performance.

Microsoft decided to let the operating system itself handle evaluating settings, such as the size of the disk cache and paging file, and adjust them dynamically as resource demands change.

Windows NT does most of the task of optimizing overall performance of the system without requiring manual changes to Registry parameters.

C.   Reasons to Monitor Performance

Although there is little to tune in NT itself, you still have several reasons to monitor system performance, as follows:

- *To optimize specific tasks.*

  If you have a particular application on your server that you want to optimize, monitoring system performance can tell you whether changing your hardware will help your application run faster.

- *To troubleshoot performance problems.*

  One of the most difficult kinds of performance problems to troubleshoot is diagnosing transient network problems.

- *To plan for future needs.*

  Another reason to monitor performance is that it enables you to detect changes in the way that the server is being used by users.

D.   Configuration Changes that Affect Performance

You can, however, change many things that affect overall system performance, including adding or upgrading hardware components, removing software components, changing Windows NT performance parameters, and moving or rescheduling time-intensive tasks.

1. Adding or Upgrading Hardware Components

Hardware optimization may be necessary to truly upgrade your server's performance. You may consider upgrading the following components: processor capability, memory capacity, disks, network capabilities, and fault-tolerance issues.

a. Processor

Optimization considerations include:

- Upgrade the speed of the processor.
- Add another processor (for example, two Pentium processors on an SMP system).
- Upgrade the secondary cache.

b. Memory

Optimization considerations include:

- You can never have too much RAM. Having adequate RAM reduces the need for paging memory to and from the hard disk.

- Shadowing of the ROM BIOS in RAM does not improve performance under Windows NT. Disabling this feature can, therefore, make more memory available to the system.

c. Disks

Optimization considerations include:

- Replace slow disks with faster ones.

- Use NTFS for partitions larger than 400 MB.

- Use a defragmentation tool if disks become fragmented.

- Upgrade from IDE to SCSI.

- Use a controller with the highest possible transfer rate and best multitasking functionality.

- Isolate disk I/O-intensive tasks on separate physical disks and/or disk controllers.

- Create a stripe set to gain the advantage of simultaneous writes to multiple disks if your hardware supports it. Stripe sets write data to the drives in 64K segments. Stripe sets without parity offer no fault-tolerance. Should a drive fail, all data on the stripe set will be lost. You should use stripe sets with parity when it is available.

d. Network

Optimization considerations include:

- Get a network card with the widest data bus available on your system.

- Divide your network into multiple networks, attaching the server to each network with a different adapter.

e. Fault Tolerance

Optimization considerations include:

- If using software-based fault tolerance such as mirroring (RAID 1) or striping with parity (RAID-5), use a hardware-based solution instead.

- If the goal is the greatest availability of data, you could consider mirroring (via Windows NT fault-tolerant drivers) two hardware-based RAID-5 arrays.

2. Removing Unnecessary Software Components

You can remove any software components that are using precious processor and memory resources. These software components fall into three categories: device drivers, network protocols, and services.

1. *Device drivers.* Any drivers that are loaded into memory but not used should be removed.

2. *Network protocols.* Remove any unnecessary network protocols. You can remove the bindings for a protocol selectively.

3. *Services.* Any services that this server does not need to provide should be disabled, or configured to start manually.

3. Replacing Inefficient Software

If your system has applications or drivers that use system resources inefficiently, you may not be able to make a particular application run faster.

4. Changing Windows NT Performance Parameters

Several relatively easy-to-change settings can make a substantial difference in performance, as discussed in the following sections.

a. Optimizing the Paging File

You configure the size of the paging file in the Virtual Memory dialog box. To open the Virtual Memory dialog box, click on the Change button in the Performance tab of the Control Panel System application.

The following are general recommendations regarding the virtual memory settings:

- Consider spreading the paging file across multiple physical disks if your hardware supports writing to those disks at the same time.

- Move the paging file to the disk with the lowest amount of total disk activity.

- If you plan to use Windows NT's Recovery feature, which writes out debugging information if a stop error occurs to disk, the swap file located on your system partition must be larger than the amount of physical RAM present on the system.

- Monitor the size of the paging file under peak usage and then set the minimum size to that value.

- To determine the amount of RAM to add to reduce paging activity, use a tool, such as Performance Monitor, to determine the amount of memory each application needs. Then remove applications (noting their working set sizes) until paging activity falls within acceptable limits.

b. Optimizing the Server Service

Another setting that can affect performance is the configuration of the Server service. To access the Server dialog box, choose the Services tab in the Control Panel Network application, select the Server service, and click on the Properties button.

By default, Windows NT Server is configured to work best as a file server for 64 or more users. Table 5.1.1 shows the optimal Server service settings.

Table 5.1.1   Server Service Optimization

Setting	Description
Minimize Memory Used	Up to 10 connections
Balance	Up to 64 connections
Maximize Throughput for File Sharing	64 or more connections, large file cache (best suited for file and print servers)
Maximize Throughput for Network Applications	64 or more connections, small file cache (best suited for PDCs, BDCs and for application servers)

c. Optimizing Other Services

Other services on your system may have Registry settings that you need to adjust for optimal performance. Table 5.1.2 lists some common values for standard Windows NT services that would be a good starting point for evaluation.

Table 5.1.2   Some Common Registry Values for Standard Windows NT Services

Service	Value
Net Logon	Pulse, Pulse Concurrency, Pulse Maximum
Directory Replication	Interval, Guard Time
Computer Browser	Hidden, IsDomainMaster, MaintainServerList
Spooler	DefaultSpoolDirectory, PriorityClass

5. Rescheduling Resource-Intensive Tasks

Demands for resources on a server often fluctuate widely at different times of day. It makes sense, then, that you should shift demands for resources to times when you have a surplus of the resource available.

6. Moving Tasks to Another System

You may be able to move the demand to another machine that has idle resources. If you have two I/O-intensive applications running on a server, consider moving one application to a different server to even out the workload.

E.   Before Making Changes

You have to be able to isolate which resource on the system has become the bottleneck; then you have to discover the source of the demand for that resource. You can use Performance Monitor, discussed in the next section after the exercises, to do this kind of investigative work.

5.1.1   Exercise: Practicing Performance Optimization

This exercise is a paper-based exercise. You are presented with a scenario and need to perform the following tasks:

- Determine the goals of the server.
- Identify the problems currently in place.
- Determine the best solutions to resolve these problems.

Scenario: You are a network administrator of a LAN environment. You have one NT Server acting as a PDC and 50 clients on NT Workstation in your domain. In addition to serving as a PDC, your server also acts as a file, print, and application server.

The primary protocol you want to use is TCP/IP, but when installing NT, you choose to install TCP/IP, NetBEUI, and IP/SPX. Currently, you have four SCSI drives in the server, but you are not using any stripe sets with parity or disk mirroring.

From the information presented, complete the following:

1. What should the primary goal(s) of the PDC be?

2. What problems (list at least three based on the information presented) might present themselves in this environment?

3. What is an immediate solution you could make to impact network performance on the PDC?

4. What are some potential changes you might make to enhance this environment?

5.1   Practice Problems

In the following multiple choice questions, more than one answer can be correct; pick all answers that apply.

1. For the most part, how much time should you spend tuning and optimizing Windows NT?

    A. At least an hour a day.

    B. After the initial installation, you should plan on spending most of the first week tuning and optimizing Windows NT.

    C. You should never have to.

    D. NT, for the most part, is self-tuning and requires very little user intervention. On occasion, you should monitor portions of the OS.

2. Name the major tool for gathering information and identifying bottlenecks.

    A. Tune-T.

    B. NT Monitor.

    C. Performance Monitor.

    D. Server Manager.

    E. NT doesn't provide any tools for tuning and performance monitoring.

3. Before you can tune a file server for optimum performance, which one of the following questions must you answer?

    A. How much money do you have available to spend on new hardware?

    B. What types of tasks is the file server expected to perform?

    C. This question has no answer; simply put, tuning is the process of installing the fastest hardware in your computer.

    D. In what type of business is the company using file server? For certain companies, you cannot tune NT because of U.S. government restrictions.

4. A curious user tells you that while reading a major computer periodical, she came across this statement: "All computer systems have a bottleneck of some type." Why is this so?

    A. All computer systems are only as fast as their slowest component. You might remove one bottleneck, but you will always expose another.

    B. The article was incorrect. For example, your file server has absolutely no bottlenecks.

    C. The article was referring to non-Windows NT systems. Microsoft has designed the system to continually self-adjust, thus eliminating bottlenecks.

    D. Because you always upgrade components as soon as new ones are available, you eliminate any potential bottlenecks before they become apparent.

5. Which statement is true regarding the type of hardware you should place in a heavily used file server?

    A. The equipment in the server is not important because nobody actually uses the server to run applications.

    B. You should always spend the most money on the server hardware.

    C. When designing a file server, always pick the hardware that exploits the full bus speed if possible (for example, SCSI hard drives, PCI bus network cards, and so on).

    D. You should use the same type of computer hardware as the workstations so that users get good response time, because hardware from the same vendor works better together.

5

6. To optimize the network components in an NT Workstation or Server, which *one* of the following should you do?

    A. You do not need to do anything. NT automatically optimizes the network components.

    B. You should remove unused adapter cards and protocols.

    C. You should always have TCP/IP, NetBEUI, and NWLink installed, even if your computers are using only one protocol. This leaves more paths open in case one protocol becomes unusable.

    D. You should disable the server service for a workstation, and disable the workstation service for a server.

7. Select the name of the piece of software that automatically swaps data in physical RAM out to disk and back.

    A. The Virtual Memory Manager

    B. The Virtual Device Driver

    C. Himem.exe

    D. Emm386.exe

8. Choose the paging file that Windows NT creates.

    A. RAMPAGE.SYS

    B. SYS$RAM.SYS

    C. PAGEFILE.SYS

    D. VIRAM.SYS

9. What are some of the things you can do to make the system use virtual memory more efficiently? (Choose all that apply.)

    A. Spread the paging file across multiple hard drives.

    B. Move the paging file to the drive where the Windows NT System files are located.

    C. Move the paging file from the drive where the Windows NT System files are located.

    D. Monitor the size of the paging file under peak usage and then set the minimum size of the paging file to that value, thereby saving time when the system has to expand the paging file.

10. Performance on NT depends on what two variables?

    A. Hardware

    B. Pagefile.sys location(s)

    C. Software

    D. RISC or Intel processor

11. What is optimal performance?

    A. Making NT work faster by editing the registry.

    B. Getting the best result with the hardware and software available.

    C. Making threads process at a higher priority.

    D. Making processors work at their maximum.

12. In addition to servicing LOGON validations from users, what additional tasks are performed at a BDC acting as a File and Print Server? (Choose all that apply.)

    A. Acting as Master Browsers in the domain

    B. Directory replication updates

    C. Servicing resource requests from users

    D. Account database updates from the PDC

13. Windows NT optimizes what components automatically? (Choose all that apply.)

    A. Disk cache

    B. Paging file

    C. Monitor settings

    D. Bindings

14. What hardware changes have an effect on system performance? (Choose all that apply.)

    A. Mouse

    B. Monitor

    C. Processor

    D. Memory

15. What are considerations for hard disks in regard to optimization of a file server? (Choose all that apply.)

    A. Use faster disks.

    B. Combine multiple hard disks into a stripe set with parity.

    C. Use the FAT file system.

    D. Use SCSI over IDE.

16. Why should you use stripe sets?

    A. They require less overhead.

    B. They are easier on system for I/O management.

    C. They enable NT to do simultaneous writes (if supported by hardware).

    D. You should not use stripe sets.

17. Which are considerations with regard to optimizing NT with network cards? (Choose all that apply.)

    A. Get a network card with the widest data bus available.

    B. Always use NetBEUI when available.

C. Never use NetBEUI.

D. Divide your network into multiple networks, attaching the server to each network with a different adapter.

18. How many drives do you need to implement fault tolerance under NT Server?

    A. 1

    B. 2

    C. 3

    D. 4

19. You are deciding how to implement fault tolerance on your NT Server. You've heard that using hardware fault tolerance is better than using NT's software fault tolerance. Why is one better than the other?

    A. NT's built-in fault tolerance works only with NTFS.

    B. Software fault tolerance is more reliable than hardware.

    C. Hardware fault tolerance takes the load of parity calculation off the processor.

    D. Hardware fault tolerance does not work with NT because of the HAL.

20. What can you do with device drivers to optimize NT?

    A. Remove unneeded drivers.

    B. Pause any unnecessary drivers through the devices applet in the Control Panel.

    C. Create hardware profiles that use only the drivers needed during that boot-up phase.

    D. There is no need to do anything. NT automatically purges unneeded drivers.

5

5.1   Answers and Explanations: Exercise

1. In this environment, the primary goals of the PDC are to validate users from the LAN, and serve as the file, print, and application server—all in the most efficient way possible.

2. Possible problems, from the information presented, include:

    - The PDC becomes a bottleneck in the network if it becomes too busy serving client requests.

    - The extra protocols can have detrimental effects on network performance.

    - In a single server environment, fault tolerance is crucial. If a drive in the server were to go bad, the data on that drive would be lost.

    - If the PDC were to be taken off-line, access to network resources on the server, including domain validation, would be denied.

3. To make an immediate impact on the network performance of the PDC, you should remove all unnecessary network protocols. If TCP/IP is the desired protocol, it must be configured as such on the server and on the workstations.

4. Potential changes include:

    - Adding a BDC to the domain to act as a file, print, and application server

    - Evaluating the hardware to see whether hardware upgrades are appropriate

    - Implementing fault-tolerance support—either disk mirroring or stripe sets with parity

    - Removing unnecessary protocols and evaluating bindings of the remaining protocols to see whether they are effective in their current state

5.1   Answers and Explanations: Practice Problems

1. **D**   Windows NT, for the most part, is self-tuning. There are portions of the OS, such as memory and network usage, that should be monitored to optimize performance.

2. **C**   Performance Monitor is the major tool for gathering information and identifying bottlenecks.

3. **B**   The question to ask is, "What types of tasks is the file server expected to perform?" Based on the answer to that question, one can determine what the primary goals of that server should be and optimize accordingly.

4. **A**   All computer systems are only as fast as their slowest component.

5. **C**   When designing a file server, always pick the hardware that exploits the full bus speed if possible (for example, SCSI hard drives, PCI bus network cards, and so on).

6. **B**   You should remove unused adapter cards and protocols in order to optimize the network components in an NT Workstation or Server.

7. **A**   Virtual Memory Manager automatically swaps data in physical RAM out to disk and back.

8. **C**   PAGEFILE.SYS is the name of the paging file that Windows NT creates.

9. **A, C, D**   Spread the paging file across multiple hard drives. Move the paging file to the drive where the Windows NT System files are located. Move the paging file from the drive where the Windows NT System files are located. Monitor the size of the paging file under peak usage and then set the minimum size of the paging file to that value, thereby saving time when the system has to expand the paging file.

10. **A, C** Performance on NT depends on hardware and software.

11. **B** Optimal performance is getting the best result with the hardware and software available.

12. **B, C, D** BDCs can also act as file, print, and application servers. Most BDCs will also participate in Directory Replication.

13. **A, B** Windows NT optimizes the disk cache and the paging file automatically.

14. **C, D** Processor and memory changes have an effect on system performance.

15. **A, B, D** You always want the faster hard drives available; stripe sets can improve performance; and SCSI drives are preferred over IDE.

16. **C** Stripe sets enable NT to do simultaneous writes if it is supported by the hardware.

17. **A, D** Considerations with regard to optimizing NT with network cards include getting a network card with the widest data bus available and dividing your network into multiple networks by attaching the server to each network with a different adapter.

18. **B** Two drives are needed to implement fault tolerance on NT Server.

19. **C** Hardware fault tolerance takes the load of parity calculation off the processor.

20. **A** You can remove unneeded drivers to optimize NT.

5.1 Key Words

Boot partition

Mirrored set fault-tolerance RAID Level 1

Optimal performance

Paging file

Secondary cache

Stripe set

Stripe set with parity

System partition

5

5.2   Using Performance Monitor

The most useful tool for measuring performance on NT systems is Performance Monitor.

You can use Performance Monitor for the following tasks:

- Measuring the demand for resources on your system
- Identifying bottlenecks in your system performance
- Monitoring the behavior of individual processes
- Monitoring the performance of remote systems
- Generating alerts to inform you that an exception condition has occurred
- Exporting performance data for analysis using other tools
- Collecting data to determine a baseline for the computer system.

You can configure Performance Monitor to record a variety of statistical measurements (called *counters*) for a variety of system hardware and software components (called *objects*). Each object has its own collection of counters.

Windows NT Server exam objectives specify that you should be familiar with how to use Performance Monitor to measure processor, memory, disk, and network functions.

A.   Bottleneck—The Limiting Resource

When you understand the tools you need for measuring your system's performance, you are ready to dig into the data to determine how to improve it.

The simplest way to detect the bottleneck on your system is to examine the amount of time that the four major bottleneck areas: memory, disk, processor, and network. Typically, the component that uses the most time to complete its portion of the task is the bottleneck.

B.   Overall Performance Indicators

A reasonable place to start in monitoring performance for a server in Windows NT is to watch a number of general counters in Performance Monitor.

1. The Processor Object

The following are useful counters for the processor object. In looking at the processor, be certain to remember that high levels of processor activity can result from two situations other than handling a processor-intensive task:

- A severe memory shortage with the processor busy managing virtual memory (swapping pages of memory to and from the disk).
- The system is busy handling a large number of interrupts.

The following are useful counters for the processor object:

- **% Processor Time.** This counter measures the amount of time the processor spent executing a non-idle thread.

- **Interrupts/sec.** This counter measures the number of interrupts the processor handles per second.

- **System:** Processor Queue Length. This counter measures the number of threads waiting in the queue for an available processor. Generally, if the number of threads in the queue exceeds two, you have a problem with processor performance.

2. The Memory Object

In general, the symptoms of a memory shortage on the system are a busy processor and a high level of disk activity on the disk that contains the page file.

a. Pages/sec

This counter measures the number of times that a memory page had to be paged in to memory or out to the disk.

b. Available Bytes

This counter measures the amount of physical memory available. When this value falls below 4 MB, you are getting excessive paging.

c. Committed Bytes

This counter measures the amount of virtual memory that has been committed to physical RAM or to pagefile space. If the amount of committed bytes exceeds the physical memory of a system, more RAM is required on the system.

d. The PhysicalDisk and LogicalDisk Objects

Before you can use Performance Monitor to monitor disk activity, you must enable the disk performance counters. Otherwise, all values for the disk counters report zeroes in Performance Monitor.

To turn on the disk performance counters, log on as a user with administrative privileges and type the following:

```
diskperf -y
```

To start the disk counters on a remote computer, add the computer name to the `diskperf` command:

```
diskperf -y Error! Reference source not found.
```

To complete performance analysis on an NT Server with RAID 5 you must execute diskperf -ye to enable the disk counters.

e. PhysicalDisk: % Disk Time

This counter reports the percentage of time that the physical disk was busy reading or writing.

f. PhysicalDisk: Avg. Disk Queue Length

The average disk queue length is the average number of requests for a physical disk (both read and write requests).

g. LogicalDisk: % Disk Time

This counter reports the percentage of time that the logical disk (for example, C) was busy.

h. LogicalDisk: Avg Disk Queue Length

This counter measures the number of read and write requests waiting for the logical disk to become available.

3. The Server Object

The Server component is responsible for handling all SMB-based requests for sessions and file and print services. If the Server service becomes the bottleneck, requests from clients are denied, forcing retries and creating slower response times and increased traffic. Here are the counters:

- **Bytes Total/sec.** This counter measures the number of bytes sent to and received from the network.

- **Logon/sec.** This counter measures the logon activity to predict if you need to add a BDC on the segment.

- **Pool Nonpaged Failures.** This counter measures the number of times that a request from the server to allocate memory from the nonpaged pool failed. It is generally an indication that the computer's physical memory is not sufficient.

- **Pool Paged Failures.** This counter measures the number of times that a request from the server to allocate memory from the paged pool failed. It is generally an indication that the computer's physical memory or its pagefile size is not sufficient.

C. Establishing Baseline Performance Data

Many of the counters that Performance Monitor provides cannot be interpreted without some baseline data to which to compare it.

It is a good idea to log performance from your servers at various times of the day, regularly, so that you have appropriate baselines with which to compare.

5.2.1 Exercise: Creating a Chart in Performance Monitor

This exercise helps you do the following: become familiar with the process of creating and reading a Performance Monitor chart; understand the basic components of the Performance Monitor main window and the Add to Chart dialog box; and learn how to turn on disk performance counters by using the diskperf command.

Estimated Time: 25 minutes

1. Choose Start, Programs, Administrative Tools, and click on Performance Monitor. The Performance Monitor window appears.

2. Choose Edit, Add to Chart. The Add to Chart dialog box appears. You also can open the Add to Chart dialog box by clicking on the plus sign in the toolbar of the Performance Monitor window.

3a. The Computer text box at the top of the Add to Chart dialog box tells Performance Monitor which computer you want to monitor. The default is the local system. Click on the ellipses button to the right of the Computer text box for a browse list of computers on the network.

3b. The Object combo box tells Performance Monitor which object you want to monitor. As you learned earlier in this chapter, an object is a hardware or software component of your system. You can think of an object as a *category* of system statistics. Click on the down arrow to the right of the Object combo box to see a list of object options. Scroll through the list of objects. Look for the Processor, Memory, PhysicalDisk, LogicalDisk, Server, and Network Segment objects described earlier in this chapter. Choose the PhysicalDisk object. If you have more than one physical disk on your system, a list of your physical disks appears in the Instances box to the right of the Object box. The Instances box lists all instances of the object selected in the Object box. If necessary, choose a physical disk instance.

3c. The Counter list box displays the counters (the statistical measurements) available for the object in the Object box. Scroll through the list of counters for the PhysicalDisk object. If you feel like experimenting, select a different object in the Object box. Notice that the different object is accompanied by a different set of counters. Switch back to the PhysicalDisk object and choose the % Disk Time counter. Click on the Explain button. Notice that a description of the % Disk Time counter appears at the bottom of the dialog box.

3d. Click on the Done button in the Add to Chart dialog box. The dialog box closes and you see the Performance main window.

4. In the Performance Monitor main window, you'll see a vertical line sweeping across the chart from left to right. You also might also see a faint colored line at the bottom of the chart recording a % Disk Time value of 0. If so, this is because you have not enabled the disk performance counters for your system. (If the disk performance counters are enabled on your system, you should see a spikey line that looks like the readout from an electrocardiogram. Go to step 5.)

   If you need to enable the disk performance counters, choose click on the Start button go to the command prompt. Enter the command: diskperf -y. Reboot your system and repeat steps 1–4. (You do not have to browse through the Object and Counter lists this time.)

5. You should now see a spikey line representing the percent of time that the physical disk is busy reading or writing. Choose Edit, Add to Chart. Select the PhysicalDisk object and choose the counter Avg. Disk Queue Length. Click on the Add button; then choose the counter Avg. Disk Bytes/Read. Click on the Add button. Click on the Done button.

6. Examine the Performance Monitor main window. All three of the counters you selected should be tracing out spikey lines on the chart. Each line is a different color. A table at the bottom of the window shows which counter goes with which color. The table also gives the scale of the output, the instance, the object, and the computer.

5

7. Below the chart (but above the table of counters) you find a row of statistical parameters labeled Last, Average, Min, Max, and Graph Time. These parameters pertain to the counter selected in the table at the bottom of the window. Select a different counter and some of these values change. The Last value is the counter value over the last second. Graph Time is the time it takes (in seconds) for the vertical line that draws the chart to sweep across the window.

8. Start Windows NT Explorer. Select a file (a graphics file or a word processing document) and choose Edit, Copy. (This will copy the file you selected to the Clipboard.) Go to another directory and choose Edit, Paste. (This will create a copy of the file in the second directory.) Minimize Explorer and return to the Performance Monitor main window. The disk activity caused by your Explorer session will be reflected in the spikes of the counter lines.

9. Choose Options, Chart. The Chart Options dialog box appears, providing a number of options governing the chart display. The Update Time frame enables you to choose an update interval. The update interval tells Performance Monitor how frequently it should update the chart with new values. (If you choose the Manual Update option, the chart updates only when you press Ctrl+U or choose Options, Update Now.) Experiment with the Chart Options dialog box, or click on the Cancel button.

10. Choose File, Exit to exit Performance Monitor. The Save Chart Settings and Save Chart Settings As options in the File menu enable you to save the collection of objects and counters you are using now so you can monitor the same counters later without having to set them up again. The Export Chart option enables you to export the data to a file that you can open with a spreadsheet or database application. The Save Workspace option saves the settings for your chart as well as any settings for alerts, logs, or reports specified in this session. You will learn more about alerts, logs, and reports in Exercise 5.2.2.

5.2.2   Exercise: Performance Monitor Alerts, Logs, and Reports

In this exercise, you learn about the alternative views (Alert view, Log view, and Report view) available through the View menu of Performance Monitor, and you learn how to log performance data to a log file.

Estimated time: 25 minutes

1. Choose Start, Programs, Administrative Tools, and Performance Monitor. The Performance Monitor main window appears.

2. Open the View menu. You see the following four options:

   - The Chart option plots the counters you select in a continuous chart (refer to Exercise 5.2.1).

   - The Alert option automatically alert a network official if a predetermined counter threshold is surpassed.

   - The Log option saves your system performance data to a log file.

   - The Report option displays system performance data in a report format.

   The setup is similar for each of these view formats. All use some form of the Add to Chart dialog box. All have options configured through the first command at the top of the Options menu. (The name of the first command at the top of the Options menu changes depending on the active view.) It was the Chart command in Exercise 5.2.1.

3a. Choose View, Alert.

3b. Click on the plus sign in the toolbar or choose Edit, Add to Alert. The Add to Alert dialog box appears; it is similar to the Add to Chart dialog box, except you will notice two additional items at the bottom.

The options in the Alert If frame enable you to enter a threshold for the counter. The Over and Under radio buttons specify whether you should receive an alert if the counter value is over or under the threshold value. The Run Program on Alert text box enables you to specify a command line that will execute if the counter value reaches the threshold you specify in the Alert If box. Use the Run Program on Alert text box to execute a command or script that will send a message to your beeper, send you an e-mail message, or notify your paging service.

> **Do not specify a batch file in the Run Program on Alert text box. Performance Monitor uses Unicode format, which can confuse the command-prompt interpreter. (The < and > symbols, which are used in Unicode format, are interpreted as a redirection of input or output.)**

3c. The default object in the Object combo box should be the Processor object. The default counter in the Counter list box should be % Processor Time. Enter the value **5%** in the Alert If box and select the Over radio button.

In the Run Program on Alert text box, type **SOL** and select the First Time radio button. This configuration tells Performance Monitor to execute Windows NT's Solitaire program when the % Processor Time exceeds five percent.

It is important to select the First Time radio button; otherwise, Performance Monitor will execute a new instance of Solitaire every time the % Processor Time exceeds five percent, which happens every time Performance Monitor executes a new instance of Solitaire. In other words, if you try this experiment without selecting the First Time radio button, you'll probably have to close Performance Monitor using the X button or reboot your system to stop the incessant shuffling and dealing.

3d. Click on the Add button, and then click on the Done button. The Alert Legend at the bottom of the Performance Monitor window describes the active alert parameters. The Alert Log shows every instance of an alert.

3e. Make some change to your Desktop. (Hide or reveal the taskbar, change the size of the Performance Monitor window—anything that will cause a five percent utilization of the processor.) The Solitaire program should miraculously appear on your screen. In a real alert situation, Performance Monitor would execute an alert application instead of starting a card game.

3f. Choose Edit, Delete Alert.

4a. Choose View, Log. The Log view saves performance data to a log file instead of displaying it on-screen.

4b. Choose Edit, Add to Log. Notice that only the objects appear in the Add to Log dialog box. The counters and instances boxes do not appear because Performance Monitor automatically logs all counters and all instances of the object to the log file.

Select the Memory Object and click on Add. If you want, you can select another object, such as the Paging File object, and then click on Add again. When you are finished adding objects, click on Done.

4c. Choose, Options Log. The Log Options dialog box appears, enabling you to designate a log file that Performance Monitor will use to log the data.

In the File Name text box, enter the name **exer2.log**.

You also can specify an update interval. The update interval is the interval at which Performance Monitor records performance data to the log. The Manual Update radio button specifies that the file won't be undated unless you press Ctrl+U or choose Options, Update Now.

Click on the Start Log button to start saving data to the log. Wait a few minutes, and then return to the Log Options dialog box and click on the Stop Log button.

4d. Choose View, Chart.

4e. Choose Options, Data From. The Data From dialog box enables you to specify a source for the performance data that will appear in the chart. Note that the default source is Current Activity. (That is why the chart you created in Exercise 5.2.1 took its data from current system activity.)

The alternative to the Current Activity option is to use data from a log file. Click on the Log File radio button; click on the ellipses button to the right of Log File; and select the exer2.log file you created in step 4c. Click on OK.

4f. Choose Edit, Add to Chart.

Click on the down arrow of the Object combo box. Notice that your only object choices are the Memory object and any other objects you selected in step 4b. Select the Memory object. Browse through the counter list and select Pages/sec. Click on the Add button. Select any other memory counters you want to display and click on the Add button. Click on Done.

4g. The log file's record of the counters you selected in 4f appear in the chart in the Performance main window. Notice that, unlike the chart you created in Exercise 5.2.1, this chart does not continuously sweep out new data. That is because this chart represents static data from a previous, finite monitoring session.

4h. Choose Edit, Time Window. A time window enables you to focus on a particular time interval within the log file.

In this example (because you only collected data for a few minutes), the Time Window option might seem unnecessary. If you collected data for a longer period, however, and you want to zero in on a particular event, a time window can be very useful.

Set the beginning and end points of your Time window by adjusting the gray start and stop sliders on the Time Window slide bar. The Bookmarks frame enables you to specify a log file bookmark as a start or stop point. (You can create a bookmark by choosing Options, Bookmark while collecting data to the log file or by clicking on the book in the Performance Monitor toolbar.)

Click on OK to view the data for the time interval.

5a. Choose View, Report.

Choose Options, Data From.

In the Data From... dialog box, select the radio button labeled Current Activity. Report view displays the performance data in a report rather than in a graphics format.

5b. Choose Edit, Add to Report.

Select the processor object and choose the % Processor Time, % Interrupt Time, and Interrupts/sec counters (hold down the Ctrl key to select all three), and then click on Add. Select the PhysicalDisk object and choose the % Disk Time, Avg. Disk Queue Length, and Current Disk Queue Length counters. Click on the Add button. Select the Memory object and choose the Pages/sec, Page Faults/sec, and Available Bytes counters. Click on the Add button. Click on Done.

5c. Examine the main report window. Performance Monitor displays a report of the performance data in a hierarchical format, with counters listed under the appropriate object.

6. Choose File, Exit to exit Performance Monitor.

5

5.2   Practice Problems

In the following questions, more than one answer can be correct; pick all answers that apply.

1. Which Performance Monitor object and counter measures the amount of time that the CPU is busy?

   A.   Processor: % Busy Time

   B.   Processor: % Processor Time

   C.   System: % Processor Time

   D.   System: TotalProcessorUsage

2. While monitoring system performance in Performance Monitor, you notice that the number of interrupts per second have doubled. You haven't increased the number of users or added any new applications to the server. What does an increase of this counter mean?

   A.   Nothing. It is normal for this counter to increase over time.

   B.   It could mean that you have a potential hardware problem, and that a piece of hardware is generating many more interrupts than normal.

   C.   It indicates that the network card is the bottleneck in the system and should be replaced.

   D.   It indicates that the CPU is the bottleneck in the system and should be replaced or upgraded.

3. You're trying to explain the System: Processor Queue Length counter in Performance Monitor to a coworker. Which statement below best describes the purpose of this counter?

   A.   It measures the amount of activity on the CPU.

   B.   It indicates the number of threads waiting for CPU time.

   C.   It indicates the number of users waiting to log on to the domain.

   D.   It indicates the total CPU usage across all CPUs in the system. You see a number for this counter only if your computer has more than one CPU.

4. You're trying to get some statistics that measure how the network is performing. Which Performance Monitor counter can you measure?

   A.   Server: Pool Nonpaged Failures%Network frames

   B.   Server: Total Network Bytes/sec

   C.   Network Interface: Bytes Total/sec

   D.   Network Segment: %Network UtilizationBytes

5. You notice an increase in the number of Pool Nonpaged Failures. What does that indicate?

   A.   That you need to add more RAM to the server.

   B.   That the hard disk is failing, and the system must continually retry to allocate page file space.

   C.   That the system is using the RAM installed in the system, and is good sign that the server is running efficiently.

   D.   That you need to upgrade the RAM in the system by installing faster EDO memory.

6. What tool do you use to monitor objects in NT?

   A.   Network Monitor

   B.   Event Viewer

   C.   Performance Monitor

   D.   Diskperf

7. What would be an example of an object that you would monitor on a database server? (Choose all that apply.)

   A. Security subsystem lookups

   B. Disk access time

   C. Response time for queries

   D. Response time for thread execution

8. Which of the following are reasons to use Performance Monitor? (Choose all that apply.)

   A. To optimize specific tasks

   B. To troubleshoot performance problems

   C. To diagnose program crashes

   D. To plan for future needs

9. How do you install Performance Monitor?

   A. Through Control Panel, use the Add remove Programs applet.

   B. Through Control Panel, use the Network Applet.

   C. Run setup from the Admin, Nettools, Perfmon directory on the CD-ROM.

   D. Performance Monitor is installed as part of the NT Setup program.

10. Where is Performance Monitor located?

    A. Control Panel, Performance Monitor.

    B. Control Panel, System.

    C. Administrative tools folder.

    D. You have to launch Performance Monitor through WinMSD.

11. Which counter would be most effective in identifying which application is causing your NT Server to run slowly?

    A. Processor: %Processor Time

    B. Memory: Page Faults

    C. Process: %Processor Time

    D. Memory: Pages/sec

12. While monitoring the Performance Monitor counter Processor: Interrupts/ Sec you discover an unusual increase of this counter as compared to previous measurements with the same amount of system activity. What could this mean?

    A. You have added services.

    B. You have added applications.

    C. You might have a hardware problem.

    D. You network card is probably receiving many interrupts at this time that could have an adverse effect on the processor.

13. Of the following, what can Performance Monitor do?

    A. Log minimums, maximums, and averages of various counters for critical system objects.

    B. Send administrative alerts.

    C. Provide a GUI of your system performance.

    D. Track network activity on a server.

14. A user calls and tells you that the NT Workstation is running very slowly. How can you monitor this performance? (Choose the best answer.)

    A. Go to the workstation and use Performance Monitor.

    B. Connect to the user's computer through Performance Monitor and monitor over the network.

    C. You must connect to the user's computer's C$ share, and then run Network Monitor.

    D. You cannot monitor the user's computer, as NT Workstation does not have a Performance or Network Monitor.

15. You would like to monitor your disk performance and you are aware that you must use the diskperf -y command to do so. Why do you have to enable this?

    A. This command enables Performance Monitor to write a signature to drive O.

    B. This command enables Performance Monitor to have access to the MBR.

    C. This command enables Performance Monitor's disk monitoring features.

    D. You have to use this command only on SCSI drives.

16. What does the counter Memory: Available Bytes track in Performance Monitor?

    A. Amount of memory available in RAM

    B. Amount of memory available in pagefile.sys

    C. Amount of memory available combined with pagefile.sys and RAM

    D. Amount of memory available to the application in the foreground

17. What does the counter Memory: Pages/sec track in Performance Monitor?

    A. How many pages the Virtual Memory Manager can swap out of RAM to pagefile.sys in one second.

    B. How many pages the Virtual Memory Manager can swap out of RAM to pagefile.sys in one nanosecond.

    C. How many pages the Virtual Memory Manager can swap out of RAM to pagefile.sys in one millisecond.

    D. The overall activity of pages swapped.

18. What does the counter Memory: Committed bytes track in Performance Monitor?

    A. The amount of bytes currently in RAM

    B. The amount of bytes currently in pagefile.sys

    C. The amount of bytes currently in use and needed by all applications

    D. The amount of bytes currently in RAM and in pagefile.sys

19. While using Performance Monitor, you track the performance of Physical Disk: Disk Queue length. You suspect that the disk is a bottleneck. What setting would indicate that this disk is the bottleneck?

    A. The value was less than 2

    B. The value was less than 4

    C. The value was more than 2

    D. The value was more than 4

20. While using Performance Monitor, you track the performance of Physical Disk: Disk Queue length. You determine that disk is a bottleneck. What can you do to improve this? (Choose all that apply:)

    A. RAID

    B. Memory

    C. Faster disk interface

    D. Asynchronous disk drivers

5.2 Answers and Explanations: Practice Problems

1. **B** Processor: % Processor Time measures the amount of time that the CPU is busy.

2. **B** An increase in interrupts without an increase in users or applications to the server generally means that a hardware device is acting improperly.

3. **B** A thread is the smallest unit of executable code.

4. **D** Network Segment: %Network UtilizationBytes is the Performance Monitor counter that you can measure.

5. **A** Typically, adding RAM is the most common activity to increase performance on an NT machine.

6. **C** Performance Monitor is the tool you use to monitor objects in NT.

7. **C** Response time for queries is an example of an object that you would monitor on a database server.

8. **B, D** You use Performance Monitor to troubleshoot performance problems and to plan for growth.

9. **D** Performance Monitor is installed as part of the NT Setup program.

10. **C** Performance Monitor is in the Administrative tools folder.

11. **A** Processor: %Processor Time is the most effective counter to identify which application is causing your NT Server to run slowly.

12. **C** If you discover an unusual increase of the counter Processor: Interrupts/Sec compared to previous measurements with the same amount of system activity, you have a hardware problem.

13. **A, B, C, D** Performance Monitor can do all of these.

14. **B** Performance Monitor does enable remote monitoring of NT workstations.

15. **C** The diskperf -y command enables Performance Monitor's disk monitoring features.

16. **A** The counter Memory: Available Bytes tracks the amount of memory available in RAM.

17. **D** The counter Memory: Pages/sec tracks overall activity of pages swapped.

18. **C** The counter Memory: Committed bytes tracks the amount of bytes currently in use and needed by all applications.

19. **C** You determine that the disk is a bottleneck because the value is more than 2.

20. **A, C, D** Implementing RAID alleviates performance degradation; faster controllers speed up disk access; and asynchronous disk drivers boost performance.

5.2 Key Words

BDC	Bottleneck
Bytes total/sec	Counters
Interrupts/sec	Objects
Pages/sec	PDC

Practice Exam: Monitoring and Optimization

Use this practice exam to test your mastery of Planning. This practice exam is 16 questions long. Keep in mind that the passing Microsoft score is 76.4 percent. There will be two types of questions:

- Multiple Choice—Select the correct answer.

- Multiple Multiple Choice—Select all answers that are correct.

Begin as soon as you are ready. Answers follow the test.

1. You have a server that is receiving requests from users running IPX/SPX only, yet you have TCP/IP installed so that you may browse IP resources from this machine. How can you configure bindings to improve performance on this server?

   A. Remove TCP/IP.

   B. Unbind IPX/SPX from the Workstation service and unbind TCP/IP from the server service.

   C. Unbind TCP/IP from the Workstation service and unbind IPX/SPX from the server service.

   D. You cannot change the protocol binding on services.

2. What is the most common upgrade that you can do for NT Server to improve performance?

   A. Monitor performance on a regular basis.

   B. Add another processor.

   C. Add memory.

   D. Add a faster disk controller.

3. What hardware implementations should you use to improve data-transfer performance? (Choose all that apply:)

   A. Use only SCSI host adapters.

   B. Use host adapters capable of asynchronous I/O.

   C. Implement stripe sets with parity either through NT's Disk Administrator or hardware RAID solutions.

   D. Distribute data across several servers to accomplish load balancing.

4. Where can you modify the Virtual Memory setting in NT 4.0? (Choose the best answer.)

   A. Through WinMSD

   B. Through Control Panel, System, Virtual Memory

   C. Through Control Panel, 386/Pentium

   D. Through Regedit

5. In the Virtual Memory Setting dialog box, you are presented with a number of choices. One of the choices, Minimize Memory Used, is available. When would you select this option?

   A. When the number of users is greater than 64

   B. When the number of users is 10 or fewer

   C. On an application server or in a domain with just one domain controller

   D. When the number of users is greater than 10, but fewer than 64

6. In the Virtual Memory Setting dialog box, you are presented with a number of choices. One of the choices, Balance, is available. When would you select this option?

   A. When the number of users is greater than 64

   B. When the number of users is 10 or fewer

   C. On an application server or in a domain with just one domain controller

   D. When the number of users is greater than 10, but fewer than 64

7. In the Virtual Memory Setting dialog box, you are presented with a number of choices. One of the choices, Maximize Throughput for File Sharing, is available. When would you select this option?

   A. When the number of users is greater than 64

   B. When the number of users is 10 or fewer

   C. On an application server or in a domain with just one domain controller

   D. When the number of users is greater than 10, but fewer than 64

8. In the Virtual Memory Setting dialog box, you are presented with a number of choices. One of the choices is Maximize Throughout for Network Applications. When would you select this option?

   A. When the number of users is greater than 64

   B. When the number of users is 10 or fewer

   C. On an application server or in a domain with just one domain controller

   D. When the number of users is greater than 10, but fewer than 64

9. While using Performance Monitor, you track the performance of Physical Disk: %disk time. You suspect that the disk is a bottleneck. What setting would lead you to such a conclusion?

   A. The value was less than 90.

   B. The value was less than 100.

   C. The value was more than 90.

   D. The value was more than 100.

10. While using Performance Monitor, you track the performance of Physical Disk: %disk time. You determine that the disk is a bottleneck. How can you immediately improve the performance of this bottleneck? Choose the best answer:

    A. Add memory.

    B. Distribute processes to other machines.

    C. Use SCSI host adapters.

    D. Use faster hard drives.

11. What is the Server Object tracking in Performance Monitor?

    A. NT Server's capability to handle more than 10 concurrent connections

    B. NT Server's capability to handle more than 64 concurrent connections

    C. SMB-based requests from clients

    D. Both SMB-based and NCP-based requests from clients

12. If the server service becomes a bottleneck, what effect(s) could this have on your system? Choose all that apply:

    A. Requests from clients are denied.

    B. Logon requests might not happen.

    C. Response times are much longer.

    D. PDCs and BDCs will not communicate

5

13. What does the counter Network: Bytes Total/sec measure?

    A. Bytes sent to the network

    B. Bytes sent from the network

    C. Bytes sent to and from the network

    D. Bytes discarded from the network

14. You are monitoring the counter Network: Bytes Total/sec in Performance Monitor. On each server, you tally the total amount, and you realize that this amount is nearly the total amount of maximum throughput for your network medium. What does this mean you need to do to increase productivity?

    A. You need to install faster network adapters.

    B. You need to segment the network.

    C. You need to add more memory.

    D. You need to upgrade to NDIS 4.0 drivers.

15. What does the counter pool nonpaged failures and pool paged failures measure?

    A. The number of times the server service generated a page fault

    B. The number of pages swapped from RAM to the pagefile.sys

    C. The number of times that a request from the server to allocate memory failed

    D. The number of times interrupts from a network card caused the Virtual Memory Manager to swap pages

16. You are measuring the counter pool nonpaged failures and pool paged failures. The results of your test will indicate what component of your system is causing trouble?

    A. Network Card

    B. Processor

    C. Memory

    D. Hard Disk

Practice Exam Answers

1. **B** By unbinding the protocols, you free up resources on your server.

2. **C** The most common upgrade that you can do for NT Server to improve performance is to add memory.

3. **A, B, C, D** You can use all the mentioned hardware implementations to improve data-transfer performance.

4. **B** Use Control Panel, System, Virtual Memory applet.

5. **B** You would select Minimize Memory Used from the Virtual Memory Setting dialog box when the number of users is 10 or fewer.

6. **D** You would select Balance from the Virtual Memory Setting dialog box when the number of users is greater than 10, but fewer than 64.

7. **A** You would select Maximize Throughput for File Sharing from the Virtual Memory Setting dialog box when the number of users is greater than 64.

8. **C** You would select Maximize Throughput for Network Applications from the Virtual Memory Setting dialog box on an application server or in a domain with just one domain controller.

9. **C** If the Physical Disk: %disk time value is more than 90, you have a bottleneck.

10. **B, C, D** Distribute processes to other machines, use SCSI host adapters, and use faster hard drives.

11. **C** SMBs are Server Message Blocks.

12. **A, B, C** The server service is started by default, and its primary job is to share resources.

13. **C** Network: Bytes Total/sec measures bytes sent to and from the network.

14. **B** You need to segment the network.

15. **C** The counter pool nonpaged failures and pool paged failures measure the number of times that a request from the server to allocate memory failed.

16. **C** Measuring the counter pool nonpaged failures and pool paged failures shows that memory is causing trouble.

5

CHAPTER 6

Troubleshooting

This chapter helps you prepare for the "Troubleshooting" section of Microsoft's Exam 70-67, "Implementing and Supporting Microsoft Windows NT Server 4.0." Microsoft provides the following objectives for the Troubleshooting section:

- Choose the appropriate course of action to take to resolve installation failures.

- Choose the appropriate course of action to take to resolve boot failures.

- Choose the appropriate course of action to take to resolve configuration errors.

- Choose the appropriate course of action to take to resolve printer problems.

- Choose the appropriate course of action to take to resolve RAS problems.

- Choose the appropriate course of action to take to resolve connectivity problems.

- Choose the appropriate course of action to take to resolve resource access problems and permission problems.

- Choose the appropriate course of action to take to resolve fault-tolerance failures. Fault-tolerance methods include: tape backup, mirroring, stripe set with parity, and disk duplexing.

6.1   Troubleshooting Installation

Microsoft lists the following objective for the Windows NT Server exam: Choose the appropriate course of action to take to resolve installation failures.

Microsoft has identified the following common installation problems and solutions:

- **Media errors.** If there seems to be a problem with the Windows NT Installation CD-ROM or floppy disks, ask Microsoft Sales to replace the disk. Call 800-426-9400.

- **Insufficient disk space.** Delete unnecessary files and folders, compress NTFS partitions, reformat an existing partition or use Setup to create more space, create a new partition with more space.

- **Non-supported SCSI adapter.** Boot to a different operating system (that can use the SCSI adapter) and run WINNT from the installation CD-ROM, try a network installation, replace the unsupported adapter with a supported adapter on the Hardware Compatibility List.

- **Failure of dependency service to start.** Verify the protocol and adapter configuration in the Control Panel Network application, make certain that the local computer has a unique name.

- **Inability to connect to the domain controller.** Verify account name and password, make sure the domain name is correct, make sure the Primary Domain Controller is functioning properly, and verify protocol and adapter configuration settings in the Control Panel Network application. If you just finished installing or upgrading, make sure the domain account for the computer has been reset (added to the network again).

- **Error in assigning domain name.** Make certain that the domain name isn't identical to some other domain or computer name on the network.

Server cannot be installed strictly from disks or floppies. To install Server 4.0 on a previous version of NT and keep all settings, install it in the same directory the old version was in. If you install into any other directory, you have not upgraded, but created a dual-boot machine. Windows 95 cannot be upgraded to NT Server as there are incompatibilities in the Registry, drivers, and so on. You must install NT in a separate directory from Windows 95 and reinstall all applications.

Three startup disks are made at the time of install. If you lose these disks, you can recreate them by running WINNT /OX. CONVERT.EXE is used to convert FAT partitions to NTFS. There is no such utility for converting NTFS back to FAT.

6.1   Practice Problems

1. Which of the following should be one of the first steps undertaken to resolve a dependency service that fails to start after a Windows NT installation?

   A. Boot to a different operating system and run WINNT from there.

   B. Compress NTFS partitions.

   C. Verify the local computer has a unique name from the Control Panel.

   D. Call Microsoft Sales to replace the disks.

2. Which of the following should be one of the first steps undertaken to resolve an error a non-supported SCSI adapter during a Windows NT installation?

   A. Boot to a different operating system and run WINNT from there.

   B. Compress NTFS partitions.

   C. Verify the local computer has a unique name from the Control Panel.

   D. Call Microsoft Sales to replace the disks.

3. Which of the following should be one of the first steps undertaken to resolve an error of insufficient disk space during a Windows NT installation?

   A. Boot to a different operating system and run WINNT from there.

   B. Compress NTFS partitions.

   C. Verify the local computer has a unique name from the Control Panel.

   D. Call Microsoft Sales to replace the disks.

4. Which of the following should be one of the first steps undertaken to resolve an error with the installation CD during a Windows NT installation?

   A. Boot to a different operating system and run WINNT from there.

   B. Compress NTFS partitions.

   C. Verify the local computer has a unique name from the Control Panel.

   D. Call Microsoft Sales to replace the disks.

5. Windows NT Server 4.0 can be installed from which media? (Choose any that apply.)

   A. CD-ROM

   B. 5" floppies

   C. 3.5" disks

   D. A network share point

6. To install NT Server 4.0 on a previous version of NT, and keep all settings:

   A. Install in the same directory the old version was in.

   B. Install in a new directory.

   C. Do nothing, it will automatically find and install over the old version.

   D. Run the MIGRATE utility.

7. To create a dual-boot machine with a previous version of NT:

   A. Install in the same directory the old version was in.

   B. Install in a new directory.

   C. Do nothing, it will automatically find and install over the old version.

   D. Run the MIGRATE utility.

6

8. To upgrade Windows 95 to Windows NT Server:

    A. Install in the same directory the old version was in.

    B. Install in a new directory.

    C. Do nothing, it will automatically find and install over the old version.

    D. Run the MIGRATE utility.

    E. None of the above.

9. When installing NT Server, how many startup disks must be made?

    A. 1

    B. 2

    C. 3

    D. 4

    E. No startup disks must be made

10. If you lose the startup disks made during NT Server's install, how can you remake them?

    A. WINNT32

    B. WINNT

    C. WINNT /OX

    D. WINNT /STARTUP

11. The utility used to convert FAT partitions to NTFS is:

    A. NTFS.EXE.

    B. CONVERT.EXE.

    C. MIGRATE.EXE.

    D. There is no utility to perform this operation.

6.1 Answers and Explanations: Practice Problems

1. **C** A duplicate computer name on the domain can prevent all services from starting. Make certain the computer has a unique name.

2. **A** Booting to an operating system that can use the SCSI adapter can enable you to use the CD and try a network installation.

3. **B** Compressing the partition can free up more disk space, allowing the installation to successfully execute.

4. **D** Microsoft Sales can replace the faulty disks. The phone number is 800-426-9400.

5. **A, D** NT Server can be installed from a network share point, or CD-ROM. 3.5″ floppies are needed to start the CD install, but Server cannot be installed strictly from disks or floppies.

6. **A** To install Server 4.0 on a previous version of NT and keep all settings, install it in the same directory the old version was in. If you install into any other directory, you have not upgraded, but created a dual-boot machine.

7. **B** To install Server 4.0 on a previous version of NT and keep all settings, install it in the same directory the old version was in. If you install it into any other directory, you have not upgraded, but created a dual-boot machine.

8. **B** Windows 95 cannot be upgraded to NT Server, as there are incompatibilities in the Registry, drivers, and so on. You must install NT in a separate directory from Windows 95 and reinstall all applications.

9. **C**   Three startup disks are made at the time of install. If you lose these disks, you can recreate them by running WINNT /OX.

10. **C**   Three startup disks are made at the time of install. If you lose these disks, you can recreate them by running WINNT /OX.

11. **B**   CONVERT.EXE is used to convert FAT partitions to NTFS.

6.1   Key Words

Domain name

NTFS partitions

FAT

Startup disks

6

6.2   Troubleshooting Boot Failures

The boot process is one of the most common sources of problems in Windows NT. The cause may be a lost or corrupt boot file. Try booting from the Windows NT boot disk and perform an emergency repair (a process described later in this chapter) if necessary.

Microsoft lists the following objective for the Windows NT Server exam: Choose the appropriate course of action to take to resolve boot failures.

A.   Booting Up

The boot process begins when your computer accesses the hard drive's Master Boot Record (MBR) to load Windows NT. If your system fails during the Power On Self Test (POST), the problem isn't NT-related; instead, it is a hardware issue. What happens after the MBR's program loads depends on the type of computer you are using.

1. The Intel Boot Sequence

On Intel x86-based computers, the boot sector of the active partition loads a file called NTLDR. Similar to IO.SYS for MS-DOS or Windows 95, NTLDR is a hidden, system, read-only file in the root of your system partition, responsible for loading the rest of the operating system. NTLDR carries out the following steps:

1. Switches the processor to the 32-bit flat memory model necessary to address 4 GB of RAM.

2. Starts the minifile system driver necessary for accessing the system and boot partitions. This minifile system driver contains just enough code to read files at boot time. The full file systems are loaded later.

3. Displays a Boot Loader menu that gives the user a choice of operating system to load, and waits for a response. The options for the Boot Loader menu are stored in a hidden, read-only file in the root of your system partition named BOOT.INI.

4. Invokes, if Windows NT is the selected system, the hardware detection routine to determine the hardware required. NTDETECT.COM (the same program that detects the hardware during NTSETUP) performs the hardware detection. NTDETECT.COM builds the hardware list and returns it to NTLDR. NTDETECT.COM is hidden, system, and read-only in the root of the system partition.

5. Loads the kernel of the operating system. The kernel is called NTOSKRNL.EXE, and you can find it in the <winnt_root>\SYSTEM32 directory. At this point, the screen clears and displays OS Loader V4.xx.

6. Loads the Hardware Abstraction Layer (HAL). The HAL is a single file (HAL.DLL) that contains the code necessary to mask interrupts and exceptions from the kernel.

7. Loads SYSTEM, the HKEY_LOCAL_MACHINE\SYSTEM hive in the Registry. You can find the corresponding file in the <winnt_root>\SYSTEM32\CONFIG directory.

8. Loads the boot-time drivers. Boot-time drivers have a start value of 0. These values are loaded in the order in which they are listed in HKEY_LOCAL_MACHINE\SYSTEM\CurrentControlSet\ Control\ServiceGroupOrder. Each time a driver loads, a dot is added to the series following the OS Loader V4.00 at the top of the screen. If the /sos switch is used in BOOT.INI, the name of each driver appears on a separate line as each is loaded. The drivers are not initialized yet.

9. Passes control, along with the hardware list collected by NTDETECT.COM, to NTOSKRNL.EXE.

After NTOSKRNL.EXE takes control, the boot phase ends and the load phases begin.

2. The RISC Boot Sequence

On a RISC-based computer, the boot process is much simpler because the firmware does much of the work that NTLDR does on the Intel platform. RISC-based computers maintain hardware configuration in their firmware (also called non-volatile RAM), so they don't need NTDETECT.COM. Their firmware also contains a list of valid operating systems and their locations, so they don't need BOOT.INI either.

RISC-based machines don't look for the Intel-specific NTLDR to boot the operating system; instead, they always look for a file called OSLOADER.EXE. This file is handed the hardware configuration data from the firmware. It then loads NTOSKRNL.EXE, HAL.DLL, and SYSTEM, and the boot process concludes.

3. Booting to Windows 95, MS-DOS, or OS/2

On Intel-based computers, you can install Windows NT with Windows 95 or MS-DOS. The boot loader screen offers the user a choice of Windows NT Workstation 4, Microsoft Windows, and MS-DOS. If the user chooses a non-Windows NT operating system, a file called BOOTSECT.DOS is loaded and executed. BOOTSECT.DOS is a hidden, system, read-only file in the root of the system partition. It contains the information that was present in the boot sector before Windows NT was installed. If a user chooses Windows 95 from the boot menu, for example, BOOTSECT.DOS loads IO.SYS and passes control to it.

4. BOOT.INI

To understand the BOOT.INI file, you must understand two things—the ARC syntax and the actual use of the file. Both topics are discussed in the sections that follow.

a. ARC

Because not all machines use MS-DOS–style paths (for example, c:\winnt) for referring to locations on a hard drive, Windows NT uses a cross-platform standard format called Advanced RISC Computer (ARC), within BOOT.INI. An ARC-compliant path consists of four parameters:

Parameter	Description
scsi(x) or multi(x)	identifies the hardware adapter
disk(y)	SCSI bus number: always 0 if multi
rdisk(z)	Physical drive number for multi; ignored for SCSI
partition(a)	Logical partition number

The first three parameters are zero-based; that is, the first physical IDE drive is rdisk(0) and the second is rdisk(1). The partition parameter, however, is one-based, so the first partition on the drive is rdisk(0)partition(1).

All of the parameters—even the ones that are ignored—must be present in the path. For instance, multi(0)disk(0)rdisk(0)partition(1) is a valid path even though disk(0) is essentially unnecessary. multi(0)rdisk(0)partition(1) is not valid.

The first parameter almost always is multi, even for a SCSI controller. The only time you even see SCSI in a BOOT.INI file is if the BIOS on the disk controller is turned off. If this is the case, don't worry; an additional hidden, system, read-only file, NTBOOTDD.SYS, is present in the root of the system partition. NTBOOTDD.SYS is a device driver necessary for accessing a SCSI controller that doesn't have an on-board BIOS or doesn't use INT 13 to identify hard disks. If you have this file present, you probably see a scsi(x) entry in BOOT.INI. If you don't, you probably have upgraded from Windows NT 3.1 (where this setting was more common) without ever deleting the file.

The same holds true for a RISC-based computer; look at the firmware entries for the operating system paths and you should see the same kind of ARC-compliant paths.

b. The BOOT.INI in Use

NTLDR may invoke the Boot Loader menu, but BOOT.INI, an editable text file, controls it. (It is read-only, so you must remove that attribute before editing it.) BOOT.INI is the only INI file that Windows NT uses—if, indeed you can actually say that NT uses it. After all, Windows NT is not loaded when this file is called on.

BOOT.INI has only two sections: [boot loader] and [operating systems], covered next.

[boot loader]—The [boot loader] section of BOOT.INI defines the operating system loaded if the user doesn't make a selection within a defined period of time. By default, you see something like this:

```
[boot loader]
timeout=30
default=multi(0)disk(0)rdisk(0)partition(1)\WINNT
```

The timeout parameter is the length of time (in seconds) that NTLDR has to wait for the user to make a decision. If timeout is set to 0, the default operating system loads immediately. If it is set to -1, the menu displays until the user makes a decision.

The default parameter defines the actual path to the directory that contains the files for the default operating system.

You can edit BOOT.INI directly, but remember that a mistyped character in NOTEPAD.EXE or EDIT.COM could result in your system not booting properly.

[operating systems]—The [operating systems] section contains a reference for every operating system available to the user from the Boot Loader menu, as well as any special switches necessary to customize the Windows NT environment. One of these entries must match the default= entry in the [boot loader] section. Otherwise, you end up with two entries for the same OS on-screen, one of which has (default) following it.

Note that the paths are in ARC format with a label in quotation marks, which display as an on-screen selection. Here's an example of an [operating systems] section:

```
multi(0)disk(0)rdisk(0)partition(1)\WINNT=Windows NT Workstation "Version
4.00"
```

c. BOOT.INI Switches

The following table delineates several useful switches that you can include in the [operating systems] section of BOOT.INI. The only way to include them is to manually edit the BOOT.INI file (take the read-only attribute off first and save the file as a text file).

Switch	Description
/basevideo	Tells Windows NT to load the standard VGA driver rather than the optimized driver written for your video card. Selecting the VGA mode entry uses the standard VGA 640×480, 16-color driver that works with almost every video card.
/sos	Enumerates to the screen each driver as it loads during the kernel load phase. If Windows NT hangs during this phase, you can use the /sos switch to determine which driver caused the problem.
/noserialmice=[COMx|COMx,y,z_]	When Windows NT boots, NTDETECT.COM looks for, among other things, the presence of serial mice. Sometimes this detection routine misfires and identifies modems or other devices as serial mice. Then, when Windows NT loads and initializes, the serial port is unavailable and the device is unusable because Windows NT is expecting a serial mouse. This switch tells NTDETECT.COM not to bother looking for serial mice. Used with a specific COM port(s), NTDETECT.COM still looks for serial mice, but not on the port(s) specified.
/crashdebug	Turns on the Automatic Recovery and Restart capability, which you can also configure using the Control Panel System application. In fact, when you configure this capability through Control Panel, you are adding this switch to the OS path in BOOT.INI.

continues

Switch	Description
/nodebug	Programmers often use a special version of Windows NT that includes debugging symbols useful for tracking down problems with code. This version of Windows NT runs slowly compared to the retail version, owing to the extra overhead in tracking every piece of executing code. To turn off the monitoring in this version of NT, add the /nodebug switch to the OS path in BOOT.INI.
/maxmem:n	Memory parity errors can be notoriously difficult to isolate. The /maxmem switch helps. When followed with a numeric value, this switch limits Windows NT's usable memory to the amount specified in the switch. This switch also is useful for developers using high-level workstations, who want to simulate performance on a lower-level machine.
/scsiordinal:n	If your system has two identical SCSI controllers, you need a way to distinguish one from the other. The /scsiordinal switch is used to assign a value of 0 to the first controller and 1 to the second.

5. Kernel Initialization Phase

After all the initial drivers have loaded, the screen turns blue and the text height shrinks; the kernel initialization phase has begun. Now the kernel and all the drivers loaded in the previous phase are initialized. The Registry begins to flesh out. The CurrentControlSet is copied to the Clone Set, and the volatile HARDWARE key is created. The system Registry hive then is scanned once more for higher-level drivers configured to start during system initialization.

6. Services Load Phase

Here the session manager scans the system hive for a list of programs that must run before Windows NT fully initializes. These programs may include AUTOCHK.EXE, the boot-time version of CHKDSK.EXE that examines and repairs any problems within a file system, or AUTOCONV.EXE, which converts a partition from FAT to NTFS. These boot-time programs are stored in the following:

```
HKEY_LOCAL_MACHINE\SYSTEM\CurrentControlSet\Control\Session
Manager\BootExecute
```

Following these programs, the page file(s) are created based on the locations specified in:

```
HKEY_LOCAL_MACHINE\SYSTEM\CurrentControlSet\Control\Session Manager\Memory
Management
```

Next, the SOFTWARE hive loads from <winnt_root>\SYSTEM32\CONFIG. Session Manager then loads the CSR subsystem and any other required subsystems from:

```
HKEY_LOCAL_MACHINE\System\CurrentControlSet\Control\Session
Manager\SubSystems\Required
```

Finally, drivers that have a start value of 2 (Automatic) load.

7. Windows Start Phase

After the Win32 subsystem starts, the screen then switches into GUI mode. The Winlogon process is invoked, and the Welcome dialog box appears. Although users can go ahead and log on at this point, the system might not respond for a few more moments while the Service Controller initializes automatic services.

The critical file at this point is SERVICES.EXE, which actually starts Alerter, Computer Browser, EventLog, Messenger, NetLogon, NT LM Security Support Provider, Server, TCP/IP NetBIOS Helper, and Workstation. A missing or corrupt SERVICES.EXE cripples your Windows NT-based computer.

After a user successfully logs on to the system, the LastKnownGood control set is updated and the boot is considered good. Until a user logs on for the first time, though, the boot/load process technically remains unfinished, so a problem that Windows NT cannot detect but that a user can see (such as a video problem) can be resolved by falling back on the LastKnownGood configuration.

8. Control Sets and LastKnownGood

A *control set* is a collection of configuration information used during boot by Windows NT. A special control set, called LastKnownGood, plays a special role in troubleshooting the boot process.

After the system boots and a user logs on successfully, the current configuration settings are copied to the LastKnownGood control set in the Registry. These settings are preserved so that if the system cannot boot successfully the next time a user attempts to log on, the system can fall back on LastKnownGood, which, as the name implies, is the last configuration known to facilitate a "good" boot. LastKnownGood is stored in the Registry under

```
HKEY_LOCAL_MACHINE\SYSTEM\CurrentControlSet
```

The key to understanding LastKnownGood lies in recognizing that it updates the first time a user logs on to Windows NT after a reboot.

To boot with the LastKnownGood configuration, press the spacebar when prompted during the boot process. You are presented with the Hardware Profile/Configuration Recovery menu. Select a hardware profile and enter L for the LastKnownGood configuration.

Windows NT occasionally will boot using LastKnownGood automatically, but only if the normal boot process produces severe or critical errors in loading device drivers.

LastKnownGood does not do you any good if files are corrupt or missing. You must use the Emergency Repair Process for aid with that.

6

B.　Troubleshooting the Boot Process

If one of the important boot files is missing or corrupt, Windows NT can't boot correctly. If NTLDR, NTDTECT.COM, BOOTSECT.DOS, or NTOSKRNL.EXE fail, NT displays a message that tells you the name of the missing file. Use the Emergency Repair Process to restore the system.

If BOOT.INI is missing, NTLDR tries to start Windows NT without consulting BOOT.INI or the boot menu. This works as long as Windows NT is installed in the default \Winnt directory on the first partition of the first disk. If Windows NT is installed in a different directory, however, NTLDR cannot find it and issues an error message stating that the file, \winnt root\system32\ntoskrnl.exe, is missing or corrupt.

If BOOT.INI contains an invalid path name, or if a BOOT.INI path includes an invalid device, the boot fails. Verify all BOOT.INI paths. If possible, boot from a floppy and edit BOOT.INI to fix the problem. The Emergency Repair Process described later in this chapter can restore BOOT.INI if the error stems from a recent change.

If you need to boot Windows NT from the floppy drive, you can use Setup Boot disks created using the Winnt.exe or Winnt32.exe utilities with the /ox switch.

C.　The Emergency Repair Process

As discussed in Chapter 2, the installation process enables you to create an emergency repair directory and emergency repair disk, both of which are backup copies of Registry information (which come in handy if you can't boot Windows NT owing to missing or corrupt files). The following sections examine ways in which the Emergency Repair Process can aid a troubled Windows NT installation.

1. Emergency Repair Directory Versus Emergency Repair Disk

Installation always creates the emergency repair directory. You can find it in <winnt_root>\REPAIR. You can create an emergency repair disk as well.

Both the directory and disk are computer-specific. Keep a separate emergency repair disk for each computer and tag it with the serial number of the computer.

Table 6.2.1 lists and describes the files on the emergency repair disk.

Table 6.2.1　Files on the Emergency Repair Disk

Files	Description
SETUP.LOG	A text file that contains the names of all the Windows NT installation files, along with checksum values for each. If any of the files on your hard drive are missing or corrupt, the Emergency Repair Process should detect them with the aid of this hidden, system, and read-only file.
SYSTEM._	A compressed copy of the Registry's SYSTEM hive. This is the Windows NT control set collection.

Files	Description
SAM._	A compressed copy of the Registry's SAM hive. This is the Windows NT user accounts database.
SECURITY.__	A compressed copy of the Registry's SECURITY hive. This is the Windows NT security information, which includes SAM and the security policies.
SOFTWARE._	A compressed copy of the Registry's SOFTWARE hive. This hive contains all Win32 software configuration information.
DEFAULT._	A compressed copy of the system default profile.
CONFIG.NT	The VDM version of the MS-DOS CONFIG.SYS file.
AUTOEXEC.NT	The VDM version of the MS-DOS AUTOEXEC.BAT file.
NTUSER.DA_	A copy of the file NTUSER.DAT (which contains user profile information) from the directory winnt_root\profiles\Defaultuser.

2. RDISK.EXE

Both the emergency repair disk and directory are created during installation, but neither are updated automatically at anytime thereafter. To update the emergency repair information, use the hidden utility RDISK.EXE (located in \<winnt_root>\SYSTEM32).

RDISK offers two options for administrators: Update Repair Info and Create Repair Disk.

a. Update Repair Info

The Update Repair Info button updates only the emergency repair directory, although it does prompt for the creation/update of an emergency repair disk immediately following successful completion of the directory update. Always update the directory before creating the disk, because the disk will be created using the information in the directory.

b. Create Repair Disk

If the information in the repair directory is up-to-date, you may choose to create or update an emergency repair disk. You don't have to use a pre-formatted disk for the repair disk. RDISK formats the disk regardless.

A significant limitation of RDISK is that it will not update DEFAULT._, SECURITY, or SAM, in the repair directory (or disk). In other words, you may update your repair disk week-to-week, but none of your account changes are being backed up. To do a complete emergency repair update, you must run RDISK.EXE using the /S switch.

3. Starting the Emergency Repair Process

Whether you use the emergency repair directory or the emergency repair disk, you need to recognize that you can't boot from either or use either from within Windows NT. To actually invoke the Emergency Repair Process, you must access the original three Windows NT Setup disks. If you don't have the original disks handy, you generate them from the CD by using the WINNT /OX command on a DOS-based machine.

6

The Setup process offers the choices either to install Windows NT or repair an existing installation. Pressing R on this screen invokes the Emergency Repair Process.

After you select your repair options, Setup attempts to locate your hard drive. After Setup locates your hard drive, it asks you whether you want to use an emergency repair disk or you want Setup to search for your repair directory. You then encounter a series of restoration choices based on the repair options you selected and the problems Setup uncovers as it analyzes your system. The next few sections discuss the emergency repair options.

a. Inspect Registry Files

At this point, the process gets computer-specific. If your registry becomes corrupt, only your own emergency repair disk can save you—no one else's can. You granularly select to repair any combination of the SYSTEM, SOFTWARE, DEFAULT, and SECURITY/SAM hives, which are copied from the repair directory/disk.

b. Inspect Startup Environment

The files required to boot Windows NT are discussed earlier in this chapter. If any of these files become corrupted, choose Inspect Startup Environment to repair them. You can use anyone's emergency repair disk for this option because these files are generic across all Windows NT installations.

c. Verify Windows NT System Files

This option systematically inspects every file in the Windows NT directory tree and compares them with the checksum values in SETUP.LOG. If it determines that any files are missing or corrupt, the repair process attempts to replace them. Again, you need the original disks or CD before you can do so.

d. Inspect Boot Sector

If you upgrade to a new version of DOS and suddenly find that you cannot boot to Windows NT anymore, your boot sector probably has been replaced. The MS-DOS or Windows 95 SYS command is notorious for trashing the Windows NT boot sector. The emergency repair disk solves this problem, and you don't even need a computer-specific ERD—you can borrow anybody's.

6.2.1 Exercise: Booting with SOS

In Exercise 6.2.1, you learn how to initiate a Windows NT boot by using the /sos switch, which enumerates each driver as the drivers load during the kernel load phase.

Estimated time: 20 minutes

1. Remove the Read-only flag on the BOOT.INI file. Start the Notepad accessory application and open the boot.ini file in the root directory of the system partition. In the Notepad Open dialog box, don't forget to select All Files in the box labeled Files of type. The extension may not appear in the browse list. (The filename may appear as *boot*, without the extension. If you aren't sure you have the right file, right-click on the file and select Properties.) Examine the MS-DOS name setting in the File Properties dialog box.

2. Figure 6.2.1 shows the boot.ini file in Notepad. Find the line with the text string "Windows NT Server Version 4.00 [VGA]." Make sure the string is followed by the switches /basevideo and/sos. If you're confident your system uses a VGA video driver, skip to step 6; otherwise, continue with step 3.

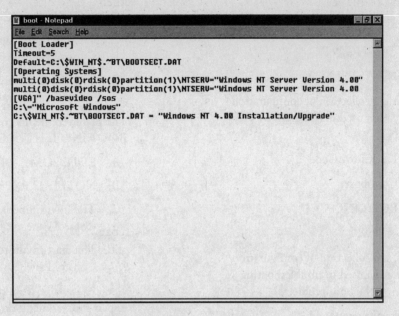

```
boot - Notepad
File  Edit  Search  Help
[Boot Loader]
Timeout=5
Default=C:\$WIN_NT$.~BT\BOOTSECT.DAT
[Operating Systems]
multi(0)disk(0)rdisk(0)partition(1)\NTSERV="Windows NT Server Version 4.00"
multi(0)disk(0)rdisk(0)partition(1)\NTSERV="Windows NT Server Version 4.00
[VGA]" /basevideo /sos
C:\="Microsoft Windows"
C:\$WIN_NT$.~BT\BOOTSECT.DAT = "Windows NT 4.00 Installation/Upgrade"
```

Figure 6.2.1   A boot.ini file.

3. Save the boot.ini file to a different filename (such as boot.tmp) by using the File, Save As command.

4. Delete the /basevideo switch in the line with the text string "Windows NT Server Version 4.00 [VGA]." The /sos switch should remain. Change the text in the square brackets from "VGA" to "sos."

5. Save the file as boot.ini.

   You may have to use the Save As command to save boot.ini. Verify the filename in the File name box. Step 3 may have changed the default filename.

6. Close Notepad and shut down your system.

7. Reboot Windows NT. When the boot menu appears, choose the "sos" option (or the VGA option if you skipped steps 3–5).

8. Watch the drivers display on-screen as they load. (Watch carefully, they will disappear quickly from the screen.) The drivers, like the boot.ini entries, will appear in ARC format. If you experience a boot failure, you can use this technique to determine which driver crashed or hung the system.

9. Log on to Windows NT. Restore the boot.ini file to its original state, either by inserting "VGA" and "/basevideo" using Notepad or by copying the boot.tmp file back to boot.ini. When you're finished, open boot.ini and make sure it is back to normal.

   Note that Step 9 is very important. You may not use the VGA boot option for months or even years, and when you do, you may not remember that you tried this exercise.

6

6.2 Practice Problems

1. Which of the following files are not on the Emergency Repair Disk?

   A. SETUP.LOG

   B. NTUSER.DA_

   C. CONFIG.NT

   D. NTSYSTEM.DA_

2. Which is a collection of configuration information used during boot by Windows NT?

   A. LastKnownGood

   B. Control set

   C. BOOT.INI

   D. NTLDR

3. Which is a collection of configuration information used in troubleshooting Windows NT boot problems?

   A. LastKnownGood

   B. Control set

   C. BOOT.INI

   D. NTLDR

4. The user screen switches into GUI mode after which phase of startup?

   A. Kernel Initialization

   B. Services Load

   C. Windows Start

   D. Win32 subsystem

5. Before editing the BOOT.INI file, you should (choose two):

   A. Backup the existing file.

   B. Turn off the system attribute.

   C. Turn off the read-only attribute.

   D. Rename the file with a TXT extension.

6. The BOOT.INI file can be changed with which of the following? (Choose all that apply.)

   A. EDIT.COM

   B. NOTEPAD.EXE

   C. The Environment tab of the Control Panel System application

   D. The Startup/Shutdown tab of the Control Panel System application

7. The preferred method of changing the BOOT.INI file is via:

   A. EDIT.COM

   B. NOTEPAD.EXE

   C. The Environment tab of the Control Panel System application

   D. The Startup/Shutdown tab of the Control Panel System application

8. Choices available from the Emergency Repair Process menu do *not* include:

   A. Inspect Registry Files

   B. Event Viewer

   C. Inspect Startup Environment

   D. Verify Windows NT System Files

9. LastKnownGood boot information is stored in the Registry under:

   A. HKEY_LOCAL_MACHINE

   B. HKEY_LOCAL_MACHINE\ SYSTEM

   C. HKEY_LOCAL_MACHINE\ SYSTEM\CurrentControlSet

   D. HKEY_LOCAL_MACHINE\ SYSTEM\CurrentControlSet\ LastKnownGood

10. Two of the files needed during an Intel-based boot that are *not* needed for a RISC boot operation are:

    A. NTDETECT.COM

    B. NTLDR

    C. OSLOADER.EXE

    D. NTOSKRNL.EXE

11. To update the SAM information on the Emergency Repair Disk, which switch must you use with RDISK?

   A. /SAM

   B. /S

   C. /OX

   D. SYSTEM

   E. None of the above

12. Which of the following items will RDISK *not* update, by default, in the Emergency Repair Directory?

   A. SAM

   B. SETUP.LOG

   C. DEFAULT._

   D. SYSTEM._

13. Which of the following items will RDISK update, by default, in the Emergency Repair Directory?

   A. SAM

   B. SETUP.LOG

   C. DEFAULT._

   D. SYSTEM._

14. Which is responsible for building the hardware list during boot operations?

   A. HAL.DLL

   B. NTLDR

   C. NTOSKRNL.EXE

   D. NTDETECT.COM

15. Two files that are common to RISC-based boots as well as Intel-based boots:

   A. OSLOADER.EXE

   B. HAL.DLL

   C. NTDETECT.COM

   D. NTOSKRNL.EXE

16. Which is a system file that is read-only, and hidden in the root of your system partition?

   A. HAL.DLL

   B. NTLDR

   C. NTOSKRNL.EXE

   D. NTDETECT.EXE

17. Which is a system file that is in the <winnt_root>\SYSTEM32 directory of your system?

   A. HAL.DLL

   B. NTLDR

   C. NTOSKRNL.EXE

   D. NTDETECT.COM

18. To boot with the LastKnownGood configuration:

   A. Start WINNT with the /L switch.

   B. Select the option from the Boot Loader menu.

   C. Use the /lastknowngood switch in the BOOT.INI file.

   D. Press the spacebar, when prompted, during the boot process.

19. The utility used to update the emergency repair information is:

   A. RDISK.EXE

   B. REPAIR.EXE

   C. DISKPERF

   D. Server Manager

20. Which two items are updated by running the RDISK utility?

   A. The Emergency Repair Directory

   B. The Emergency Repair Disk

   C. The LastKnownGood control set

   D. HKEY_LOCAL_USER

6

21. On Intel x86-based computers, the boot sector of the active partition loads a file called:

    A. NTLDR

    B. IO.SYS

    C. BOOT.INI

    D. MSDOS.SYS

22. Selecting VGA mode during boot uses which settings? (Select all that apply.)

    A. 16 color

    B. 256 color

    C. 640×480

    D. 800×600

23. This BOOT.INI file switch tells Windows NT to load the standard VGA driver rather than the optimized driver written for you video card:

    A. /basevideo

    B. /sos

    C. /crashdebug

    D. /nodebug

24. What are two ways to turn on the Automatic Recovery and Restart capability?

    A. Use the /crashdebug switch in the BOOT.INI file.

    B. Use the /recovery switch in the BOOT.INI file.

    C. From the System application in the Control Panel.

    D. From Server Manager.

25. This BOOT.INI file switch turns on the Automatic Recovery and Restart capability:

    A. /basevideo

    B. /sos

    C. /crashdebug

    D. /nodebug

26. This BOOT.INI file switch limits the amount of usable memory to a specified amount:

    A. /basevideo

    B. /maxmem

    C. /noserialmice

    D. /nodebug

27. This BOOT.INI file switch turns off the tracking of each piece of executing code during the loading of Windows NT:

    A. /basevideo

    B. /sos

    C. /crashdebug

    D. /nodebug

28. This BOOT.INI file switch tells NTDETECT.COM to not look for the presence of serial mice:

    A. /basevideo

    B. /sos

    C. /noserialmice

    D. /nodebug

29. If you need to recreate the Setup Boot disks, which command should be used?

    A. WINNT32

    B. WINNT

    C. WINNT /OX

    D. REPAIR

30. This BOOT.INI file switch is useful in differentiating between multiple SCSI controllers in a system:

    A. /scsiordinal

    B. /scsi

    C. /nononscsi

    D. /nodebug

31. If NT hangs during the loading of system drivers, which switch should be added to the BOOT.INI file to assist with troubleshooting?

    A. /nodebug

    B. /crashdebug

    C. /sos

    D. /drivers

32. This BOOT.INI file switch lists every driver to the screen as it loads during the kernel load phase:

    A. /basevideo

    B. /sos

    C. /crashdebug

    D. /nodebug

33. The NTOSKRNL.EXE file is found, by default, on an x86-based NT Server in:

    A. <winnt_root>

    B. <winnt_root>\SYSTEM32

    C. <winnt_root>\SYSTEM32\ CONFIG

    D. <winn_root>\SYSTEM

34. Choices available from the Emergency Repair Process menu do *not* include:

    A. Inspect Security Environment

    B. Inspect Boot Sector

    C. Inspect Startup Environment

    D. Verify Windows NT System Files

35. If Windows NT is installed in a location other than the default directory and an error message indicating that NTOSKRNL.EXE is missing or corrupt occurs, what is the most likely cause of the error?

    A. The BOOT.INI file is missing or corrupt.

    B. The Registry has not saved the new location.

    C. The NTOSKRNL.EXE has been moved.

    D. The LastKnownGood was automatically invoked.

36. The section of the BOOT.INI file that contains a reference for every OS on the Boot Loader menu is:

    A. [initialize]

    B. [common]

    C. [boot loader]

    D. [operating systems]

37. The section of the BOOT.INI file that defines the default operating system that will be loaded if a choice is not made on the Boot Loader menu is:

    A. [initialize]

    B. [common]

    C. [boot loader]

    D. [operating systems]

38. The sections of the BOOT.INI file include (choose all correct answers):

    A. [initialize]

    B. [common]

    C. [boot loader]

    D. [operating systems]

39. Which of the following files are *not* on the Emergency Repair Disk?

    A. DEFAULT._

    B. NTUSER.DA_

    C. BOOT.INI

    D. SYSTEM._

40. A hidden, read-only, system file in the root of the system partition, it contains information that was present in the boot sector prior to the install of Windows NT:

    A. NTBOOT.INI

    B. NTLDR

    C. BOOT.INI

    D. BOOTSECT.DOS

6

41. Windows NT installation always creates an emergency repair directory. This is located in:

   A. <winnt_root>

   B. <winnt_root>\SYSTEM

   C. <winnt_root>\REPAIR

   D. <winnt_root>\SYSTEM\REPAIR

42. If you upgrade to a new version of DOS and find that you suddenly cannot boot to NT anymore, a possible cause is:

   A. Your boot sector has been replaced.

   B. The BOOT.INI file has been deleted.

   C. NTOSKRNL.EXE has been moved.

   D. The two operating systems are not compatible.

43. It is a single file that contains the code necessary to mask interrupts and exceptions from the kernel:

   A. HAL.DLL

   B. NTLDR

   C. NTOSKRNL.EXE

   D. NTDETECT.COM

44. It is an editable text file that controls the Boot Loader menu:

   A. NTBOOT.INI

   B. NTLDR

   C. BOOT.INI

   D. BOOTSECT.DOS

45. It is the file responsible for starting the minifile system driver necessary for accessing the system and boot partitions on an NT system:

   A. NTLDR

   B. IO.SYS

   C. BOOT.INI

   D. MSDOS.SYS

46. Which of the following files are not the Emergency Repair Disk?

   A. NTLDR

   B. NTUSER.DA_

   C. CONFIG.NT

   D. SYSTEM._

47. The option to Verify Windows NT System Files during the Emergency Repair Process relies upon information contained in what file?

   A. SOFTWARE._

   B. CONFIG.NT

   C. SAM

   D. SETUP.LOG

48. Which file of those on the Emergency Repair Disk contains the names of all Windows NT installation files?

   A. AUTOEXEC.NT

   B. SETUP.LOG

   C. NTLDR

   D. WINNT.LOG

49. The HKEY_LOCAL_MACHINE\ SYSTEM file is found, by default, on an x86-based NT Server in:

   A. <winnt_root>

   B. <winnt_root>\SYSTEM32

   C. <winnt_root>\SYSTEM32\ CONFIG

   D. <winn_root>\SYSTEM

50. The BOOT.INI file allows for the use of several troubleshooting switches. Those switches are added to which section of the file?

   A. [initialize]

   B. [common]

   C. [boot loader]

   D. [operating systems]

51. Which is *not* a valid BOOT.INI switch?

    A. /maxmem

    B. /msgsvc

    C. /noserialmice

    D. /nodebug

52. Which is *not* a valid BOOT.INI switch?

    A. /maxmem

    B. /readonly

    C. /noserialmice

    D. /nodebug

53. Boot-time drivers are stored in the Registry under:

    A. HKEY_LOCAL_MACHINE

    B. HKEY_LOCAL_MACHINE\
    SYSTEM

    C. HKEY_LOCAL_MACHINE\
    SYSTEM32

    D. HKEY_LOCAL_MACHINE\
    SYSTEM\CurrentControlSet\
    Control\ServiceGroupOrder

54. The LastKnownGood control set is updated:

    A. After a user successfully logs on to a system

    B. After the Win32 subsystem starts

    C. During Shutdown

    D. During the Kernel Initialization phase

55. To recreate the Setup Boot disks with the WINNT command, the system of choice would be:

    A. A DOS machine with a CD-ROM drive and floppy drive

    B. A Windows NT Workstation machine with a CD-ROM drive and floppy drive

    C. A Windows NT Server machine with a CD-ROM drive and floppy drive

    D. Any RISC-based machine with a CD-ROM drive and floppy drive

56. On an Intel-x86 computer, which set of files is required to boot Windows NT?

    A. NTLDR; BOOT.INI;
    NTDETECT.COM;
    NTOSKRNL.EXE;
    NTBOOTDD.SYS

    B. NTLDR; BOOT.MNU;
    NTDETECT.EXE; OSLOADER;
    NTBOOTDD.SYS

    C. OSLOADER; NTOSKRNL.EXE;
    NTDETECT.COM;
    NTBOOTDD.SYS

    D. NTLDR; HAL.DLL; BOOT.INI;
    NTDETECT.COM;
    NTOSKRNL.EXE

57. Evan calls on Friday, right before it is time to go home. He wants to know if you can reduce the amount of time his computer takes to boot. He also wants to change the default operating system from MS-DOS to NT Workstation. Which utility should be used?

    A. Control Panel, Boot.

    B. Control Panel, System.

    C. Server Manager.

    D. Configure on a user-by-user basis in the users' profiles.

6

6.2   Answers and Explanations: Exercise

In the preceding exercise, you learned how to initiate a Windows NT boot using the /sos switch. Through careful observation, you saw how it enumerates each driver as the driver is loaded during the kernel load phase.

6.2   Answers and Explanations: Practice Problems

1. **D**   A compressed copy of the Registry's SYSTEM hive is stored as SYSTEM._ instead of NTSYSTEM.DA.

2. **B**   A control set is a collection of configuration information used during boot, whereas LastKnownGood is a special single control set used for troubleshooting.

3. **A**   A control set is a collection of configuration information used during boot, whereas LastKnownGood is a special single control set used for troubleshooting.

4. **D**   After the Win32 subsystem starts, the screen switches into GUI mode.

5. **A, C**   Always back up the file because an error can cause serious harm; take off the default read-only attribute to save your changes.

6. **A, B, D**   An editable text file, BOOT.INI, can be changed with any text editor, but doing so from the Startup/Shutdown tab is preferred because one typographical error in the file can cause serious boot problems.

7. **D**   An editable text file, BOOT.INI, can be changed with any text editor, but doing so from the Startup/Shutdown tab is preferred because one typographical error in the file can cause serious boot problems.

8. **B**   Event Viewer is a stand-alone utility and not a part of the Emergency Repair Process.

9. **C**   HKEY_LOCAL_MACHINE\ SYSTEM\CurrentControlSet houses the LastKnownGood information.

10. **A, B**   Much of the work of NTDETECT.COM and NTLDR are performed by the firmware on the RISC platform.

11. **B**   Neither the DEFAULT._, SAM, or SECURITY._ items are updated with RDISK unless the /S option is used.

12. **A, C**   Neither the DEFAULT._, SAM, or SECURITY._ items are updated with RDISK unless the /S option is used.

13. **B, D**   Neither the DEFAULT._, SAM, or SECURITY._ items are updated with RDISK unless the /S option is used.

14. **D**   NTDETECT.COM builds the hardware list and returns the information to NTLDR.

15. **B, D**   NTDETECT.COM is used only on Intel boots, whereas OSLOADER.EXE is used only on RISC boots. HAL.DLL and NTOSKRNL.EXE are common to both boot operations.

16. **B**   NTDLR is the system file responsible for the majority of the early boot operations.

17. **C**   NTOSKRNL.EXE is the kernel file and it is loaded during boot by the NTLDR.

18. **D**   Pressing the spacebar during the boot process presents you with the Hardware Profile/Configuration Recovery menu. Select a hardware profile and enter **L** for LastKnownGood configuration.

19. **A**   RDISK will update Emergency Repair Directory and Emergency Repair Directory.

20. **A, B**   RDISK will update Emergency Repair Directory and Emergency Repair Directory.

21. **A** Similar to the IO.SYS file in MS-DOS environments, the NTLDR file is a hidden, read-only, system file in the root of the system partition.

22. **A, C** Standard VGA consists of 16 colors displayed at 640×480.

23. **A** The /basevideo switch performs this operation.

24. **A, C** The /crashdebug switch enables this, as does the System application in the Control Panel.

25. **C** The /crashdebug switch performs this operation.

26. **B** The /maxmem switch performs this operation.

27. **D** The /nodebug switch performs this operation.

28. **C** The /noserialmice switch performs this operation. At times, other devices connected to the serial port can be falsely identified as mice. After boot, the serial port is unavailable because the system expects a mouse to be there.

29. **C** The /OX switch, used with WINNT, will recreate the Setup Boot disks.

30. **A** The /scsiordinal switch performs this operation.

31. **C** The /sos switch causes all drivers to be displayed on the screen as they are loaded.

32. **B** The /sos switch performs this operation.

33. **B** The <winnt_root>\SYSTEM32 directory holds the NTOSKRNL.EXE file.

34. **A** The Boot Sector, Startup Environment, and NT System files can all be inspected and verified during the Emergency Repair Process.

35. **A** The BOOT.INI file contains a pointer to the NTOSKRNL.EXE location.

36. **D** The BOOT.INI file contains only two sections, [boot loader] and [operating systems]. The first defines the default operating system, whereas the second contains a reference for each OS on the menu.

37. **C** The BOOT.INI file contains only two sections, [boot loader] and [operating systems]. The first defines the default operating system, whereas the second contains a reference for each OS on the menu.

38. **C, D** The BOOT.INI file contains only two sections, [boot loader] and [operating systems]. The first defines the default operating system, whereas the second contains a reference for each OS on the menu.

39. **C** The BOOT.INI file is not on the Emergency Repair Disk.

40. **D** The BOOTSECT.DOS file contains information about previous operating systems and calls the correct files if a choice other than NT is made from the Boot Loader menu.

41. **C** The directory where the emergency repair directory resides is <winnt_root>\REPAIR.

42. **A** The DOS and Windows 95 SYS command will often overwrite the boot sector—which can be restored from the Emergency Repair Disk.

43. **A** The HAL.DLL file contains the code necessary to mask interrupts and exceptions from the kernel.

44. **C** The NTLDR calls the Boot Loader menu, but it is the BOOT.INI file that controls it and its choices.

45. **A** The NTLDR file is responsible for carrying out the vast majority of the early initialization operations, including starting the minifile system driver.

6

46. **A**   The NTLDR is not on the Emergency Repair Disk.

47. **D**   The SETUP.LOG file contains names and checksum values of files used during NT installation.

48. **B**   The SETUP.LOG file has the name and checksums of all Windows NT installation files. It can find corrupted files and report which ones need to be fixed.

49. **C**   The SYSTEM component of the Registry is stored in <winnt_root>\SYSTEM32\CONFIG.

50. **D**   The [operating systems] section contains information about each operating system offered on the menu, whereas the [boot loader] lists only the default operating system if one is not chosen from the Boot Loader menu.

51. **B**   There is not a /msgsvc switch for the BOOT.INI file.

52. **B**   There is not a /readonly switch for the BOOT.INI file.

53. **D**   This is the hive of the Registry responsible for boot-time driver information.

54. **A**   When a user successfully logs into a system, the LastKnownGood control set is updated.

55. **A**   WINNT works on DOS machines, whereas WINNT32 is used on all other choices.

56. **A**   The files needed to load NT on an Intel-x86 platform are NTLDR; BOOT.INI; NTDETECT.COM; NTOSKRNL.EXE; and NTBOOTDD.SYS

57. **B**   The System utility will enable you to choose a default operating system and reduce boot time.

6.2   Key Words

Boot

Master Boot Record (MBR)

NTLDR

Control set

Advanced RISC Computer (ARC)

6.3   Troubleshooting Configuration Errors

Microsoft lists the following objective for the Windows NT Server exam: Choose the appropriate course of action to take to resolve configuration errors.

Some common device problems are resource conflicts (such as interrupt conflicts) and SCSI problems. Use Windows NT diagnostics to check resource settings. If the error is the result of a recent configuration change, you can reboot the system and boot to the LastKnownGood configuration.

If a Windows NT service doesn't start, check Event Viewer; or, check the Control Panel Services application to make sure the service is installed and configured to start. Windows NT includes some important tools, as follows:

- Event Viewer

- Windows NT Diagnostics

- System Recovery

A.   Event Viewer

If your Windows NT-based computer manages to boot successfully, yet still isn't performing correctly, the first thing to check is the system event log, where all critical system messages are stored.

Windows NT includes the Event Viewer application in the Administrative Tool program group for viewing the messages stored in the system, security, and application log files (see fig. 6.3.1).

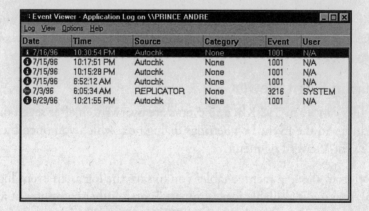

Figure 6.3.1   Event Viewer.

1. System Log

The system log, the default view in Event Viewer, is maintained by the operating system. It tracks three kinds of events:

- **Errors.** Symbolized by Stop signs, and indicative of the failure of a Windows NT component or device, or perhaps an inability to start. These errors are common on notebook computers when Windows NT fails to start the network components because PCMCIA network cards are not present.

- **Warnings.** Symbolized by exclamation points, and indicative of an impending problem. Low disk space on a partition triggers a warning, for example.

- **Information Events.** Symbolized by the traditional "I" in a blue circle, and indicative of an event that isn't at all bad but is still somehow significant. Browser elections often cause information events.

2. Security Log

The security log remains empty until you enable auditing through User Manager. After enabling auditing, the audited events reside here. The security log tracks two types of events:

- **Success Audits.** Symbolized by a key, and indicative of successful security access.

- **Failure Audits.** Symbolized by a padlock, and indicative of unsuccessful security access.

3. Application Log

The application log collects messages from native Windows NT applications. If you aren't using any Win32 applications, this log remains empty.

4. Securing Event Logs

Ordinarily, anyone can view the event log information. Some administrators, however, might not want guests to have this sort of access. There is one restriction, enabled through the Registry, that you can place on Event Viewer—you can prohibit guests from accessing the system or application logs from the following Registry location, in which <log_name> is either System or Application:

```
HKEY_LOCAL_MACHINE\System\CurrentControlSet\Services\EventLog\å<log_name>
```

You need to add a value called RestrictGuestAccess of type REG_DWORD and set it equal to 1. To re-enable guest access to either log, set the appropriate RestrictGuestAccess value to 0 or just delete the value altogether.

5. Configuring Event Viewer

By default, log files can reach 512 KB, and events are overwritten after seven days. You can change these settings in the Event Log Settings dialog box, which you open by choosing Log Settings in the Event Viewer Log menu.

The Save As option in the Log menu enables you to save the log as an event log file (with an EVT extension), making it available for examination on another computer at a future time, or as a comma-separated value text file (also with a TXT extension) for importing into a spreadsheet or database.

6. Using Event Viewer

At some point, every Windows NT user receives this infamous message:

```
One or more services failed to start. Please see the Event Viewer for
details.
```

This message appears when the first user logs on to the system after at least one Windows NT component fails to load successfully. As directed, you should immediately proceed to Event Viewer.

To find the source of the problem, look at the system log, under the Event heading. Somewhere toward the top of the column, you should find an Event code of 6005. By default, the logs list the most recent events at the top of the list, so start scanning at the top of the list or you may not find the most recent 6005 event. Event 6005 means that the EventLog service was successfully started.

To examine an event message, double-click on an event to open the Event Detail dialog box.

Note the identifying information for the event:

- Date of the event
- Time of the event
- User account that generated the event, if applicable (usually found in the security log)
- Computer on which the event occurred
- Event ID (the Windows NT Event code)
- Source Windows NT component that generated the event
- Type of event (Error, Warning, and so on)
- Category of event (Logon/Logoff audit, for example)
- Description of the event
- Data in hexadecimal format, useful to a developer or debugger

B. Windows NT Diagnostics

Windows NT Diagnostics provides a tidy front-end to much of the information in the HKEY_LOCAL_MACHINE Registry subtree. Like its ancestor, MSD from Windows 3.1, Windows NT Diagnostics can create incredibly detailed and valuable system configuration reports. One thing you cannot do with Windows NT Diagnostics is edit the system configuration. Figure 6.3.2 shows the Windows NT Diagnostics dialog box.

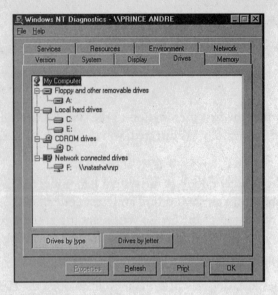

Figure 6.3.2　The Windows NT Diagnostics dialog box.

The Windows NT Diagnostics dialog box includes the following nine tabs:

- **Version.** Displays information stored under HKEY_LOCAL_MACHINE\Software\Microsoft\Windows NT\CurrentVersion, including the build number, registered owner, and Service Pack update information.

- **System.** Displays information stored under HKEY_LOCAL_MACHINE\Hardware, including CPU and other device identification information.

- **Display.** Displays information on the video adapter and adapter settings.

- **Drives.** Lists all drive letters in use and their types, including drive letters for floppy drives, hard disks, CD-ROM and optical drives, and network connections. Double-click on a drive letter to display a drive Properties dialog box. The General tab of the drive Properties dialog box shows byte and cluster information for the drive, while the File System tab shows file system information.

- **Memory.** Displays current memory load, as well as physical and virtual memory statistics.

- **Services.** Displays service information stored under HKEY_LOCAL_MACHINE\System\CurrentControlSet\Services, including status. Click on the Devices button to display driver information stored under HKEY_LOCAL_MACHINE\System\CurrentControlSet\Control, including status.

- **Resources.** Displays device information listed by interrupt and by port, and also by DMA channels and UMB locations in use.

- **Environment.** Displays environment variables for command prompt sessions (set under Control Panel System).

- **Network.** Displays network component configuration and status.

C. System Recovery

The Recovery utility is a tool you can use to record debugging information, alert an administrator, or reboot the system in the event of a Stop error. (A *Stop error* causes Windows NT to stop all processes.) To configure the Recovery utility, start the Control Panel System application and click on the Startup/Shutdown tab.

The bottom frame of the Startup/Shutdown tab is devoted to Recovery options. The options are as follows:

- Write an event to the system log.

- Send an administrative alert.

- Write debugging information to (specify a filename). In the event of a Stop error, the Savedump.exe program dumps everything in memory to the pagefile and marks the location of the dump. When you restart your system, Windows NT copies the memory dump from the pagefile to the file specified in the Startup/Shutdown tab. You can then use a program called Dumpexam.exe in the \Support directory of the Windows NT CD-ROM to study the contents of the memory dump and determine the cause of the Stop error.

- Automatically reboot. You might not want to have your server sit idle after a Stop error. This option instructs Windows NT to automatically reboot after a Stop error.

D. Backing Up the Registry

Before discussing Registry files, you should be familiar with the term hive. A *hive* is a binary file that contains all the keys and values within a branch of the Registry.

Two files are associated with each hive: one file is named after the hive and has no extension, and the other is identically named with a LOG extension (with the exception of SYSTEM, which has a SYSTEM.ALT counterpart for reasons to be explained shortly). Both files reside in the \<winnt_root>\SYSTEM32\CONFIG directory. Most of the hives loaded at any given time are residents of HKEY_LOCAL_MACHINE, and the others belong to HKEY_USERS. Here is a list of the Registry hives:

HKEY_LOCAL_MACHINE\SAM (SAM, SAM.LOG)

HKEY_LOCAL_MACHINE\SECURITY (SECURITY, SECURITY.LOG)

HKEY_LOCAL_MACHINE\SOFTWARE (SOFTWARE, SOFTWARE.LOG)

HKEY_LOCAL_MACHINE\SYSTEM (SYSTEM, SYSTEM.ALT)

HKEY_USERS\.DEFAULT (DEFAULT, DEFAULT.LOG)

HKEY_USERS\<user_sid> (<user_profile>, <user_profile>.LOG)

6

The LOG files provide fault tolerance for the Registry. Whenever configuration data is changed, the changes are written to the LOG file first. Then the first sector of the actual hive is flagged to indicate that an update is taking place. The data is transferred from the log to the hive, and the update flag on the hive is then lowered. If the computer were to crash after the flag had been raised but before it had been lowered, some, if not all the data, would quite possibly be corrupt. If that happened, when Windows NT restarted it would detect the flag still raised on the hive, and it would use the log to redo the update.

The only exception to this rule is the SYSTEM file. Because the SYSTEM hive contains critical information that must be loaded intact to load enough of the operating system to process the log files, a duplicate of SYSTEM is maintained as SYSTEM.ALT. This file functions identically to a log file, except that the entire file (rather than just the changes) is mirrored. If the computer were to crash during an update to the SYSTEM branch of the Registry, the integrity of the SYSTEM hive is still preserved. If the data had not yet been fully committed to SYSTEM.ALT, the SYS-TEM hive is still preserved in its original configuration. If the data had not yet been fully committed to SYSTEM, SYSTEM.ALT would be used to redo the update.

LOG files are so transitory that they would be useless by the time the backup completes, and should not be included in the backup. The files of greatest import are SYSTEM and SOFT-WARE.

Registry files almost always are in a state of flux and are constantly open for read/write access. The Windows NT Backup program usually skips over these files for that reason. Probably the best way to back up the SYSTEM and SOFTWARE files is to use the Repair Disk application, another hidden application in the \<winnt_root>\SYSTEM32 directory. The section "RDISK.EXE," earlier in this chapter, discussed the Repair Disk utility, otherwise known as RDISK.EXE.

E.   Backing Up Individual Keys

You can create your own hive files by saving an entire branch of the Registry starting from any key you choose. You do so by choosing Registry, Save Key in Registry Editor. To load the hive into the Registry of another Windows NT computer, choose Registry, Restore Key.

If you want to work with the key only temporarily, you can use the Restore Volatile command rather than the Restore Key command. The key still loads into the Registry at the selected location, but it doesn't reload the next time the system restarts.

6.3.1   Exercise: Back up an Individual File

In Exercise 6.3.1, you learn how to start the NTBACKUP utility and back up an individual file.

Estimated time: 10 minutes

1.   Start the Backup program by choosing Administrative Tools from the Programs section of the Start Menu. Next, select Backup.

2.   Double-click on the root drive, and then Windows, followed by system and viewers.

3. Select the QUIKVIEW.EXE program. Notice what happens to the tree—not only is the file selected, but all the directories above it in the path now have a gray box showing that a portion of their contents has been chosen.

4. Choose Backup and observe as this file is backed up to your tape drive.

6.3.2   Exercise: Restore an Individual File

In Exercise 6.3.2, you learn how to start the NTBACKUP utility and restore the file backed up in Exercise 6.3.1.

Estimated time: 10 minutes

1. Start the Backup program by choosing Administrative Tools from the Programs section of the Start Menu. Next, select Backup.

2. Double-click on the tape drive, and find the file you backed up in the early exercise.

3. Reverse the steps in Exercise 6.3.1 and restore QUIKVIEW.EXE from the tape to your system.

6.3.3   Exercise: Utilize Event Viewer

In Exercise 6.3.3, you learn how to start the Event Viewer utility and examine the System log file.

Estimated time: 15 minutes

1. Start the Event Viewer program by choosing Administrative Tools from the Programs section of the Start Menu.

2. Next, select Event Viewer. Notice that the System log comes up by default.

3. Select the Log option and change to Security, then Application, and back to System.

4. From View, choose Filter Events, then select only for the information entries to display.

5. Select View, All Events to remove the filter.

6. Exit Event Viewer.

6.3.4   Exercise: Examine Windows NT Diagnostics

In Exercise 6.3.4, you learn how to start the Windows NT Diagnostics utility and look at your system.

Estimated time: 10 minutes

1. Start the Diagnostics program by choosing Administrative Tools from the Programs section of the Start Menu.

2. Next, select Windows NT Diagnostics. Notice the tabs which appear.

3. Click through each of the tabs and observe the information each presents.

4. Exit Windows NT Diagnostics.

6.3   Practice Problems

1. The Recovery tool can do which three of the following:

   A. Record debugging information.

   B. Alert an administrator of a stop event.

   C. Alert two administrators on different domains of a stop event.

   D. Reboot the system in response to a stop event.

2. A common cause of information events in the System log would be:

   A. Browser elections

   B. Failure of a service to start

   C. Hard drive errors

   D. Configuration errors

3. By default, who can view Event Log information:

   A. Administrators

   B. Members of Domain Users

   C. Guests

   D. Anyone

4. There is only one restriction you can place on who can see Event Log information. That restriction applies to whom?

   A. Administrators

   B. Members of Domain Users

   C. Guests

   D. Anyone

5. The default directory that system dumps are written to is:

   A. C:\

   B. %SystemRoot%

   C. SYSTEM

   D. DUMP

6. The default filename that system dumps are written to is:

   A. Dump.hex

   B. Dump.txt

   C. Memory.dmp

   D. Memory.txt

7. The Save As option in the Event Viewer log menu will let you save the files as comma-delimited fields. When you choose to do so, what extension is used on the files?

   A. TXT

   B. EVT

   C. DAT

   D. CHK

8. The Save As option in the Event Viewer log menu, by default, saves the event log file with what extension?

   A. TXT

   B. EVT

   C. DAT

   D. CHK

9. What program creates EVT extension hex files?

   A. Event Viewer

   B. Performance Monitor

   C. DiskPerf

   D. System

10. Which extension indicates hex files that were saved from the Event Viewer?

    A. TXT

    B. EVT

    C. DAT

    D. CHK

11. To see information about DMA channels and VMB locations in the Windows NT Diagnostics tool, select which tab?

    A. Services

    B. Memory

    C. Resources

    D. Network

12. Event Viewer can view which three log files?

    A. System

    B. Application

    C. Security

    D. Netlogon

13. If a Windows NT service fails to start, what tool should you use?

    A. Performance Monitor

    B. Event Viewer

    C. Tracert

    D. System Recovery

14. The Windows NT Diagnostics dialog box includes all of the following tabs *except*:

    A. Memory

    B. Network

    C. Global

    D. Resources

15. The System Tab in the Windows NT Diagnostics box displays information stored in the Registry under which hive:

    A. HKEY_LOCAL_MACHINE\
       SOFTWARE

    B. HKEY_LOCAL_MACHINE\
       HARDWARE

    C. HKEY_LOCAL_MACHINE\
       SOFTWARE\MICROSOFT\
       WINDOWS NT\CurrentVersion

    D. HKEY_LOCAL_MACHINE\
       SYSTEM

16. Version information is stored in the Windows NT Registry under which hive:

    A. HKEY_LOCAL_MACHINE\
       SOFTWARE

    B. HKEY_LOCAL_MACHINE\
       SOFTWARE\MICROSOFT\
       WINDOWS NT

    C. HKEY_LOCAL_MACHINE\
       SOFTWARE\MICROSOFT\
       WINDOWS NT\CurrentVersion

    D. HKEY_LOCAL_MACHINE\
       SYSTEM

17. Service information is stored in the Windows NT Registry under which hive:

    A. HKEY_LOCAL_MACHINE\
       SOFTWARE

    B. HKEY_LOCAL_MACHINE\
       SOFTWARE\MICROSOFT\
       WINDOWS NT

    C. HKEY_LOCAL_MACHINE\
       SOFTWARE\MICROSOFT\
       WINDOWS NT\CurrentVersion

    D. HKEY_LOCAL_MACHINE\
       SYSTEM

18. A common cause of warning events in the System log would be:

    A. Browser elections

    B. Failure of a service to start

    C. Low disk space on a hard drive partition

    D. Configuration errors

19. To see information about network component configuration in the Windows NT Diagnostics tool, select which tab:

    A. Services

    B. Memory

    C. Resources

    D. Network

6

20. A common cause of error events in the System log would be:

   A. Browser elections

   B. PCMCIA cards not present on a notebook computer

   C. Low disk space on a hard drive partition

   D. Configuration errors

21. Tools for looking at configuration errors include all of the following *except*:

   A. Event Viewer

   B. Performance Monitor

   C. Windows NT Diagnostics

   D. System Recovery

22. The Windows NT Diagnostics dialog box includes all of the following tabs *except*:

   A. Services

   B. Resources

   C. Environment

   D. Profiles

23. Two common causes of device problems are:

   A. Interrupt conflicts

   B. Installation of graphic-intensive game packages

   C. Installation of new software

   D. SCSI problems

24. To see information stored in HKEY_LOCAL_MACHINE\ SYSTEM\CurrentControlSet\Services in the Windows NT Diagnostics tool, select which tab?

   A. Services

   B. Memory

   C. Resources

   D. Network

25. Failure Audits are displayed in the Security log—when viewed with Event Viewer—as:

   A. A stop sign

   B. A key

   C. An exclamation mark

   D. A padlock

26. Success Audits are displayed in the Security log—when viewed with Event Viewer—as:

   A. A stop sign

   B. A key

   C. An exclamation mark

   D. A padlock

27. Which two symbols are displayed in the Security log—when viewed with Event Viewer:

   A. A stop sign

   B. A key

   C. An exclamation mark

   D. A padlock

28. By default, on a busy system with large event log files that reach their maximum default size, you can choose how much information should be maintained in terms of:

   A. hours

   B. days

   C. weeks

   D. months

29. If you are not using any Win32 applications on a system, what are the contents of the Application log:

   A. It is empty.

   B. Only the Win16 application information.

   C. It mirrors the System log.

   D. Only events for those applications manually selected.

30. The backup Registry file for SAM is:

    A. SAM.BACKUP

    B. SAM.BAK

    C. SAM.ALT

    D. SAM.LOG

31. Recovery options are configured by:

    A. Using Regedit to change parameters.

    B. Running the SYSTEM command-line utility.

    C. Changing values in the bottom frame of the Startup/Shutdown tab.

    D. Running Server Manager.

32. By default, on a busy system with large event log files that reach their maximum default size, how many days of information are kept before the information is overwritten?

    A. 1

    B. 7

    C. 14

    D. 21

33. Debugging information from a Stop error can be verified in a dump file using:

    A. Savedump.exe

    B. Dump.exe

    C. Dumpchk.exe

    D. Dumpexam.exe

34. The backup Registry file for System is:

    A. SYSTEM.BACKUP

    B. SYSTEM.BAK

    C. SYSTEM.ALT

    D. SYSTEM.LOG

35. Debugging information from a Stop error can be made viewable in a dump file using:

    A. Savedump.exe

    B. Dump.exe

    C. Dumpchk.exe

    D. Dumpexam.exe

36. The Event Viewer is found on a Windows NT Server in which program group:

    A. User Manager

    B. System

    C. Administrative Tool

    D. Diagnostics

37. Two common reasons for configuration errors are:

    A. Installation of a new device

    B. Failing hard drives

    C. Installation of new software

    D. Incorrect SCSI settings

38. Debugging information from a Stop error is written to a dump file using:

    A. Savedump.exe

    B. Dump.exe

    C. Dumpchk.exe

    D. Dumpexam.exe

39. Until an administrator enables auditing, what are the contents of the Security log?

    A. Only configuration errors.

    B. It is empty.

    C. It mirrors the System log.

    D. Only share permission errors.

40. The Security log tracks which two types of events?

    A. Success Audits

    B. Failure Audits

    C. Permission Audits

    D. Registry Audits

6

41. If your Windows NT-based computer manages to boot successfully, yet still is not performing correctly, the first thing to check is:

    A. The system event log

    B. The Performance Monitor

    C. Server Manager

    D. BOOT.INI

42. Which of the following logs is the default log displayed in Event Viewer?

    A. System

    B. Application

    C. Security

    D. Netlogon

43. When looking at a series of stop errors in a System log, the most likely source of all the errors is:

    A. The stop error at the top of the list

    B. The stop error at the bottom of the list

    C. Each error stands alone

    D. The error most replicated

44. The System log, which can be viewed with Event Viewer, tracks which three kinds of events?

    A. Warnings

    B. Information

    C. Configuration

    D. Errors

45. Which of the following events is *not* tracked in the System log?

    A. Warnings

    B. Information

    C. Configuration

    D. Errors

46. Windows Diagnostics is a front-end to information contained where?

    A. HKEY_LOCAL_MACHINE

    B. HKEY_LOCAL_USER

    C. USER

    D. SYSTEM

47. To see information about virtual memory statistics in the Windows NT Diagnostics tool, select which tab?

    A. Services

    B. Memory

    C. Resources

    D. Network

48. Error events are symbolized in the System log—as displayed in Event Viewer—by which of the following symbols?

    A. Stop sign

    B. Exclamation mark

    C. Question mark

    D. An "I" in a blue circle

49. Information events are symbolized in the System log—as displayed in Event Viewer—by which of the following symbols?

    A. Stop sign

    B. Exclamation mark

    C. Question mark

    D. An "I" in a blue circle

50. Warning events are symbolized in the System log—as displayed in Event Viewer—by which of the following symbols?

    A. Stop sign

    B. Exclamation mark

    C. Question mark

    D. An "I" in a blue circle

51. Which of the following would not be a symbol found in the System log—as displayed by Event Viewer?

    A. Stop sign

    B. Exclamation mark

    C. Question mark

    D. An "I" in a blue circle

52. The Windows NT Diagnostics dialog box includes all of the following tabs except:

    A. Version

    B. Connections

    C. System

    D. Display

53. The backup Registry file for Security is:

    A. SECURITY.BACKUP

    B. SECURITY.BAK

    C. SECURITY.ALT

    D. SECURITY.LOG

54. Marco, a remote administrator, claims to have received a message during the boot process reading that a dependency service failed to start. Where should you inform him to look for more information?

    A. The file server error log

    B. In Event Viewer, under the security log

    C. In Event Viewer, under the system log

    D. In Server Manager, under the system log

6.3 Answers and Explanations: Exercises

In Exercise 6.3.1, you learned how to start the NTBACKUP utility. An important correlation to make is that NTBACKUP works only with tape devices. Without a tape device, you cannot do the exercise, or utilize any function of NTBACKUP. Additionally, you learned how to back up an individual file.

In Exercise 6.3.2, you started the NTBACKUP utility once more and saw how to restore the file backed up in Exercise 6.3.1.

In Exercise 6.3.3, you learned how to start the Event Viewer utility. You also saw that the default file to examine is the System log file, and you looked at it.

In Exercise 6.3.4, you learned how to start the Windows NT Diagnostics utility and look at your system.

6.3 Answers and Explanations: Practice Problems

1. **A, B, D** An individual user or group can be notified of a stop event, but not two administrators on different domains.

2. **A** Browser elections are a common cause of information events in the System log.

3. **D** By default, anyone can view Event Log information. Editing the Registry, you can prevent Guests from seeing the log information, but that is the only restriction available.

4. **D** By default, anyone can view Event Log information. Editing the Registry, you can prevent Guests from seeing the log information, but that is the only restriction available.

5. **B** By default, memory dumps are written to Memory.dmp—a non-viewable hex file in the %SystemRoot% directory.

6. **C** By default, memory dumps are written to Memory.dmp—a non-viewable hex file.

7. **A** By default, the files are saved as EVT hex files, but can also be saved as comma-delimited TXT files for importing into spreadsheets or databases.

8. **B** By default, the files are saved as EVT hex files, but can also be saved as comma-delimited TXT files for importing into spreadsheets or databases.

9. **A** By default, the files are saved as EVT hex files, but can also be saved as comma-delimited TXT files for importing into spreadsheets or databases.

10. **B** By default, the files are saved as EVT hex files, but can also be saved as comma-delimited TXT files for importing into spreadsheets or databases.

11. **C** DMA channel and VMB location information is displayed under the Resources tab.

12. **A, B, C** Event Viewer will show the contents of the System, Application, and Security log files.

13. **B** Event Viewer will show the System log, which indicates what services have started and which ones have failed.

14. **C** Global is a type of group, a function of the user and User Manager for Domains rather than Windows NT Diagnostics.

15. **B** HKEY_LOCAL_MACHINE\ HARDWARE stores information about what is available on the machine.

16. **C** HKEY_LOCAL_MACHINE\ SOFTWARE\MICROSOFT\ WINDOWS NT\CurrentVersion stores information about the current version of NT on the machine.

17. **D** HKEY_LOCAL_MACHINE\ SYSTEM\CurrentControlSet\Services stores information about the current services available to NT on the machine.

18. **C** Low disk space in a partition is a common cause of warning events in the System log.

19. **D** Network component configuration information is displayed under the Network tab of the Windows NT Diagnostics tool.

20. **B** On notebook computers, the absence of a PCMCIA card is a common cause of an error event in the System log.

21. **B** Performance Monitor is used to gather statistics on running services and processes, and not to diagnose configuration errors.

22. **D** Profiles are a function of the user and User Manager for Domains rather than Windows NT Diagnostics.

23. **A, D** SCSI problems and interrupt conflicts are common causes of device problems.

24. **A** Services information in the Registry is displayed under the Services tab of the Windows NT Diagnostics tool.

25. **D** Success Audits are displayed as a key and Failure Audits are displayed as a padlock.

26. **B** Success Audits are displayed as a key and Failure Audits are displayed as a padlock.

27. **B, D** Success Audits are displayed as a key and Failure Audits are displayed as a padlock.

28. **B** The default on a busy system is for the event log files to be overwritten every 7 days. This can be changed to any other day value.

29. **A** The Application log only stores information on Win32 applications.

30. **D** The backup files all have the LOG extension except for System, which is ALT.

31. **C** The bottom frame of the Startup/Shutdown tab contains configuration information for the Recovery options.

32. **B** The default on a busy system is for the event log files to be overwritten every 7 days. This can be changed to any other day value.

33. **C** The Dumpchk utility is used to verify the contents of a debugging file.

34. **C** The backup files all have the LOG extension except for System, which is ALT.

35. **D** The Dumpexam utility is used to make the contents of a debugging file viewable.

36. **C** The Event Viewer is located in the Administrative Tool program group.

37. **A, C** The most common causes of configuration errors are the installation of new software or devices.

38. **A** The Savedump utility is used to write out debugging information.

39. **B** The Security log remains empty until auditing is enabled.

40. **A, B** The Security log tracks only success and failure audits.

41. **A** The system event log will show all services that have started, or attempted to start, and results of that operation.

42. **A** The System log is the default log displayed when Event Viewer is started.

43. **B** The System log is written to in sequential order, with new entries at the top. The error most likely to be causing others is the first one written to the file and at the bottom of the list.

44. **A, B, D** The System log tracks warnings, errors, and information events.

45. **C** The System log tracks warnings, errors, and information events.

46. **A** The Windows Diagnostic tool is a front end to the Registry information stored in HKEY_LOCAL_MACHINE.

47. **B** Virtual memory statistics are displayed under the Memory tab of the Windows NT Diagnostics tool.

48. **A** Warning events are shown with an exclamation mark, errors by a stop sign, and information by an "I" in a blue circle.

49. **D** Warning events are shown with an exclamation mark, errors by a stop sign, and information by an "I" in a blue circle.

50 **B** Warning events are shown with an exclamation mark, errors by a stop sign, and information by an "I" in a blue circle.

51. **C** Warning events are shown with an exclamation mark, errors by a stop sign, and information by an "I" in a blue circle.

52. **B** Windows NT Diagnostics contains information about NT, which would not include current connections.

53. **D** The backup files all have the LOG extension except for System, which is ALT.

54. **C** The system log contains information about services

6.3 Key Words

Errors

Information events

Hive

Warnings

Stop error

6

6.4 Troubleshooting Printer Problems

Microsoft lists the following objective for the Windows NT Server exam: Choose the appropriate course of action to take to resolve printer problems. When you try to isolate printing problems, the following guidelines can be helpful:

- Check the cable connections and the printer port to verify that the printing device is on and the cables are all securely fitted. This precaution may seem rather obvious, but the simplest of things cause some of the most perplexing problems.

- To verify that the correct printer driver is installed and configured properly, establish the type of printing device (such as PCL, PostScript, and so on) and verify that the correct driver type has been installed. If necessary, reinstall the printer driver. If a printer driver needs updating, use the Printers folder to install and configure the new printer driver.

- Verify that the printer is selected, either explicitly in the application or as the default printer. Most Windows NT applications have a Printer Setup menu or toolbar button. When printing by means of OLE or some other indirect means, you need to specify a default printer.

- Verify that enough hard disk space is available to generate the print job, especially on the partition that has the spooler directory specified, which, by default, is the boot partition (that is, the winnt_root partition).

- Run the simplest application possible (for example, Notepad) to verify that printing can occur from other applications within Windows NT. If problems are encountered printing from the application (other than a Win32-based application), check the appropriate application subsystem (for example, DOS, Win16, POSIX, and OS/2).

- Print to a file (FILE:) and then copy the output file to a printer port. If this works, the problem is the spooler, or is data-transmission related. If this doesn't work, the problem is application- or driver-related.

A. Spooling Problems

By default, spooled print jobs reside in the \<winnt_root>\SYSTEM32\SPOOL\PRINTERS directory until completely printed. If a Windows NT-based computer is acting as a print server for the network, make sure plenty of free disk space is available on the partition that contains the default spool directory. Also, keeping this partition defragmented improves printing performance. Because Windows NT doesn't include a defrag utility, you need to use a third-party utility (or boot to MS-DOS if you are using the FAT file system).

If you have more room on another partition, you may change the default spool directory in the Advanced tab of the Server Properties dialog box. You can also change the spool directory in the Registry by adding a value called DefaultSpoolDirectory of type REG_SZ to the following and entering the path to the new spool directory:

```
HKEY_LOCAL_MACHINE\System\CurrentControlSet\Control\Print\Printers
```

You need to restart the spooler service (or the computer itself) for the change to take effect.

You can also assign a separate spool directory for each individual printer. Enter the path to the new spool directory as the data for the value SpoolDirectory in the following, where <Printer> is the name of the printer you want to redirect:

```
HKEY_LOCAL_MACHINE\System\CurrentControlSet\Control\Print\åPrinters\<Printer>
```

Again, you need to restart the spooler service for this change to take effect.

B.   Printing from Non-Windows–Based Applications

Non-Windows–based applications—for example, MS-DOS–based applications—require their own printer drivers if the application requires any kind of formatted output other than plain ASCII text. WordPerfect for MS-DOS, for example, does not even allow the user to print a document unless there is a WordPerfect-specific and printer-specific driver installed, for example, because non-Windows-based applications are not written to conform to or take advantage of the Windows APIs. Also, remember that you may need to use the NET USE LPT1: \\servername\printername command to enable the DOS-based application to print.

C.   Handling the Computer Crashing

When a document prints, two files are created for the print job in the spool directory (by default, <winnt_root>\SYSTEM32\SPOOL\PRINTERS). One of the files, which has an .SPL extension, is the actual print job spool file. The other file, which has an .SHD extension, is a shadow file that contains information about the job, including its owner and priority. These files remain in the spool directory until the jobs finish printing, at which point they are deleted.

In the event of a system crash, some spool and shadow files may be left over from jobs that were waiting to be printed. When the spooler service restarts (along with the rest of the system), the printer should process these files immediately. They are, however, sometimes corrupted during the crash and get stuck. Be certain, therefore, to check the spool directory every so often, and delete any spool and shadow files with old date/time stamps. How old is old depends on how long it takes to print a job on your printer. Certainly anything from days, weeks, or months ago should be deleted.

If a print job appears stuck in the printer and you cannot delete it, stop the spooler service in Control Panel Services and delete the SPL and/or SHD file for that job from the spool directory (match the date/time stamp on the files and in Print Manager to determine which files are causing the problem).

D.   Printing Too Slow or Workstation Too Sluggish

Windows NT Workstation assigns priority 7 to the spooler service, which puts printing on an equal footing with other background applications. Windows NT Server, which favors printing over background applications, assigns priority 9 to the spooler, which puts it neck-and-neck with the foreground applications.

If a Windows NT-based workstation moonlighting as a print server appears to print too slowly, consider raising the priority by one or two classes. If the workstation is responding sluggishly to the user while printing, consider lowering the priority by a class or two. Don't alter the priority by more than two levels under any circumstances without a full understanding of the performance consequences involved.

To change the priority class for the Spooler service, add a value called PriorityClass of type REG_DWORD to HKEY_LOCAL_MACHINE\System\CurrentControlSet\Control\Print and set it equal to the priority class desired. If this value is set to 0 or isn't present, the default is used (7 for Windows NT Workstation, or 9 for Windows NT Server).

6

6.4   Practice Problems

1. If you cannot print to a printer, one of the first things tried should be:

   A. Change print drivers.

   B. Reconfigure the print spool.

   C. Try a different printer to see if the problem appears there.

   D. Stop and restart the printing services.

2. By default, spooled print jobs reside where?

   A. \<winnt_root>

   B. \<winnt_root>\SYSTEM32

   C. \<winnt_root>\SYSTEM32\ SPOOL

   D. \<winnt_root>\SYSTEM32\ SPOOL\PRINTERS

3. If an NT-based computer will function as a print server for the network, what is one of the most critical components?

   A. Free disk space

   B. Frequent backups

   C. A fast processor

   D. Accelerated PCI local bus video

4. What priority level is assigned to the print spooler service by Windows NT Server?

   A. 1

   B. 3

   C. 9

   D. 15

5. You can change the location of the spool directory by:

   A. Changing the entry is the Spool tab of the Control Panel\Printers option

   B. In the Registry, adding a value called DefaultSpoolDirectory to HKEY_LOCAL_MACHINE\ System\CurrentControlSet\ Control\Print\Printers

   C. Mapping a drive to the new location

   D. Changing port settings at the printer

6. A potential solution to problems with printing from non-Window–based applications to a printer that works fine in Windows is:

   A. Install additional printer drivers.

   B. Elect to use RAW data instead of EMF.

   C. Stop spooling services, and send data directly to the printer.

   D. Configure the printer on a different port.

7. If DOS-based applications will not print, what command should you first try?

   A. PRINT

   B. NET PRINT

   C. NET PRINT LPT1: _ HYPERLINK \\\\servername\\printername __\\servername\printername_

   D. NET USE LPT1: \\servername\printername

8. Files in the printer spool should have which two of the following extensions?

   A. TXT

   B. SHD

   C. SHT

   D. SPL

9. Files in the printer spool remain there for what duration?

   A. Until there is a clean boot of the system

   B. Until the system is shut down

   C. Until the job finishes printing

   D. Until the administrator empties the spool

10. What becomes of spooled print jobs in the event of a computer crash?

    A. When the system restarts, the printer should process these files immediately.

    B. They wait until the administrator restarts them before continuing.

    C. They do not restart.

    D. They perform a checksum operation to identify corruption that may have occurred.

11. If a print job appears stuck in the printer after recovering from a system crash, and you cannot delete it, you should:

    A. Continue rebooting the computer until the problem goes away.

    B. Stop the spooler service in Control Panel Services and delete the files for that job in the spool directory.

    C. Invest in a more industrial printer.

    D. Use Regedit to change stuck job parameters.

12. What priority level is assigned to the print spooler service by Windows NT Workstation?

    A. 15

    B. 10

    C. 7

    D. 1

13. If a Windows NT-based workstation moonlighting as a print server appears to print too slowly, what action should be be taken on the priority level of the print service?

    A. Raise the priority by one or two classes.

    B. Raise the priority by three to four classes.

    C. Lower the priority by one or two classes.

    D. Make no change—the priority level does not affect this service.

6.4   Answers and Explanations: Practice Problems

1. **C**   Always try to isolate the problem as much as possible before taking other actions.

2. **D**   By default, print jobs are in \<winnt_root>\SYSTEM32\SPOOL until they are completely printed.

3. **A**   If a Windows NT-based computer is acting as a print server for the network, make sure plenty of free disk space is available on the partition that contains the default spool directory. Spooled print jobs can be quite large and can eat up disk space more quickly than you might think, especially during peak printing periods.

4. **C**   Windows NT Server assigns a default priority level of 9 to the print spooler service.

5. **B**   You can change the spool directory in the Registry by adding a value called DefaultSpoolDirectory of type REG_SZ to HKEY_LOCAL_MACHINE\ System\CurrentControlSet\Control\ Print\Printers and entering the path to the new spool directory.

6. **A**   Non-Windows-based applications— for example, MS-DOS–based applications—require their own printer drivers if the application requires any kind of formatted output other than plain ASCII text.

7. **D**   You might need to use the NET USE LPT1: \\servername\printername command to enable the DOS-based application to print.

8. **B, D**   When a document prints, two files are created for the print job in the spool directory (by default, <winnt_root>\ SYSTEM32\SPOOL\PRINTERS). One of the files, which has an .SPL extension, is the actual print job spool file. The other file, which has an .SHD extension, is a shadow file that contains information about the job, including its owner and priority.

6

9. **C** When a document prints, two files are created for the print job in the spool directory (by default, <winnt_root>\ SYSTEM32\SPOOL\PRINTERS). One of the files, which has an .SPL extension, is the actual print job spool file. The other file, which has an .SHD extension, is a shadow file that contains information about the job, including its owner and priority. These files remain in the spool directory until the jobs finish printing, at which point they are deleted.

10. **A** In the event of a system crash, some spool and shadow files might be left over from jobs that were waiting to be printed. When the spooler service restarts (along with the rest of the system), the printer should process these files immediately.

11. **B** If a print job appears stuck in the printer and you cannot delete it, stop the spooler service in Control Panel Services and delete the SPL and/or SHD file for that job from the spool directory (match the date/time stamp on the files and in Print Manager to determine which files are causing the problem).

12. **C** Windows NT Workstation assigns a default priority level of 7 to the print spooler service.

13. **A** If a Windows NT-based workstation moonlighting as a print server appears to print too slowly, consider raising the priority by one or two classes. If the workstation is responding sluggishly to the user while printing, consider lowering the priority by a class or two.

6.4 Key Words

Printer

Spool

Priority

6.5   Troubleshooting RAS

Microsoft lists the following objective for the Windows NT Server exam: Choose the appropriate course of action to take to resolve RAS problems.

If RAS isn't working, check the Event Viewer. Several RAS events appear in the system log. You might also check the Control Panel Dial-Up Networking Monitor application. The Status tab of Dial-Up Networking Monitor displays statistics on current conditions, including connection statistics and device errors.

RAS supports TCP/IP, NWLink, and NetBEUI protocols for both dial-in and dial-out connections. TCP/IP benefits from being available on a number of different platforms, easily routable, and the compatibility choice of the Internet.

If you are having problems with PPP, you can log PPP debugging information to a file called PPP.Log in the \<winnt_root>\System32\Ras directory. To log PPP debugging information to PPP.Log, change the Registry value for the following subkey to 1:

```
\HKEY_LOCAL_MACHINE\System\CurrentControlSet\Services\Rasman\PPP\Logging
```

Microsoft has identified the following common RAS problems and some possible solutions:

- **Authentication.** RAS authentication problems often stem from incompatible encryption methods. Try to connect using the `Allow any authentication including clear text` option. If you can connect using clear text and you can't connect using encryption, you know the client and server encryption methods are incompatible.

- **Callback with Multilink.** If a client makes a connection using Multilink over multiple phone lines, with Callback enabled, the server will call back using only a single phone line (in other words, Multilink functionality is lost). RAS can use only one phone number for callback. If the Multilink connection uses two channels over an ISDN line, the server can still use Multilink on the callback.

- **AutoDial at Logon.** At logon, when Explorer is initializing, it might reference a shortcut or some other target that requires an AutoDial connection, causing AutoDial to spontaneously dial a remote connection during logon. The only way to prevent this is to disable AutoDial, or to eliminate the shortcut or other target causing the AutoDial to occur.

6

6.5   Practice Problems

1. If RAS is suspected of failing, what should be one of the first tools used to look for problems?

    A.   Performance Monitor

    B.   Event Viewer

    C.   Server Manager

    D.   User Manager for Domains

2. What tool displays statistics on current conditions of RAS?

    A.   Performance Monitor

    B.   In Control Panel, the Status tab of Dial-Up Networking Monitor

    C.   Event Viewer

    D.   User Manager for Domains

3. Which of the following statements are true of PPP logging (choose two):

    A.   It is enabled by default.

    B.   Information is written to the PPP.Log.

    C.   You must edit the Registry to turn it on.

    D.   It also contains logging information on modems.

4. The PPP.Log is stored, by default, where:

    A.   \<winnt_root>\System32\Ras

    B.   \<winnt_root>\System32

    C.   \<winnt_root>

    D.   C:\

5. If you can connect using clear text, and you can't connect using encryption, what is the most likely problem?

    A.   Connection speeds are too low to support verification.

    B.   Encryption is not enabled at both client and server.

    C.   The client and server encryption methods are incompatible.

    D.   The server requires additional resources.

6. If you suspect the client and server encryption methods of being incompatible, what should you try?

    A.   Try to connect using the Allow any authentication including clear text option.

    B.   Try to avoid using any form of encryption.

    C.   Try to discourage users from seeking dial-in functionality.

    D.   Try to connect using the Incompatible encryption methods option.

7. Which of the following statements is true in regards to Callback with MultiLink:

    A.   RAS can use multiple phone numbers for callback.

    B.   RAS can use only one phone number for callback by default, but can use multiple phone numbers after this function is enabled.

    C.   RAS can utilize callback only over ISDN lines.

    D.   RAS can use only one phone number for callback.

8. If a non-ISDN client makes a connection using Multilink over multiple phone lines, with Callback enabled, the server will call back using:

    A.   Only a single phone line

    B.   Multiple phone lines

    C.   An ISDN line

    D.   One phone line unless, the default has been changed to Utilize Multiple

9. Which three of the following are RAS problem areas, as identified by Microsoft:

    A.   Autodial at Logon

    B.   Authentication

    C.   Heterogeneous connectivity

    D.   Callback with MultiLink

10. Juan complains that AutoDial spontaneously attempts to dial a remote connection during his logon. How should an administrator address this problem?

    A. Move Juan to another machine.

    B. Disable AutoDial.

    C. Restrict Juan's profiles and groups.

    D. Reinstall Windows NT.

11. RAS can use which protocols for dial-in connections (choose all correct answers):

    A. TCP/IP

    B. NWLink

    C. NetBEUI

    D. SMTP

6.5 Answers and Explanations: Practice Problems

1. **B** If RAS isn't working, check the Event Viewer. Several RAS events appear in the system log.

2. **B** In Control Panel, the Status tab of Dial-Up Networking Monitor displays statistics on current conditions, including connection statistics and device errors.

3. **B, C** If you are having problems with PPP, you can log PPP debugging information to a file called PPP.Log in the \<winnt_root>\System32\Ras directory. To log PPP debugging information to PPP.Log, change the Registry value for \HKEY_LOCAL_MACHINE\System\ CurrentControlSet\Services\Rasman\ PPP\Logging to 1.

4. **A** PPP.Log in the \<winnt_root>\System32\Ras directory.

5. **C** RAS authentication problems often stem from incompatible encryption methods.

6. **A** If you can connect using clear text, and you can't connect using encryption, you know the client and server encryption methods are incompatible. You should try to connect using the Allow any authentication including clear text option.

7. **D** RAS can use only one phone number for callback.

8. **A** If a client makes a connection using Multilink over multiple phone lines, with Callback enabled, the server will call back using only a single phone line—in other words, Multilink functionality is lost.

9. **A, B, D** Autodial at Logon, Authentication, and Callback with MultiLink have all been identified as potential RAS problem areas by Microsoft.

10. **B** At logon, when Explorer is initializing, it might reference a shortcut or some other target that requires an AutoDial connection, causing AutoDial to spontaneously dial a remote connection during logon. The only way to prevent this is to disable AutoDial, or to eliminate the shortcut or other target causing the AutoDial to occur.

11. **A, B, C** RAS supports TCP/IP, NWLink, and NetBEUI protocols for both dial-in and dial-out connections.

6.5 Key Words

RAS

TCP/IP

6

6.6   Troubleshooting Connectivity Problems

Network problems often are caused by cables, adapters, or IRQ conflicts, or problems with transmission media. Protocol problems also can disrupt the network. Use a diagnostics program to check the network adapter card. Use a cable analyzer to check the cabling. Use Network Monitor to check network traffic, or use a network protocol analyzer.

Microsoft lists the following objective for the Windows NT Server exam: Choose the appropriate course of action to take to resolve connectivity problems.

A.   Pinging Other Computers

If you are using TCP/IP, the IP address and the subnet mask must be given when installed in a non-routed environment. You often can isolate problems by *pinging* the other computers on your network. Pinging is a common diagnostic procedure:

1. Ping the 127.0.0.1 (the loopback address).

2. Ping your own IP address.

3. Ping the address of another computer on your subnet.

4. Ping the default gateway.

5. Ping a computer beyond the default gateway.

Check the Control Panel Services application to ensure that the Server service and the Workstation service (and any other vital services that might affect connectivity) are running properly. Check the Bindings tab in the Control Panel Network application to ensure that the services are bound to applications and adapters.

B.   Network Monitor

Windows NT Server 4 includes a tool called Network Monitor. Network Monitor captures and filters packets and analyzes network activity. The Network Monitor included with Windows NT Server can monitor only the specific system on which it is installed.

To install Windows NT Server's Network Monitor, start the Network application in Control Panel and click on the Services tab. Click on the Add button and select Network Monitor and Tools from the network services list. After Network Monitor is installed, it appears in the Administrative Tools program group. Figure 6.6.1 shows the Network Monitor main screen.

The Network Monitor window is divided into four sections, or *panes*. The Graph pane (in the upper-left corner) shows the current network activity in a series of five bar charts. Note the scroll bar to the right of the Graph section. To view the bar charts (not shown in fig. 6.6.1), scroll down or drag the lower border down, exposing the hidden charts. The five bar graphs are as follows:

- % Network Utilization
- Frames Per Second
- Bytes Per Second
- Broadcasts Per Second
- Multicasts Per Second

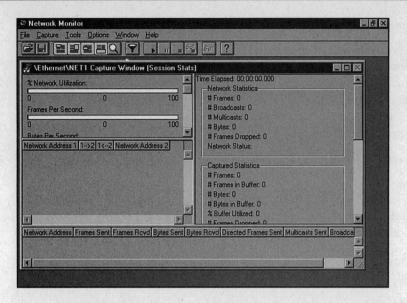

Figure 6.6.1 The Network Monitor main screen.

Below the Graphs pane you see the Session Stats pane. The Session Stats pane indicates the exchange of information from two nodes on the network, the amount of data, and the direction of travel. This data is limited to a per-session basis.

All the Stats panes report only on the first 128 sessions it finds. You can specify a particular session creating a capture filter. The Session Stats pane collects information on the following four areas:

- Network Address 1. The first node included in a network session.

- 1→2. The number of packets sent from the first address to the second.

- 1←2. The number of packets sent from the second address to the first.

- Network Address 2. The second node included in the network session.

On the right side of the display windows is the Total Stats pane, which reveals information relevant to the entire activity on the network. Whether statistics are supported depends on the network adapter. If a given network adapter isn't supported, Unsupported replaces the label.

The Total Stats information is divided into the following five categories:

- *Network Statistics*

  Total Frames
  Total Broadcasts
  Total Multicasts
  Total Bytes
  Total Frames Dropped
  Network Status

- *Captured Statistics*

  Captured Frames
  Captured Frames in Buffer
  Captured Bytes
  Capture Bytes in Buffer
  Percentage of Allotted Buffer Space in Use
  Captured Packets Dropped

- *Per Second Statistics*

  Frames
  Bytes/second
  Broadcasts/second
  Multicasts/second
  % Network Utilization

- *Network Card (MAC) Statistics*

  Total Frames
  Total Broadcasts
  Total Multicasts
  Total Bytes

- *Network Card (MAC) Error Statistics*

  Total Cyclical Redundancy Check (CRC) Errors
  Total Dropped Frames Due to Inadequate Buffer Space
  Total Dropped Packets Due to Hardware Failure(s)

At the bottom of the display window, you see the Station Stats pane. The Station Stats pane displays information specific to a workstation's activity on the network. You can sort on any category by right-clicking on the column label.

The following eight categories constitute the Station Stats pane:

- Network Address

- Frames Sent

- Frames Rcvd

- Bytes Sent

- Bytes Rcvd

- Directed Frames Sent

- Multicasts Sent

- Broadcasts Sent

6.6   Practice Problems

1. Which of the following are common causes of network problems? (Select all correct answers.)

   A. IRQ conflicts

   B. Workstation RAM

   C. Cables and adapters

   D. Transmission media

2. Which of the following tools should be used to check the network adapter card:

   A. Cable analyzer

   B. Diagnostics program

   C. Network Monitor

   D. Performance Monitor

3. Which of the following tools should be used to check the network cabling:

   A. Cable analyzer

   B. Diagnostics program

   C. Network Monitor

   D. Performance Monitor

4. Which of the following tools should be used to check the network traffic:

   A. Cable analyzer

   B. Diagnostics program

   C. Network Monitor

   D. Performance Monitor

5. The Ping utility can be useful in diagnosing network problems. Which address is the "loopback" address?

   A. 0.0.0.0

   B. 0.0.0.1

   C. 127.0.0.1

   D. 255.255.255.255

6. You have used Ping to troubleshoot your problems. After having used the loopback address and having received successful results, what should you try?

   A. Ping the default gateway.

   B. Ping your own IP address.

   C. Ping a computer on your subnet.

   D. Ping a computer beyond the default gateway.

7. When troubleshooting network problems, what information can be gleaned from the Services application in the Control Panel?

   A. Ensure that the Server service is running properly.

   B. Verify that a remote host is up and running.

   C. Verify that the default gateway is operable.

   D. Identify bottlenecks on the system.

8. To verify that services are bound to applications and adapters, which tab should you check in the Control Panel Network application?

   A. Services

   B. Bindings

   C. Protocols

   D. System

9. You have used Ping to troubleshoot your problems. After having pinged your own IP address and having received successful results, what should you try?

   A. Ping the default gateway.

   B. Ping the loopback address.

   C. Ping a computer on your subnet.

   D. Ping a computer beyond the default gateway.

10. Which troubleshooting tool included with NT captures and filters packets and analyzes network activity?

   A. Event Viewer

   B. Performance Monitor

   C. SMTP

   D. Network Monitor

11. Which statement regarding the version of Network Monitor included with Windows NT is true?

   A. It can monitor only the system upon which it was installed.

   B. It can monitor any system on the network.

   C. It is not included with NT, but rather a component of the resource kit.

   D. It will not collect TCP/IP information until SMTP is installed.

12. You have used Ping to troubleshoot your problems. After having pinged a computer on your subnet and having received successful results, what should you try?

   A. Ping the default gateway.

   B. Ping your own IP address.

   C. Ping the loopback address.

   D. Ping a computer beyond the default gateway.

13. Network Monitor appears on which program group tab:

   A. System

   B. Server Manager

   C. Resource Kit

   D. Administrative Tools

14. To install Windows NT Server's Network Monitor, start the Network application in Control Panel and click on which tab:

   A. Install

   B. Services

   C. System

   D. Network

15. You have used Ping to troubleshoot your problems. After having pinged the default gateway and having received successful results, what should you try?

   A. Ping the loopback address.

   B. Ping your own IP address.

   C. Ping a computer on your subnet.

   D. Ping a computer beyond the default gateway.

16. Network Monitor's display is broken into a number of sections called:

   A. Views

   B. Windows

   C. Panes

   D. Corners

17. The Graph pane in Network Monitor shows:

   A. The exchange of information from two nodes on the network

   B. Activity on the entire network

   C. Current network activity, as a series of bar charts

   D. Information specific to a workstation's activity on the network

18. The Station Stats pane in Network Monitor shows:

    A. The exchange of information from two nodes on the network

    B. Activity on the entire network

    C. Current network activity, as a series of bar charts

    D. Information specific to a workstation's activity on the network

19. The Session Stats pane in Network Monitor shows:

    A. The exchange of information from two nodes on the network

    B. Activity on the entire network

    C. Current network activity, as a series of bar charts

    D. Information specific to a workstation's activity on the network

20. The Total Stats pane in Network Monitor shows:

    A. The exchange of information between two nodes on the network

    B. Activity on the entire network

    C. Current network activity as a series of bar charts

    D. Information specific to a workstation's activity on the network

21. Within the Graph Pane of Network Monitor, which of the following is *not* displayed as a bar graph:

    A. % Network Utilization

    B. Total Frames Dropped

    C. Frames Per Second

    D. Bytes Per Second

22. The Session Stats pane of Network Monitor can report on how many sessions at a time:

    A. 1

    B. 32

    C. 64

    D. 128

23. The Session Stats pane collects all of the following information *except*:

    A. The network address of the first node included in a session

    B. The network address of the second node included in a session

    C. The total number of frames dropped from each address

    D. The number of packets sent from each address

24. Within the Graph Pane of Network Monitor, which of the following is not displayed as a bar graph:

    A. % Network Utilization

    B. Multicasts Per Second

    C. Network Status

    D. Bytes Per Second

25. Total Stats information in Network Monitor is divided into which of the following categories? (Choose three.)

    A. Network Statistics

    B. Dropped Frame Statistics

    C. Captured Statistics

    D. Per Second Statistics

26. The Station Stats portion of Network Monitor keeps track of all of the following *except*:

    A. Bytes/second

    B. Bytes Sent

    C. Bytes Recd

    D. Frames Sent

6

27. Within the Graph Pane of Network Monitor, which of the following is not displayed as a bar graph:

    A. Captured Frames

    B. Multicasts Per Second

    C. Broadcasts Per Second

    D. Frames Per Second

28. The Station Stats portion of Network Monitor keeps track of all of the following *except*:

    A. Broadcasts Sent

    B. Bytes Sent

    C. %Network Utilization

    D. Frames Sent

29. Network Card (MAC) Error Statistics would contain which of the following statistical categories? (Choose all correct answers.)

    A. Total Cyclical Redundancy Check (CRC) Errors

    B. Total Dropped Frames Due to Inadequate Buffer Space

    C. Total Dropped Packets Due to Hardware Failure(s)

    D. Total Dropped Bytes Due to Failure(s)

30. The Station Stats portion of Network Monitor keeps track of all of the following *except*:

    A. Directed Frames Sent

    B. Frames Sent

    C. Bytes Resent

    D. Frames sent

31. Network Card (MAC) Statistics would consist of which of the following (select all correct answers):

    A. Total Dropped Frames Due to Inadequate Buffer Space

    B. Total Broadcasts

    C. Total Multicasts

    D. Total Dropped Bytes Due to Failure(s)

32. The Station Stats portion of Network Monitor keeps track of all of the following *except*:

    A. Network Address

    B. Bytes Sent

    C. Bytes Recd

    D. Frames Resent

33. The minimum number of nodes needed to constitute a session for Session Stats in Network Monitor is:

    A. 0

    B. 1

    C. 2

    D. 3

6.6 Answers and Explanations: Practice Problems

1. **A, C, D** Network problems often are caused by cables, adapters, IRQ conflicts, or problems with transmission media.

2. **B** Use a diagnostics program to check the network adapter card. Use a cable analyzer to check the cabling. Use Network Monitor or a network protocol analyzer to check network traffic.

3. **A** Use a diagnostics program to check the network adapter card. Use a cable analyzer to check the cabling. Use Network Monitor or a network protocol analyzer to check network traffic.

4. **C** Use a diagnostics program to check the network adapter card. Use a cable analyzer to check the cabling. Use Network Monitor or a network protocol analyzer to check network traffic.

5. **C** 127.0.0.1 is the loopback address that Ping can use to verify the status of the internal\local operation.

6. **B** The sequence is: Ping the loopback address, your own IP address, then the address of another computer on your subnet. Following that, Ping the default gateway, and finally a computer beyond the default gateway.

7. **A** Checking the Control Panel Services application can ensure that the Server service and the Workstation service (and any other vital services that might affect connectivity) are running properly.

8. **B** Check the Bindings tab in the Control Panel Network application to ensure that the services are bound to applications and adapters.

9. **C** The sequence is: Ping the loopback address, your own IP address, the default gateway, and finally a computer beyond the default gateway.

10. **D** Network Monitor captures and filters packets and analyzes network activity.

11. **A** The Network Monitor included with Windows NT Server can monitor only the specific system on which it is installed, unlike the Network Monitor in Microsoft's Systems Management Server package, which can monitor other systems on the network.

12. **A** The sequence is: Ping the loopback address, your own IP address, then the address of another computer on your subnet. Following that, Ping the default gateway, and finally a computer beyond the default gateway.

13. **D** After Network Monitor is installed, it appears in the Administrative Tools program group.

14. **B** To install Windows NT Server's Network Monitor, start the Network application in Control Panel and click on the Services tab. Click on the Add button and select Network Monitor from the network services list. After Network Monitor is installed, it appears in the Administrative Tools program group.

15. **D** The sequence is: Ping the loopback address, your own IP address, then the address of another computer on your subnet. Following that, Ping the default gateway, and finally a computer beyond the default gateway.

16. **C** The Network Monitor window is divided into four sections, or *panes*.

17. **C** The Graph pane (in the upper-left corner) shows the current network activity in a series of five bar charts.

18. **D** The Station Stats pane displays information specific to a workstation's activity on the network.

19. **A** The Session Stats pane indicates the exchange of information from two nodes on the network, the amount of data, and the direction of travel. This data is limited to a per-session basis.

20. **B** The Total Stats pane reveals information relevant to the entire activity on the network. Whether statistics are supported depends on the network adapter.

21. **B** The five graphs shown are:

% Network Utilization

Frames Per Second

Bytes Per Second

Broadcasts Per Second

Multicasts Per Second

6

22. **D** The Session Stats pane of Network Monitor can report on only the first 128 sessions that it finds.

23. **C** The total number of frames dropped is displayed in Total Stats, and not Session Stats.

24. **C** The five graphs shown are:

% Network Utilization

Frames Per Second

Bytes Per Second

Broadcasts Per Second

Multicasts Per Second

25. **A, C, D** The five categories of Total Stats are:

Network Statistics

Captured Statistics

Per Second Statistics

Network Card (MAC) Statistics

Network Card (MAC) Error Statistics

26. **A** The following eight categories constitute the Station pane:

1. Network Address

2. Frames Sent

3. Frames Rcvd

4. Bytes Sent

5. Bytes Rcvd

6. Directed Frames Sent

7. Multicasts Sent

8. Broadcasts Sent

27. **A** The five graphs shown are:

% Network Utilization

Frames Per Second

Bytes Per Second

Broadcasts Per Second

Multicasts Per Second

28. **C** The following eight categories constitute the Station pane:

1. Network Address

2. Frames Sent

3. Frames Rcvd

4. Bytes Sent

5. Bytes Rcvd

6. Directed Frames Sent

7. Multicasts Sent

8. Broadcasts Sent

29. **A, B, C** Network Card (MAC) Error Statistics consist of: Total Cyclical Redundancy Check (CRC) Errors, Total Dropped Frames Due to Inadequate Buffer Space, and Total Dropped Packets Due to Hardware Failure(s).

30. **C** The following eight categories constitute the Station pane:

1. Network Address

2. Frames Sent

3. Frames Rcvd

4. Bytes Sent

5. Bytes Rcvd

6. Directed Frames Sent

7. Multicasts Sent

8. Broadcasts Sent

31. **B, C**   Network Card (MAC) Statistics consist of: Total Frames, Total Broadcasts, Total Multicasts, and Total Bytes

32. **D**   The following eight categories constitute the Station pane:

    1. Network Address

    2. Frames Sent

    3. Frames Rcvd

    4. Bytes Sent

    5. Bytes Rcvd

    6. Directed Frames Sent

    7. Multicasts Sent

    8. Broadcasts Sent

33. **C**   The Session Stats pane indicates the exchange of information between two nodes on the network, the amount and data, and direction of travel.

6.6   Key Words

IP address

Subnet mask

Subnet

6

6.7   Troubleshooting Access and Permission Problems

If you can't log on, you may be using an incorrect username or password. Also, ensure the correct account database is selected in the drop list at the bottom of the dialog box. You can logon to the domain or to the local workstation account database. If you still can't log on, try logging on using another account. If other accounts are working normally, check the settings for your account in User Manager for Domains. If you can't log on from any account, repair the accounts database by using the emergency repair process. One of the worst culprits for logon problems is the Caps Lock key. Make certain that the user isn't typing the password in all caps.

Microsoft lists the following objective for the Windows NT Server exam: Choose the appropriate course of action to take to resolve resource access problems and permission problems.

If a user can't access a file, a share, a printer, or some other resource, check the resource permissions. Try connecting using a different account. Try accessing a similar resource to see whether the problem also appears there. Make certain that the user has spelled the name of the resource correctly.

Check the Control Panel Services application to ensure that the NetLogon service, the Server service, and the Workstation service are running properly, and check the Bindings tab in the Control Panel Network application to ensure that the services are bound to applications and adapters.

You can also check User Manager for Domains to ensure that the user's group memberships haven't changed or that a change to a group rights setting hasn't inadvertently denied the user access to the resource. Finally, check System Policy Editor for restrictions on the user's access to computers or other resources.

6.7   Practice Problems

1. What are two likely reasons for failure to log on to a network from a workstation you have used in the past?

   A. Incorrect password

   B. Incorrect username

   C. Incorrect media

   D. Incorrect frame type

2. If you cannot log on from a workstation you were using earlier, and are certain username and password are correct, what should be checked next?

   A. Verify you are logging on to the correct domain or workgroup.

   B. Check the media.

   C. Verify frame types.

   D. Look for CRC errors.

3. You cannot log on to the network from a workstation you have used earlier, and are certain that username, password, and domain name are correct. What is the next logical step to try?

   A. Down the network and begin an Emergency Repair procedure.

   B. Verify the proper permissions are on the SAM database.

   C. Attempt to log on using another account.

   D. Look for CRC errors.

4. If you cannot log on to a workstation using any account, what is the next logical step in solving the problem?

   A. Repair the accounts database by using the emergency repair process.

   B. Verify the proper permissions are on the SAM database.

   C. Look for CRC errors.

   D. Verify frame types.

5. One of the most common logon problems is:

   A. Programmable keyboards

   B. Hashing table errors

   C. Duplicate SIDs

   D. The Caps Lock key

6. If a user can't access a file, a share, a printer, or some other resource, start by checking:

   A. The resource permissions

   B. The Global groups

   C. The Local groups

   D. TechNet

7. To ensure that a user's group memberships have not changed, thus denying them permissions to a resource, use:

   A. Network Monitor

   B. User Manager for Domains

   C. Server Manager

   D. Performance Monitor

8. If there is a suspected logon problem from a workstation, you should check the Control Panel Services application to ensure that which of the following services are running properly:

   A. The NetLogon service

   B. The Server service

   C. The Workstation service

   D. The Bindings service

9. Checking the Bindings tab in the Control Panel Network application verifies which of the following? (Choose two.)

   A. Services are bound to applications.

   B. Correct frame types have been selected.

   C. Dirty RAM is not causing a failure to update SAM.

   D. Services are bound to adapters.

10. You use which tool to find restrictions on the user's access to computers?

    A.   Network Monitor

    B.   User Manager

    C.   User Manager for Domains

    D.   System Policy Editor

6.7   Answers and Explanations: Practice Problems

1. **A, B**   If you can't log on, you might be using an incorrect username or password.

2. **A**   Enable the check box beneath the password to make certain that you are logging on to the correct domain or workgroup (or the local machine).

3. **C**   Try logging on using another account. If other accounts are working normally, check the settings for your account in User Manager for Domains.

4. **A**   If you can't log on from any account, repair the accounts database by using the emergency repair process.

5. **D**   One of the worst culprits for logon problems is the Caps Lock key. Make certain that the user isn't typing the password in all caps.

6. **A**   If a user can't access a file, a share, a printer, or some other resource, check the resource permissions.

7. **B**   You can use User Manager for Domains to ensure that the user's group memberships haven't changed or that a change to a group rights setting hasn't inadvertently denied the user access to the resource.

8. **A, B, C**   Check the Control Panel Services application to ensure that the NetLogon service, the Server service, and the Workstation service are running properly.

9. **A, D**   Checking the Bindings tab in the Control Panel Network application will verify that the services are bound to applications and adapters.

10. **D**   Check System Policy Editor for restrictions on the user's access to computers or other resources.

6.8 Recovering from Fault-Tolerance Failures

Even if you are employing a high-tech RAID fault-tolerance system, a well planned backup routine is still your best defense against lost data. Windows NT includes a backup utility (NTBACKUP.EXE). Backup is part of the Administrative Tools group.

Microsoft lists the following objective for the Windows NT Server exam: Choose the appropriate course of action to take to resolve fault-tolerance failures. Fault-tolerance methods include: tape backup, mirroring, stripe set with parity, disk duplexing.

A. Backing Up Files and Directories

The Backup main window shows the disk drives presently accessible to the Backup utility. Double-click on a drive and to see an Explorer-type directory tree. Note that every directory or file has a small box beside it. Click on the box to back up the file or directory and all child files/directories beneath it.

To start a backup, click on the Backup button in the toolbar or choose Operations, Backup. The Backup Information dialog box appears, offering a number of backup options (see fig. 6.8.1). Note the Log Information frame at the bottom of the Backup Information dialog box. You can write a summary or a detailed description of the backup operation to a log file.

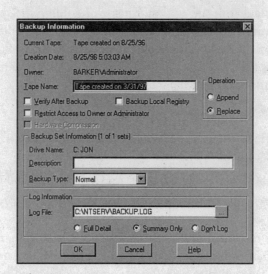

Figure 6.8.1 The Backup Information dialog box.

B. Restoring Files and Directories

To restore a file or directory using the Backup utility, open the Tapes window (if you don't see the Tapes window on your screen, pull down the Window menu and choose Tapes) and select the backup set you want to restore. Like the Drives window, the Tapes window enables you to expand directories and select individual files for restoration.

Select the files/directories you want to restore and click on the Restore button in the toolbar (or choose Operations, Restore). The Restore Information dialog box appears. Select the desired restore options and click on OK to restore the files/directories.

You also can run the NTBACKUP utility from the command prompt. This enables you to automate the backup process through batch files, so you can perform backups at regular intervals. You can only back up directories with the ntbackup command (not individual files). The syntax is as follows:

```
ntbackup operation  path
```

where *operation* is the name of the operation (backup, restore, and so on), and *path* is the path to the directory you're backing up. The NTBACKUP command includes a number of switches, including the following:

/a cause the backup set to be appended after the last backup set. (If you don't specify /a will overwrite existing backup sets on the tape.)

/v verifies the backup operation.

/d "text" enables you to add a description of the data in the backup set.

/t {option} enables you to specify the backup type (normal, incremental, daily, differential, copy).

C.   Breaking a Mirror Set

A mirror set is the only fault-tolerant option capable of holding the system and boot partitions. When a partition in a mirror set fails, it becomes an orphan. To maintain service until the mirror is repaired, the fault-tolerant device directs all I/0 requests to the healthy partition. If the boot and/or system partitions are involved, a fault-tolerant boot disk is required to restart the system. To create a fault-tolerant boot disk, follow these steps:

1. Format a floppy disk using Windows NT.

2. If you are using an I386 system, copy NTLDR, NTDETECT.COM, NTBOOTDD.SYS (for SCSI disks not using SCSI BIOS), and BOOT.INI to the disk.

    If you're using a RISC-based computer, copy OSLOADER.EXE and HAL.DLL.

3. Modify the BOOT.INI file so that it points to the mirrored copy of the boot partition.

To fix a mirror set, you must first break it by choosing Fault Tolerance, Break Mirror. This action exposes the remaining partition as a separate volume. The healthy partition is given the drive letter that was previously assigned to it in the set, and the orphaned partition is given the next logical drive letter, or one that you manually selected for it.

After the mirror (RAID level 1) has been re-established as a primary partition, selecting additional free space and restarting the process of creating a mirror set can form a new relationship.

D. Regenerating a Stripe Set with Parity

Like a mirror set, the partition that fails in a stripe set with parity (RAID level 5) becomes an orphan. Also, the fault-tolerant device redirects I/O requests to the remaining partitions in the set to enable reconstruction. So that this can be done, the data is stored in RAM by using the parity bits (which may affect the system's performance).

To regenerate a stripe set with parity, follow these steps:

1. Select the stripe set with parity by clicking on it.

2. Select an area of free space as large or larger than the stripe set. The size of the stripe set becomes the size of the smallest amount of free space on any drive multiplied by the number of drives.

3. Choose Fault Tolerance, Regenerate.

You must close the Disk Administrator and restart the system before the process can begin. After the system restarts, the information from the existing partitions in the stripe set are read into memory and re-created on the new member. This process completes in the background, so the stripe set with parity isn't active in the Disk Administrator until it finishes.

E. Troubleshooting Partitions and Disks

When you install Windows NT, your initial disk configuration is saved on the emergency repair disk and in the directory \<winnt_root>\Repair. The RDISK utility does update the disk configuration information stored on the repair disk and in the Repair directory. You can also save or restore the disk configuration by using Disk Administrator.

You should periodically update emergency configuration information in case you ever need to use the Emergency Repair Process or you ever want to you upgrade to a newer version of Windows NT. Otherwise, NT restores the original configuration that was saved when you first installed Windows NT.

6.8.1 Exercise: Familiarize Yourself with Disk Administrator

In Exercise 6.8.1, you learn how to use Disk Administrator to perform some routine tasks.

Estimated time: 20 minutes

1. Start the Disk Administrator program by choosing Administrative Tools from the Programs section of the Start Menu. Next, select Disk Administrator.

2. Select Tools, and then Assign Drive Letter. Change the C: drive to J: and notice how simple the operation is. The mappings are all internal.

3. Change the J: drive back to C:

4. Make note of the size of each partition and the amount of free space.

5. If Fault Tolerance is in use, note the information pertinent to it from the Fault Tolerance menu of Disk Administrator.

6. Exit Disk Administrator.

6.8 Practice Problems

1. What is the best defense against lost data?

    A. RAID hardware implementation

    B. RAID software implementation

    C. Backups

    D. Volume sets

2. The Windows NT backup utility is called:

    A. NTBACK.EXE

    B. NTBACKUP.EXE

    C. BACKUP.EXE

    D. BACKUP.COM

3. When installed, the Backup utility is a part of what program group?

    A. Server Manager

    B. User Domain for Workgroups

    C. Administrative Tools

    D. Backup

4. To start a Backup process in the Windows NT Backup Utility, you could do either of which two options:

    A. Click on the Backup button in the toolbar.

    B. Choose Operations, Backup.

    C. Type BACKUP at a command-line prompt.

    D. Type BACKUP at the RUN line.

5. The Backup operation can be detailed in a log file by making the appropriate radio box selection on the Backup Information screen in what three ways?

    A. Full Detail

    B. Limited Detail

    C. Summary Only

    D. Don't Log

6. To restore a file or directory using the Backup utility, what must be done first?

    A. You must reboot the system.

    B. You must disable logging.

    C. You must select the backup set you want to restore.

    D. You must load the Restore utility from the Resource kit.

7. The Backup utility can be run in which three ways:

    A. Click on the Backup button in the toolbar.

    B. Choose Operations, Backup.

    C. Type NTBACKUP at a command-line prompt.

    D. Type BACKUP at the RUN line.

8. What is an advantage of running NTBACKUP from the command line?

    A. There is none.

    B. It takes up less RAM.

    C. It enables you to automate the backup process.

    D. It enables you to choose files as well as directories.

9. What is a disadvantage of running NTBACKUP from the command line?

    A. There is none.

    B. It takes up more RAM.

    C. It does not allow you to automate the backup process.

    D. It does not allow you to choose files; only directories.

10. Which NTBACKUP command-line switch will cause the backup set to be appended after the last backup set?

    A. /a

    B. /v

    C. /d

    D. /t

11. Which NTBACKUP command-line switch will verify the backup operation?

    A. /a

    B. /v

    C. /d

    D. /t

12. Which NTBACKUP command line-switch enables you to set the backup type to incremental?

    A. /a

    B. /v

    C. /d

    D. /t

13. Which NTBACKUP command-line switch enables you to add a description of the data in the backup set?

    A. /a

    B. /v

    C. /d

    D. /t

14. When a partition in a mirror set fails, it becomes known as:

    A. An orphan

    B. A discard

    C. A non-member

    D. A Lansing-75

15. After a drive in a mirror set fails, all I/O requests are:

    A. Spooled

    B. Directed to the other partition

    C. Ignored

    D. Withdrawn

16. If a mirrored drive fails on a system partition:

    A. The system continues to act normally until the failed drive can be replaced.

    B. The system shuts down automatically and NT must be reinstalled.

    C. A fault-tolerant boot disk might be required to restart the system.

    D. Only a Lansing-75 (or higher) will continue to process requests.

17. Which files are necessary on a fault-tolerant boot disk for an I386 system (choose all that apply):

    A. OSLOADER.EXE

    B. NTDETECT.COM

    C. HAL.DLL

    D. BOOT.INI

18. Which files are necessary on a fault-tolerant boot disk for a RISC-based system? (Choose all that apply.)

    A. OSLOADER.EXE

    B. NTDETECT.COM

    C. HAL.DLL

    D. BOOT.INI

19. In the event of a mirror failure, which file must be modified to point to the mirrored copy of the boot partition?

    A. NTBOOTDD.SYS

    B. BOOT.INI

    C. NTBOOT.INI

    D. NTLDR

20. Which file is needed on a fault-tolerant boot disk for systems with SCSI controllers that are non-BIOS enabled:

    A. NTBOOTDD.SYS

    B. BOOT.INI

    C. NTBOOT.INI

    D. NTLDR

6

21. To fix a mirror set, you must first:

    A. Break it by choosing Fault Tolerance, Break Mirror.

    B. Replace the bad drive with a new one.

    C. Stop transaction logging.

    D. Expose the bad partition as a separate volume.

22. When you break a mirror set due to a fault, what drive letter is given to the faulty drive, by default?

    A. The one it originally had.

    B. The next logical letter.

    C. It does not need one.

    D. The last free letter of the alphabet.

23. After a broken mirror has been re-established as a primary partition, selecting additional free space and restarting the process of creating a mirror set will do what?

    A. Remove all old references.

    B. Re-enable transaction logging.

    C. Form a new relationship.

    D. Start parity checking again.

24. When a partition in a stripe set with parity fails, it becomes known as:

    A. An orphan

    B. A discard

    C. A non-member

    D. A Lansing-75

25. To recreate a stripe set with parity after replacing a failed drive:

    A. First break the set it by choosing Fault Tolerance, Break Mirror.

    B. Choose Fault Tolerance, Regenerate.

    C. Do nothing, the stripe set will recreate itself.

    D. Enable Pulse via the Regedit utility.

26. If you employ fault-tolerance via a stripe set with parity over six drives, what must you do if two drives fail (and are replaced) after a lightning strike?

    A. Choose Fault Tolerance, Regenerate.

    B. Restore the lost data from tape backup.

    C. Do nothing; the stripe set will recreate itself.

    D. Enable Pulse via the Regedit utility.

27. The Regenerate command is located beneath Fault Tolerance in what utility?

    A. Network Monitor

    B. Disk Administrator

    C. Emergency Repair

    D. Server Manager

28. What utility updates the disk configuration information stored on the repair disk and in the Repair directory?

    A. Server Manager

    B. Network Monitor

    C. RDISK

    D. Regenerate

29. In addition to RDISK, you can also save or restore the disk configuration information by using:

    A. Disk Administrator

    B. Server Manager

    C. Network Monitor

    D. Regenerate

30. Volume information can be viewed on the NT Server by using which utility?

    A. Disk Administrator

    B. Server Manager

    C. Network Monitor

    D. Regenerate

31. When first using NTBACKUP, the default is that all files and directories are:

    A. Checked for inclusion in the backup.

    B. There is no default setting.

    C. Not checked to be included in the backup.

    D. Marked to archive, but not backup.

32. Which utility is used to create an emergency repair disk?

    A. Disk Administrator

    B. ERD.EXE

    C. BOOTNT.COM

    D. RDISK.EXE

33. Fault-Tolerance can be provided at which two RAID levels in Windows NT?

    A. 1

    B. 2

    C. 3

    D. 5

34. What is the minimum number of physical disks needed to implement mirroring?

    A. 1

    B. 2

    C. 3

    D. 4

35. What is the minimum number of physical disks needed to implement disk striping with parity?

    A. 1

    B. 2

    C. 3

    D. 4

36. What is the minimum number of physical disks needed to implement disk striping without parity?

    A. 1

    B. 2

    C. 3

    D. 4

37. Data can be recovered in the event of *either* a hardware *or* software failure using which redundancy techniques? (Choose all correct answers.)

    A. Disk mirroring

    B. Disk duplexing

    C. Disk striping

    D. Disk striping with parity

38. If disk striping with parity is implemented on three drives with free space of 250 MB, 400 MB, and 900 MB, respectively, what is the size of the stripe set?

    A. 250 MB

    B. 750 MB

    C. 1550 MB

    D. 2700 MB

39. What is the maximum number of drives RAID level 1 will support?

    A. 1

    B. 2

    C. 4

    D. unlimited

40. The System and boot partitions can be included in which fault-tolerance strategies? (Choose all correct answers.)

    A. Mirror

    B. Stripe set with parity

    C. Stripe set

    D. Volume set

6

41. Which can be thought of as the graphical equivalent of FDISK.EXE?

    A. Disk Administrator

    B. ERD.EXE

    C. BOOTNT.COM

    D. RDISK.EXE

42. If disk striping with parity is implemented on five drives with free space of 100 MB, 200 MB, 300 MB, 400 MB and 500 MB, respectively, what is the size of the stripe set?

    A. 100 MB

    B. 500 MB

    C. 1000 MB

    D. 1500 MB

6.8   Answers and Explanations: Exercise

In Exercise 6.8.1, you learned how to use Disk Administrator to perform some routine tasks. This is a tool you should become very familiar with and consider indispensable.

6.8   Answers and Explanations: Practice Problems

1. **C**   Even if you are employing a high-tech RAID fault-tolerance system, a good backup routine is still your best defense against lost data.

2. **B**   Windows NT includes a backup utility called NTBACKUP.EXE.

3. **C**   Backup is part of the Administrative Tools group.

4. **A, B**   To start a backup, click on the Backup button in the toolbar or choose Operations, Backup.

5. **A, C, D**   You can write a summary or a detailed description of the backup operation to a log file as Full Detail or Summary Only. You can also choose to not create a log file.

6. **C**   To restore a file or directory using the Backup utility, open the Tapes window and select the backup set you want to restore.

7. **A, B, C**   You also can run the NTBACKUP utility from the command prompt.

8. **C**   This enables you to automate the backup process through batch files, so you can perform backups at regular intervals.

9. **A**   The command line utility is less intuitive in nature than the graphical version.

10. **A**   Ntbackup /a cause the backup set to be appended after the last backup set. (If you don't specify /a will overwrite existing backup sets on the tape.)

11. **B**   Ntbackup /v verifies the backup operation.

12. **D**   Ntbackup /t {option} enables you to specify the backup type (normal, incremental, daily, differential, copy).

13. **C**   Ntbackup /d "text" enables you to add a description of the data in the backup set.

14. **A**   When a partition in a mirror set fails, it becomes an orphan.

15. **B**   To maintain service until the mirror is repaired, the fault-tolerant device directs all I/0 requests to the healthy partition.

16. **C**   If the boot and/or system partitions are involved, a fault tolerant boot disk is required to restart the system.

17. **B, D**   If you are using an I386 system, NTLDR, NTDETECT.COM, NTBOOTDD.SYS (for SCSI disks not using SCSI BIOS), and BOOT.INI are needed on the disk.

18. **A, C, D**   OSLOADER.EXE and BOOT.INI are needed on a RISC-based fault tolerant boot disk.

19. **B** BOOT.INI must be modified to point to the mirrored copy of the boot partition.

20. **A** NTBOOTDD.SYS must be included on a fault tolerant disk if SCSI drives are used without SCSI BIOS.

21. **A** To fix a mirror set, you must first break it by choosing Fault Tolerance, Break Mirror. This action exposes the remaining partition as a separate volume.

22. **B** The healthy partition is given the drive letter that was previously assigned to it in the set, and the orphaned partition is given the next logical drive letter or one that you manually selected for it.

23. **C** After the mirror has been re-established as a primary partition, selecting additional free space and restarting the process of creating a mirror set can form a new relationship.

24. **A** When a partition in a mirror set or a stripe set with parity fails, it becomes an orphan.

25. **C** The Regenerate command is used to reestablish a stripe set with parity after replacing the fault disk.

26. **B** A stripe set with parity keeps a system running during the failure of one drive but cannot handle more than that.

27. **B** Disk Administrator is the utility for all disk-related operations.

28. **C** The RDISK utility does update the disk configuration information stored on the repair disk and in the Repair directory.

29. **A** You can also save or restore the disk configuration by using Disk Administrator.

30. **A** The Disk Administrator is used to view all information relevant to the drives, partitions, and volumes.

31. **C** By default, files are not marked for backup, and you must select which ones you want to include in the set.

32. **D** RDISK is used to create an emergency repair disk.

33. **A, D** RAID level 1 (mirroring) and RAID level 5 (disk striping with parity) are both supported by Windows NT.

34. **B** Two physical disks are needed to implement disk mirroring.

35. **C** Three physical disks are needed to implement disk striping with parity.

36. **B** Two physical disks are needed to implement disk striping without parity. It is not considered a fault-tolerant solution because it does not support data redundancy.

37. **A, B, D** Disk Striping does not offer fault tolerance or data redundancy whereas mirroring, duplexing, and striping with parity do.

38. **B** The size of the stripe set becomes the size of the smallest amount of free space on any drive multiplied by the number of drives.

39. **B** Disk mirroring (RAID level 1) supports only two drives.

40. **A** A mirror is the only fault tolerant strategy capable of containing the system and boot partitions.

41. **A** Disk Administrator is the graphical equivalent of FDISK.EXE. It enables you to partition drives, create stripe sets, etc.

42. **B** The size of the stripe set becomes the size of the smallest amount of free space on any drive multiplied by the number of drives.

6.8   Key Words

Mirror set

Disk Administrator

Fault-tolerance

Orphan

6

Practice Exam: Troubleshooting

Use this practice exam to test your mastery of Connectivity. This practice exam is made up of 20 questions. Keep in mind that the passing Microsoft score is 76.4 percent. There will be two types of questions:

- Multiple Choice—Select the correct answer.

- Multiple Multiple Choice—Select all answers that are correct.

Begin as soon as you are ready. Answers follow the test.

1. The utility used to convert NTFS partitions to FAT is:

   A. NTFS.EXE

   B. CONVERT.EXE

   C. MIGRATE.EXE

   D. There is no utility to perform this operation.

2. Spencer calls to say that he was playing around and accidentally changed the SCSI controller card driver, and now the computer won't boot NT. It stops at the blue screen and gives him a system error. What should Spencer do?

   A. Boot into DOS and rerun the Windows NT Setup program.

   B. Purchase and install the SCSI device that he selected.

   C. Reinstall NT.

   D. Select the LastKnownGood configuration during NT booting, then remove the incorrect driver.

3. Annie works in the South Building. She calls to say that the message "I/O Error accessing boot sector file multi(0)disk(0)rdisk(0)partition (1):\bootsect.dos," is showing up on her screen. Which one of the critical boot files is *really* missing?

   A. NTLDR

   B. NTDETECT.COM

   C. BOOTSECT.DOS

   D. MSDOS.SYS

4. What information does the BOOTSECT.DOS file contain?

   A. A copy of the information that was originally on the boot sector of the drive before NT was installed. You use it to boot an operating system other than NT.

   B. A copy of the information needed to boot a RISC-based computer.

   C. The file that detects the hardware installed on a PC with a Plug-and-Play BIOS.

   D. The file that contains the boot menu selections.

5. If BOOTSECT.DOS becomes corrupted on one machine, can you copy it from another machine?

   A. Yes, the file is standard on every machine.

   B. Only if the other machine is identical to the corrupted one in every way.

   C. Only with the RDISK utility.

   D. No, the file is machine specific.

6. Marco calls back to say that he is looking for a particular message in the system log under Event Viewer, but there are so many messages that he can't find the one you told him to look for. Can he display messages of a certain type?

    A. He cannot. Event Viewer shows all the messages in the system log.

    B. He must set up Event Viewer to store only messages of the type he is looking for and then restart the system.

    C. He can filter the log by choosing View, Filter Events.

    D. He must first export the data to an ASCII file and then use the Edit program to find the specific data sought.

7. The pointy-headed manager informs you that an inventory of all company PCs running NT Workstation and NT Server needs to be done. Which NT utility can you use to find the amount of RAM, type of CPU, and other information about the computers in question?

    A. You must purchase the 32-bit version of PC Tools. This program gives you the required information.

    B. No tools will run under NT because they would have to access the hardware directly, which isn't allowed under NT.

    C. You must manually edit the Registry and search for the information you need.

    D. Use the Windows NT Diagnostics utility.

8. Kristin knows just enough to be dangerous. She calls and says that while running Windows NT Diagnostics, she attempted to change the type of CPU that was reported but could not. Why?

    A. NT Diagnostics only shows information. You cannot make any modifications using this tool.

    B. The type of CPU cannot be changed with NT Diagnostics. The user must use Registry Editor to make the change manually.

    C. The user must make the CPU change in CMOS setup, not in NT Diagnostics.

    D. Kristin does not have sufficient permissions to make the change.

9. If a Windows NT-based workstation moonlighting as a print server appears too sluggish to the user while printing is taking place, what action should be done on the priority level of the print service?

    A. Raise the priority by one or two classes.

    B. Raise the priority by three to four classes.

    C. Lower the priority by one or two classes.

    D. Make no change—the priority level does not affect this service.

10. To change the priority class of a print service, edit which component of the Registry?

    A. HKEY_LOCAL_MACHINE\ System\CurrentControlSet

    B. HKEY_LOCAL_MACHINE\ System\CurrentControlSet\Control

    C. HKEY_LOCAL_MACHINE\ System\CurrentControlSet\Control\Print

    D. HKEY_LOCAL_MACHINE\ System\CurrentControlSet\ Control\Printers

6

11. RAS can use which protocols for dial-out connections? (Choose all correct answers.)

    A. TCP/IP

    B. NWLink

    C. NetBEUI

    D. SMTP

12. Of the protocols RAS supports for dial-in and dial-out, which benefits from being available on a number of different platforms and is easily routable?

    A. TCP/IP

    B. NWLink

    C. NetBEUI

    D. SMTP

13. Which statement regarding the version of Network Monitor included with Windows NT Resource Kit is true?

    A. It can monitor only the system upon which it was installed.

    B. It can monitor any system on the network.

    C. It is not included with the Resource Kit, but rather a component of the NT distribution disks.

    D. It will not collect TCP/IP information until SMTP is installed.

14. Common causes of physical network problems include which two of the following:

    A. Transmission media

    B. NIC cards

    C. Fax/Data modems in Workstations

    D. Insufficient video RAM

15. Which of the following tools should be used to check network traffic:

    A. Cable analyzer

    B. Diagnostics program

    C. A network protocol analyzer

    D. Performance Monitor

16. Mary calls to say that she is having trouble with networking in a non-routed TCP/IP environment. What two pieces of information had to be given to enable networking in this environment:

    A. Number of servers

    B. IP address

    C. Subnet mask

    D. Host name

17. Karen calls to report that she cannot log on to the system. She is getting a message that says "NT cannot log you on. Check your userid and password information and try again" As an administrator, what should you check first?

    A. Make sure that she types in the correct password and userid combination. Also check that she has entered the password in the correct case and is specifying the correct domain name.

    B. Nothing. It's a normal message that a user would get when the server is down for maintenance.

    C. Log on as administrator and restart the domain controller to clear out any unused connections. When the server comes back up, Karen should be able to log on.

    D. Check the System log in Event Viewer.

18. If disk striping with parity is implemented of three drives with free space of 250 MB, 400 MB, and 900 MB, respectively, what is the size of the data that can be stored on the stripe set?

    A. 250 MB

    B. 500 MB

    C. 750 MB

    D. 2700 MB

19. When do changes take place in Disk Administrator?

    A. When they are implemented.

    B. When they are committed.

    C. When you exit the program.

    D. When you reboot the server.

20. What is stored in the BOOT.INI file?

    A. Information about the previous operating system.

    B. Properties associated with the video card.

    C. Information on services and drivers that fail to start.

    D. The ARC path of partitions.

Answers and Explanations: Practice Exam

1. **D** There is no such utility for converting NTFS back to FAT.

2. **D** Booting with LastKnownGood boot gets around recent driver change problems.

3. **C** Never try to make a problem harder than it is. If the error message says BOOTSECT.DOS is missing, it is probably BOOTSECT.DOS that is missing.

4. **A** BOOTSECT.DOS is a copy of the information that was originally on the boot sector of the drive before NT was installed. You use it to boot an operating system other than NT.

5. **B** BOOTSECT.DOS can be borrowed from another machine if the two machines are identical in every way.

6. **C** You can filter the log by choosing View, Filter Events.

7. **D** The Windows NT Diagnostics utility is perfect for this task.

8. **A** NT Diagnostics only shows information. You cannot make any modifications using this tool.

9. **C** If a Windows NT-based workstation moonlighting as a print server appears to print too slowly, consider raising the priority by one or two classes. If the workstation is responding sluggishly to the user while printing, consider lowering the priority by a class or two.

10. **C** To change the priority class for the Spooler service, add a value called PriorityClass of type REG_DWORD to HKEY_LOCAL_MACHINE\ System\CurrentControlSet\Control\Print and set it so that it is equal to the priority class desired.

11. **A, B, C** RAS supports TCP/IP, NWLink, and NetBEUI protocols for both dial-in and dial-out connections.

12. **A** TCP/IP benefits from being available on a number of different platforms, being easily routable, and having the compatibility choice of the Internet.

13. **B** The Network Monitor included with Windows NT Server can monitor only the specific system on which it is installed, unlike the Network Monitor in Microsoft's Systems Management Server package, which can monitor other systems on the network.

14. **A, B** Network problems often are caused by cables, adapters, IRQ conflicts, or problems with transmission media.

15. **C** Use a diagnostics program to check the network adapter card. Use a cable analyzer to check the cabling. Use Network Monitor to check network traffic, or use a network protocol analyzer.

6

16. **B, C**   The IP address and the subnet mask must be given when TCP/IP is installed in a non-routed environment.

17. **A**   If users can't log on, they might be using an incorrect username or password.

18. **B**   The size of the stripe set becomes the size of the smallest amount of free space on any drive multiplied by the number of drives. The stripe set is then divided by the number of drives to come up with the parity information, and what remains is used for data storage.

19. **B**   Disk Administrator changes are not made until you commit the changes.

20. **D**   BOOT.INI stores the ARC path to partitions. It must be edited to reflect changes in the event of a mirrored drive failure.

Practice Exam 1

Implementing and Supporting Microsoft Windows NT Server 4.0

NT Server exam instructions:

You have 90 minutes to complete 67 questions. The Passing score is 764 out of 1000. There will be two types of questions:

- Multiple Choice—Select the correct answer.
- Multiple Multiple Choice—Select all answers that are correct.

We suggest that you set a timer to track your progress while taking the practice exam, since the time-constraint on the tests is often a big obstacle to overcome.

Begin after you set your timer.

Practice Exam Begins

1. In the Control Panel, the Virtual Memory settings are controlled by which applet?
   - A. Devices icon
   - B. Server icon
   - C. Services icon
   - D. System icon
   - E. None of the above

2. Windows NT Server will automatically load which of the following services? Select all that apply:
   - A. Computer Browser
   - B. Schedule
   - C. RPC Locator
   - D. Server
   - E. Workstation

3. Which permissions can be assigned to a given directory (folder) under Windows NT Server (using NTFS partition)?
   - A. No Access
   - B. Deny
   - C. Change
   - D. Full Control
   - E. Share Folder
   - F. Scan

4. When copying files from a Windows NT NTFS partition to a Windows NT FAT partition, what will happen to the file-level permissions for the file that is copied?

   A. They are retained.

   B. The new file permissions granted will be Full Control rights.

   C. FAT permissions override NTFS permissions.

   D. All NTFS permissions are dropped.

5. What is the best reason for the creation of a user's home directory on a Windows NT PDC?

   A. So that there is a centralized location to back up all the data from the user.

   B. To allow other users to gain access of that user's data.

   C. So that data can be shared with all users from other trusted domains.

   D. Increased performance.

6. Printing priorities that can be assigned to a printer are in a range from:

   A. 1 through 255

   B. 1 through 100

   C. 1 through 64

   D. 1 through 99

   E. 1 through 10

   F. Printer priorities cannot be changed.

7. You want to ensure that your backup procedures and restore processes are fully completed and accurate. Which of the following options would you select to make sure a backup/restore was successful?

   A. Perform a backup on a single file to a tape device; and verify that the file exists on the tape. Next, restore the file on the hard drive to verify the backup and restore process.

   B. Select Verify when performing a complete backup.

   C. Select Verify when performing a complete restore.

   D. Restore files to a different path option from your backup procedure and compare the restore files with the original files.

   E. Perform a backup once a month.

8. You are the administrator of your Windows NT Domain and decide to delegate the responsibilities to perform auditing to other users on your team. By default, which members of the following groups can perform auditing?

   A. Backup Operator's group

   B. Server Operator's group

   C. Everyone's group

   D. Administrator's group

   E. None of the above

9. You are working on your Windows NT Workstation using the User Manager for Domains utility from the Server Tools option on the CD-ROM. You are about to create new users for the domain you are in. Where is the user account information being stored?

   A. On the Windows NT Workstation on which you are currently working

   B. Windows NT Backup Domain Controller

   C. Windows NT Member Server

   D. Windows NT Primary Domain Controller

   E. Windows NT Primary Domain Controller from the other Domain

10. You are in charge of your MIS team. You noticed that users are complaining about missing files. You want to be able to track files and directory accesses. Which of the following must be selected to achieve this, assuming NTFS partitions?

    A. Logon and Logoff

    B. Process Tracking

    C. Use of User Rights

    D. User and Group Management

    E. File and Object Access

11. You are working at night in a high-volume manufacturing plant. Your network consists of 150 Member Servers, four Backup Domain Controllers, 355 Windows NT Workstations, and 56 Windows 95 clients. An alarm goes off, indicating that your Primary Domain Controller has gone down. What will be your first reaction to this situation?

    A. Install a new Primary Domain Controller.

    B. Upgrade one of the Backup Domain Controllers to Primary.

   C. Do nothing, one of the four Backup Domain Controllers will promote itself to Primary.

   D. Upgrade any one of the Windows NT Workstations to Primary Domain Controller.

   E. Select the closest physical Backup Domain Controller and promote it to Primary Domain Controller.

   F. Do nothing.

12. How does a member of the Domain Administrator's Group receive the proper rights to administrate every computer with the domain design?

    A. Domain administrators automatically have full access to all computers in the domain.

    B. The Domain Administrator's Global Group content is automatically added to the Local Group Power Users when the computer is joined to the domain.

    C. The Domain Administrator's Local Group contents are automatically added to the Local Group Administrator's Group by default.

    D. The Domain Administrator's Global Group is added to the Local Group Administrators automatically when the computer joins the domain.

13. Windows NT Server 4.0 DS (Directory Services) provides which of the following features? Select all that apply:

    A. Single-user logon

    B. Automated backup operations

    C. Decentralized administration

    D. Centralized administration

    E. Universal access to resources

    F. Single access to a resource

14. In which situation would a Windows NT Domain configuration be used in preference to a workgroup model?

   A. When no security is required.

   B. When the maximum number of users for a workgroup model has exceeded 100 users.

   C. When there is no clearly defined system administrator and everyone must share administrative responsibilities.

   D. When security is required.

15. Which of the following files on a Windows NT Application server under NTFS should be backed up on a daily basis? Select all that apply:

   A. User data on the server

   B. Directories

   C. Operating system files

   D. MS-DOS boot files

   E. System Registry

   F. SQL database

16. You are working in the network communication room and need to send a message to all users that the Windows NT Server will be off-line for six hours. How do you send the message to the connected users in your domain?

   A. Use the SEND option in the Network Client Admin Utility.

   B. Use the SEND option in User Manager for Domains.

   C. Use the SEND option in Events Manager.

   D. Use the SEND option in Server Manager.

   E. There is no such option.

17. Which of the following administrative utilities is used to manage administrative alerts?

   A. User Profile Manager

   B. System Policy Editor

   C. WinMSD

   D. Server Manager

   E. Disk Administrator

   F. Alert Monitor

18. You have just created a printer on your Windows NT Print Server and then shared the printer. What must a client do when he is connecting to that shared printer so that the print driver will make the client's workstation print to the shared printer?

   A. Copy the print driver to the client's memory as the client logs on the NT Domain.

   B. Share the print driver with the printer.

   C. Make sure that the print driver is compatible with ALPHA, MIPS, INTEL chipsets.

   D. The client does nothing. This procedure is automatic when the client prints the document to that shared printer.

19. Which application would you use on your Primary Domain Controller to view the roles of all the computers in your network?

   A. Explorer

   B. Server Manager

   C. User Manager for Domains

   D. Network Administrator

   E. Control Panel, System

   F. None of the above

20. Your network uses three protocols—TCP/IP, NetBEUI, and NWLink. The binding order of these protocols on your Windows NT Server and Windows NT Workstation is the following: NetBEUI, NWLink, and TCP/IP. The users on your network are accessing resources using NWLink. Where must the binding order sequence of your three protocols be changed to increase the performance of your network?

   A. On the Windows NT Server only.

   B. On the Windows NT Workstation only.

   C. On the PDC only.

   D. On the BDC only.

   E. On the PDC, BDC, and Windows NT Workstations.

21. Susan is installing TCP/IP protocol on a Windows NT server that is a member in the domain. Susan manually assigns a TCP/IP address to the member server. What other parameters must she specify to install TCP/IP protocol on her Windows NT server?

   A. The DHCP server IP address scheme

   B. The WINS server IP address scheme

   C. The default gateway address

   D. The subnet mask

22. There are several WFW 3.11 Workstations that are part of your Windows NT domain that need access to resources that are located on a NetWare 3.12 server. How can you set up the WFW 3.11 Workstations so that they can access the NetWare 3.12 server without adding additional client software to their workstations?

   A. By installing NWLink protocol on the Windows NT Server.

   B. By installing IPX/SPX protocol on the Windows NT Server.

   C. By installing IPX/SPX protocol on the WFW 3.11 Workstations.

   D. By installing Gateway Services for NetWare on the WFW 3.11 clients.

   E. By installing Gateway Services for NetWare on the Windows NT Server.

   F. By doing nothing.

23. There are 75 Windows NT Workstations running NT 4.0 on your network. These workstations print to a Windows NT member server that is acting as a print server. You just downloaded from the Internet an updated print driver that must be implemented. What is the best way to update the new print driver to all 75 Windows NT Workstations?

   A. Go to all 75 Windows NT Workstations and update the driver.

   B. Update the driver on the Windows NT PDC.

   C. Update the driver on the Windows print server.

   D. Update the driver on the Windows NT print server, and when the workstations connect, the driver will install on each workstation.

24. You have 200 MS-DOS computers on your network. You decided to install Windows NT 4.0 Workstation on all 200 computers. How would you install Windows NT Workstation 4.0 on all 200 MS-DOS computers?

   A. Connect to a network share directory that contains the

Windows NT 4.0 CD-ROM
and run SETUP.EXE from the
\i386 directory.

B. From a MS-DOS prompt, type
WINNT32.EXE from the \i386
directory.

C. You cannot install Windows NT
4.0 OS with MS-DOS already
installed.

D. Connect to a network share
directory that contains the
Windows NT 4.0 CD-ROM
and run WINNT.EXE from the
\i386 directory.

E. FDISK.EXE and slice the disk.

25. You have RAS services running on
your Windows NT Server. You have a
RAS problem occurs and you want to
troubleshoot this problem. You have
enabled the RAS log file called
device.log. In your Windows NT RAS
Server, where is device.log located?

A. WINNT directory

B. WINNT\SYSTEM directory

C. C:\

D. WINNT\SYSTEM32\REPL
directory

E. WINNT\SYSTEM32\RAS
directory

26. Which of the following is an example
of RAID 0 on Windows NT Server?

A. Four disk drives

B. Two logical partitions

C. Two disk drives mirrored

D. Two disk drives duplexed

E. Two hard drives

27.   You have been notified by management that you will receive a new tape
device to be installed in your Windows NT Server. You already have a
spare SCSI controller in your lab. You

installed the tape device and controller in your server. What should you do
to enable these devices? Select all that
apply:

A. Install the driver for the tape
device.

B. Install the driver for SCSI.

C. Install the driver for the controller.

D. Do nothing.

E. Reboot.

F. Install the driver for the first
controller again.

28. You have a Primary Domain Controller installed on your new network.
You installed Visual FoxPro application on your PDC. How would you
tune your server for clients to access
this server to query the FoxPro
Database?

A. Minimum memory used

B. Balance

C. Maximize throughput for file
sharing

D. Maximize throughput for
network applications

E. It's dynamic

29. Mike wants to design a fault-tolerance
solution to his SQL NT server. He
has a UPS connected to the server, but
this unit has a very limited battery
supply time. Which fault-tolerance
solution should Mike design? Select
all that apply:

A. Volume sets

B. Stripe sets without parity

C. Stripe sets with parity

D. Mirror sets

E. Duplex sets

F. Both A and B

G. Both D and B

H. None of the above

30. You have received a piece of hardware and installed it in your Windows NT server. You have installed the driver for the hardware device, and the Windows NT server cannot boot anymore. What is the easiest way to troubleshoot this boot problem for your Windows NT Server?

    A. FDISK.

    B. Reinstall Windows NT Server.

    C. Boot to the Emergency Repair Disk—restore the registry.

    D. Select Windows NT VGA Boot Mode.

    E. Select Last Known Good.

    F. Boot to MS-DOS, and then run WINNT /B switch for repair.

31. You are running Windows NT Workstation 4.0 and have one partition, C drive. The file format is FAT and you have one page file on the local drive. How would you convert this format to NTFS?

    A. Format C: /NTFS

    B. Convert C:/FAT /NTFS

    C. NTFS C:

    D. Convert C: /NTFS /FAT /Y

    E. Cannot convert FAT to NTFS on only one partition

    F. Convert C: /FS:NTFS /V

    G. None of the above

32. You want to use a Null Modem. Which of the following are valid statements for a Null Modem? Select all that apply:

    A. To test and evaluate a Remote Access Server locally

    B. To enable subnet routing from location x to location y over Frame Relay

    C. To have a Windows NT Workstation attached to two different networks that are not physically attached by a 10BaseT cable

    D. To have Windows NT Workstation log into a DOMAIN A without a network interface card installed and protocol binded

    E. Cannot use NULL MODEM cable under Windows NT

33. What is the minimum amount of hardware configurations for disk duplexing?

    A. One drive and two controllers

    B. Two drives and one controller

    C. Two drives and four controllers

    D. Disk duplexing is not supported under Windows NT

    F. Two drives and three controllers

    G. Two drives and two controllers with the same controller architecture

    H. Two drives and two controllers without the same controller architecture

34. You have a UNIX network and want to introduce Windows NT Server. What is the best protocol to use to connect to a UNIX environment?

    A. NetBEIU

    B. IPX/SPX

    C. NWLink

    D. DLC

    E. TCP/IP

    F. None of the above

35. You have created a printer pool under Windows NT Server 4.0. You have configured 10 print devices. Which condition must be met to have all 10 print devices communicate in the printer pool?

    A. All 10 devices must have the same protocol.

B. All 10 devices must be located on the same physical floor.

C. You cannot create a printer pool in NT 4.0.

D. All print devices must use COM2 port.

E. All print devices must use LPT1 port.

F. All devices must be connected to the same Print Server destination.

36. Frank is a design graphics artist in his art department. He is running on Windows NT 4.0 Workstation with 1.5GB SCSI disk on a Pentium 166 Mhz system. His default spooler folder is on the 1.5GB hard drive known as C:. He is running out of space, so he added another drive with a 4 GB capacity. How can Frank move his default spooler folder to the new hard drive known as D:?

A. Modify the print driver.

B. Reinstall Windows NT Workstation.

C. Modify Printer Control Option in Settings, Control Panel.

D. Modify the Registry by using the command \HKEYLocalMachine\ System\Microsoft\Printers.

E. Modify the Registry by using the command HKEYLocalMachine\ System\CurrentControlSet\ Control\Print\Printers.

F. None of the above.

37. You have field sales representatives moving around the country on a weekly basis. They want to gain access to the company's network over the Internet by a RAS service. What method would you use to provide

access to network over the Internet and provide security?

A. TCP/IP

B. PPP (Point to Point Protocol)

D. ISDN connection

E. X.25 connection

F. SLIP connection

G. PPTP connection

38. In which configuration can a Windows NT system partition and boot information be supported?

A. RAID 0

B. RAID 5

C. RAID 1

D. RAID 10 (Software)

E. Volume sets

F. Stripe sets without parity

G. Windows NT does not support the above options

39. John has access to the Disk Administrator program, and he tried to delete the Windows NT System Partition. What results would you expect from the system?

A. Continue with Deletion (YES) or (NO)

B. System Partition Deleted

C. Dialog Box appears and prompts you to "Commit Changes Now"

D. System Reboots Automatically

E. Error message appears

40. Sam misplaced his three Windows NT Server 4.0 setup disks. He needs to re-create them. How can Same accomplished this task?

A. Call Microsoft Support.

B. Run WINNT32.EXE /B.

C. Run WINNT32.EXE /R.

D. Run SETUP.EXE.

E. Run WINNT.EXE.

41. Susan is a domain administrator for the Sales domain. She constantly is updating the logon scripts for her 350-user database. What is the best method she can use to ensure that the logon scripts are replicated correctly?

    A. Store the logon scripts in the following directory: WINNT\SYSTEM32\REPL\EXPORTS and replicate to all domain controllers.

    B. Store the logon scripts in the following directory: WINNT\SYSTEM32\REPL\EXPORTS and replicate to all Windows NT Workstations.

    C. Store the logon scripts in the following directory: WINNT\SYSTEM32\REPL\IMPORTS and replicate to all Windows NT Workstations.

    D. Store the logon scripts in the following directory: WINNT\SYSTEM32\REPL\EXPORTS and replicate to all Windows NT PDC Domain Controllers.

    E. Store the logon scripts in the following directory: WINNT\SYSTEM32\REPL\EXPORTS, create a subdirectory under EXPORTS, and replicate to all Backup Domain Controllers.

42. How can Lucy convert from NTFS back to FAT?

    A. Run CONVERT.EXE NTFS FAT.

    B. Run CONVERT.EXE NTFS C:\FS:FAT.

    C. Run CONVERT.EXE /FAT.

    D. Cannot be converted.

    E. Lucy must format the disk, choose FAT, and then reinstall the operating system, applications, and data.

43. You just installed a new printer on your Windows NT 4.0 Print Server. You go to a Windows NT Workstation and submit a print job for testing by right-clicking on the new printer object and then selecting properties and pressing the Print Test Page button. When the job prints, it comes out as garbage. What is the most likely cause of the problem?

    A. DLC protocol is not installed.

    B. Ran out of disk space.

    C. The Print Spooler is corrupted.

    D. The Print Router is corrupted.

    E. Incorrect print driver is installed.

44. By default, the initial paging file is determined by which of the following formulas?

    A. 24 + initial memory

    B. 16 + initial memory

    C. 12 + initial memory

    D. 32 + initial memory

    E. Random number

    F. None of the above

45. Which of the following protocols can be used as a dial-out protocol for Windows NT Server?

    A. TCP/IP only.

    B. NWLink only.

    C. NetBEUI, NWLink.

    D. NWLink, NetBEUI, and TCP/IP.

    E. None of the above can be used as a dial-out protocol.

46. Mike wants to set up Directory Replication in his network. Which of the following configurations would accomplish this goal? Select all that apply:

    A. Windows NT Member Server.

    B. Windows NT Primary Domain Controller.

C. Windows NT Backup Domain
   Controller.

D. Windows NT Workstation.

E. Directory Replication is not
   supported.

47. You're running Windows NT Server
    4.0 and you launched 3GL Screen
    Saver. You noticed that the system is
    running SQL queries extremely
    slowly. Which counters would you use
    from Performance Monitor to deter-
    mine whether the CPU is being hit
    hard? Select all that apply:

A. %USAGE PEAK

B. %MEMORY PAGES/SEC

C. %PROCESS

D. %PROCESSOR TIME

E. System Object Processor Queue
   Length

F. %Interrupt Time

G. %DPC

48. You wanted to use a null modem
    cable in Windows NT Server 4.0.
    Which of the following ways are true
    tests? Select all that apply:

A. Subnet routing

B. Testing another Windows NT
   RAS Server locally in your test
   lab

C. Using Windows 95 Workstation
   to access the domain of which
   they are a member without any
   hardware network interface cards

D. None of the above

49. You have a UNIX system across the
    campus in your college network. You
    have just installed Windows NT
    Workstation on your local network.
    To be able to use the router from
    building A to building B, what
    protocol must you install on Windows
    NT Workstation?

A. DLC

B. SNA

C. NetBEUI

D. NWLink

E. TCP/IP

F. X.25

G. Frame Relay

50. You hire Stacy to work in your IS
    dept. Stacy's responsibility for the first
    two weeks is to create user accounts in
    your Windows NT domain. You do
    not want to give Stacy full administra-
    tive rights. You created her account,
    and by default she belongs to the
    Domain User Account. In which
    group would you place Stacy to enable
    her to create accounts?

A. Domain Administrator group

B. Backup Operator group

C. Server Operator group

D. Account Operator group

E. None of the above

F. All of the above

51. Mike just purchased a laptop to work
    both at the office and at home. When
    he comes to work in the morning, he
    inserts his laptop into the docking
    station, which contains an external
    CD-ROM writer. Later, Mike leaves
    the office and goes home to work on a
    spreadsheet document. When he boots
    his laptop running Windows NT
    Workstation, an error message appears:
    "One or more services failed to start.
    See the Event Viewer for details." Mike
    does not want the device drivers to
    load on his CD-ROM unit that is
    attached to his docking station while
    he works at home. How can Mike
    accomplish this without any errors
    appearing when he's booting at home?

A. Reinstall Windows NT at home.

B.   Create a separate user account
     for home.

C.   Create a separate user account
     for work.

D.   Boot with the emergency repair
     disk.

E.   Create a roaming account for
     home.

F.   Create a separate hardware
     profile.

52.   You have an MS-DOS application
      that does not support UNC redirec-
      tion to a remote printer. Which of the
      following options makes it possible to
      print out to a remote printer from
      your MS-DOS application under
      Windows NT Workstation 4.0?

A.   NT does not support MS-DOS
     printing.

B.   Map LPT1 \\print server
     name\printer name.

C.   Install MS-DOS Printing
     Services from your Windows
     NT Server CD-ROM.

D.   Download redirection program
     from http://www.microsoft.com/
     support/printing.

E.   Map a physical port to the
     network printer in your network.

F.   None of the above.

53.   You just installed seven Windows NT
      Version 4.0 Workstations in your
      network. They are installed with
      NWLink protocol only and you can
      see all seven NT Workstations. You go
      home over the weekend and come in
      on Monday morning to add another
      Windows NT Workstation. After you
      installed the NT Workstation Version
      3.51, you could not see the original
      seven. What is most likely the cause of
      this problem?

A.   The protocol is corrupted.

B.   Reboot NT Workstation again.

C.   There is a mismatch in Windows
     NT Workstation Build Numbers.

D.   Windows NT Version 4.0 is not
     compatible with Windows NT
     Version 3.51.

E.   There is a frame mismatch.

54.   You have 10 workstations connected
      to your local Windows NT Server.
      Which of the following optimization
      methods would be the best choice in
      this situation?

A.   Maximize throughput for
     Network Applications

B.   Maximize throughput for File
     Sharing

C.   Minimize memory used

D.   Balance

E.   None

55.   You discovered that you could use
      Windows NT Server as a router. You
      purchase two network adapter cards
      and physically install them in your
      server. The two networks that you
      must connect have the following IP
      addresses assigned to each segment:
      Segment # 1—150.50.0.0 and
      Segment #2—150.51.0.0. You must
      configure the IP addresses of the two
      network cards in your NT Server.
      Which of the following addresses
      would you choose?

A.   150.50.0.99, 150.50.0.100

B.   150.50.0.0, 150.50.0.1

C.   150.50.0.1, 150.51.0.1

D.   150.50.0.50, 150.51.50.1

E.   None of the above

56.   Chris wants to use LFN on both
      Windows 95 and Windows NT 4.0
      Workstation products on one ma-
      chine. Which of the following file
      system structures would satisfy Chris'
      requirements?

A. HPFS

B. NTFS

C. FAT32

D. FAT

E. CDFS

F. FAT8

57. You executed the Windows NT registry by REGEDT32.EXE from a command prompt. You edited an entry in the network section and then rebooted the Windows NT server. Your Windows NT Server comes up with a blue screen. What is the best way to get the server back to the original state?

A. Boot to ERD.

B. Reinstall.

C. Boot to MS-DOS, and then execute NTOSKRNL.EXE.

D. Boot to MS-DOS, and then execute NTLDR.EXE /B.

E. Press the spacebar, select Last Known Good by selecting L, and then press Enter.

58. You installed a Windows NT Server running DHCP. You created a scope of addresses with an IP expiration of 20 days. You changed a Windows NT Workstation from static address to DHCP to get an IP address from the server. The next day your DHCP Server crashes. How long will it take for the NT Workstation to request for a renewal of the IP address?

A. 20 days

B. 1 day

C. 5 days

D. 15 days

E. Infinity

F. 0 days

G. 10.5 days

H. 17.5 days

59. You have installed a color laser printer and want your users to use it, but it will not be available off-hours. What will happen to all the print jobs that are queued to the new color laser printer during the regular peak hours during the day, but are not printed at that time?

A. The print jobs must be printed no matter what.

B. The print jobs must be redirected to another printer.

C. The print jobs will be removed automatically if no printer is available.

D. The print jobs will be stored in a temp. directory.

E. The print jobs will be stored in the print spooler.

60. You have TCP/IP installed on your network. You want to gather some performance analysis remotely from a Windows NT Server in your local domain. On your Windows NT Workstation, you invoke perfmon.exe from the command prompt. What must you do before tracking the TCP/IP performance counters on your network from your local Windows NT Workstation?

A. Install SNMP Service on all systems.

B. Install SNMP Service on your workstation.

C. Install SNMP Service on all BDCs.

D. Install SNMP Service on your PDC.

E. Install SNMP Service on the server.

61. What is the most likely cause of the following error message when booting up Windows NT Server or Workstation Product: "Can't find NTLDR."

    A. The disk is corrupt.
    B. You are using IDE only.
    C. Mirroring is corrupted.
    D. Raid 5 is corrupted.
    E. There is a floppy in the disk drive.

62. Tim has an account in the Newriders Domain. Tim is currently set up to log into the Newriders Domain. What must Tim do if he wants to use a resource in the Sams Domain?

    A. Set up a two-way trust relationship by using User Manager for Domains.
    B. Set up a one-way trust relationship from Newriders Domain to trust Sams Domain.
    C. Set up a one-way trust relationship from Sams Domain to Trust Newriders Domain.
    D. Do nothing.

63. You have an SCSI drive in your Windows NT Server environment. The boot partition is located by the following path: c:\winnt, which is SCSI. Jumpers on the board disable the BIOS for the SCSI adapter card. You want to create a recovery disk. Which of the following files need to be placed on the recovery disk? Select all that apply:

    A. SCSI.DRV
    B. SCSI.SYS
    C. OSLOADER.EXE
    D. BOOTSCSI.DOS
    E. BOOT.INI
    F. NTLDR
    G. NTDETECT.COM
    H. FAT.SYS
    I. NTBOOTDD.SYS
    J. All of the above

64. Which of the following is required in order for a Windows NT Workstation 4.0 running CSNW to access a NetWare 3.12 server? Select all that apply:

    A. NWLink Protocol
    B. TCP/IP Protocol
    C. GSNW
    D. User Account on Windows NT
    E. User Account on NetWare Server 3.12

65. You have just installed RAS on your Windows NT server. Which of the following encrypted authorization methods provides the most secure environment for RAS connections in this network?

    A. PAP
    B. SPAP
    C. CHAP
    D. LDAP
    E. MS-CHAP

66. You have installed Windows NT 3.51 Server. What will be the best way to upgrade the server to Windows NT 4.0?

    A. Run WINNT.EXE from the NT 4.0 CD-ROM \i386.
    B. Run WINNT32.EXE from the NT 4.0 CD-ROM \i386.
    C. Run WINNT32.EXE from the NT 3.51 directory.
    D. Run WINNT.EXE from the NT 3.51 directory.
    E. Run WINNT32.EXE /NEW from the NT 4.0 CD-ROM \i386.

67. You have a Windows NT RAS server and WINS running on your network. You have Windows NT Workstation clients connecting to your RAS Server

(using TCP/IP). Where should the LMHOSTS and HOST files be placed for the best performance on your network to your RAS clients?

A. In the LMHOST file on the RAS Server only.

B. In the LMHOST and HOST file on the RAS Server only.

C. In the LMHOST and HOST file on all remote clients.

D. In the LMHOST and HOST file on only one remote client.

E. It is not necessary to have LMHOST and HOST files on Windows NT RAS clients.

Answers and Explanations

1. **D** The System icon contains the Virtual Memory setting. By default, Windows NT uses the formula, 12 MB + physical memory, as the base start for Virtual Memory. To change the Virtual Memory, go to the Performance Property Page, select Change Button, and then select the drive for the Virtual Memory value. Performance is the best when the paging file is off the operating system drive.

2. **A, C, D, E** The Schedule service is used to work the with AT utility. The Task Scheduler starts each time Windows NT boots if this service is set to automatic. The at command schedules commands and programs to run on a computer at a specified time and date. The Schedule service must be running to use the at command. Note that in Control Panel, Services there are three options for startup: Disabled, Manual, and Automatic.

The at command runs the command on every specified day(s) of the week

or month (for example, every Thursday, or the third day of every month). Specify date as one or more days of the week (M,T,W,Th,F,S,Su) or one or more days of the month (using numbers 1 through 31). Separate multiple date entries with commas. If the date is omitted, the current day of the month is assumed.

A. /next:date[,...]

Runs the specified command on the next occurrence of the day (for example, next Thursday). Specify date as one or more days of the week (M,T,W,Th,F,S,Su) or one or more days of the month (using numbers 1 through 31). Separate multiple date entries with commas. If date is omitted, the current day of the month is assumed.

3. **D** By default under Windows NTFS, creating a new folder will assign the group Everyone full control access to that folder created. You must then reset the permissions for that folder if you want to reassign rights. You can view the properties content of the folder by right-clicking on it.

4. **D** When moving a file from NTFS (security based on Folder/File structure), the FAT file structure does not support advanced security indexes on each file/folder format. So, for example, if a file contained Change permissions, it will lose that file right attribute when copied to a FAT partition.

5. **A** The Home Directory is a place where users can save their data on the NT Server. Because the server is backed up from proper backup procedures, all the users' data are saved and organized.

6. **D** You can change the order of documents in the print queue only if you have Full Control access permissions. Members of the Administrators, Server Operators, Print Operators, or Power Users groups have Full Control permission by default. Priority 1 is the lowest, and priority 99 is the highest; you can control the priority by moving the slide bar from the property sheet of any print object by right-clicking on it.

7. **D** Backing up files to a device media, such as DAT system, and then restoring those files to a different path, verifies complete backup and restores functionality.

8. **D** Auditing is turned off by default under Windows NT. Only the Administrators (members of the Administrator group) can turn on Auditing. Auditing is activated through the User Manager for Domains, Policies menu. Auditing Events are placed in the Event Viewer, which is located in the Administrator Tools Group. With Event Viewer, you can troubleshoot various hardware and software problems. You can also use Event Viewer to monitor Windows NT Server security events, which are significant system or program problems about which users should be notified.

9. **D** Windows NT Primary Domain Controller contains the master database for all users groups. A read-only copy of the directory services database is replicated to all Backup Domain Controllers in the domain model. User Manager for Domains enables you to manage security for domains and computers. This includes creating and managing user accounts and groups, and managing

the domain's security policies such as accounts (passwords), user rights, auditing, and trust relationships.

10. **E** You must select File and Object Access. This way you can track user access to a directory or a file on an NTFS partition that is set for directory or file auditing, and you can monitor files that are sent to printers when the printers are set for printer auditing.

Audit Policy

Selected activities of users can be tracked by auditing security events and then placing the entries in a computer's security log. Use the Audit policy to determine the types of security events that will be logged.

When administering domains, the Audit policy affects the security logs of the domain controller and of all servers in the domain, because they share the same Audit policy.

When administering a computer running Windows NT Workstation or a Windows NT Server that is not a domain controller (a member server), this policy affects only the security log of that computer.

Because the security log is limited in size, carefully click on events to be logged. The maximum size of each computer's security log is defined in Event Viewer. Entries in a security log can be reviewed using Event Viewer. Managing your computer's security with User Manager for Domains enables you to manage security for domains and computers. This includes creating and managing user accounts and groups, and managing the domain's security policies such as accounts (passwords), user rights, auditing, and trust relationships.

11. **E**   Windows NT BDC will not automatically promote itself to PDC status. You must go to the closest BDC and promote it to PDC in Server Manager Utility. You can use Server Manager to administer domains and computers. With Server Manager, you can display the member computers of a domain, manage server properties and services for a selected computer, share directories, and send messages to connected users.

    You can also use Server Manager to reassign a backup domain controller as the primary domain controller, synchronize computers with the primary domain controller, and add or remove computers in a domain.

12. **D**   Global groups can cross trusted domains. A Global group can be imported to a Local group. By default, members of the Global group domain will be added to the Administrator Local group when the computer joins the Domain.

13. **A, D, E**   With Directory Services, users can have a single logon to the domain model and have access to all resources assigned to them if the users are placed into groups. Directory Services also provides full centralized administration—up to 40,000 users.

14. **B**   Using a domain model provides centralized security by requiring the users to be checked against a security system before being allowed into the Domain. If the user is not a member of the Domain, the user does not have access to resources. User Manager for Domains enables you to manage security for domains and computers. This includes creating and managing user accounts and

groups, and managing the domain's security policies such as accounts (passwords), user rights, auditing, and trust relationships.

15. **A, E, F**   User data is one of the most important pieces of data that should be backed up routinely, because workstations in an environment usually do not have backup devices attached. The SQL database is the heart of most businesses today. It usually contains the financial, accounting, payroll, and mission-critical data that must be backed up on a consistent basis. The Windows NT Registry database is the most important data in the operating system. The registry defines security, applications installed on your server, and users defined in the master database. The System Registry is the mission-critical system file of the Windows NT operating system.

16. **D**   To send a message to all attached to a Windows NT Server, the Server Manager utility located in the Administrator Tools is the best method. You can use Server Manager to administer domains and computers. With Server Manager, you can display the member computers of a domain, manage server properties and services for a selected computer, share directories, and send messages to connected users.

    You can also use Server Manager to reassign a backup domain controller as the primary domain controller, synchronize computers with the primary domain controller, and add or remove computers in a domain.

17. **D**   You can use Server Manager to administer domains and computers. With Server Manager, you can display the member computers of a domain,

manage server properties and services for a selected computer, share directories, and send messages to connected users.

18. **D** The driver is downloaded automatically when the user accesses the shared printer on the network (only if you specify all platforms the Print Server supports at the time you create the printer).

19. **B** Server Manager is used to administer domains and computers on your network. Server Manager can display the member computers of a domain, manage server properties and services for a selected computer, share directories, and send messages to connected users. You can also use Server Manager to reassign a backup domain controller as the primary domain controller, synchronize computers with the primary domain controller, and add or remove computers in a domain.

20. **B** The protocol that is used the most frequently on your network, in this case NWLink, should be bound first. The Windows NT Server can accept any protocol directed to it, but the Windows NT Workstation network performance is controlled by the Windows NT Workstation only.

21. **D** When installing the protocol TCP/IP, the IP address and the subnet mask parameters must be specified on the server.

22. **E** The Gateway Service for NetWare provides access to the NetWare 3.12 server for Workstations that are part of the Microsoft Network. Because these workstations do not have any NetWare client loaded, the Windows NT Server will automatically load

NWLink protocol by default when Gateway Service for NetWare Service is loaded. Essentially, the NT Server mounts the Novel volume.

23. **D** When the workstation connects to the print server, the new updated driver will be copied automatically to each workstation without the user having to do an installation procedure.

24. **D** When you are in Real Mode (MS-DOS), you can run the WINNT.EXE command. This will start the installation process. If you are running the Windows NT 3.51 release, you can use the WINNT32.EXE command for an upgrade. (Installation and Configuration.)

25. **E** The DEVICE.LOG file is located in the WINNT\SYSTEM32\RAS directory. This log traps sessions between the Modem and RAS services.

26. **E** RAID 0 is disk striping without parity. This serves as a performance gain by moving data across two drives at the same time. In this case, RAID 0 does not offer fault tolerance. By defining the two separate physical drives with Disk Administrator, such as Device 0 and Device 1, each drive is striped.

27. **A, C, E** You must install the drivers for all new hardware to be recognized in Windows NT. After the drivers are loaded into memory, you must reboot the server to update the HKEY_LOCAL_MACHINE registry database.

28. **C** Maximize throughput for network applications is used for databases that use memory-caching in their programs.

29. **C, D, E**   Fault tolerance is supported by disk mirroring (two separate physical drives); disk duplexing (two separate physical drives and two separate controllers); and RAID 5, which is disk striping with parity (at least three physical drives).

30. **E**   After installing the new device driver, select Last Known Good by pressing the spacebar at boot up. This will load the original Current Control Set Registry Driver database and recover the system.

31. **F**   You can convert FAT into NTFS format by going to a CMD prompt and typing **Convert C: /FS:NTFS /V**. (/FS represents File System; NTFS represents NTFS file format; and /V represents Verbose Mode.)

32. **A, B, C**   You can use a Null Modem cable to test and stimulate a RAS server locally by using RS232 signaling. Null Modem cable can attach two workstations on two different networks by using the COM ports as the medium of transfer. Frame relay is a packet switch service that does not provide for error detection and correction, which results in minimal routing delays.

33. **G**   You must have two drives and any combination of two controllers that support different technologies; for example, drive one can be attached to IDE controller, whereas drive two can be attached to a SCSI controller. It is recommended to have both controllers of the same technology.

34. **E**   TCP/IP is the protocol that is routable and is the de facto protocol used on the Internet.

35. **F**   To have a printer pool, all devices must be connected to the same Windows NT print server

36. **E**   Modify the spooler folder to the new hard drive by editing the key entry DefaultSpoolDirectory from C:\winnt\system32\spool\printers to D:\winnt\system32\spool\printers.

37. **G**   PPTP is Point to Point Tunneling Protocol that provides security over the Internet into Windows NT RAS server.

38. **C**   Disk Mirroring (RAID 1) supports both system partition and boot partition information.

39. **E**   You cannot delete the system partition that contains Windows NT files. You can, however, delete other partitions—this should be done with extreme caution.

40. **E**   WINNT.EXE is the format used to make the SETUP disks. This format is used in REAL MODE—MS-DOS, Windows 3.x, or Windows 95, for example. When used with the /ox switch, you can create all three boot disks without installing any other Windows NT source files. You can also create boot disks while running Windows NT by using the WINNT32 /ox switch.

41. **E**   When scripts are located in a subdirectory under the Exports directory all files are replicated to all Import Servers, such as Backup Domain Controllers. In the case of a failed PDC, the BDC will authenticate and process any logon scripts to the users due to the replication that takes place from PDC to BDC.

42. **D**   You can convert from FAT to NTFS, but you cannot convert from NTFS to FAT without reformatting the disk. This is a one-way process only.

43. **E**   With a incorrect print driver installed, the document spooling to the print device can be distorted. This is especially true for Post Script drivers that are installed incorrectly.

44. **C**   The initial page file is 12 plus the amount of physical memory that is installed on the server. For example, if the Windows NT Server has 64 MB of RAM, the initial page file is 64 MB plus 12, which equals 76 MB.

45. **D**   All three protocols are supported by both dial-in and dial-out services under Windows NT RAS.

46. **B** and **C**   The configurations that enable user authentication are a PDC and a BDC controller.

47. **D, E**   The percentage of elapsed time a processor spends executing a non-idle thread is measured by the %Processor Time Counter. The number of processors contributing to the processor's usage can be found by evaluating the System Object Queue Length counter. If the processor is over 80% and the System Object Queue Length is greater than the value of 2, a much faster CPU would be recommended. Windows 95 can use dialup networking to be authenticated by a Domain Controller just like NT RAS for a Windows NT Workstation, by asynchronous connection, but without NIC cards.

48. **B, C**   Just remember that a null modem cable is really RS232C cable. You can test a Windows NT Workstation connection to the Windows NT RAS Server without any modems involved by using the null modem cable assembly.

49. **E**   TCP/IP is a routable protocol that can pass through the routers by configuring TCP/IP to route. All UNIX systems use TCP/IP protocol as a de facto because it is the primary protocol used in the Internet.

50. **D**   You can create user accounts when you are a member of the Account Operator Local group, but more importantly, you cannot assign user rights.

51. **F**   When you create a separate hardware profile using Control Panel, System Properties, and choosing Hardware Profiles Property page, you can set what drivers can be loaded from mobile (home) to permanent (docking station at work). After the Windows NT Workstation boots, you must select the spacebar to invoke a different hardware profile.

52. **E**   Map the physical port using the following syntax: net use LPTx: \\server \name\print_share name.

53. **E**   Frame mismatches can cause this error. For example, if the frame is set to 802.2 and you have another workstation configured to use frame 802.3, the frame type structure headers are different. This mismatching means you can't see the frame from the Data Link Layer or the Data Packet.

54. **C**   When you have 10 network connections or fewer, the best optimization would be set to Minimize Memory Used.

55. **C**   You must manually add IP addresses to a router because it is static, not dynamic, such as DHCP. The address range from segment #1 matches 150.50.0.x and segment #2 matches 150.51.0.x on the other segment. This will bridge the two segments together.

56. **D**   FAT supports both Windows 95 and Windows NT 4.0 Workstation

for LFN support. FAT32 is not supported by the Windows NT 4.0 product line.

57. **E** Last Known Good selects the last configuration database from the registry database (a copy of the most recent registry that successfully booted Windows NT).

58. **H** The Windows NT Workstation will broadcast a request to any DHCP server when 87.5% of the lease time has expired (or again at reboot).

59. **E** Any print jobs that are delayed will be stored in the print spooler.

60. **E** The TCP/IP performance counters become available for monitoring when the SNMP Service is installed on the machine you're monitoring.

61. **E** When you leave a floppy disk in the floppy drive system, most computers look into the drive first before booting to the C drive, by default. When Windows NT reboots, the NTLDR file cannot be located from the master boot device (usually the C drive), by default.

62. **B** As long there is an account setup in the domain, a user can join that domain from his workstation by using the settings in Network option and changing the Domain setting within the Control Panel environment.

63. **E, F, G, I** When SCSI is used and the BIOS are disabled, remember to include BOOTSECT.DOS driver.

64. **A, E** When running CSNW, NWLink protocol must be configured to talk IPX to the NetWare server. To gain access inside the NetWare server, a user account also must be created.

65. **E** MS-CHAP, which is RSA Message Digest 4 or RSA MD4, uses the RC4 algorithm and supports the DOD DES encryption. It will encrypt all data structures (including passwords) that are processed during a RAS session connection.

66. **B** When running Windows NT 3.51, you must execute the WINNT32 executable because it runs a 32-bit run code for the upgrade. The best choice is to run it unattended by WINNT32.EXE /U from the NT 4.0 CD-ROM \i386.

67. **C** For the best performance in static name resolution for a Windows NT RAS Server and Windows NT RAS Clients, place both files on the RAS Clients' local cache hard drives. This eliminates traffic by name resolution requests with the WINS server. The LMHOST file is a local text file that maps IP addresses to the computer names of Windows NT networking computers outside the local subnet. In Windows NT, this file is stored in the \systemroot \System32\Drivers\Etc directory.

Practice Exam 2

Implementing and Supporting Microsoft Windows NT Server 4.0

NT Server exam instructions:

You have 90 minutes to complete 55 questions. The Passing score is 764 out of 1,000. There will be two types of questions:

- Multiple Choice—Select the correct answer.
- Multiple Multiple Choice—Select all answers that are correct.

The answers and explanations follow the actual test and include the objective covered in the question. We suggest that you set a timer to track your progress while taking the practice exam, as the time-constraint on the tests is often a big obstacle to overcome. Begin after you set your time.

Practice Exam Begins

1. Jeff is logged in as the local administrator on his NT workstation computer. He needs to have his computer joined to the domain Developers. How can Jeff join his computer to the Developers Domain? Choose all that apply:

    A. The domain administrator for Developers can add Jeff's workstation on the PDC. Then, Jeff can join the domain in the Network option of Control Panel.

    B. Jeff can add his computer to the domain using Server Manager and his administrator password.

    C. The domain administrator can add Jeff to the domain Developers by using the Network option on the PDC.

    D. The administrator of the Developers domain can add Jeff's machine to the domain by using the Network option in Control Panel on Jeff's machine after supplying the domain administrator username and password.

2. You want to change a member server on your domain to a BDC. What is the correct procedure to do so? Choose one:

   A. Promote the member server to a BDC.

   B. Copy the user accounts database to the member server so that it can validate users.

   C. Reinstall the member server as a BDC.

   D. Use the services option in Control Panel to start the BDC service for the member server.

3. Increasing the Pulse registry entry on the PDC does what? Choose one:

   A. Frees memory on the PDC for use by other processes.

   B. Decreases the frequency that BDCs are synchronized, freeing processor time on the PDC.

   C. Increases communication with the BDCs, causing domain information to be updated more frequently.

   D. Increases the number of BDCs allowed on the Domain.

4. The developers department has hired a new user named Mary. You would like to add a user account for Mary with the same attributes as an existing worker in the department. Using User Manager for Domains, what procedure would you follow? Choose one:

   A. Select the existing user and choose New User from the user pulldown.

   B. Create a new user for Mary, and then copy the existing user's profile to Mary's account.

   C. Create a new user, and then use Edit, Copy Permissions to copy the existing user's permissions.

   D. Select the existing user's account and choose User, Copy.

5. You have created roaming profiles for users in your domain. Your coworkers suggest that you rename the NTUser.dat to NTUser.man. What will this accomplish? Choose one:

   A. This enables users to choose whether or not to run the profile at login.

   B. This has no affect on the profile.

   C. This enables the user to change the profile.

   D. This keeps the user from saving any changes to the profile.

6. The users in your domain would like to be able to log in at any workstation while retaining desktop attributes specific to each user. How would you implement this? Choose one:

   A. As long as the users are logging onto the domain at each work-station, their individual profiles will be used by default.

   B. Use the User Manager for Domains to specify the full UNC profile path for each user.

   C. A copy of each user's profile must be placed on the NETLOGON share.

   D. Set up replication to copy all user profiles to each machine.

7. Where would you look to find out why RAS connections from many different users to your NT Server are being dropped after users have been connected for various amounts of time? Choose one:

   A. The device.log.

   B. Use the administrative tools Event Viewer on the RAS Server.

   C. The ras.log.

   D. The remote machine's Event Viewer.

8. Which of the following statements are true of PPP (Point-to-Point Protocol)? Choose all that apply:

   A. Built-in error correction

   B. Built-in password encryption

   C. Used by RAS clients only

   D. Supports secure authentication

9. The development department in your company will share a single new server with one large capacity hard drive. This department is divided into five groups. The managers of these groups have asked you to create separate locations on the hard drive that will have controlled access for each group. Which of the following methods can you use? Choose one:

   A. Create a single primary partition with directories for each group. Share the directories with appropriate permissions for each group.

   B. Create five separate Extended partitions, one for each group. Share each partition with the appropriate permissions.

   C. Create five separate primary partitions shared with the appropriate permissions for each group. Additionally, create one primary partition for the operating system.

   D. Create a single primary partition and subdivide it into five smaller logical drives.

10. Which statements are true of a FAT file system under Windows NT? Choose all that apply:

    A. You can use filenames up to 255 characters.

    B. FAT is generally slower than NTFS.

    C. The maximum file, directory, or partition size under FAT is 2 GB.

    D. FAT does not offer the security features offered by NTFS.

11. Your company needs to implement a fault-tolerance method for the PDC that currently contains one 4 GB hard drive. You have decided that 8 GB of data storage is necessary. Your co-worker suggests that you implement RAID Level 5 (Disk Stripping.) Select the true statements regarding this plan. Choose all that apply:

    A. This will be more efficient than disk mirroring (RAID Level 1).

    B. The more disks you use, the more efficient RAID Level 5 becomes.

    C. A minimum of three partitions will be needed to implement this plan.

    D. In the case of a disk failure, this plan will recover lost data faster than RAID Level 1.

12. Which of the following is not true of TCP/IP? Choose all that apply:

    A. It is routable.

    B. It is a widely accepted standard.

    C. It provides compatibility with Novel NetWare IPX/SPX networks.

    D. It was designed for Microsoft Networks.

13. Which of the following are not one of the eight default Windows NT domain local groups? Choose all that apply:

    A. Administrators

    B. Users

    C. Backup Operators

    D. Power Users

    E. Replicator

14. Which of the following are true of the Guest account? Choose all that apply:

    A. It is permanent.

    B. Its group memberships can be changed.

    C. It can be disabled.

    D. It inherently has restricted permissions.

15. Your company has hired some temporary employees. You would like to allow them some access to the domain, yet you want them to be able to log on only at a single machine. How would you accomplish this? Choose one:

    A. Using User Manager for Domains, add a new user. Use the Logon To option to specify the computer.

    B. Add the user locally to the workstation that you want them to be able to log on to.

    C. Under user manager for domains, add a new user, and then use the permission pulldown to restrict access to a single machine.

    D. Add the user locally to the workstation you would like them to be able to log on to. Then add this user to the domain's Guest group.

16. Which of the following statements are not true about ACLs (Access Control Lists) in an NTFS file or folder? Choose all that apply:

    A. They are retained after backup/restore to any NTFS volume.

    B. They are retained when moved to the same volume.

    C. They are retained when copied to any other NTFS folder or volume.

    D. They are retained when moved to another NTFS volume.

17. Martha would like to know if she can access the share "info" from your Server. Martha is a member of the global Software group and the global Software Engineers group. Software is a member of your local Reviewers group. Software Engineers group is a member of your local Testers group.

    The "info" share on your server grants the Reviewers group Read and the Testers group Change access. The NTFS permissions in this share grant the Testers group Read and the Reviewers group Full Control access. What access will Martha have to this share? Choose one:

    A. Read and Change

    B. Read and Full Control

    C. Read

    D. Full Control

    E. Change

18. Which of the following can be configured through Scope Options of DHCP? Choose all that apply:

    A. Default gateway

    B. WINS server address

    C. WINS node type

    D. DNS server address

    E. DNS domain name

19. What attributes are true for NetBEUI? Choose all that apply:

    A. Fast for small networks

    B. Easy to administer

    C. Routable

    D. Frequent Broadcasts

20. You have a group of NT Workstations that need to be able to access files on a NetWare server. You would like to set up a gateway via an NTServer. Which of the following steps are necessary on the NetWare Server? Choose all that apply:

A. Create a user account for the NT Server's gateway service.

B. Put the user account in a group called NTGateway on the NetWare Server.

C. Assign Trustee Rights to the previously mentioned accounts.

D. Put the Gateway Service Account in a group called NWLINK.

21. Your company's support department has 10 users. They have a computer running NT Server that has been optimized for its current workload. The department is adding 15 users over the next month. What server setting should you configure to keep the machine optimized for the new number of users? Choose one:

A. Virtual Memory

B. Foreground and Background Task Balance

C. Workstation service

D. Server service

22. What is true of a hardware-based security host? Choose all that apply:

A. It sits between the RAS server and modem.

B. It provides encryption.

C. It adds a layer of password protection.

D. It requires two or more data lines.

23. You have a RAS Server that will be used by employees using a PPP client. This client supports CHAP encryption for logon authentication only. You want to provide the highest level of security possible. What type of authentication should you use? Choose one:

A. Clear text

B. Microsoft Encrypted Authentication

C. Data Encryption

D. PAP encryption

24. You would like to use DHCP to configure TCP/IP settings on your remote clients. Which of the following configuration settings cannot be set on your remote clients that are using RAS to connect? Choose all that apply:

A. DNS Server address

B. Default Gateway address

C. WINS server address

D. IP address

E. Default WWW server address

25. What location should you place your system policy, config.pol, and logon scripts on your Windows NT workstation to have them replicated to your Window NT Server machine? Choose one:

A. NT workstation cannot be used as an export replication machine.

B. The files must be placed in the Replication share on your NT Workstation computer.

C. The files should be placed in the %systemroot%\system32\repl\export directory.

D. The files should be placed in the %systemrroot%\system32\repl\exports\scripts directory.

26. Your Software department has just purchased a new computer that they would like to use to store source code. They would like to make the computer fault-tolerant. What are the minimum disk requirements? Choose one:

   A. Two disk drives with one controller

   B. Two disk drives with two controllers

   C. Three disk drives with one controller

   D. Three disk drives with three controllers

27. What fault-tolerant levels of RAID are standard with Windows NT Server? Choose all that apply:

   A. 5

   B. 4

   C. 3

   D. 2

   E. 1

28. Your company has four servers (one PDC and three BDCs). You also have NT Workstation 3.51, NT Workstation 4.0, and Windows 95 clients. You will configure one of the servers as a print server. On which machines will you need to load the appropriate drivers? Choose one:

   A. The Print Server and the Windows 95 clients

   B. The PDC only

   C. The Print server only

   D. The PDCs and the BDCs

   E. The PDC and the Print Server (if they are not the same machine)

29. In order to establish a printer pool, you must do what? Choose all that apply:

   A. Configure the printers with the appropriate driver.

   B. Select "Enable Print Pooling."

   C. Configure all printers in the pool with the same name.

   D. Add a "Pooled" port.

   E. Connect all the printers to the same port.

30. Which of the following clients cannot download print drivers from an NT 4.0 print server? Choose all that apply:

   A. Windows for Workgroups

   B. Windows 95

   C. Windows NT 3.51 Server

   D. Windows NT 4.0 Workstation

   E. Windows NT 4.0 Server

31. Your support department has just purchased a new machine to use as an application server. They will use the hard drive from the old server for the system and boot drive, plus they have budgeted to purchase some additional hardware. How would you suggest they spend their money and configure the server for maximum performance in disk I/O? Choose one:

   A. Buy as many drives as needed to support their needs and set up a Stripe set.

   B. Set up as many mirrored sets (with one controller per set) as needed to meet their requirements.

   C. Buy as many drives as needed and set up a Stripe set with parity.

   D. Purchase multiple drives, each with its own controller, to set up a Stripe set.

32. Which of the following are true for point-to-point Tunneling Protocol? Choose all that apply:

    A. It uses the Internet for connections.

    B. It has lower hardware costs than other network solutions.

    C. It provides security.

    D. It has high transmission costs.

    E. It has higher administration costs compared to other protocols.

33. Which statements about NTFS are true? Choose all that apply:

    A. NTFS is the only file system for NT that can support filenames over 8.3.

    B. NTFS can easily be converted to FAT.

    C. NTFS is the most commonly supported file system.

    D. NTFS has less overhead than FAT.

    E. None of the above.

34. Which protocols can be used by Windows NT Server for Remote Access Service? Choose all that apply:

    A. TCP/IP

    B. NetBEUI

    C. IPX

    D. SNMP

35. Jim, who is currently a member of the support group, calls to request access to the Accounting Group share. You add him to the Accounting Group, which currently has Change access to this share. Jim calls back an hour later complaining that he still cannot access the Accounting share. Which option might fix the problem? Choose one:

    A. Wait until synchronization has occurred.

    B. Have Jim log off and then log back on.

    C. The next time the PDC is rebooted, the access permission will be correct.

    D. Wait until directory replication occurs.

36. Your company has purchased several 4 GB drives for setting up servers throughout your building. The Marketing department needs fault-tolerant data storage of at least 12 GB. Excluding space for Boot and System partitions, what is the minimum number of drives the Marketing department must have in its server in order to set up RAID 5 and still meet the 12 GB minimum requirement? Choose one:

    A. 2

    B. 3

    C. 4

    D. 5

    E. 6

37. By creating a paging file on each physical disk, you will:

    A. Improve overall performance, because more than one disk I/O can be performed simultaneously.

    B. Be able to use less disk space for the paging file.

    C. Make it easier to convert to RAID 5 if you need to do so later.

    D. Degrade overall performance.

38. Which of the following cannot be implemented using a DHCP server? Choose all that apply:

    A. IP addresses

    B. DNS server address

    C. WINS server address

    D. Profile path

    E. NetBios name resolution type

39. The administrator of the domain XYZ has noticed problems with the application server's performance. The administrator suspects that the processor needs to be upgraded. Using Performance Monitor, which counter values would prove the suspicions about the processor activity being too high? Choose two:

    A. System Object processor Queue length < 2

    B. System Object processor Queue length > 2

    C. % Processor Time = 1%

    D. % Processor Time = 99%

40. You have a NetWare 4.X network to which you would like to add a Windows NT server to utilize as an application server. In order to do this, you must install what to enable your NetWare Clients to access applications on your server? Choose one:

    A. TCP/IP protocol

    B. The NWLink protocol

    C. IPX Service

    D. Gateway Services for NetWare

41. You are considering converting all of your existing NetWare clients to NT. If you decide not to convert them, what must be done to each NetWare client PC so that they can connect to the NT Servers? Choose one:

    A. Install Gateway Services for NetWare on the NT Server.

    B. Install Gateway and Client Services for NetWare on the NT Server.

    C. Install file and print services for NetWare on each client.

    D. Install a Microsoft Redirector on each client.

42. You would like to have DHCP broadcast across two subnets. Which service is required on an NT Server in order to accomplish this? Choose one:

    A. Gateway Services for DHCP

    B. DHCP relay agent

    C. RIP for TCP/IP

    D. BOOTP

43. You would like to migrate all of your NetWare Clients to Windows NT by using the Migration Tool for NetWare. What needs to be loaded on the NT Server in order to complete the migration? Choose one:

    A. File and print services for NetWare

    B. Directory Replicator for NetWare

    C. Gateway Services for NetWare

    D. RIP for NetWare

44. You would like to upgrade NT Server from 3.51 to 4.0 from a distribution share on the network. Which command line would you execute in order to perform a floppyless upgrade while running NT 3.51? Choose one:

    A. winnt.exe /F

    B. setup.exe

    C. winnt32.exe /F

    D. winnt32.exe /B

45. You currently have 1,000 domain users that are complaining about logons being too slow. You notice that the Logons/sec counter in performance monitor is high. What can be done to speed up the time it takes to log on to the Domain? Choose one:

    A. Add another PDC.

    B. Increase the Logon Concurrency entry in the registry.

C. Increase the Pulse Concurrency entry in the registry.

D. Add another BDC.

46. You have an NT Server with two physical drives. Currently, the system and boot files are on the first drive and the page file is on the second. By splitting the page file between the two drives, what benefits will you receive? Choose all that apply:

A. You will get better performance.

B. You will get a crash dump file if the system fails.

C. You will get fault tolerance.

D. You will decrease page swapping.

47. You are attempting to figure out the best time to schedule your weekly backups for the NT Servers on your network. How can you gather this information? Choose one:

A. Review the Event Log.

B. Use the Chart option Performance Monitor.

C. Use the Log option in Performance Monitor.

D. Review the System Load log.

48. When repairing a damaged Windows NT installation, the repair option "Verify Windows NT System files" does what? Choose one:

A. It prompts for replacement of each Registry file.

B. It verifies that NT is an option in boot.ini.

C. It replaces files such as NTLDR and NTOSKRNL.EXE.

D. It verifies and/or fixes boot sector and NTLDR.

49. Using the NTBackup utility, which of the following options must be selected in order to perform a successful backup of the local registry on an NT Server? Choose all that apply:

A. Select the local drive to backup.

B. Select the "Backup Local Registry" check box.

C. Select the "Registry" check box.

D. Select the directory that contains the registry.

50. You currently have an NT server running virus scan software that automatically detects and cleans viruses. You accidentally left a floppy in the server while rebooting it. After the server comes back up, a virus alert pops up notifying you that the server was infected with a boot sector virus and the contents of the boot sector have been cleaned to remove the virus. The next time the server is restarted, the server will not boot successfully because it cannot find the operating system. What steps need to be taken in order to fix the problem? Choose one:

A. Boot from the emergency repair disk and restore the boot partition.

B. Boot the server with the Windows NT installation disks and use Server Manager to restore the boot partition.

C. Boot the server with the Windows NT installation disks and use the emergency repair disks to restore the boot partition.

D. Boot the system using an NT boot disk and use the emergency repair disk to restore the boot partition.

51. You have a total of five hard disks in your NT Server. The first disk contains the boot and system partitions. The remaining four disks are configured as a stripe set with parity containing user data files. The first disk fails and needs to be replaced. What step must you take in order to recover from this failure? Choose one:

   A. Re-install NT Server to disk one.

   B. You need to recover all five disks from tape backup.

   C. Re-install NT Server to disk one, and then restore the other four disks from tape backup.

   D. Re-install NT Server to disk one and then restore the registry information tape backup.

52. You have installed a new video card in your NT Server because the old one has failed. The new video card is from a different vendor. What must be done to get the NT Server working with the new video card? Choose one:

   A. Boot with the three NT Installation disks and then load the driver for the new video card.

   B. Boot with the three NT Installation disks and then perform an emergency repair to change the video driver to Standard VGA.

   C. Choose the VGA option for Windows NT Server during the boot process. After the system comes up, install the driver for the new video card.

   D. Install the new driver.

53. The system partition in your server has just failed. Fortunately, the system partition was part of a mirror set. So, now all you have to do is create a fault-tolerant boot disk so that you can boot the system into Windows

NT from the mirrored partition. Both the physical disks are SCSI without the SCSI BIOS enabled. They are both connected to the same SCSI controller card. Which ARC name should be used in the boot.ini file on the boot disk to ensure that the disk boots the server successfully into Windows NT? Choose one:

   A. scsi(0)disk(0)rdisk(0)partition(1)

   B. multi(0)disk(1) rdisk(0)partition(1)

   C. scsi(0)disk(1)rdisk(0)partition(1)

   D. multi(0)disk(0) rdisk(0)partition(1)

54. Which of the following statements are true of disk striping with parity? Choose all that apply:

   A. Striping requires less disk overhead than mirroring.

   B. Striping has better read performance than mirroring.

   C. Striping supports up to 32 hard disks.

   D. Striping requires two hard disks.

55. You have the memory.dmp file that your NT Server created after a system failure. What utility can you use to decode the data in that file? Choose one:

   A. dumpexam.exe

   B. rdisk.exe

   C. dumpflop.exe

   D. dumpchk.exe

Answers and Explanations

1. **A, D** Only domain administrators have the ability to add a computer to a domain. After this has been done, a local administrator can join a machine to the domain, as in answer A. In answer D, the machine is added and joined in a single step. (Installation and Configuration.)

2. **C** The only way to create a BDC is during installation of NT server. A member server can never be promoted to a BDC. (Installation and Configuration.)

3. **B** The Pulse registry entry controls the amount of time between synchronization of the BDCs and the PDC on the domain. Increasing this time decreases the workload on the PDC. (Monitoring and Optimization.)

4. **D** Copying an existing account enables the creation of a new user with identical attributes. (Managing Resources.)

5. **D** The .man extension on a profile makes it unchangeable by the user. (Managing Resources.)

6. **B** The profile path can be set only in the User Manager for Domains, and it must be a full UNC path in order to be accessed from any machine. (Managing Resources.)

7. **A** Device errors, such as modem errors, are written to the device.log file. Because multiple users are having the same problem, the problem is likely to be on the server end. (Troubleshooting.)

8. **A, B, D** PPP can be used by RAS Clients and Servers. (Connectivity.)

9. **A** B is incorrect because only one extended partition can reside on a hard drive. C is incorrect because a hard drive can contain only four primary partitions. B is incorrect because primary partitions cannot be divided into logical drives. (Planning.)

10. **A, B, D** The maximum file, directory, or partition size under FAT is 4 GB. (Planning.)

11. **A, B, C** is incorrect because you need to have at least one additional partition for the boot and system partition. D is incorrect because RAID Level 5 needs to regenerate missing data, whereas RAID Level 1 has a complete copy of missing data. (Planning.)

12. **A, B** NWLink is required for Novel compatibility, and NetBEUI was designed for Microsoft Networks. (Connectivity.)

13. **D** Default NT domain local groups are Administrators, Users, Guests, Backup Operators, Replicator, Print Operators, Server Operators. (Managing Resources.)

14. **A, B, C** The Guest account has no inherent power or lack of power. Group membership for the account establishes its scope. (Managing Resources.)

15. **A** By default, a domain user has the capability to log on to all domain machines. The Logon To option in User Manager for Domains gives you the ability to restrict user accounts to certain machines. (Managing Resources.)

16. **C, D** In both cases, the ACLs are inherited from the destination folder. (Planning.)

17. **E** The files have Full Control privilege on NTFS because multiple privileges will result in the least restrictive privileges. The share will have Change privileges for the same reason. When calculating the result between the share and the file privileges, the most restrictive privilege is used, which in this case is Change. (Managing Resources.)

18. **A, B, C, D, E**   All these options are configurable under the Scope option of DHCP. (Connectivity.)

19. **A, B, D**   NetBEUI is not routable. (Connectivity.)

20. **A, B, C**   These three are the only steps that need to be performed on the NetWare server in order to set up a gateway via an NT Server. (Connectivity.)

21. **D**   The Server services can be set to Balance, which is optimal for up to 64 connections.(Monitoring and Optimization.)

22. **A, C**   A hardware-based security host requires only the normal communication lines set up for RAS communication, and it does not supply encryption. (Connectivity.)

23. **B**   This is the most secure encryption and it supports CHAP. (Connectivity.)

24. **E**   The following addresses can be assigned through DHCP to RAS clients: IP Address, Default Gateway Address, WINS Server Address, WINS Node Type, DNS Server Address, and DNS Domain Names. (Connectivity.)

25. **A**   Only NT server can be used as an export replication machine. (Installation and Configuration.)

26. **A**   Disk mirroring (RAID 1) requires only two drives and a single controller. (Planning.)

27. **A, E**   The following levels of RAID are options under NT: RAID 0 (Striping), RAID 1 (Mirroring/Duplexing), and RAID 5 (Striping with Parity). (Planning.)

28. **C**   Each machine will load the appropriate drivers from the print server as needed. (Installation and Configuration.)

29. **A, B**   All printers in a Printer Pool must be able to utilize the same printer driver. "Enable Print Pooling" must be selected on the print server. (Installation and Configuration.)

30. **A**   All Microsoft clients except for WFW clients can download drivers from 4.0 print servers. (Installation and Configuration.)

31. **D**   Stripe sets with multiple controllers allow concurrent I/O request, dramatically improving performance. (Planning.)

32. **A, B, C**   PPP uses the Internet for connections, is less expensive when compared to other network solutions, and requires higher administrative costs. (Connectivity.)

33. **E**   FAT file systems under NT can support long filenames. NTFS can not be converted to FAT. NTFS is only usable by Windows NT, and it uses more overhead than FAT. (Planning.)

34. **A, B, C**   The following protocols can be used with RAS: Netbeui, TCP/IP, and IPX. (Connectivity.)

35. **B**   Permissions are contained in the user's access token. This token is generated when the user logs on. Jim will have access to the Accounting share the next time he logs on. (Troubleshooting.)

36. **C**   The formula for % of disk space available is *(no. of disks −1)/no. of disks × 100%*. In this case, (4−1)/4 ×100% = 75%. 75% of the total disk space, 16 GB (4 disks × 4 GB), is 12 GB. (Planning.)

37. **A**   When a page file is split between physical disks, performance is improved because disk I/O is shared between the separate disks. (Monitoring and Optimization.)

38. **D** These options can be configured using the Defaults, Global, and Scope options on the DHCP server. (Connectivity.)

39. **B, D** The System Object processor Queue length should always be two or less, and the 99% Processor time shows that the processor is loaded so much that it has no free time while tasks are waiting. (Monitoring and Optimization.)

40. **B** NWLink protocol must be loaded on any NT server for NetWare Clients to access it. (Connectivity.)

41. **D** Microsoft Redirector is all that the client PCs need in order to communicate with the NT Server. (Connectivity.)

42. **B** DHCP Relay Agent allows DHCP to broadcast over multiple subnets. (Installation and Configuration.)

43. **C** Gateway Services for NetWare enable workstations connected to your NT Server to also access NetWare drives. (Connectivity.)

44. **D** Winnt32.exe is the 32-bit installation program for NT. The /B parameter invokes a floppyless install. (Installation and Configuration.)

45. **D** One way to speed up the logon process is to add another BDC. When the PDC is busy, the logons will be validated by any available BDC. (*Note* Another method is to make sure that the PDC Server service is optimized for Network Applications. This increases logons from 6-7 per second to around 20 per second.) (Monitoring and Optimization.)

46. **A, B** You will get some performance increase because you will be able to do concurrent reads from the page file. When any part of the page file exists on the system drive, a system failure will generate a crash dump file. (Monitoring and Optimization.)

47. **C** The logging option of the performance monitor will save information over long periods of time that can reviewed later. (Monitoring and Optimization.)

48. **C** All the other answers are tasks performed by other valid installation repair options, but C is the task performed for "Verify Windows NT System files" for repairing the NT system boot files. (Troubleshooting.)

49. **A, B, D** The local drive and directory that contains the registry must be selected along with the "backup local registry" check box. If you do not choose any one of those options, the registry backup will fail. (Installation and Configuration.)

50. **C** The windows NT installation disks must be loaded first in order to repair anything from the emergency repair disk. (Troubleshooting.)

51. **D** NT server will need to be installed to disk one and the registry will need to be recovered in order to recover the shares on the user data files that reside on the remaining four disks. (Troubleshooting.)

52. **C** The VGA option for Windows NT is added by default to the boot.ini file during the installation of NT. This option is used for troubleshooting video problems with NT. (Troubleshooting.)

53. **C**   SCSI represents a disk on which SCSI BIOS is not enabled, and MULTI represents a disk other than SCSI or a SCSI accessed by the SCSI BIOS. DISK indicates the hard drive of the controller that you are using. RDISK is ignored for SCSI controllers and represents the ordinal number of the disk you are using. PARTITION refers to the partition number and is always assigned beginning with the number 1. SCSI/MULTI, DISK, and RDISK all begin with the number 0. (Troubleshooting.)

54. **A, B, C**   If you have four hard drives, mirroring utilizes only 50% of disk space and striping would utilize 75%. With disk striping, data is split over multiple drives and can be read simultaneously. Disk striping supports from three to 32 harddisks. (Planning.)

55. **A**   DUMPEXAM.EXE writes information from the dump file to a text file so that you can find out what caused the system failure. (Troubleshooting.)

Glossary

Account lockout—You can specify to lock out an account after a given number of unsuccessful logon attempts.

Account Operators group—Group that holds the right to administer user accounts.

Account policy—Way to administer security for accounts (such as password age, account lockout, and more).

Administrators group—Group that holds the right to administer the local server.

Advanced RISC Computer (ARC)—A non-Intel x86-based computer.

AT.EXE—An executable used to schedule batch files to run at a given time. Can be used to start or stop services, as well as to start other executables such as NTbackup.

Auditing—Logs accesses to files and directories. Helps to track object usage and security credentials.

AutoDial—A Windows NT feature that automatically associates network connections with Phonebook entries. If a resource is needed that is only accessible via a dial-up connection, Windows NT will attempt to make the connection automatically.

BackOffice support—MS BackOffice application most often requires NT Server to operate.

Backup browsers—The backup browser gets a copy of the browse list from the master browser (on the subnet) and distributes the browse list to subnet clients who request it.

Backup Operators group—Group that holds rights to backup servers.

BDC—Backup Domain Controller; added as "load-balancing" mechanism to validate users to the domain. Can also serve as a file, print, and application server. Receives regular updates from the PDC of the domain accounts database so that it may also validate users logging onto the domain.

Bindings—Network Bindings are software interfaces between network cards, protocols, and services; the Bindings tab enables you to tweak the arrangement of bindings to increase performance on your NT machine.

Boot—The process of initializing the operating system.

Boot partition—Partition that contains the NT operating system files.

Bottleneck—A resource snag that limits the rate at which a task can complete.

Bridge—Links networks and is commonly used to overcome node per-segment limitations.

Built-in groups—Groups that are created when Windows NT is installed.

Bytes total/sec—Performance Monitor counter that measures the number of bytes sent to and received from the network.

Callback—A security feature incorporated into RAS that disconnects the incoming caller and calls back at a predetermined number.

CDFS—CD File System; implemented on CD-ROMs.

Centralized user management—User information (logon information and so on) is stored in a central location.

Characterization file—Contains all the printer-specific information, such as memory, page protection, soft fonts, graphics resolution, paper orientation and size, and so on; it's used by the two dynamic link libraries whenever they need to gather printer-specific information.

Client Services for NetWare (CSNW)—Enables Windows NT Workstation to access file and print resources on a NetWare server. Used in conjunction with NWLink.

Compact.exe—Utility to compress files from the command prompt.

Compression—Used to minimize the storage space needed for files.

Control set—A set of controls used to determine the configuration.

Counters—Statistical measurements used to track levels of performance on system and hardware components in Performance Monitor.

Creating groups—Task of creating new groups, either local or global (on domain controllers only).

Creating users—Task of adding new user accounts to a server.

Creator Owner group—Special group for owners of resources.

CSNW—See *Client Services for NetWare*.

Decentralized user management—User information is spread across different machines; changes have to be made to all machines when a user account is being changed.

Deleting groups—Task of deleting a group. You cannot delete built-in groups.

Deleting users—Task of deleting user accounts from a server.

Devices—Control Panel applet used to start, stop, or disable device drivers.

DHCP—Dynamic Host Configuration Protocol; a service installed on NT Server to dynamically assign hosts an IP address and other TCP/IP related information.

Directory Replication—A facility that enables you to configure Windows NT Servers to automatically transmit updated versions of important directories to other computers on the network.

Disabling users—Task of disabling a user account that doesn't delete the account, but prevents the use of it.

Disk Administrator—A graphical utility used in Windows NT Server to manage all aspects of drives.

Disk duplexing—Disk mirroring implemented using a second controller.

Disk mirroring—Duplicating one disk to another.

DNS—Domain Name Service; used to map computer names to IP addresses and vice versa.

Domain—A network model in which user management is done in central locations. Also a collection of computer accounts. Only NT Workstations and servers can be true members of a domain.

Domain name—The name of the networking entity.

Domain Admins group—Global group of administrators.

Domain Guests group—Global group of guests.

Domain master browser—The domain master browser requests subnet browse lists from the master browsers and merges the subnet browse lists into a master browse list for the entire domain. This computer is always the Primary Domain Controller.

Domain Users group—Global group of users.

Errors—Problems that create NT Server conditions about which to be concerned.

Event Viewer—Program to view system, security, and application events.

Everyone group—Special group of which everyone is automatically member.

Extended partition—Partition that can be subdivided.

FAT—File Allocation Table; primary file system used for DOS. Alternative format for media to NTFS.

FAT32—Enhanced FAT introduced with Windows 95b.

Fault-tolerance—Capability to recover from hardware errors, such as a failing drive.

File Delete Child—Special security option available for POSIX compliance.

Gateway Services for NetWare (GSNW)—Enables Windows NT Server systems to access NetWare file and print resources directly, and to act as a gateway to NetWare resources. Non-NetWare clients on a Windows NT network then can access NetWare resources through the gateway as if they were accessing Windows NT resources without any need for NetWare client licensing.

Guests group—Local group of guests that can log on to the server.

Global groups—Groups defined on the domain controller and available to all servers.

Group—Logical grouping of user accounts that performs similar tasks and needs the same rights and permissions.

GSNW—See *Gateway Services for NetWare*.

GuardTime—A REG_WORD value that defines how long a directory must be stable before its files can be replicated. The range is 0 to one half of the Interval value.

Hardware profile—A method of configuring what devices and services should be started upon start up time depending on the location of the hardware or the tasks to be completed.

Hardware requirements—The requirements your computer must meet in order to be able to run specific software or hardware components.

Hive—A structure and component of the Windows NT Registry.

Hot fixing—Automatic error correction implemented in NTFS for moving data from bad sectors on a hard disk.

HPFS—High performance file system; used by OS/2 as the primary file system.

Information events—Problems of a non-critical nature of which you should be aware.

Integrated Services Digital Network (ISDN)—A digital media provided by telephone companies that provides faster communications and higher bandwidth than traditional phone lines.

Interactive group—Special group everyone becomes a member of when logged on locally.

Internet—International Wide Area Network using the TCP/IP protocol.

Interrupts/sec—Performance Monitor counter that measures the amount of interrupts the processor handles per second.

Interval—A REG_WORD value that defines how often an export server checks for updates. The range is from one to 60 minutes, and the default is five minutes.

IP address—Dotted decimal notation of unique address per host.

IPCONFIG—The command used to retrieve current IP information about a host.

IPX/SPX—Network protocol used by NetWare servers.

ISDN—See *Integrated Services Digital Network*.

Local groups—Groups available on a server computer only.

Local profile—Profile stored on the local computer.

Logon scripts—Scripts that run when users log on to a Windows NT computer.

Managing shares—Usually done with Server Manager and enables you to fine tune shares.

Mandatory profile—Profile that can't be changed by a user.

Master Boot Record (MBR)—The primary boot record used at each boot.

Member Server—An NT server computer that is part of a domain but does not act as a domain controller. May exist in a domain or workgroup environment.

Migration Tool for NetWare—Used as an automatic and relatively simple method to transfer file and directory data, along with user and group account data and logon scripts and directory rights from a NetWare server to a Windows NT domain controller.

Mirror sets—Two disks mirrored together to replicate data. Data written to one physical disk is mirrored on another physical disk—ensures fault-tolerance.

Mirrored set-fault tolerance RAID Level 1—Requires two hard drives in NT Server. Data written to a mirrored partition on Disk 0 will be "mirrored" on a partition, equal in size, on Disk 1.

Monitoring shares—Auditing turned on for shares.

Multilink—Combines multiple physical links into a single logical link to increase bandwidth. Can be used for bundling multiple ISDN channels, or two or more standard modems.

Multiprocessor—Term relating to the capability of an operating system to use more than one processor.

Net share—Command to share a directory from the command prompt.

NetBEUI— NetBIOS Extended User Interface; a protocol stack that ships with Microsoft LAN Manager.

NetBIOS—Network Basic Input/Output System defines a software interface and a naming convention, not a protocol. The NetBEUI protocol provides a protocol for programs designed around the NetBIOS interface. However, NetBEUI is a small protocol with no networking layer and because of this, it is not a routable protocol suitable for medium-to-large intranets.

NetWare Directory Service (NDS)—A distributed database of network resources primarily associated with NetWare 4.x systems.

Network Client Administrator—Utility that creates the NT client-based administration tools setup directory.

Network group—Special group of which everyone becomes member when connected to a network share on a server.

Novell NetWare—Server software from Novell.

NTFS—NT file system; a file system designed for Windows NT that is fault-tolerant and can be used to set permissions for files.

NTFS partitions—Disk partitions formatted with NTFS rather than FAT.

NTFS permissions—Permissions of files and directories on an NTFS volume.

NTLDR—The load program\routine for NT.

NWLink—The NWLink IPX/SPX compatible transport provides support for IPX/SPX Sockets and NetBIOS APIs.

Objects—System and hardware components tracked by counters in Performance Monitor.

Operating system—The software required to run any other programs, such as word processors or spreadsheet applications.

Optimal performance—Getting the best performance from the software and hardware currently in place.

Orphan—A remaining disk from a broken mirror set.

Pages/sec—Performance Monitor counter that measures the number of times that a memory page had to be paged into memory or out to disk.

Paging file—The area of hard disk commonly referred to as virtual memory. This is where pages are stored when they are not active in RAM. Windows NT, by default, controls the size of the paging file.

Partition—Unit of storage on a disk.

Partitioning—The method of dividing a physical hard disk into smaller units.

PC Cards (PCMCIA)—Control Panel applet used to add and configure PCMCIA device drivers. Also used to identify cards that NT does not support.

PDC—Primary Domain Controller; the first NT Server online in a Domain. Maintains a Master Database of all user account information in the domain.

Per server licensing—For each per server license you purchase, one concurrent network connection is allowed access to the server. When the maximum specified amount of concurrent connections is reached, NT returns an error to a connecting user and prohibits access. An administrator, however, can still connect to the server to increase the amount of per server licenses.

Per seat licensing—Each computer that accesses a Windows NT Server requires a separate client access license. Clients are free to connect to any server, and there are unlimited connections to the server. Each client participating in the network must have a per seat license.

Phonebook entries—Phonebook entries are, in essence, the address book for all established telephone links assigned in the Dial-Up Networking dialog box.

PING—Packet Internet Groper; a tool used to test the validity of an IP address.

Platform independent—NT is platform-independent as it exists in versions for Intel, Alpha, and others.

Point-to-Point Protocol (PPP)—A protocol normally used in conjunction with TCP/IP routers and PCs for communicating over a dial-up or a leased line WAN link.

Point-to-Point Tunneling Protocol (PPTP)—Similar protocol to PPP, but it encapsulates enhanced security through encryption.

Policy file mode—Mode of operation for System Policy Editor; edits the system policy file that is used for different users and computers for your domain.

Policy templates—Template files used for System Policy Editor when creating system policies.

Ports—Control Panel applet that lists the available serial ports. Also used to add a port under Windows NT.

Power Users group—Group on servers that are nearly as powerful as Administrators.

Preferred Server—A NetWare server selected from a list of available NetWare servers in conjunction with GSNW and CSNW during the NT logon process. The Preferred Server indicates which NetWare server you want to validate your NetWare Logon process.

Primary partition—Partition that can't be subdivided.

Priority—An arbitrary ranking that places one process ahead or behind another in processing order.

Print Operators group—Group that holds rights to administer printers.

Print processor—Responsible for completing the rendering process. The tasks performed by the print processor differ depending on the print data's data type.

Print router—The print router receives the print job from the spooler and routes it to the appropriate print processor.

Printer—A device that delivers output—the actual hardware from which the print job is produced. Also, software between the operating system and the physical printing device.

Printer graphics driver DLL—This dynamic link library consists of the rendering or managing portion of the driver; it's always called by the Graphics Device Interface.

Printer interface driver—This dynamic link library consists of the user interface or configuration management portion of the printer driver; it's used by an administrator to configure a printer.

Printer pool—A collection of identical printing devices configured as one printer to increase printing productivity by printing jobs on the first available printing device.

Profiles—Stored information about a user's settings for desktop, network neighborhood, program files, and more.

RAID—Redundant array of inexpensive disks; a system used for fault-tolerance. Windows NT Server uses RAID 1, disk mirroring, and RAID 5, stripe sets with parity.

RAS—Remote Access Service; the ability to remotely dial in to the server.

Regedt32.exe—The application that enables you to edit your NT registry.

Registry mode—Mode of operation for System Policy Editor; edits the local registry.

Remote access—Accessing a computer from a dialup link.

Remote Access Service (RAS)—Windows NT RAS extends the power of NT networking to remote user via dial-up connectivity.

Renaming users—Task of renaming a user account. Doesn't affect the SID assigned to this account.

Replicator group—Special group for replication tasks.

Roaming profile—Profile that is located on a network server share and is downloaded to every computer a user logs on.

Router— A router helps LANs and WANs achieve interoperability and connectivity and can link LANs that have different network topologies (such as Ethernet and Token Ring).

SCSI adapters—Control Panel applet used to install SCSI adapter drivers and IDE drivers.

Secondary cache—(Also called Level 2 (L2) cache.) Internal cache is called Level 1 cache (L1) and can generally outperform L2 cache. The real factor with cache is the cache controller and system design.

Serial Line Internet Protocol (SLIP)—A protocol that carries IP over an asynchronous serial communications line.

Server Manager—Utility to manage server on the network.

Server Message Block (SMB)—A jointly developed file-sharing protocol by Microsoft, Intel, and IBM. SMB specifies a series of commands utilized to pass information between computers using the following four message types: file, printer, session control, and message.

Server Operators group—Group that holds rights to administer a server.

Service Advertising Protocol (SAP)—A NetWare protocol that enables servers to advertise their services to the network.

Services for Macintosh—A service that enables the system administrator to create shares for Macintosh users as well as creating printer queues for Macintosh.

Share permissions—Permissions that are applicable to share points.

Sharing—Creating a share point on a server that can be accessed from the network.

Special groups—Groups that cannot be administered, but are used by NT for local or remote users.

Spool—Temporary holding place for jobs waiting to print; operates in the background to manage the printing process.

Startup disks—The disks used to start the system.

Stop error—The most critical type of error possible in NT.

Stripe set—Hardware solution to increase performance by writing data to multiple drives (2-32 drives in NT server and Workstation) in 64K segments. However, stripe sets offer no fault-tolerance. See *stripe set with parity*.

Stripe set with parity—RAID Level 5 hardware and software solution to increase performance by writing data to multiple drives (3-32 drives in NT Server) in 64K segments. (Data is written in chunks with parity information to different hard disks that form a stripe set.) Stripe sets with parity offer fault-tolerance support, because parity information is written to each disk in the stripe set in rotation.

Subnet—A division of a network into sub-networks.

Subnet mask—An address that breaks the IP address into individual subnets. Used to mask a portion of the IP address so that the TCP/IP protocol can distinguish the host id from the network id.

System partition—Partition that contains the NT loader (the files necessary to boot the operating system).

System policy editor—Program that enables you to edit system policies via a user interface.

Take Ownership—Permission that someone can take ownership of a file or directory.

TCP/IP—Transmission Control Protocol; A suite of protocols used to connect dissimilar hosts on a network. This is the primary protocol used on the Internet.

Telephony Application Program Interface (TAPI)—TAPI is a device driver for the PCs phone system. It provides a standard interface with telephony applications. TAPI manages communications between the computer and the phone system.

User—Account representing a person allowed to logon to a domain.

User Manager—Program to manage user and groups, as well as user rights, account policy, and trust relationships.

User rights—Specific rights to which users have been assigned.

Volume sets—Areas of free space combined into a single logical drive.

Warnings—Problems that create NT Server conditions about which to be alert.

Windows 95—Operating system created as a successor to Windows 3.1.

Windows 95 clients—Computers running Windows 95 in a network.

Windows NT clients—Computers running Windows NT in a network.

Windows NT Server—The server operating system version of NT optimized for file sharing and server applications.

Windows NT Workstation—The workstation version of NT optimized for single-users.

WINNT.exe—16-bit installation program used to install Windows NT.

WINNT32.exe—32-bit installation program used to install Windows NT 4.0 from a previous version of NT.

WINS—Windows Internet Naming Service; a service installed on Windows NT that dynamically registers and records NetBIOS names and the IP addresses associated with them.

Workgroup—A network model in which each computer manages its own resources (including user accounts).

All About the Exam

The exam incorporates a variety of questions from a question bank intended to determine if you have mastered the subject. Here are some tips to keep in mind as you prepare for your exam:

- Make sure you understand the material thoroughly.

- Go through all of the practice problems. Reread those sections that you were having trouble with.

- Make sure you are comfortable with the style of the scenario questions. These will probably be the most challenging part of the exam.

- Review the exam objectives.

The Microsoft Certification Process

Microsoft has a variety of certifications available for their products. You can find out more about their certifications on the Web page: `http://www.microsoft.com/train_cert/`.

How to Become a Microsoft Certified Product Specialist (MCPS)

The Microsoft Certified Product Specialist is the entry level of Microsoft's certifications, and requires passing a minimal number of exams. Microsoft Certified Product Specialists are required to pass one operating system exam, proving their expertise with a current Microsoft Windows desktop or server operating system, and one or more elective exams from the MCSE or MCSD tracks. The following list shows the operating system exam choices that are eligible:

- **Exam 70-073:** Implementing and Supporting Microsoft Windows NT Workstation 4.02 *OR* Exam 70-042: Implementing and Supporting Microsoft Windows NT Workstation 3.51

- **Exam 70-067:** Implementing and Supporting Microsoft Windows NT Server 4.0 *OR* Exam 70-043: Implementing and Supporting Microsoft Windows NT Server 3.5

- **Exam 70-030:** Microsoft Windows 3.1
- **Exam 70-048:** Microsoft Windows for Workgroups 3.11—Desktop
- **Exam 70-063:** Implementing and Supporting Microsoft Windows 95
- **Exam 70-160:** Microsoft Windows Architecture I
- **Exam 70-161:** Microsoft Windows Architecture II

All exams for Microsoft's premium certifications (Microsoft Certified Systems Engineer and Microsoft Certified Solution Developer) are available as electives and provide further verification of skills with Microsoft BackOffice products, development tools, or desktop applications.

How to Become a Microsoft Certified Systems Engineer (MCSE)

The Microsoft Certified Systems Engineer is probably the most rapidly growing certification in the world. It proves that you are knowledgeable in advanced operating systems such as Windows 95 and Windows NT, that you excel in networking related skills, and that you have a broad enough background to understand some of the elective products.

MCSE candidates need to pass four operating system exams and two elective exams. The MCSE certification path is divided into two tracks: the Windows NT 3.51 track and the Windows NT 4.0 track.

Table B.1 shows the core requirements (four operating system exams) and the elective courses (two exams) for the Windows NT 3.51 track.

Table B.1

Windows NT 3.51 MCSE Track			
Take These Two Required Exams (Core Requirements)	Plus, Pick One Exam from the Following Operating System Exams (Core Requirement)	Plus, Pick One Exam from the Following Networking Exams (Core Requirement)	Plus, Pick Two Exams from the Following Elective Exams (Elective Requirements)
Implementing and Supporting Microsoft Windows NT Server 3.51 #70-43	Implementing and Supporting Microsoft Windows 95 #70-63	Networking Microsoft Windows for Workgroups 3.11 #70-46	Implementing and supporting Microsoft SNA Server 3.0 #70-13
AND Implementing and Supporting Microsoft Windows NT Workstation 3.51 #70-42	*OR* Microsoft Windows for Workgroups 3.11-Desktop #70-48	*OR* Networking with Microsoft Windows 3.1 #70-47	*OR* Implementing and Supporting Microsoft Systems Management Server 1.2 #70-18

Take These Two Required Exams (Core Requirements)	Plus, Pick One Exam from the Following Operating System Exams (Core Requirement)	Plus, Pick One Exam from the Following Networking Exams (Core Requirement)	Plus, Pick Two Exams from the Following Elective Exams (Elective Requirements)
	OR Microsoft Windows 3.1 #70-30	*OR* Networking Essentials #70-58	*OR* Microsoft SQL Server 4.2 Database Implementation #70-21
			OR Implementing a Database Design on Microsoft SQL Server 6.5 #70-27
			OR Microsoft SQL Server 4.2 Database Administration for Microsoft Windows NT #70-22
			OR System Administration for Microsoft SQL Server 6.5 #70-26
			OR Microsoft Mail for PC Networks 3.2-Enterprise #70-37
			OR Internetworking Microsoft TCP/IP on Microsoft Windows NT (3.5-3.51) #70-53
			OR Internetworking Microsoft TCP/IP on Microsoft Windows NT 4.0 #70-59

continues

Table B.1   Continued

Windows NT 3.51 MCSE Track			
Take These Two Required Exams (Core Requirements)	Plus, Pick One Exam from the Following Operating System Exams (Core Requirement)	Plus, Pick One Exam from the Following Networking Exams (Core Requirement)	Plus, Pick Two Exams from the Following Elective Exams (Elective Requirements)
			OR Implementing and Supporting Microsoft Exchange Server 4.0 #70-75
			OR Implementing and Supporting Microsoft Internet Information Server #70-77
			OR Implementing and Supporting Microsoft Proxy Server 1.0 #70-78

Table B.2 shows the core requirements (four operating system exams) and elective courses (two exams) for the Windows NT 4.0 track. Tables B.1 and B.2 have many of the same exams listed, but there are distinct differences between the two. Make sure you read each track's requirements carefully.

Table B.2

Windows NT 4.0 MCSE Track			
Take These Two Required Exams (Core Requirements)	Plus, Pick One Exam from the Following Operating System Exams (Core Requirement)	Plus, Pick One Exam from the Following Networking Exams (Core Requirement)	Plus, Pick Two Exams from the Following Elective Exams (Elective Requirements)
Implementing Microsoft Windows NT Server 4.0 #70-67	Implementing Microsoft Windows 95 #70-63	Networking dows for Workgroups 3.11 #70-46	Implementing and Supporting Microsoft SNA Server 3.0 #70-13

Take These Two Required Exams (Core Requirements)	Plus, Pick One Exam from the Following Operating System Exams (Core Requirement)	Plus, Pick One Exam from the Following Networking Exams (Core Requirement)	Plus, Pick Two Exams from the Following Elective Exams (Elective Requirements)
AND Implementing and Supporting Microsoft Windows NT Server 4.0 in the Enterprise #70-68	*OR* Microsoft Windows for Workgroups 3.11-Desktop #70-48	*OR* Networking with Microsoft Windows 3.1 #70-47	*OR* Implementing and Supporting Microsoft Systems Management Server 1.2 #70-18
	OR Microsoft Windows 3.1 #70-30	*OR* Networking Essentials #70-58	*OR* Microsoft SQL Server 4.2 Database Implementation #70-21
	OR Implementing and Supporting Microsoft Windows NT Workstation 4.02 #70-73		*OR* Microsoft SQL Server 4.2 Database Administration for Microsoft Windows NT #70-22
			OR System Administration for Microsoft SQL Server 6 #70-26
			OR Implementing a Database Design on Microsoft SQL Server 6 #70-27
			OR Microsoft Mail for PC Networks 3.2-Enterprise #70-37
			OR Internetworking Microsoft TCP/IP on Microsoft Windows NT (3.5-3.51) #70-53

B

Table B.2   Continued

Windows NT 4.0 MCSE Track

Take These Two Required Exams (Core Requirements)	Plus, Pick One Exam from the Following Operating System Exams (Core Requirement)	Plus, Pick One Exam from the Following Networking Exams (Core Requirement)	Plus, Pick Two Exams from the Following Elective Exams (Elective Requirements)
			OR Internetworking Microsoft TCP/IP on Microsoft Windows NT 4.0 #70-59
			OR Implementing and Supporting Microsoft Exchange Server 4.0 #70-75
			OR Implementing and Supporting Microsoft Internet Information Server #70-77
			OR Implementing and Supporting Microsoft Proxy Server 1.0 #70-78

How to Become a Microsoft Certified Solution Developer (MCSD)

The Microsoft Certified Solution Developer (MCSD) program is targeted toward people who use development tools and platforms to create business solutions. If you are a software developer or programmer working with Microsoft products, this is the certification for you.

Table B.3

Microsoft Certified Solution Developer Program

Take These Two Required Exams (Core Requirements)	Plus, Pick Two Exams from the Following Elective Exams (Elective Requirements)
Microsoft Windows Architecture I #70-160	Microsoft SQL Server 4.2 Database Implementation #70-21
AND Microsoft Windows Architecture II #70-161	Database Design on Microsoft SQL Server 6.5 #70-27
	Developing Applications with C++ Using the Microsoft Foundation Class Library #70-24
	Programming with Microsoft Visual Basic 4.0 #70-65 *OR* Developing Applications with Microsoft Visual Basic 5.0 #70-165
	Microsoft Access 2.0 for Windows-Application Development #70-51 *OR* Microsoft Access for Windows 95 and the Microsoft Access Developer's Toolkit #70-69
	Developing Applications with Microsoft Excel 5.0 Using Visual Basic for Applications #70-52
	Programming in Microsoft Visual FoxPro 3.0 for Windows #70-54
	Implementing OLE in Microsoft Foundation Class Applications #70-25

How to Become a Microsoft Certified Trainer (MCT)

MCTs are product evangelists who teach Microsoft Official Curriculum (MOC) courses to computer professionals through one or more of Microsoft's authorized education channels. MCTs have special access to current Microsoft product information and invitations to Microsoft conferences and technical training events. This certification is designed for those who want to teach official Microsoft classes. The process for becoming a certified trainer is relatively simple and consists of both a general approval for the MCT program as well as an approval for each course you want to teach.

MCT Application Approval

There are three steps to the MCT application approval process:

1. Read the MCT guide and the MCT application at `http://www.microsoft.com/train_cert/mct/`.

2. Send a completed MCT application to Microsoft, including proof of your instructional presentation skills.

3. Send proof of your MCP status to Microsoft.

After you have completed these tasks, you will have satisfied the general part of the MCT application process. You have to do this only the first time.

MCT Course Certification Approval

The second part of becoming an MCT is that MCTs must be separately certified for each individual class they teach. There are four required steps to become certified to teach a Microsoft Official Curriculum course:

1. Pass any required prerequisite MCP exams to measure your knowledge.

2. Study the Official Microsoft Trainer Kit for the course for which you seek certification.

3. Attend the MOC course for which you seek certification.

4. Pass any additional exam requirement(s).

After you've completed both the MCT application and the MCT course certification, you'll be authorized to begin teaching that MOC class at an official Microsoft Authorized Technical Education Center (ATEC).

Registering and Taking the Exam

When you are ready to schedule your exam, contact the Sylvan Prometric test registration center that will be most convenient for you from the following table:

Country	Telephone Number
Australia	1-800-808-657
Austria	0660-8582
Belgium	0800-1-7414
Canada	800-755-3926
China	10800-3538
France	1-4289-8749

Germany	0130-83-9708
Guam	001-61-800-277583
Hong Kong	800-6375
Indonesia	001-800-61571
Ireland	1-800-626-104
Italy	1-6787-8441
Japan	0120-347737
Korea	007-8611-3095
Malaysia	800-2122
Netherlands	06-022-7584
New Zealand	0800-044-1603
Philippines	1-800-1-611-0126
Puerto Rico	800-755-3926
Singapore	800-616-1120
Switzerland	155-6966
Taiwan	008-061-1142
Thailand	001-800-611-2283
UK	0800-592-873
United States	800-755-3926
Vietnam	61-2-9414-3666

If this is your first time registering for a Sylvan Prometric exam, Sylvan will assign you an identification number. They will ask to use your Social Security or Social Insurance number as your identification number, which works well for most people because it's relatively easy for them to remember. You also have the option of having them assign you a Sylvan ID number if you prefer not to disclose your private information.

If this is not your first exam, be prepared to give Sylvan your identification number. It's very important that you use the same identification number for all of your tests—if you don't, the exams won't be credited to your certification appropriately. You have to provide Sylvan Prometric with the additional information: mailing address and phone number, e-mail address, organization or company name, and method of payment (credit card number or check).

Sylvan requires that you pay in advance. Microsoft certification exams prices are related to the currency exchange rates between countries. Exams are U.S. $100, but certification exam prices are subject to change, and in some countries, additional taxes might apply. Please verify the price with your local Sylvan Registration Center when registering. You can generally schedule exams up to six weeks in advance, or as late as the day before.

You can always cancel or reschedule your exam if you contact Sylvan Prometric at least two working days before the exam, or by Friday if your test is scheduled on Monday. If you cancel, exams must be taken within one year of payment.

Same-day registration is available in some locations if space is available. You must register at least 30 minutes before test time. The day of the test, plan to arrive a few minutes early so that you can sign in and begin on time. You will be provided with something to write notes to yourself on during the test, but you are not allowed to take these notes with you after the test.

You are not allowed to take in books, notes, a pager, or anything else that might contain answers to any of the questions.

Hints and Tips for Doing Your Best on the Tests

The Microsoft Certification exams are all between 75 and 90 minutes long. The more familiar you are with the test material and the actual test's style, the easier it is for you to concentrate on the questions during the exam.

You can divide your time between the questions however you like. There are 55 questions on this exam. If there are any questions you don't know the answers to, mark them to come back to later if you have time. You will have 75 minutes for the actual exam, but you will be scheduled for 90 minutes so that you can spend up to 15 minutes on a practice pre-test (on unrelated subjects) to get familiar with how the test engine works. Make sure that you think about whether you want to try out the practice test before you sit down to take it—some people find that the additional familiarity helps them, but others find that it increases their stress level.

Things to Watch For

Make sure that you read each question and all of its possible answers thoroughly. This is especially important for the scenario questions. Many people lose points because they select the first answer that looks right to them when there is a better answer following on their screens.

After you've made sure that you understand the question, eliminate those answers you know to be wrong. If you still have two or three choices, consider which of them would be the *best* answer and select it.

Marking Answers for Return

In the event that you aren't quite sure of an answer, you have the option of marking it by selecting a box in the upper-left and returning to the question at the end when you are given the option of reviewing your answers. Pay particular attention to related questions you find later in the test in case you can learn enough from them to figure out the answer to the question you were unsure of before. If you pay close attention, you will probably find that some of the other questions help to clarify questions of which you were uncertain.

Attaching Notes to Test Questions

When you finish a Microsoft exam, you are allowed to enter comments on the individual questions as well as on the entire test. This feature enables you to give the team that reviews Microsoft exams some feedback. If you find a question that is poorly worded or seems ambiguous, this is the place to let them know about it.

B

Index

REGISTRATION CARD

MCSE TestPrep: Windows NT Server 4

Name _____ Title _____

Company _____ Type of business _____

Address _____

City/State/ZIP _____

Have you used these types of books before? ☐ yes ☐ no

If yes, which ones? _____

_____

How many computer books do you purchase each year? ☐ 1–5 ☐ 6 or more

How did you learn about this book? _____

Where did you purchase this book? _____

Which applications do you currently use? _____

_____

Which computer magazines do you subscribe to? _____

_____

What trade shows do you attend? _____

_____

_____

Comments: _____

_____

_____

Would you like to be placed on our preferred mailing list? ☐ yes ☐ no

---

☐ **I would like to see my name in print!** You may use my name and quote me in future New Riders products and promotions. My daytime phone number is: _____

New Riders Publishing 201 West 103rd Street ◆ Indianapolis, Indiana 46290 USA

Fax to `317-817-7448`

Fold Here